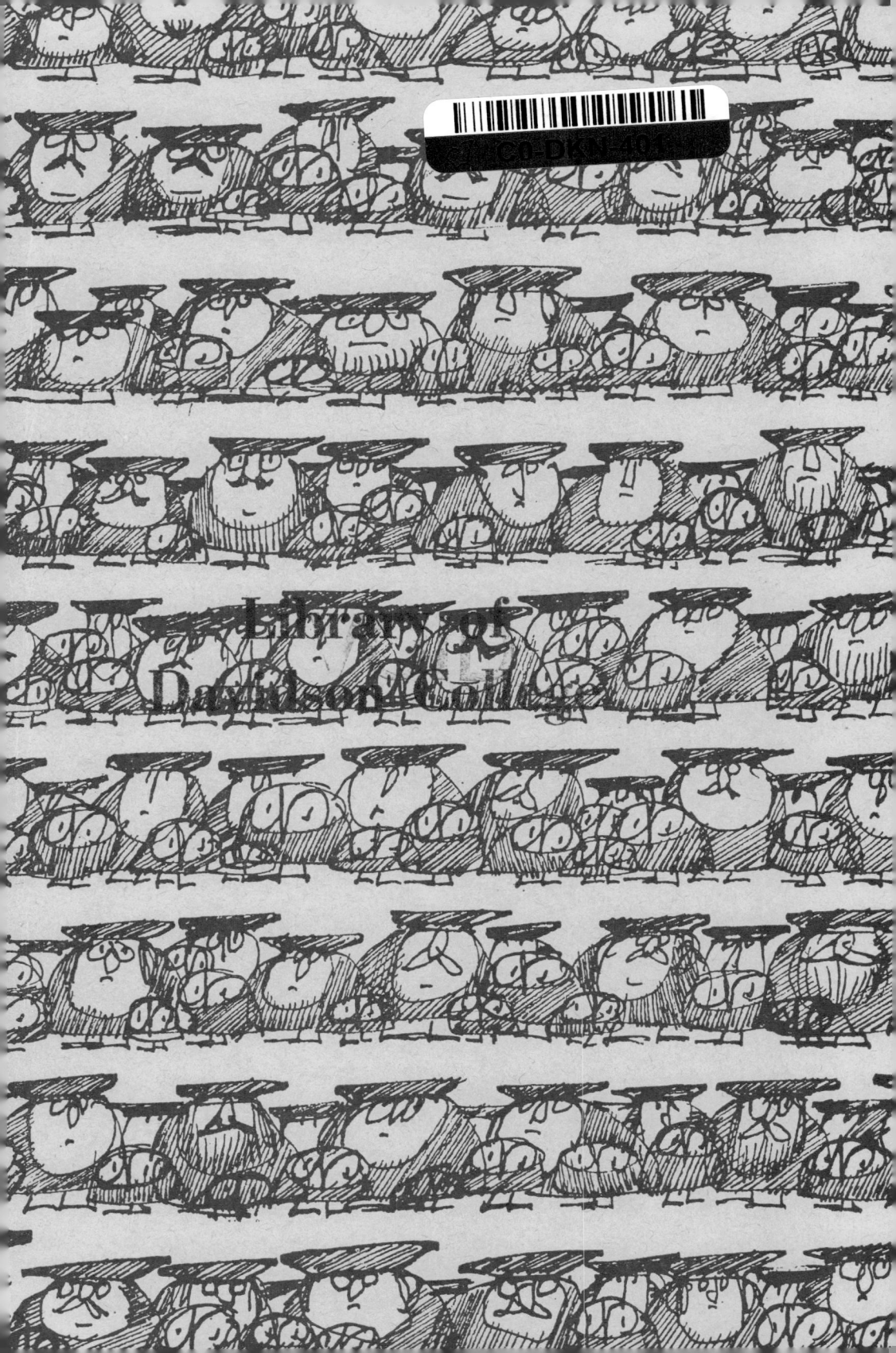

THE EXPLODING UNIVERSITY

THE EXPLODING UNIVERSITY

BY

CHRISTOPHER DRIVER

HODDER AND STOUGHTON

LONDON   SYDNEY   AUCKLAND   TORONTO

Printed in Great Britain for Hodder and Stoughton Limited, St. Paul's House,
Warwick Lane, London, E.C.4 by C. Tinling & Co. Ltd, London and Prescot.

For my parents and
other teachers

'There are forces in the world which work, not in an arithmetical, but in a geometrical ratio of increase. Education, to use the expression of Plato, moves like a wheel with an ever multiplying rapidity. Nor can we say how great may be its influence, when it becomes universal . . .'

Benjamin Jowett, in his introduction to Plato's *Republic*, 1892

'Reform a university: You may as well reform a cheese—there is a certain flavour about a university as there is about a cheese, springing from its antiquity, which may be very easily lost by mishandling.'

Lord Cecil, to the House of Lords, 1923

Contents

9

Contents

Introduction

In the library of a Russian boat on the Sea of Japan, where I would not have been but for the demands of this book, I found a copy of Maxim Gorky's *My Universities*. The point of the title is that like most good writers, Gorky had no universities, though he learnt much from the revolutionary Russian students of Kazan in the 1880s. 'Student unrest began. I could not understand it, could not grasp its aims or causes. I saw the gay to-do, but failed to perceive the genuine struggle behind it; and I felt that for the bliss of studying at the University, even torture might be endured . . . Looking in at Semyonov's bakery, I learned that the workers there were planning a trip to the University, to beat up the students. "We'll take some iron weights along," the bakers declared, with cheery malice. I tried to argue with them. But suddenly, with what was almost horror, I discovered that I had no desire to champion the students, that I could find nothing to say in their defence . . . '[1] Gorky's university was not the campus but the steppe, and the casually cruel peasants from whom he learnt that one of the most terrible things about ignorance is the mistrust that accompanies it. For the peasants, everything that happened was a surprise, usually unpleasant, and generalisation from experience was impossible. Yet even as Gorky and Barinov floated down the Volga on their barge, Russian science and industry were poised for the take-off which the Communist Revolution may have advanced but which even Tsarism could not have long delayed. Later in my own journey, on the Trans-Siberian railway, the burly conductress of my carriage handed me a potted patriotic history of the Soviet Union. It recorded that during the great famine after the October Revolution, Lenin recognised the new republic's need of scientists and artists, and asked Maxim Gorky to arrange special rations for them. The exact truth of this episode may, for all I know, be rather different, but there could not be a clearer demonstration to the *jeunes contestataires* of several continents that when a socialist society's survival is at stake, there is no damned nonsense about equality. (Similarly in the Soviet Union today, I am told, the scientists at the new university city of Akademgorok, near Novosibirsk in Siberia, enjoy freedoms denied to most other people, such as access to the BBC in English, and to the unpublished novels of Solzhenitsyn.)

[1] Tr. Margaret Wettlin (Progress Publishers, Moscow).

Russia will not again be mentioned in these pages, which prudence and pressure of time have limited to the United States, Britain, Germany, France, Italy, and Japan. These are developed countries whose political systems and educational philosophies are assumed to have something in common, though it is not easy to specify what; and whose university populations have lately exploded, first in numbers, then in revolts. But it will do no harm to begin by following Gorky, and to spend a page or two on 'my universities'. For the reader of a book like this, who may well know much and feel passionately about at least one university, is entitled to know what ballast is being put aboard before the boat is pushed out. It is impossible to write neutrally about education, though several people are misguided enough to try. One is for it or against it, lucky or unlucky in one's teachers, sly or stupid at playing the examination game. Experience in this quarter often affects in later life not merely one's income and recreations but one's political outlook and attitude to authority, which at today's universities are variables just as important as literacy or numeracy.

Critical reflection on his formal education does not come easily to an Englishman. We usually possess, or think we possess, racier subject-matter in the social milieu within which our education was conveyed. The children of the well-to-do think of clandestine homosexuality and flowered waistcoats; the others, of quick draws on cigarettes behind the school coke-stacks. Sir Osbert Sitwell, asked by *Who's Who* where he was educated, put down 'during the holidays from Eton'. This only took to its logical conclusion what most Englishmen prefer to think—that they were educated almost anywhere but the classroom. Considering this, I am surprised that there are so many able-minded people in England who are prepared to teach. I count myself fortunate to have met, at different ages, half a dozen men who could and did bring Latin, Greek, and English literature alive for me. Several of them—especially Norman Saunders, formerly master of the Upper Bench at Rugby—are distinguished scholars in their own right, and if in their youth it had been as easy to become a university teacher as it is now, I suppose they might never have 'taught school'. If so, the worse for our own children, who may then never encounter minds of this quality until their own are irretrievably set.

No student revolutionary worth his salt-mines will regard a classical education at an English public school, rounded off at Oxford, as a good qualification for attempting a book of this nature; and no technocrat will consider that an innumerate, parasitical writer is worth the £10,000 (at today's prices) which the whole process must have cost my parents, the State, and past benefactors of the institutions which I attended. But it was worth it to me. I shall never programme a computer or dissect a mouse, but I still wince like a much-tried music teacher at a false quantity in a classical quotation. That always sounds like a ridiculous fuss about nothing, but Latin and Greek resemble music in that their elementary precisions of metre and inflection possess a beauty of their own, a beauty which remains hidden until one has understood the meaning, and held the two in equipoise. The habit of thinking and composing as though in Latin or Greek, even when the vocabulary has fled, is not something to take up and put down in adolescence, like a passion for Proust or Firbank, but a beaten track in the brain, fixed as the emotional patterns which Bowlby and Winnicott impute to infants. Any competent critic could analyse out of this essay the sentence-constructions and pedantries of the spoiled classic, though if he had himself been trained to the academic study of English, he would almost certainly express himself rather worse.

The profit-and-loss account of a classical education is of course not solely linguistic. I would now defend the classics as the earliest and still the most satisfying example of area studies. They do not help anyone to solve the contemporary problems of Greece and Asia Minor, except to remind him that democracy and independent thought were no more popular there in Socrates' time. But Aeschylus is said to have been Marx's favourite poet, and the nature of *realpolitik* emerges just as clearly from Thucydides' record of the Melian debate as it does from the more copious documentation which surrounds the Gulf of Tonkin resolution. The person who has at least partially understood the life, art, thought, and politics of that older civilisation may superimpose the model upon his own in too facile a manner, as generations of British civil servants and imperial administrators are supposed to have done, but he will never see society as a series of watertight compartments, or regard history as bunk.

In the eyes of an American or a Japanese, the British are obsessed with history and the impossibility of changing anything. Not long ago I read in a newspaper that 'plans for a joint City and University Festival in Oxford have been postponed for several years'. Pessimism so profound, and so precisely calculated, would be inconceivable in a campus news release anywhere else in the world. Even in Britain, however, there has developed a new kind of impatience, a different time-scale of expectations for the achievement of change, an acute despair because inequality cannot be abolished by Monday week. In his preface to a new book on equality in Britain,[2] Professor Richard Titmuss—a social analyst in the radical tradition of Tawney and Laski—comments on the trend, 'There are many deep and profound causes of this difference in outlook, beliefs, and expectations. One of the many contributory factors in an age of rising expectations is the substitution of over-simplified social theories for the study of history; of how men comprehend the complexities of power and the stubbornness of institutions and, in the end, brought about some betterment in the human condition.'

Not only the classics and Oxford, but also certain other of my 'universities,' force me to the same conclusion. No one, for instance, can belong to a church—even a Protestant church whose members are voluntarily

[2] George Taylor and N. Ayres, *Born and bred unequal* (London, 1969).

13

congregated for presumably similar objectives—without realising that neither individual goodwill nor a humane communal ideology are strong enough to prevent an institution from accumulating a creeper-like cladding of conservatism and insensitivity, which entwines itself round human beings and is transmitted from generation to generation, even the youngest. On the other hand, no one can work for a great liberal newspaper, whose own roots go deep into the culture of a particular region in a particular country, without picking up—along with skills more directly relevant to the writing of books—the sense of an institution whose private absurdities, and public compromises with the economic and political structure of society, have not prevented it from becoming a force for good greater than the sum of the individuals who write its columns, cut its stories, sell its space.

All this that is true of churches and newspapers is much more true of universities. Professors and administrators often sound hurt and surprised when this is not understood, whether by rebellious students, critical Congressmen, or a mass electorate. But understanding cannot be easy for people whose experience of organic institutions is limited to the nuclear family and the company of coevals in club or school, from which they pass on to the mobile, morally null connections which everyone has to make in search of entertainment or a living wage. It is a great strength of both the oldest and the newest universities in Britain, as of Harvard and Yale and numerous liberal arts colleges in the United States, that their alumni can hardly help bearing away with them some memory of a social structure on an intimate scale in which more than one generation and more than one interest group was involved. There is a very different 'feel' to Japanese or German universities, where a student's lifelong associations are with the particular social, political, or professional club which he joined on arrival, and only secondarily with the institution as a whole.

But that is to anticipate. Before going further, I ought to indicate the principles on which this book has been constructed. I also need to pay a few debts, for one of the principles I have followed is the one uttered by Nicolai Alexandrovich Lobachevsky, the professor in Mr. Tom Lehrer's song, whose advice to ambitious academics was the single word, 'Plagiarise'. But there exist in fact surprisingly few cross-cultural comparisons of university systems and institutions. The inimitable classic in the field is Abraham Flexner's *Universities: American, English, German*, first published in 1930, and re-issued by the Oxford University Press in 1968 with an illuminating critical introduction by Clark Kerr. Dr. Kerr remarks that the student of present-day universities may read the opposing views of Newman[3] and Flexner with greater benefit than he will receive from most of the more contemporary analyses; this is true. But Flexner spent a

[3] John Henry, Cardinal Newman, *The Idea of a University* (London, 1873).

14

lifetime in higher education as practitioner and observer, and all this, as well as the two or three years which he spent in gathering material and in writing, went into his book.

My own work, first contemplated in 1968 after a world crisis in the hitherto mostly placid relationship between universities and the wider community in advanced nations, has occupied about eighteen months, of which only six could be spent on tour. My springboards have been the indulgence of my publishers, the name of the (Manchester) *Guardian* for whom I did some reporting on the way round, and the natural curiosity of a man educated as I have described. My approach to universities, those most highly specialised of all institutions, was to interest myself in anything which took my own fancy, or stimulated other people's comments. The technique employed is hard to describe, but anyone who has ever taken part in a television programme will be familiar with the photographic mounted cavalry who remain for most of the time at a discreet distance, but for certain shots spur their machines in close and aim with a zoom lens at the whites of the eyes. The total effect is not balanced: it could not be, so I did not try too hard to make it so. Still less is it statistical and comprehensive, but by fortunate coincidence Dr. Barbara B. Burn of the University of Massachusetts has more or less simultaneously conducted for the Carnegie Commission a survey of higher education in nine countries, including four of 'mine': Britain, Germany, France, and Japan. I was pleased to discover from the manuscript, which she and the Commission kindly allowed me to see, that it adds much basic and up-to-date descriptive and statistical information to the more impressionistic material contained here.[4] My omissions horrify me when I think of them, but I was greatly cheered to read, in W. H. G. Armytage's *Civic Universities*, a British academic's reminiscence of Flexner's visit: 'I entertained him royally at Clare College and expended two whole evenings explaining the difference between the two universities. He went away and wrote a chapter upon Oxford and then said, in effect, that Cambridge was just the same. I have seldom been more annoyed.' I have myself avoided this trap by not visiting Cambridge at all, except to be royally entertained by Edward Shils, of King's and Chicago, who among much other good advice told me not to be afraid of walking abroad in his *altera mater* when I went to America, because although he had been several times accosted with menaces in Chicago, the only place where he had ever been successfully robbed was Cambridge.

The hospitality I have enjoyed, the help I have had, and the friends I have made while travelling for this book would break the bounds of an Introduction. But there are some people whom I must mention, even at the risk of someone attributing to them ideas or errors with which they

---

[4] *Higher Education in Nine Countries*, with chapters by Philip G. Altbach, Clark Kerr, and James A. Perkins (McGraw-Hill, New York, 1971).

had nothing to do: in Chicago, Robert Rosenthal and Michael Claffey; in Chapel Hill, Arnold Nash; in Berkeley, Hugh Richmond, Jefferson Morgan, Carl Irving and Anthony Platt; at Reed College, Marvin Levich; at Harvard, David Riesman and Richard Zorza; at Columbia, Daniel Bell; in Tokyo, Michio Nagai, Hitoshi Aiba, Ken Lendon, Gavan McCormack, Bernard Beraud, and Misa Nedderman; in Kyoto, Ryo Nakanuma, Tetsuo Kishi, and John Noone; at Koyasan, Kiyomi Soeda; in Bologna, Federico Mancini and Lucca Fontana; in Paris, François Bourricaud, François Raveau, Girod de l'Ain, and Robert Panhard; in Hamburg, Johannes Kleinstück, Jörg Richter, R. W. Leonhardt and his colleagues on *Die Zeit;* in Oxford, Robert Ogilvie; in Manchester, Lord Bowden; in Lancaster, Harold Perkin. I have claimed time, or had entertainment, or learnt something significant or scandalous, from ten times as many. Irvin and Lilian Wolloch in Washington DC, and James and Peta Fuller in New York, provided me with a home base and a *poste restante* in the United States. Alastair and Miranda Hetherington lent me a cottage in which to write. Janet Tomalin typed most of this 'damned thick book'. My agents Michael Sissons and Anthony Gornall made the whole project feasible. Paul Flora of *Die Zeit* kindly allowed me to use his delightfully expressive academic faces (originally executed as a poster for a German university centenary) as endpapers here.

To my wife Margaret I owe more than to any of these, and after six months away from home I return to Horace's lines on lifelong affection:

> felices ter et amplius
>   quos inrupta tenet copula nec malis
> divolsus querimoniis
>   suprema citius solvet amor die

Borwick Fold, Crook, Westmorland
and
6 Church Road, Highgate, London, N.6.   *April–July,* 1970

NOTE

The universities and colleges tabulated in the next four pages are those which are discussed briefly, or at length in the text.

Source (names and figures only): *The World of Learning*. Names in brackets indicate subsequent resignations.

UNIVERSITY	FOUNDED	TEACHERS	STUDENTS	EXECUTIVE HEAD	LIBRARY (vols)
United States					
Harvard University	1636	5,170	15,198	(Nathan Pusey)	7,791,538 in 90 libs.
University of California at Berkeley	1868	3,050	27,500	Roger W. Heyns	3,634,819
University of Chicago	1890	1,128	8,579	Edward H. Levi	2,850,000 (new $20m. library)
Morehouse College, Atlanta, Ga.	1867	78	1,041	Hugh M. Gloster	237,622
Reed College, Portland, Oregon	1909	137	1,200	Victor G. Rosenblum	193,000
Great Britain					
Oxford University	13th cent.	'about' 1,350	10,368	(Alan Bullock)	3,000,000 (copyright library)
University of Manchester	1903 (as univ.)	1,303	8,559	(Sir W. Mansfield Cooper)	1,000,000 (now linked with John Rylands Lib.)
UMIST		476	3,070	Lord Bowden	
University of Lancaster	1964	300	2,400	C. F. Carter	120,000

Private university, financed by endowment
research grants, fees, and donations.
President answers to Harvard Corporation
and Board of Overseers. Partly collegiate
in structure.

Wealth ($1 billion in the bank),
unrivalled research collections,
self-esteem: you-name-it-we-teach-it.

State university, financed chiefly by state
funds and federal research grants.
President of the University of California
(Charles Hitch) and Chancellors of the
9 campuses answer to Board of Regents,
2/3 of whom are gubernatorial appointments
for 16-year terms.

Supermarket of learning, from
computer science to astrology;
entrepreneurial, arriviste faculty;
bureaucratic administration; loving,
riot-prone fringe community.

Private university, financed by endowment,
research grants, fees, and donations.
President and self-governing faculty
answer to self-perpetuating board of trustees,
'most exclusive club in Chicago'.

Conversion of Baptist foundation into
temple of scholarly secularity.
Educates more professors than almost
anywhere else. Was a pioneer in social
sciences and atomic physics. Hemmed
in by ghetto.

Private (Black) liberal arts college financed
by contributions and fees. President answers
to trustees. Affiliated with Atlanta University
Center and Baptist Convention.

The Black bourgeoisie's Harvard.
Graduated Martin Luther King.
Sunday morning worship compulsory
for dormitory students. Good choir.

Private liberal arts college, financed by
fees and contributions. (No graduate school.)
President answers to trustees.

'Only the mature, motivated, and self-
directed student is likely to succeed.'
Religion and sport underplayed; brains,
art, community action, and neuroses
cherished.

Inscrutable

Survivals, human and institutional.

Governed by Court, Council, and
academic Senate. Students financed by
local authority grants, university by
University Grants Committee administering
Exchequer funds.

Atomic physics (Rutherford, etc.),
electrical engineering, Jodrell Bank,
History and Social Sciences. Ambitious
precinct development. Oligarchic
professoriat.

As Manchester, but more flexible.
First British university to have students on
all three governing bodies.

Operational research, systems
engineering, non-sectarian religion, etc.
No faculties—boards of studies
co-ordinate courses and admit students.

UNIVERSITY	FOUNDED	TEACHERS	STUDENTS	EXECUTIVE HEAD	LIBRARY (vols)
Japan					
University of Tokyo	1877	3,469	17,842	Dr. I. Kato	3,300,246
Waseda University Tokyo	1882	1,814	39,615	T. Tokoyama	600,000
France					
University of Paris	1253	4,455	115,000	Robert Mallet	4,575,000 (in 8 main libraries)
Vincennes (Centre Universitaire Experimental)	1969	170	6,000	—	just beginning
West Germany					
University of Hamburg	1919	865	20,221	Peter Fischer-Appelt	1,100,000 (Staats-und Universitäts-bibliothek)
Italy					
University of Bologna	11th cent.	203 (profes-sors)	29,500	T. Carnacini	600,000 (incl. 1,000 incunabula)

National university, financed chiefly by
state funds. President is elected, and
university run, by professors. Two campuses,
Hongo (the original one) for most seniors,
Komaba for freshmen and sophomores.

Elitism: for the Cabinet, the top Civil
Service, the Bank of Japan, etc., you
have to go to Todai. Riot-torn in 1968/9.
Attached institutes for space, solid-state
physics, earthquake and ocean research,
etc.

Private university, financed by student fees,
and contributions. Professors elect President.

The liberal intelligentsia's university.
Strong in computing science, politics
and economics, English.

National university, financed and ruled by
Ministry of Education. But see appendix
D and Chapter 4 for reorganisation under
1968 *Loi d'Orientation*.

Starting it all, both in the 13th cent. and
in 1968. Remoteness from governing
elite (groomed in *grandes écoles*) and
intellectual café culture. Squalid
educational conditions. But many
famous doctors, scientists, anthropologists, and others somewhere in the web.

An autonomous *Unité d'Enseignement et de
Recherche* under the new law.

Révolution permanente. Language
teaching, Marxist philosophy, etc.

Drittelparität (see Chapter 5).
Financed by grants from *Land* Parliament
and Federal Ministry of Culture.

All-round solidity, and medicine,
overseas economics, evangelical theology.
Social Democratic: professors
conservative, students radical.

National university, financed and ruled
(theoretically) by Rome Ministry of
Education through the Rector. Internally,
all decisions taken by professors.

Student government in the Middle
Ages, academic anarchy today.
Important research collections in city.
Marconi graduated here.

PART I

Mainly Portraits

CHAPTER ONE

A place on a map

I MANCHESTER—'A FLORENTINE DIVERSITY'

'The day has long gone by when it could be doubted if a
great industrial centre like Manchester were the suitable
or the best place for a University. Such doubters forget
the active life of Florence, where Galileo lived and
Leonardo and Michael Angelo. Where the pulse of life
is highest, in the great congregations of men, and men's
energies in manufacture and trade are at their highest
strain, there also the other energies have their likeliest
play . . . It is a dull eye which cannot penetrate through
the dirt and fog of Manchester to its underlying poetry.'
> The *Manchester Guardian*, on the fiftieth anniversary
> of Manchester University (1930)

Universities are, before anything else, places: populated packages of
bricks and concrete and Gothic mouldings and flowering shrubs, set down
in a particular park, suburb, or city, at the bidding of a particular civilisation, to grow up in their own way. Sometimes they express this by being
not so much places as anti-places, casually deposited on open or built-up
land, which earn Gertrude Stein's rebuke to Oakland, California, 'there
is no there, there'. Modern industrial countries, whose higher education
is the chief topic of this book, are especially prone to the offence of
founding a university without due care and attention, and sometimes, as
the French found at Nanterre, they are punished for it. Japan and the
United States, which between them possess about 3,000 institutions which
the official imagination labels 'colleges and universities', have both produced numerous academic anti-places, in which both staff and students
are thrown completely on their own internal resources and reading for a
sense of location. Great universities, on the other hand, wherever they
are in the world, tend to create their own environment, whether (like
Oxford) they have themselves for centuries been the undisputed epicentre
of their communities; or whether (like Hamburg or Manchester) they
have started small, as islands of culture in an ocean of mercantilism, and
gradually elbowed their way into geographical prominence; or whether
(like Akademgorok in the USSR, or Berkeley, just up the road from
Gertrude Stein's Oakland) they have by the very foreign-ness of their

presumptions defined their adopted locality for the first time. Definition of this last sort is often accepted in exasperation by the very local inhabitants whom the university has put on to an international map. An American tourist whom I once met in the precincts of Salisbury Cathedral told me that he came from Berkeley, 'only they call it Berserkeley now'.

Here, then, are two of the world's most important universities. It is best to leave aside what the 'importance' of a university might mean, and regard not just the ratings of their research and teaching in the academic league-tables, but the grit on their streets and the soot on their older buildings: in fact, the whole culture of the cities which, comparatively late in their own development, found themselves hosts to a transplant of the University Idea, as patented in an older Europe by Irnerius, Abelard, Wilhelm von Humboldt . . . What does it mean to live out this Idea in Manchester, in Chicago?

To understand in the space of a quarter of an hour what Manchester is, and what the University is doing to it and receiving from it, you must arrive in the city by train and (whatever the weather) refuse to take a taxi. The train from London now does the journey in two hours forty minutes, but that is time enough to remember that the railway and the Ship Canal were the making of Manchester, as the railway and the Great Lakes were of Chicago, and that the railway was built at an effort, and a cost, reminiscent of a minor war. In the 1840s the great Woodhead tunnel under the Pennines, on the Sheffield-Manchester line, in country which not long ago became celebrated all over the world as the site of the Moors Murders, cost the lives of 32 navvies and the limbs of hundreds more: hardly surprising when the resident engineer, asked later by a House of Commons committee if it was not safer to use patent fuses in blasting, could reply, 'Perhaps it is; but it is attended with such a loss of time, and the difficulty is so very small, I would not recommend the loss of time for the sake of all the extra lives it would save.'[1] 'The year before this answer was given, Friedrich Engels, co-author of the *Communist Manifesto*, had published his *Condition of the Working-Class in England*,[2] which was written from observations made while working in his father's factory in Manchester; and another Manchester manufacturer, John Owens, had drawn up his will, endowing a college for the city that was to be open to all applicants 'without distinction of rank or condition in society'. This was the effective beginning of Manchester University.

Manchester, then, has claims to be the place where the wounds of the first Industrial Revolution, and the social structure that neglected them, first stank in the nostrils of civilised men, and compelled them to think in terms of alternative structures. Meditate on this as your train rattles over Stockport viaduct and crosses the Manchester city boundary, past a messy industrial landscape. The train is likely to be full, for one of the great

[1] The story is told in Terry Coleman's *The Railway Navvies* (London, 1965), p. 103.
[2] London, 1846.

changes that have come over Manchester since cotton ceased to be Lancashire's staple industry is that most of the city's largest firms are, as Mancunians might themselves put it, 'foreign-owned': owned, that is, by businesses whose headquarters lie in London. But the intellectual traffic on this railway line, the most heavily used in Britain, has long been heavy. C. P. Scott of the *Manchester Guardian* used it when he went to confer with Lloyd George, the conductor Hans Richter used it to commute between the Hallé Orchestra and Covent Garden, and it was said of Sir Henry Miers (Vice-Chancellor of Manchester University 1915–1926) that one outstanding feature of his service to Manchester had been his accessibility to all members of his staff: 'He could be found invariably on two or three days a week in the dining-car of the Euston–Manchester railway train.'[3] More recently, the number of plump-cheeked, dark-suited businessmen commuting between concrete palaces in London and concrete palaces in Manchester has doubled and re-doubled, and the first visible sign of the prosperity they confer and expect is the rebuilt Piccadilly station at which they arrive.

You are bound for the University. At least, that is how it would have been described five years ago, but now the whole 'Manchester Education Precinct' is planned to cover 280 acres of the inner city, laid out on the map in the shape of a fashion boot as worn by British women in 1970, with the Royal Infirmary at the top and Piccadilly Station at the toe. So the original core of the University has reverted to the name which it took from its Victorian founder: Owens. The enlarged university quarter rubs close up against Piccadilly. You could throw a stone into it from Platform Fourteen, and if there were an overhead walkway, you could enter it from the train without touching the city. But because Manchester is Manchester, where human inconvenience has always counted for little, especially if a remedy would entail additional disbursement, you must descend to street level and cross the busy London Road into a network of blackened streets with names—'Venice', 'Bombay'—conferred by some long-forgotten Town Hall romanticist. The streets between London Road and the University were some of the worst slums in England until Hitler's bombs and more recently the Council's demolition men shovelled them away into local history. It is still, and in spite of hopes may remain, a district in which no one much wants to live, except students who have no choice in the matter. Now, it is a vast, muddy car park labelled 'UMIST' (which is the acronym of the University of Manchester Institution of Science and Technology) and studded with glass and concrete tower blocks. The Precinct, which is already known—perhaps with an assertive glance across the Atlantic to Cambridge, Mass.—as 'MEP', is intended to accommodate, and even to unify in spirit, four hardly reconcilable, separately administered groupings from the higgledy-piggledy British

[3] H. B. Charlton, *Portrait of a University 1851–1951* (Manchester, 1951), p. 127.

higher education 'system': 15,000 students and 2,500 academic staff from the University, 5,000 students and 850 staff from UMIST; 1,400 students from the city hospitals and 8,000 full and part-time students from the Polytechnic (a collection of mostly vocational colleges — Art, Music, Commerce, Teacher Training, Domestic Science — controlled by Manchester's Local Education Authority). By the mid-eighties, the 280 acres may be carrying an academic and ancillary population of 43,500. It is probably the biggest, most revolutionary, and — in its use of valuable urban land — expensive higher education project in Europe. The medical school alone will cost five and a quarter million, and several whole universities in Britain have opened their doors with less. The whole, by 1984, will probably have cost a hundred million pounds.

But keep walking, for the old Manchester has not quite disappeared yet. Here is the ornately bordered window of John Cantrill, Domestic and Ecclesiastical Decorator; there is a shabby stone chapel, long since deserted by its flock, which has been pressed into use as a miniature garment workshop. A few yards away, set back from the Oxford Road in a field of rubble, is the British National Computing Centre — surely the only National Computing Centre in the world whose pre-cast external walls are apparently held together by household screws — and outside is parked a pre-war Morris eight. Ahead, to the south, blackened by a century of smuts, lies Owens College, in William Waterhouse's exuberant Gothic; beyond it the Student Union, in the Early Mussolini manner; and the Refectory, with the coloured panels to which daring architects were encouraged by the 1951 Festival of Britain. They are three of the least well assorted university buildings in Europe, and the heart of Manchester University, and hence of the whole Precinct, is really not much more than a bus stop from which students daily contemplate the most purely characteristic element in the whole décor: the windows across the street where the Manchester Grand Division of the Order of the Sons of Temperance assures them, in gold letters on black glass, that 'The Menace to Society is drink' and that 'Abstinence and thrift are twin blessings'.

Bruised by these flippancies, Manchester University would probably reply that its real heart was not in this patch of ground and these patchy buildings at all, and that if the spirits of Leonardo and Galileo, so recklessly conjured up by the *Guardian's* leader-writer at the head of this chapter, were to visit Manchester they would be found, not in the "oomanities building' (as the University's commissionaires call it) but asking their way to the world-famous radio-astronomy laboratories at Jodrell Bank; or visiting the physical laboratories where Schuster, Bragg, Rutherford and Blackett helped to push open the doors of twentieth century science; or paying their respects to Osborne Reynolds, the University's first professor of engineering (1868), whose interests had a truly Florentine diversity: he laid the foundations for work on turbulence, heat transfer, and lubrication; and conducted serious investigations into the propulsion of ships, scaling laws for hydraulic models, the dilatancy of soils, and the stability of lifeboats. And if they inquired about contributions to art as well as to science and learning, Manchester would not be embarrassed for a reply. The Whitworth, for which the University is responsible, is a far better and more adventurous gallery than its forbidding façade suggests. It is particularly rich in old Master prints and English watercolours (including Blake's 'Ancient of Days') and in early textiles and embroideries. A tapestry was commissioned from Paolozzi to mark the opening of the modernised interior of the gallery, to which sculpture by Moore, Hepworth, Frink, and Wall, with Op and kinetic constructions by Vasarely and Winter, have been added in recent years. But in spite of this, and in spite of the City of Manchester's payment of £220,000 in 1970 for Stubbs's 'A cheetah with two Indian servants', Manchester could not now possibly catch up with the wealth of pictures in public and private hands, in say, Chicago. Too many generations of Mancunians have held too firmly to the notion that to possess beautiful things is, if not immoral, at least irrelevant to the business of life. All their aesthetic passions went into music instead,[4] and there is no visible monument to what the Hallé under Richter, Harty, and Barbirolli has meant to students, lecturers, and self-made men of Manchester in the past hundred years.[5] The Hallé is not at present a great orchestra. But the itch 'to sing and play and dance while May endureth', as the old madrigal puts it, is still strong in the University, and so many enterprising composers and executants have emerged in the last decade from the Royal Manchester College of Music that the phrase 'Manchester school' now denotes a group of musicians as securely as it once denoted economists. Nor would any Manchester conductor grumble, as Solti did in my hearing when he arrived in Chicago to take charge of the Chicago Symphony, that concerts were attended only by the rich and middle-aged.

If the last paragraph has a defensive tone, it is perhaps because Manchester University has never quite been able to forget what a superior metropolitan journal said at its founding, 'Anyone educated at Manchester would certainly be dull and probably vicious'. Vice is associated with London rather than Manchester these days, though the Education Precinct did sweep away several sex-and-violence bookshops and thirty pubs. A visitor just landed from Chicago, seeing all the wasteland and ill-lit streets that separate the university buildings from each other, would grip his stick more tightly and glance nervously behind and beside him, but either he or his sister would be as safe as anywhere in England.

But dull? That is an accusation that would be rebutted more cautiously,

[4] All? Those numerous artists and intellectuals who follow Saturday by Saturday the contrapuntal intricacies of Manchester United's football games would raise an objection here, perhaps rightly.

[5] But see Neville Cardus, *Autobiography* (London, 1947), *Second Innings* (London, 1950), and *Full Score* (London, 1970).

and by some students and some staff it would not be rebutted at all. To call a university dull is a serious charge, and a journalist, especially, should press it with caution. British academics have never quite forgiven the new University of Sussex for the atmosphere of spurious excitement that Fleet Street conferred on it as a christening present. Their verdict was neatly summed up by Michael Beloff as 'too much Quant, too little 'Kant,[6] and the point was elaborated (in a different context) by the sociologist Bryan Wilson, 'In terms of the received values of university education, a university in the news ought to be an object of suspicion.'[7] Even in this ambiguous sense, Manchester University has at least its fair share of headlines. This is partly because most British national papers print their northern editions in the city, and their reporters get to know pretty accurately which senior or junior members of the University can be relied upon for an instant quote or an interesting experiment. But it is also because many very distinguished, and a few pleasantly eccentric, individuals can be found on the professorial lists by anyone who cares to look. A university whose professors include (or included at the time of writing) Sir Brian Flowers in Physics, Sir Bernard Lovell in Radio-Astronomy, Brian Chapman and S. E. Finer in Government, M. R. D. Foot in History, A. R. Prest in Economics, Morris Gluckman in Anthropology, Peter Worsley in Sociology, cannot be accused of failure to attend to the shop-window, and it is a very negligent newspaper reader who has never encountered John Allegro's views on the sacred mushroom or John Cohen's games with the psychology of everyday life.

For a southerner, too, it is dangerously easy in Manchester to confuse the down-to-earth, or the taciturn, with the dull. Professor Chapman once told Manchester University freshmen that 'the don who pointed out that the fashionable Chelsea word "sophisticated" meant a willing intent to deceive was firmly in the Manchester tradition.'[8] In this tradition, a man says what he has to say, and stops, without any of the grace-notes and cadences that Oxbridge intellectuals affect, and without the verbal running-on-the-spot that makes American academic communication such an ordeal for English ears. Institutions, like individuals, have temperaments, and this is part of Manchester's. The style is accentuated because Manchester, in spite of its world reputation and (by British standards) large size, still believes in encouraging local talent. Glance down the staff list in a few different departments, and notice the proportion of names who carry first or second degrees from Manchester itself: 20 out of 47 in Chemistry; 21 out of 26 in Electrical Engineering; 11 out of 27 in French Studies; 10 out of 39 in History. In some cases (Electrical Engineering, for example) this reflects the virtual monopoly Manchester has had over a subject. When electrical engineers graduate, they are very

---

[6] *The Plateglass Universities* (London, 1968), p. 156.

[7] 'The needs of students' (1965), essay reprinted in Mr. Wilson's *The Youth Culture and the Universities* (London, 1970).   [8] *The Guardian*, October 9, 1967.

likely to be employed in the works at Trafford Park, in West Manchester; and that is quite likely to be where their fathers work too. (Until twenty years ago, British civic universities took most of their students from the immediate neighbourhood, and the typical undergraduate today is a first-generation student.)

In History, say, the illustration works differently. The Manchester History department under such men as Tout, Powicke, and Namier was for years probably the best in England, perhaps in Europe. But few would now put it so high, and when a subject begins to lose interest for a rising generation, or a department loses sight of an international peak it once attained, proper pride has a tendency to curdle into improper protectionism. A young social historian hotfoots it to a new university 'Because he could see no future for his subject in the interstices of the Manchester history school',[9] and rumours emerge from departmental meetings that the new professor from Oxford 'has been slapped down like a junior lecturer whose contract is unlikely to be renewed'. A somewhat similar temper reigns in the English department, where young men with bright ideas are apt to be told, 'that's the sort of thing Kermode would have suggested'—the reference being to a well-known and prolific scholar who once held a Chair at Manchester, but did not stay very long. Academics, even if they are all individually excited by the particular subjects they are teaching or exploring, can sometimes collectively generate a sense of tedium. But in so far as this is true of Manchester, there are structural explanations which must be explored. The heaviest of the weights that press 'the coming Manchester multiversity' into its present shape are, first its size; second, its administrative organisation; third, and least easily comprehended, because it underlies the first two, the burden of the difference between the job the institution grew up with, and the job society now expects of it.

Size

In 1960, when Ferdinand Zweig conducted his inquiry *The Student in an Age of Anxiety: a Survey of Oxford and Manchester Students*,[10] Manchester University had 6,159 students (5,391 in Owens and 1,768 in UMIST). Ten years previously it had 5,943, ten years later it had 12,524. Ten years from the time of writing, it will have 20,000 (15,000 in Owens and 5,000 in UMIST). Only a politician would be brash enough to suppose that an institution could remain substantially the same animal after thirty years of growth at that rate. Zweig's inquiry itself testified to the strain under which the university was working. Half his student sample enjoyed their university life, but the most thoroughly content were the ones who lived in halls rather than digs, or who worked in small rather than large departments. From the other half, who were moderately

[9] Harold Perkin, *New Universities in the United Kingdom* (OECD, 1969), p. 159.
[10] London, 1963.

31

or strongly critical of the institutions, came such comments as, 'it's too big and impersonal'; 'too large and overcrowded'; 'too cramped and restricted'; 'drab and dirty with nothing to take you out of yourself'; 'too much concentration on getting a degree instead of getting culture and education'; 'the teaching's impersonal, a gulf exists between staff and students. In my department you can go right through the course without ever speaking to the professor' 'a depressing place. No bond, no pride, no sense of belonging'. In the late sixties, such comments became the small change of student uproar all over the world, and at any time, however good the conditions, it would be a dull student who could find nothing to criticise. But the critics' case remains as strong as it was a decade ago. Since 1960, an entire new 'student village' has been built in Fallowfield, a mile or so away from the University, but even this, according to one admittedly prejudiced Warden of a small hall of residence, has so far proved 'a social flop, more noted for its problems than its solutions'. Nor can bricks and mortar answer the lament of a very senior engineering professor, 'In 1948 I could put a name and face on every student in the three year course. I couldn't even recognise them now. We have saturated all the reasonable digs in the city. Students are living in hovels and doss-houses—and being exploited there, too.'

Academically, the effects of size are less spectacular; and in some ways are clearly beneficial. In a large university, more is known, and more is lectured about, by more people, so that a junior teacher in a large Manchester department ought not to have to exhaust himself by keeping up with as wide of range of subjects and periods as his counterpart in a small new university, or for that matter in an Oxford college. In theory, students too should be able to find almost anything they are likely to seek. But it does not always work like that. In Manchester as in Berkeley, the academic power focus is the department, and it is significant that in both places committees discussing student participation in academic affairs have fixed on the department as the level at which real decisions are taken, and at which students are likely to be knowledgeable and involved enough to make, and feel that they are making, some difference.[11] But it is not easy to run a university as a conglomerate of large independent fiefdoms, each with its different code of practice and ruling clique. It would take students in Manchester much longer than the three years at their disposal to find their way round a department like English, where (by one lecturer's account) 'a proposal to teach 50 per cent Shakespeare and 50 per cent modern literature to the third year, instead of 100 per cent Shakespeare as at present, was defeated after months of discussion, on a technicality which the conservatives had saved up till the last possible minute'. Often, too,

[11] University of Manchester *Report on Student Participation in Academic Affairs* (pamphlet, March 1969); Caleb Foote and others, *The Culture of the University: Governance and Education* (San Francisco, 1968).

when an actual reform is under discussion, it is discovered that a department is not as independent as it seems—that, for example, if it wants to absolve students from keeping up Latin in their first year, there will be a howl from the classicists' trade union that work is being taken away from them.

Neither over-rapid expansion nor departmental politicking are anything new to Manchester. 'No one had foreseen the rate at which the demand for university education would rise. A new Arts building had been planned just before the war. When peace came and it was first occupied, it was so overcrowded that straight away one of the larger Arts departments had to be evicted. The victim was the English department, whose chief had as great an international reputation in scholarship as any of his Arts colleagues, but who was a mere babe in political strategy and tactics.'[12] All this happened (according to the University's centenary historian) in 1919, between people who, however antipathetic they may have been, were at least meeting each other daily rather than lecturing in Ottawa or examining in Khartoum. In 1970, this observer, who visited Manchester University just after a prolonged and damaging student sit-in, came away with the impression that the people who effectively governed the university, and especially the retiring Vice-Chancellor (Sir William Mansfield Cooper), so passionately wished themselves back in the period when personal rule was possible that they would slave to maintain it rather than attempt to devise institutional substitutes for the nod in the corridor and the wink at the dinner table. (An independent, professionally-run university newspaper to supplement the amateur student version might help.) Even some of the University's most dedicated servants could not imagine why the new Vice-Chancellor (A. L. Armitage) should want to give up the delights of a Cambridge Mastership for—as one of them put it—'an inconvenient house in a twilight area'. Mr. Armitage's sanity, it was thought, would only be saved by job-redefinition. 'The chances that a single man can perform the duties of the present Vice-Chancellor are nil. When you grow up in a job you have an expertise no one else can have.'

The nature of the job, however divided, is defined by the past, present, and future structure of the University and of its partners in the Education Precinct. Here, there have always been other influences at work, national and international, besides strictly Mancunian ones. The whole history of universities as the world knows them can be seen as a search for imitable models. In 1849 John Owens's Trustees, to whom the Oxford and Cambridge model was odious because of its religious exclusiveness, turned to 'the Scotch Universities', which had always 'embraced students of every variety and description, persons engaged in the actual occupations of business, who expect to derive aid in their pursuit from the new applica-

---

[12] Charlton, op. cit., p. 127.

B   33

tions of science to the arts'. H. E. (later Sir Henry) Roscoe, the University's second Professor of Chemistry (1857–86), and A. W. Ward, Professor of History (1866–97), took this principle further by borrowing from Germany, where both had studied as young men, the notion of how to organise a university for research, both in science and the humanities. Along with the notions came the men, for from the middle of the century onwards there was an important politically-induced migration of engineers, scholars, and merchants—not to mention artists such as Charles Hallé —from Germany to Manchester. Roscoe, like Lyon Playfair (also a Manchester chemist), was one of the very few Englishmen who penetrated behind the complacency of the 1851 Great Exhibition to the underlying threat of British industrial decline: 'unless we set up a more profound and intimate connection between Science and Practice, our continental rivals who practise with knowledge must in the long run outbid our own manufacturers who practise by rule of thumb'.[13] Roscoe became a Liberal MP, and helped to prepare public opinion for the Technical Education Act, 1889. But too much time had by then been lost.

Two consequences of this history are particularly relevant to Manchester University as it is. First, and most important, technology was incorporated into the academic mainstream as long ago as 1903. Although UMIST has its own Charter and governing body, is financed directly by the national University Grants Committee, and has its own Vice-Chancellor (Lord Bowden, who had a spell as Minister of State for Education in the 1964 Labour Government), its students, staff, and degrees are all an integral part of the University of Manchester. Had this not been so, the Education Precinct might never have been conceived—though as Lord Bowden pointed out to me in conversation, conspicuous anomalies remain, especially since the group of colleges now called the Manchester Polytechnic, financed by the local authority, shares the Precinct with UMIST and Owens. Under the 'binary policy' for higher education, enunciated by a Labour Minister of Education, Mr. Antony Crosland, in an indiscreetly-drafted section of his Woolwich speech in 1965, the British Government expects to differentiate between the status, function, constitution, and resources of polytechnics and universities. Even students' union subscriptions (paid by local authorities) vary from institution to institution. In Manchester, where staff and students meet each other, enjoy reciprocal rights to many of each other's social facilities, and from time to time marry each other, the absurdities of the structure imposed by history and Whitehall are daily apparent.

The second consequence of Manchester's Scottish and Germanic borrowings was the concentration of power and influence in the hands of the professors, as distinct from junior staff. (Students have only recently begun to count constitutionally.) This did not matter much when 'junior

---

[13] This paragraph leans heavily on Charlton, op. cit., pp. 53–57.

staff' meant only the professor's assistant, but in the History department, for example, there are now thirty-one 'lecturers' to eight 'Professors' or 'Readers'. The constitution of the University was in 1963 adapted—after years of grumbling—to give these academic second-class citizens (often fine scholars who in American universities would be tenured professors) representation on the Academic Senate, and three places on the thirty-man Council, which in Bagehot's terminology is the 'efficient principle' in the University. But the old temper still lingers. In 1970 Martin Trow and A. H. Halsey, in an attitude survey of British university teachers, reported that seventy-five per cent of their sample were dissatisfied with the concentration of power in a 'professional oligarchy'.[14] When this first became a serious problem in Manchester, in the post–1945 period, it was not envisaged that junior university staff might one day be found ranged with student revolutionaries against Senate and Vice-Chancellor. But in Manchester, as elsewhere, this too has happened.[15]

The future structure of the Education Precinct will be a federal one, with separate heads for Owens, UMIST, and the Polytechnic. However desirable it might be to have one man negotiating with both nation and city on behalf of the lot, this can hardly happen while the various institutions hang suspended from different sources of ultimate authority. At present, while so much of the Precinct is still only a gleam in a planner's eye, the structure feels loose, which at this stage of university development in Britain is probably just as well. On the other hand, the geographical shape of the scheme is already known, and large though it is, it is tight at the boundaries, so schemes which the social imagination of the sixties was too small to envisage will be hard to find room for by the end of the eighties. Already, the administrator's pruning-knife is poised over types of growth which British universities have only lately begun to need. One seventh of all Manchester students are now married, and the treasurer of the Students' Day Nursery Committee writes in the University house journal: 'Our present building—formerly a wine bar—must come down

---

[14] *Sociology*, vol. 3, No. 3, p. 321. See also their *The British Academics* (London, 1971).

[15] Young left-wing social scientists, say, might well have some difficulty in picking sides, so polarised did positions become at the time of the February 1970 sit-in. From the University Students' Union resolution of February 2:

'Noting that Armitage has been undemocratically appointed as Vice-Chancellor, this General Meeting does not recognise him as *de jure* Head of the University, and . . . therefore instructs Executive to convey to Armitage the Union's opposition to the method of his appointment and inform him that Union representatives will meet him only on this basis.'

From the Vice-Chancellor's subsequent comment in Senate (February 26):

'This refers to my successor and is a typical example of the offensive productions or certain Union elements and leadership at the present time and which is progressively driving from the Union every sensitive element. . . . The Union itself seems to be intent on committing suicide.'

in four years' time and we have not yet found other accommodation. The Committee hoped that part of the proposed new University Health Centre building could be set aside for a nursery for thirty children and the University has agreed to do this *provided* we raise the capital cost of erecting that part of the building, about £18,000. If we do not obtain this sum or the promise of it *before the end of this session* we will be removed from the precinct plans. We cannot save this sum out of profits as we find it difficult enough to break even—the Matron feeds seventy children lunch and tea five days a week for only £6.'[16]

Again, the planners are anxious to have as many staff as possible living on or near the site, but the district has been a slum for too long to be immediately attractive to academic families with children to consider. Manchester University staff have in the past been forced out either to the large inconvenient Victorian houses of Didsbury, two miles to the south, or to the green-girt suburban box-homes of Cheshire. It would take not merely new maisonettes, but a vigorous urban cultural life and perhaps an institution like the University of Chicago's experimental children's school to lure them back again. The same applies to students, who have always been tempted by their environment to live a 9 a.m. to 5 p.m. existence, and who in a university of thousands count membership of societies and attendance at meetings only in tens. These things are the small change of university administration, perhaps, but if Manchester has ambitions to be Britain's first genuine 'polyversity', it will have to be someone's business to keep them in mind. Otherwise, new Precinct will be only old slum writ large, and sooner or later either dons will rise or students sit down in protest.

What does a university do?

All this, of course, is only the frame for the mental activity which is a university's proper work, and of which only a minute proportion could be picked out for description in these pages. The two examples chosen have in common the fact that they treat traditional Manchester pre-occupations in a novel manner, and at the same time reveal the very close attention which the university feels obliged to pay to the needs which British society, almost obsessively anxious about its technical and commercial future, brings to its notice.

Take, first, a project which has occupied the Textile Technology department of UMIST for the past ten years: the Vincent shuttleless, or tramistatic, loom. The weaver's loom is one of the world's earliest industrial machines. Visit, for instance, one of the little woollen mills scattered round the valleys of North and West Wales, which weave high

[16] *Staff Comment* (February 1970), p. 17. Compare the University of Vincenes (pp. 262–299) which started work with hardly any administration, but with a 250,000F. crèche.

quality blankets and tweeds for the export and London markets, and for tourists in the summer: the mills themselves and the machines they house look as though they have survived untouched from the eighteenth century, when great clanking machines were first set down beside a convenient source of water, to multiply cloth output beyond the capacity of cottage weavers. Those looms, like all but 50,000 or so of the three to four millions in the world today, depend on a shuttle, a hollow wood-and-steel projectile which carries a bobbin of yarn to and fro across the stretched warp threads. The passage of the shuttle is proverbially rapid— 'My days are swifter than a weaver's shuttle and are spent without hope', lamented Job 2,500 years ago—and it is also responsible for most of the noise that compels weaving mill workers to learn lip-reading, and often deafens them before they reach retiring age. This was the machinery that raised Lancashire and the West Riding of Yorkshire to prosperity in the first industrial revolution,[17] but it was unlikely to satisfy an imaginative engineer at the outset of the second. 'From an engineering standpoint, it is usually considered the height of absurdity to accelerate a shuttle weighing 500g from the rest to a speed of 15 m/s and bring it to rest again 1/10 second later in order to lay down a length of weft weighing as little as 1·5 mg, especially as the energy in the shuttle is not only wasted but spends itself in damaging the components of the loom. Much noise is created . . . and if, as occasionally happens, the shuttle is ejected from the loom serious injury to an operative may result.'

The history of modern loom technology, as described by Professor J. J. Vincent of UMIST, is the history of attempts to dispense with the classical shuttle. In the past fifteen years, several machines of this kind have come into use: the Swiss Sulzer loom, whose small 'gripper' shuttles travel fast across the warp in one direction but return slowly, doubling the speed of weaving but cutting down noise, maintenance, and accidents; the Draper-Fischer flexible rapier loom; and Czechoslovak air-jet and water-jet looms, which for the first time in human history allow cloth to be made without projecting anything solid between the warp strands except the weft yarn itself. But both methods have disadvantages as well as capital and operating economies, and the water-jet method is normally only applicable to hydrophobic materials like nylon and terylene. Moreover, even though nothing solid moves across the warp with the weft, 'about 1g of air and 0·5f of water are set in motion for each insertion'. The logical conclusion of the trend was to project the weft across the warp, by its own inertia, without any associated moving mass. This is what Professor Vincent and his colleagues (Noel Hodgkinson and Neil Doggett) set out to do ten years ago, and during the last two years, with a grant from the National Research Development Corporation, they have

[17] Some of it, including Arkwright's original spinning frame, can be seen in Manchester at the Museum of Science and Technology, opened in 1969 in the former Oddfellows Hall.

been trying to make the project commercially feasible.[18] The latest version of the inertial technique uses a pair of conical rollers to project the weft like a whiplash on an unwaveringly straight line for a flight of as much as eight feet for fine cotton and twenty-five feet for canvas yarn: indeed, the team had to move their apparatus out into the corridor of the research laboratory before they could measure their achievement. Professor Vincent, however, is sure that the Czechs are hot on his heels, for even major political upheavals do not always affect the march of 'technological' discovery, and his writing reflects all the unease which British scientists and technologists in the past twenty-five years have felt about society's sluggish exploitation of their discoveries: 'The contract with the National Research and Development Council has expired at a crucial time, and it is not easy to see an immediately available source of risk capital in the current mood of the domestic industry . . . Will the Vincent loom become just one more of the many ideas that originated here but were left for other nations to exploit?'[19]

Disenchantment of this kind is one of the main reasons for the introduction, late in time but vigorous in infancy, of 'management sciences' and business schools into the curriculum of British universities. Yet the development, like so many in Britain, has not taken place because some central authority willed it, still less because need for it had been demonstrated by some methodologically sound piece of research. Certainly, a powerful influence among those responsible was emulation of American universities, which in 1968 awarded 1,000 doctorates, 15,000 masters' degrees, and 50,000 first degrees, in business and management studies. But sceptics have not been slow to point out that business schools began to make an impact on American management just as the US rate of productivity increase began to slow down, and that the Japanese and the Germans have done pretty well at economic growth in the past two decades without being much obliged to management education. In Manchester, some of the leaders in the business-education business are notably modest about their function:

> 'We have no evidence whatever that academic course experience makes a better manager. We do have some evidence that it may produce frustration. The fact that some good managers have been to business schools may be less significant than the fact that some schools have managed to attract the passing interest of some managers who were so good that they are destined to go to the top anyway . . .
> 'We are trying to evolve new disciplines and new teaching methods. But we simply do not know whether, for example, industrial managers would not learn more about management from a course in Greek

---

[18] UK Patent Application Number 43255/68; Vincent, Hodgkinson, and Doggett.

[19] J. J. Vincent, 'Looms without shuttles', in *Advance* 7 (published by UMIST), October 1969.

philosophy as exemplified in a careful selection of Greek plays (this is one of the senior executive programmes in the Massachusetts Institute of Technology) because academically speaking we know very little about the management process.'[20]

For a subject that knows so little about itself, management science is expanding fast in Manchester. The Manchester Business School, which belongs to the Owens half of the University, has thirty-two students reading for masters' degrees, with twenty diploma students, and gave shorter courses to 150 managers in 1968/9. UMIST's Department of Management Sciences had 180 to 250 students, with eighty more reading degrees combined with other subjects, fifty taking masters' degrees, and ten PhDs. These two departments alone will soon absorb nearly 100 academic staff, if they can find them, and this is without counting the courses supplied by the university's Extramural Department and by the Manchester Polytechnic, where the growth of student numbers in business and management studies is most explosive of all.

It may not close the British trade gap, but it certainly attracts student customers. In Manchester, this is partly because a new and expanding subject breaks down some of the old barriers between disciplines, partly because—as one UMIST professor remarked—'there's no way of producing an engineer except three years of bloody hard work', and interdisciplinarity holds out to students at least a chance of escape. Roger Darlington, President of the UMIST Students Union in 1969/70, who spent months persuading his sponsoring firm, Associated Electrical Industries, to let him switch from engineering to management studies, told me that to judge by the attention paid by industrial talent scouts, the most interesting courses in the university were Liberal Studies in the university's Faculty of Science, and Management Studies in UMIST. The first puts together physics, chemistry, mathematics, and engineering with anthropology, sociology and economics, in a way that allows students to discuss intelligently the formation of science policy, environmental pollution, and the evolution of particular industries. The second expects in the first two years a knowledge of sociology, accounting, law, and statistics and keeps the last year for more directly 'business' subjects like market and operational research.

In the Business School itself, at present still housed off the Precinct in a commercially leased building, the scents of the jungle and the excitement of the chase are wafted unmistakably across to the observer. 'We may get interruptions,' said Mr. Tony Eccles, reaching a hand across a desk, 'but I'm running a business game that's getting a bit hairy. It's one of our own. In most business games you are given a product which you have to sell. In this one you can choose your own product and decide where you want to go. There is room too for personal as well as group objectives. You can

[20] R. B. Dew (Professor of Management Sciences) in *Advance* 7, op. cit.

do organisationally normal things like forming a splinter group to take over your own company.[21] I know there are people going to be fired after the next decision and I shall have to try to place them in another group.'

At this point a rising young executive knocked and entered.

'Just before we take over this company, is there any way of knowing what their product strategy is?'

'It's more successful than other companies in terms of *net* profit,' Eccles replied, 'and my guess is that it is also more successful in product strategy. But it's only a guess . . . In this game I represent the Industrial Reorganisation Corporation.[22] If you fail to run the company effectively we will fire you. We won't be vindictive about it, of course. By the way, where are you getting your executives from?'

'From other companies.'

'Do they know?'

'No.'

'That's interesting,' said Eccles, as the Rising Executive exited. 'He was put in as managing director into a group that only had a chairman, in a rather friction-filled situation. They are now going to lose one or two of their best executives.'

Between interruptions of this kind Eccles, a thirty-five year old Liverpool engineering graduate who came to the academic life via Unilever, described the atmosphere of the school. With a total staff of 150 including secretaries, it is almost too big for the face-to-face settling of problems that was manageable earlier on, but has not yet broken down into tight specialisms: Eccles himself, though primarily 'a human relations and labour guy' could still run a business game with marketing and computer considerations built into it. There are no departments as such, and Eccles himself is vaguely titled 'lecturer in business environment'. The (postgraduate) students at the school must be among the most highly motivated in Britain. Only sixty out of about 2,000 applications are accepted (compare, for instance, the 1:2 ratio of acceptance to rejections for several undergraduate courses at Oxford). It is generally accepted that Business School graduates can command a cash premium of £500–£1000 p.a. on the employment market, irrespective of their personal qualities or of employers' views about the actual courses, simply because the intake itself is so highly selective. The staff, too, benefit from the level of demand: they are paid at an industrial rate, but if they care to work night and day, many of them can double their salaries by outside work.

The MBS is often—in Britain—compared with the Harvard Business

[21] The founder of the new Joe Hyman Chair of Marketing, in UMIST's Department of Management Science, himself fell victim to this kind of thing during a battle for control of Viyella in 1969.

[22] An official body formed by the 1964 Labour Government, to encourage by advice and financial assistance the rationalisation of British industry, but disbanded by the 1970 Conservative Government.

School, but size apart, such comparisons are misleading. The Harvard school began in 1908 and has operated for sixty years in a society where 'The business of America is business'. In England, on the other hand, it is arguable that the respect, scope and authority given to the industrial manager is less than it is anywhere else in the developed world. The Manchester Business School, though it opened at a time when the British aristocratic and academic attitude to trade was at last being seriously questioned, is surrounded by a world generation of students who are presenting a cold front towards 'business values'. Not that rabid revolutionaries penetrate into the Business School, or want to, but whether as a reflection of external events or as a response to the comparative novelty of the institution, MBS students demand their own form of participation. The thirty-five year olds on short courses, who are more sure of themselves, are content with informal ways of achieving this: it is the younger students who demand formal structures, 'so that they can be seen to have a role to play', as one of their teachers put it. Perhaps, indeed, there is an element of role-playing about the whole business school revolution in Britain: whereas an American advances into business with a confident step, the Briton backs into it, saying to his critical contemporaries, 'Look at me, I'm playing at business'.

An academic environment makes this posture easier to maintain, and some of the more entrepreneurial spirits in the Business School are none too happy about becoming—when the Manchester Education Precinct is more nearly complete—geographically and bureaucratically closer to the heart of the University. Nor is it difficult to imagine what the Manchester University establishment would think about *jeux d'esprit* like the jigsaw nude which Tony Eccles and a partner put on the market to see if their results in practice matched the theories they were dishing out to students. 'We did all right but we didn't make our fortunes,' Eccles told me. 'The public relations side went marvellously, with plenty of free editorial publicity in the papers. The trouble was distribution. Never forget that the permissive society in Britain begins and ends with the communications industry. Not many store buyers have heard the news yet.'

Redbrick Revived

Eccles's experience could serve as a parable of Manchester's traditional relationship with London and the rest of Britain: the city tends to be either ten years ahead or twenty behind, and only experiment shows which. The Manchester Education Precinct, in size and complexity, is on an altogether different scale from the new universities in Britain, and though these have enjoyed more generous ephemeral publicity, Manchester does not lack interested visitors. Only experiment will show whether the concept is something of world importance in higher education—for all industrial countries are trying to achieve the same essential object of numerical expansion without loss of academic quality—or whether the city will only succeed in importing the problems of large American state universities, without having enough money to spend on the solutions. So far, the plan as a whole is much too dependent on short-term expedients—like sharing between several institutions common rooms that were intended to serve only one—to solve foreseeable difficulties which are posed by the structure of British higher education, and by the projections of future student numbers. The Vice-Chancellor of UMIST, Lord Bowden, is himself one of those who believes that 'this extraordinary administrative hotchpotch' cannot long continue:

'Before very long all students who study in Manchester for three years should be able to sit for a Manchester degree, which should be assessed by the staff of a great collegiate University of Manchester. Such a policy will demand fundamental changes in the structure of the University, but . . . the administrative system is already subjected to quite intolerable strain. Manchester is much the biggest University in England which is administered by a single central machine. The faculties of science, medicine, arts, and technology are all bigger than most pre-War universities . . . We were able to cope after Robbins[23] by expanding an existing machine. Next time (and that means now) we have to begin by a total reorganisation of the whole machine, from nursery schools to graduate schools.'[24]

Here, as often, Lord Bowden seems to echo Sir Henry Roscoe, who in 1870, during his campaign against the separation of polytechnics from universities, told the Royal Commission on Scientific Instruction:

'Very great evils must result from this tendency to multiply institutions—a tendency springing, probably, from the difficulty of modifying old institutions to meet new wants.'[25]

The 'wants', in today's Britain, are not so very different from what they were in 1870, when compulsory primary education was first introduced. Only the level of education thought desirable for the mass of young people, and the age of leaving full time education, have changed. But in the origins of British civic universities, there was almost always more than a felt need for technically-educated manpower. The pioneers were founding institutions which they wanted to be recognisable as universities, but at the same time they were consciously expressing a 'counter-culture' just as novel, in the circumstances of the time, as the 'free universities' of modern Stanford or Berkeley. It was not their fault that want of money and imagination in their local patrons, and later, the

[23] Report of the (Robbins) Committee on Higher Education (Cmnd. 2154, 1963).
[24] Address to UMIST Court of Governors, December 12, 1969.
[25] Quoted in W. H. G. Armytage, *Civic Universities* (London, 1955).

academic revival of Oxford and Cambridge themselves, robbed Red-brick[26] of its initial élan, and enabled a German observer, William Dibelius, to remark in 1930 that 'if a post is to be filled, the academic qualifications of the MA of Liverpool or Leeds will not prevail against the social status of the Oxford B.A., which bears no mark of coal dust and the fumes of the brewing vats.'[27] Sir Denis Brogan, from his vantage points in Princeton and Cambridge, has more generously observed that the civic universities 'near the civic reference library, the theatres, the concert halls, the pubs and the cinemas, the art gallery and the great civic churches . . . are the normal universities of the world.'[28] For the first time, the opportunity now exists in England for this ideal to be worthily realised, on a scale sufficient to alter the sociology of a whole urban community. It will be a pity if it misses its mark again.

[26] The popular English term for the 'civic universities', of which London and Manchester are the chief. All were founded in the century between 1815 and 1914, and most of their architects built in brick. By analogy, the British universities founded during the past decade were christened 'Plateglass'. See Beloff, op. cit.

[27] *England*, translated by M. A. Hamilton (London, 1930), p. 440.

[28] Quoted in Armytage, op. cit., p. 311.

2 CHICAGO—'A PROFOUNDLY GERMAN TOWN'

'The loyalty of the community is directed towards the institution in which it participates. The words change to receive the content which the community gives to them. The effort to find agreement before the institution goes to work is meaningless.'

Edward Levi, *An Introduction to Legal Reasoning*
(Chicago 1948), p. 104 (Phoenix edition)

'The University of Chicago lives on its morale. It is located in an unpleasant city, in a nasty climate, a thousand miles from anywhere; most members of this faculty could immediately increase their salaries by going to other universities. They are here rather than elsewhere because they value their colleagues and their students and their relations with their colleagues and their students. If the web of those relations is torn, the University will fall in on itself. The faculty will cease to teach (that has been the usual result of disruptive demonstrations at other universities); the best of them will go elsewhere and so will the students most concerned for education; it will be impossible to recruit to positions of administrative leadership anyone who cares for the real life of the place. The University of Chicago will become another mediocre impersonal routine institution and will probably perish. It will deserve to.'

James Redfield, Chairman and Associate Professor,
University of Chicago Committee on Social Thought,
in an open letter to faculty and students,
April 10, 1969

In the world's mental image of Chicago, there is a time-jump from the city of Al Capone and Augie March to the city of Mayor Daley and the Conspiracy Trial. Both the individuals quoted at the head of this chapter came to know their Chicago during the years between. Edward Levi, a violin-playing, cigar-loving lawyer, the grandson of a famous Chicago rabbi and probably the most intrinsically intelligent of reigning American university presidents, has been on the staff of the University of Chicago since 1936, and President since 1968. A colleague with the mind of an Irish ward politician remarked to me that if Levi had chosen to stick with his law practice, he would have fitted neatly into 'the Jewish slot' on the

Supreme Court. Professor Redfield's personal acquaintance with the
Chicago style is closer still, and has been permanently memorialised: on
the *Chicago Tribune* building downtown, bronze casts of some of the
paper's most famous front pages are displayed, and somewhere at the foot
of the page announcing the abdication of Edward VIII, it is reported that
James Redfield, aged three, had been returned by kidnappers to his father,
who was also a professor (a renowned anthropologist) in the University
of Chicago.

'An unpleasant city, in a nasty climate, a thousand miles from any-
where . . . ' True enough, though Chicago's Americans like to think that
Detroit or Pittsburgh are much less pleasant, that the summer heat and the
knife-like winter winds make boys into men, and that the capital of the
Mid West is a considerable somewhere in its own right. So is its university.
There are, of course, other universities within Chicago's city boundaries,
and several more a few miles outside, including important ones like
Northwestern, Michigan State, and the various campuses of the University of Illinois. But between the University of Chicago, which is a private
university dependent on the donors it can touch and the research grants it
can attract, and its immediate constituency there is a uniquely close and
prickly relationship. In a short eighty years Chicago has gathered to itself
as much historical and sociological complexity as Harvard has in three
centuries.

That is how the people of Chicago would want it. In Norman Mailer's
inimitable description, the place is 'perhaps the last of the great American
cities', where 'the unheard crash of giant mills stamping new shapes on
large and obdurate materials is always pounding in one's inner ear'. Its
people have 'great faces, carnal as blood, greedy, direct, too impatient for
hypocrisy, in love with honest plunder'.[29] That is the underlying poetry
of Chicago, just as blackened chimneys and viscous canals and broad-
vowelled, pause-filled conversations are the poetry of Manchester.
Chicago is at once happy and resentful that it is not New York, just as
Manchester is at once contemptuous and ever-so-slightly envious of
London. But perhaps because both the physical and the human environment in Chicago is that much more hostile than it is in Manchester,
England, the temper of the individuals and groups who doggedly pursue
culture and learning in that environment has become more serious, more
metaphysical, than anywhere else. Reyner Banham, the architectural and
pop-cultural critic, the other day called Chicago 'a profoundly German
town'. Manchester, too, could make this claim if it cared to. In Chicago,
there are even more obvious marks of German influence and immigration,
from the names in the telephone directory to Mies van der Rohe's buildings for the Illinois Institute of Technology. But it goes deeper than that.
The significance of the University of Chicago in the history of American
and the world's higher education was its marriage in a single institution

[29] *Miami and the Siege of Chicago* (New York, 1968).

of German philosophical seriousness, expressed in a systematic exploration of the unknown through a rigorous training of the intellect, and the late nineteenth century Middle-Western version of the American dream, in which realism, regionalism, and religiosity all played their part, but in which the itch to be first on the streets with a new model for human society was perhaps the dominant force. Virtually contemporaneous with the founding of the University of Chicago was the Colombian Exposition of 1893, staged in the Midway Plaisance which then bordered, but now divides, the main buildings of the University. To this period belongs a campus song which it is difficult to envisage the class of '72 singing:

'Oh there were more profs. than students, but then we didn't care
They spent their days in research work, their evenings at the Fair
O Chicago, O Chicago, how great you've grown to be
Since first we cast our lot with thine in 1893.'

And one young Chicago dean recalls seeing a contemporary picture of the Exhibition scene, Ferris wheel and all, with a background, not of South Side Chicago and Lake Michigan, but of misty blue mountains, a Wild West of the mind.

The University of Chicago's intellectual history, and its constitution as a private university, are two keys to an understanding of it, but there is a third key in its physical setting and appearance. Its territory, or sphere of influence, is over a mile square, bounded by 47th Street to the North, 61st Street to the South, Cottage Grove to the West, and Lake Shore Drive (and beyond that, Lake Michigan) to the East. The central campus area, including the blocks originally given to the University by Marshall Field, the department store millionaire, is much smaller, with the same southern boundary. Ten minutes easy walk takes you from the Law School on 60th Street, across the tree-lined Midway, where on occasion leaders of the Blackstone Rangers gang sit on chairs to parley in front of their men like African tribal chieftains; through the main university quadrangle; and past Henry Moore's bronze *Nuclear Energy* (placed on the site where Fermi, Szilard and their team achieved the world's first self-sustaining atomic reaction) to the proposed student village north of 56th Street. Architecturally, the contrasts which the campus provides are absurd, but pleasantly sharp. The dominant style is American collegiate Gothic. Hutchinson Commons, the first student dining hall to be built in the University, is a fair imitation of Christ Church hall, Oxford. It is said that Edward Prince of Wales, when he visited Chicago during the thirties, was kind enough to agree about the resemblance, adding only that at Christ Church they never cleaned the windows. From that day on, Hutchinson's windows were never cleaned either, until a few years later President Hutchins said he could stand the gloom no longer, and ordered soap and water. Close by, snarling stone gryphons scamper up the arch leading to the Hull Biological Laboratories, as though Professor Ronald

46

Singer, chairman of the Anatomy Department, were after them with a dissecting knife; and across the road the twenty million dollar Joseph Regenstein library is under construction; a gift (with a matching grant from the Ford Foundation) which was negotiated with the donor, the widow of a chemical multi-millionaire, by one of the University's trustees. Lesser benefactions are sought and handled by the Director of Development and his staff, but as one of them explained, 'you set a million to catch a million.'

Gothic, too, is the Rockefeller Memorial Chapel, a miniature cathedral, which cost nearly two million dollars to build in the twenties. (Only a Rockefeller would call it a chapel.) On a Sunday morning or a Wednesday evening, the resounding tinkle of Bach on the seventy-two-bell carillon draws the visitor to the foot of the tower, where high up in a little room a solitary musician is stamping vigorously on his wooden keyboard. (On Good Friday 1969, while Chicago's white-owned shops closed in prudent homage on the anniversary of Martin Luther King's death, he played 'The Vicar of Bray'.) Across the street is Robie House, which Frank Lloyd Wright built in 1909, all leaded panes and horizontal planes. It has claims to be the first truly modern domestic building, and it now houses the Adlai Stevenson Institute for the study of international relations. Finally, walk back across the Midway—though after dark, however anxious you are to get indoors out of a bitingly cold Chicago wind, you may be advised not to cut across the grass, but keep to the lighted streets. On the far side stands Saarinen's most civilised Law School, behind a row of fountains aligned to trap the sun in a shifting prismatic effect, and a Pevsner sculpture, 'Construction in space in the 3rd and 4th dimension'. The shrewd professor of taxation law who chaired the building committee acquired an office overlooking the pool with a view across Midway to the old Harper Library: it is the best prospect in the University. The School itself has several subtle touches designed to bring teachers and students into accidental contact: the professors' rooms open off the library book-stacks, and they cannot fetch their mail without crossing the student lounge. But law students are graduates, studying for a lucrative profession and paying handsomely for the privilege. It is accidentally symbolic of the University's priorities that although Saarinen was also commissioned to do a couple of undergraduate high-rise dormitories, he refused to have his name on them when they were built, because the University ran short of cash and was obliged to spoil the scale of the rooms by 'doubling-up' to pack more students in.

The University of Chicago has 8,579 students, of whom about thirty per cent are in the undergraduate college, forty-three per cent doing graduate work, and twenty-seven per cent in the (graduate) professional schools: Law, Divinity, Business, Social Service Administration, and others. A student paying the full rate (which is itself much less than the true cost) has to budget on spending between three and four thousand dollars a year on board and tuition, and the cost to the University of scholarships, loans, and other forms of remission has risen from one million to eighteen million dollars in the past twenty years. The proportion of graduates is by national and international standard exceptionally high, even if the professional schools are left out of account. Oxford, England, for example has yet to achieve the proportion (recommended by the Franks Report) of one graduate to every two undergraduates. In Chicago, one out of every ten undergraduates ends up not only with a master's degree, but with a Ph.D., which is not a matter for unambiguous self-congratulation but is a reliable index of career intention: there are 2,500 Chicago alumni teaching at fifty-two leading American universities. The faculty numbers over a thousand, of whom under a third do any undergraduate teaching: tutors at Oxford, England, may find this a surprisingly small proportion. Twenty-nine Nobel Prize winners have at one time or other taught or studied at Chicago—including Dr. Charles B. Huggins, director of the Ben May Cancer Research Laboratory, who attracted a different kind of attention in 1969 by calling a press conference to say that the student revolt was a Communist plot. The University, like Chicago itself, operates in the grand manner. It has a vacuum tube a mile long for measuring the speed of light, and the projected twenty-one-volume Assyrian dictionary is just over half complete after half a century of work by sixty scholars of several generations. (To be fair, the Oxford Latin Dictionary has proceeded no faster.) The University sent an expedition to Nubia in 1962–3, which rescued the contents of a 3,000 year old grave from the Nile waters rising above Aswan, and brought home an exquisitely worked copper hand-mirror and other artefacts to add to the collection in their Oriental Institute. In the all-American ratings of graduate schools, the University of Chicago stands first in Anthropology, Fourth in Political Science, and sixth in Astronomy.[30] The University of Chicago lately sent the Dean of its Business School to be Secretary of Labour, and one of its trustees to be Secretary of the Treasury, in Mr. Nixon's administration; and its best-known and most intimidating economist, Milton Friedman, a nineteenth century liberal in the tradition of Bentham and Mill, was welcomed as a man and a brother by those Republicans who thought they understood what he was saying. The University of Chicago receives two million dollars a year in royalties from its share in the Encyclopaedia Britannica (and would have had a larger share if a faculty committee of the time had not turned up its nose at the notion). It employs Saul Bellow—not as a teacher of 'creative writing', but as a scholar in the history of literature and thought. In 1968, two people in the University's laboratory at Argonne, forty miles away, devised an artificial kidney the size of a transistor radio, which could be

[30] Allan Cartter, *An Assessment of Quality in Graduate Education* (Washington D.C., 1966).

used three or four times and then thrown away. In 1968 Professor Tetsuya Fujita investigated the effect of thunderstorms on aircraft, on a grant from the National Severe Storms Foundation; and Dr. Melanie Baehr had a programme (of great social utility in Chicago) to determine what kind of people make good cops. In 1968, the University's faculty and students put in a million call cards for books in the Library, and if you look at a day's returns, they range from the first edition of *Winnie the Pooh* to runs of *Nature* and *Mind*. In 1968, the University maintained a public relations staff of fourteen to make sure the world knew what it was doing. But so much, or nearly as much, could be said of a dozen important American universities, and the purpose of this essay is to get at the quiddity of this campus, whose occupants fall so easily into the habit of getting the car out of the garage to drive an evening guest home, even if he is staying only a block or two away.

The University of Chicago exists for, and is controlled by, its faculty, rather in the sense that an old-fashioned British teaching hospital exists for the doctors first, and patients afterwards. 'What a pity,' remarked a professor at a party, 'that the students at this place can't have as much fun as the faculty do.' Both the perception and the assumption reveal much. The faculty run the University, through the President himself and through the Council of the University Senate. At other American universities, the professors often feel and behave like strangers on a visit, but at Chicago the university is what they make of it. Their mean salary is $21,000 per annum, and a few top scientists receive more than twice that. About eighty per cent of them live within the stockade, a few minutes' walk from their departments, which for an urban American university is an astounding proportion. 'The difference between this place and Berkeley,' one woman told me, 'is that there the professors get into their cars at the end of the day and drive up to their homes in the hills twenty miles away, while we just put on our galoshes and shuffle round the corner.' They are best observed in the Quadrangle Club, a building whose oppressive solemnity would qualify it for a niche in Pall Mall next door to the Oxford and Cambridge. Indeed, one March evening while I was staying there, nearly one hundred tuxedoed guests gathered to celebrate Boat Race night. At the Quadrangle Club visiting lecturers alight from Manchester or Göttingen or Lund. Here, tenured professors lay siege to consultancies, and untenured professors angle for tenure. An enterprising Hungarian catering manager offers apple and toasted marshmallow pancakes for light scholarly lunches, and beef Wellington to mark someone's appointment to a Distinguished Service professorship. In the Quad Club, a young man from the Divinity School bitterly remarked on my first day in Chicago, 'the bosses make sick jokes about the students they expel'. To the faculty, the second most offensive and seriously regarded act of the February 1969 student sit-in was the invasion of the Quad Club by some sixty students, self-styled the Chickenshit Brigade, who stood on the tables, hectored guests, and ate some food. Their ostensible reasons for doing this were, of course, politically defined. But one visitor nevertheless found himself wondering if the event had nothing at all to do with the fact that this intellectually formidable campus lacks a good bookstore, a clutter of intimate little bars and restaurants, an art cinema, and several other casual amenities which make student life at once enjoyable and memorable. There is high thinking, but not too much high living, in Hyde Park. However, Hyde Park is a bourgeois paradise for young and old by comparison with the districts to north and south of it. The University of Chicago is pinched between two of America's urban disaster areas, and the history of the defensive action against the black ghetto, which it has conducted by varying tactics for half a century or so now, is so significant to the University's concept of its 'mission' (its own word, not mine) that it cannot be omitted. Indeed, the issues raised are liable to recur elsewhere in the world, as urban living conditions worsen and the space-hunger of higher education and academic research continue to grow. Chicago's problem is also a classic example of a social bind from which no one knows how to escape—without breaking some obligation or abandoning some value.

For a full account, the reader must look elsewhere—and be warned that the documentation, thanks not least to the University of Chicago's own professors, is extensive.[31] Between about 1915 and 1940 the Chicago school of sociologists, led by Robert Park, held a virtual monopoly over the professional study of race relations in America. Their laboratory was on their doorstep. In 1919, there had taken place in Chicago a race riot that lasted six days and resulted in the deaths of thirty-eight people, white and black. This riot, which began when a Negro boy bathing in Lake Michigan strayed across into the white section of the beach and drowned under a hail of stones, developed out of white resentment of the mass migration of southern Negroes into the city to provide cheap unskilled labour for war industries: a pattern which was to be more or less exactly repeated during the 1939–45 war. The riot was distinguished from more recent so-called race riots in Watts, Newark, and elsewhere by being, in essence, a white riot: gangs of whites pursued Negroes into their own quarters and killed them. This pattern was dramatically depicted in a sequence of photographs printed in the massive and well-informed investigative report[32] (which was locally, not federally, commissioned and organised). However, while liberal professors and other concerned Chicago citizens were engaged on this report, some of their white neighbours in the Kenwood and Hyde Park districts were taking positive action with the paper weapons which the bourgeoisie uses instead of half-bricks.

[31] Especially in Allan H. Spear, *Black Chicago, 1890–1920* (Chicago, 1967); and Peter Rossi and Robert Dentler, *The Politics of Urban Renewal* (New York, 1961).

[32] *The Negro in Chicago*, report by the Chicago Committee on Race Relations, Chicago, 1922.

The local Property Owners Association demanded a conference to deal with 'the promiscuous scattering of Negroes throughout whole districts of our city', and by 1920 their *Property Owners Journal* was arguing in terms that became familiar to English ears forty years later:

'Every coloured man who moves into Hyde Park . . . is making war on the white man. Consequently he is not entitled to any consideration and forfeits his right to be employed by the white man'
and
'There is nothing in the make-up of a Negro, physically or mentally, which should induce anyone to welcome him as a neighbour . . . They are proud as peacocks, but have nothing of the peacock's beauty.'

By the mid-twenties a formal technique for exclusion was found: the restrictive housing covenant, enforceable in the courts, forbidding the sale or lease of property to black people. The University, like most other big white real estate owners, participated with the local property-owning associations in these agreements, although it had never excluded blacks from its own student body. (*De facto* segregation in the medical school came later.) The then President of the University, Robert M. Hutchins, whose fame as an innovating liberal educationist spread far beyond Chicago and still endures, felt obliged to defend the covenants: 'However unsatisfactory they may be, they are thought to be the only means at present available by which the members of the associations can stabilise the conditions under which they desire to live'.[33]

And the student paper, the *Maroon*, whose editorial writer had not yet learnt how to be tactful, endorsed the choice:

'Any proper sense of values will condone this action. The University business office has a much deeper and more important obligation to the University community than to the negro (*sic*) community, however depressed it may be. Segregation and restrictive agreements are a necessity, given the social prejudice that exists.'[34]

The University's peace ended in 1948, when the US Supreme Court made restrictive covenants of this kind unenforceable in the courts. The swollen, overcrowded black population of Chicago began to move into Hyde Park–Kenwood. By the mid fifties, the housing stock was deteriorating fast, and when it became positively dangerous to walk the streets, the more impressionable faculty began to look longingly eastwards or westwards. (Not only the faculty, for at about this time the notion of moving the entire university to keep company with Stanford at Palo Alto in California was seriously discussed. But the cost, financial as well as human, was too great: after all, as someone said, who wants to buy a

[33] Quoted by Harold M. Baron in a paper to the Beardsley Ruml Colloquium, Chicago, April 5, 1969.
[34] Ibid.

secondhand university?) As long as Hutchins remained President, nothing was done. Two hundred professors left, and student enrolments dropped sharply. But under his successors, the University for the first time became an active agent in its environment, rather than merely a consumer of land for academic expansion. In 1954-5, an urban renewal programme was launched which was to cost the University thirty million dollars of its own money, with another thirty million from local and Federal agencies, in the ensuing decade. Edward Levi's brother Julian, Professor of Urban Studies and by temperament a match for any speculator or politician on the South Side, was put in charge of the South East Chicago Commission. According to Rossi and Dentler, one favoured technique was to ring up the company insuring a dubious property and persuade it to cancel the insurance, then get the mortgage holder to foreclose on the building on the grounds that it was uninsured.[35] Strategically, the plan was to envelop the University in a foam-rubber cushion of safely bourgeois streets. Politically, as Rossi and Dentler demonstrate in their book, the compromise was astute:

> 'Agreements on means between the racial liberals and the racial con-
> servatives raised dilemmas for both. Liberals had to reconcile espousal
> of an interracial neighbourhood with the goal of a reduction in the
> Negro population of Hyde Park–Kenwood. For the conservatives the
> goal of an all-white neighbourhood had to be reconciled with the likeli-
> hood that any Negro who could pay the price would have access to
> housing in the neighbourhood.'[36]

Someone, of course, had to be the loser. Inevitably, the losers turned out to be the poor and black. Of twenty to twenty-five thousand persons displaced by the plan, something like four out of five were black; of the households relocated within Hyde Park (where there is very little public housing) four out of five were white. In the same period, similar schemes —for commercial rather than academic motives—were being carried out elsewhere in Chicago, and the cumulative effect on the blacks was disastrous. Some 50,000 families had to go somewhere. If they were not accommodated in the stark high rise public housing projects which the city built in the heart of the ghetto, they could go to the University's next problem area, Woodlawn.

Woodlawn is the district housing 60,000 people on the south side of the Midway (sometimes known as the DMZ). The University's own South Campus expansion is encroaching on it, using blighted land which the University has long possessed. The rest awaits renewal. Between 1950 and 1960, 39,000 whites left Woodlawn and 44,000 blacks came in. By 1960 over a third of the population was under nineteen. Among young adult males, unemployment ran at thirty to thirty-five per cent—more than at the height of the Depression. Nearly twenty per cent of Woodlawn

[35] Op. cit., p. 82.
[36] Op. cit., pp. 51-2.

families have annual incomes of under $2,000 (which in America means the direst poverty). The crime rate is well over twice the city of Chicago average of 262 police calls per thousand population. Woodlawn is the main reason why the University of Chicago spends nearly a million dollars a year on its own private police force—mostly ex-city policemen who require a certain amount of methodological re-education when they join the strength, but who are very agreeable guys to go on patrol with. Even they cannot prevent all incidents, of which the rape of a girl in the Harper Memorial Library, and the gunning to death of a student, at random, from a passing car, were freshest in people's memories during my own visit. Even the alderman for the district, Leon Despres, a liberal opponent of Mayor Daley, was mugged by a group of boys on his way home one night, and shot and severely wounded by the youngest, aged thirteen.

The University's own interventions have been gentler in temper in Woodlawn than they were in Hyde Park–Kenwood. In the sixties, American Negro communities became markedly less easy to push around, or even to convince, than they were in the fifties; and Woodlawn did have, in The Woodlawn Organisation (TWO), a supposedly representative body with which uneasy co-operation was possible. The result has been a series of University initiatives in which practical utility and research or educational value have been diplomatically blended: a paediatric clinic and a mental health center run by enthusiastic doctors from the Medical School, a 'poor man's lawyer' service at the back door of the Law School, an 'upward bound' programme for one hundred socially handicapped students, and other projects of the kind that the Left all over the world damns as 'band-aids'.

The projects do not feel quite like that when you talk to the people involved, for Woodlawn is now much too prickly to accept any external research or welfare programme, especially from the University of Chicago, unless it can share the control. But certainly, the most considerable benefit which Woodlawn has reaped, or is likely to reap, from its academic neighbour is the University's services as an advocate in the corridors of Washington and City Hall. American politics are based on patronage— on the 'gravy train' principle. University of Chicago professors have enough leverage to hoist themselves, or their protegés, on to the train. The black poor—even if they are what Thomas Arnold once injudiciously described as 'the good poor'—have no leverage at all, except the threat of future riots. Besides, the best practical help that the University can offer is by several orders of magnitude too little. The creator of the Woodlawn Child Health Center, Dr. Albert Dorfman, Chairman of the University's Paediatrics Department, has defined the weaknesses:

'1 The portion of the population that can be served by medical schools represents only a tiny fraction of the need.

2. The medical personnel available to medical schools is only a small fraction of the national pool. Almost all of the faculty of medical schools are chosen, quite properly, because of abilities as teachers and investigators . . .

3. Society is unlikely to finance community health programs in the long term at present cost levels.'[37]

Innovation, in other words, is one thing: systematisation quite another. Edward Levi's own comment is pertinent:

'There is something singularly sad about a New Deal or a Great Society which can only find the way and the means for an integrated society when there is a private institution available to give enormous funds before the government can respond, and even then is unable to respond in such a way as to build upon the natural assets of the community including the institutions within it. It is as though school systems, park systems, and police departments were to be had only on a matching basis. The cities cannot be saved in this way. There are simply not enough universities to go round for the purpose.'[38]

Nor would the total funds of the University of Chicago, in particular, go far round Woodlawn. One University administrator's guess is that it might cost one billion dollars to rebuild Woodlawn as a community, whoever controlled the outlay. That represents nearly three times the University's total endowment fund. (Harvard is so far the only American private university to have a billion dollars on its books.) The problem, in other words, is insoluble by acts of self-sacrifice, even if the University had the will to make them. The consequence is a certain withdrawal—not a physical withdrawal into 'fortress Chicago', for nothing short of a Berlin-type wall would permit that, but an emotional one. This, probably, is the residual sense in which the University can still be accused—along with most white people—of 'racism'.

Of course, on any global scale of comparison, the University of Chicago enjoys vast reserves. An endowment of $394,000,000 in the five per cents, with some $25,000,000 annual income above that, from federal grants and private gifts, buys a huge amount of research and education, even in America. But to a foreigner, the genuinely rich and strange element in the financing of American higher learning is not the number of dollars at the foot of the ledger, but the routes by which they arrive, and the kind of influence they exert. In the case of Chicago, this theme cannot be illustrated without reference to the men who initially lifted the university off the ground: John D. Rockefeller and William Rainey Harper,

[37] *Chicago Today* (published by the University of Chicago), vol. 5, no. 2, (summer 1968).
[38] Address to the University of Chicago Club of Washington DC, May 3, 1968.

respectively the founder and first President of the University.[39]

Both were Baptists, Rockefeller a pious lay businessman who by his late forties had amassed a huge fortune out of Standard Oil, Harper a liberal Old Testament scholar who was frequently in trouble with denominational fundamentalists. Both were, by present-day standards, slightly cracked. Between them they made the University of Chicago, for they were ideally matched. Rockefeller, besides his genius for making money, had a rarer genius for giving it away. Harper, on the other hand, had a genius for spending it. Both were initially fired by the imagination of a young Baptist minister called Gates, who thus defined in 1888 the need for a great college, ultimately to be a university, in the rapidly growing city of Chicago:

'An institution with an endowment of several millions, with buildings, library and other appliances equal to any on the continent; an institution commanding the services of the ablest specialists in every department, giving the highest classical as well as scientific culture, and aiming to counteract the western tendency to a merely superficial and utilitarian education; an institution wholly under Baptist control as a chartered right, loyal to Christ and his church, employing none but Christians in any department of instruction; a school not only evangelical but evangelistic, seeking to bring every student into surrender to Jesus Christ as Lord.'[40]

The tone is hardly that of today's great secular university. But Harper himself wanted substantially the same thing as Gates, and he wanted it at once, holding that 'in these modern times, ten years count for as much as one hundred years did formerly'. Four years after Gates's speech, his University had had its first three million from Rockefeller, with land from Marshall Field, and opened its doors. 'The good Lord gave me my money: how could I withhold it from the University of Chicago?' Rockefeller asked. Harper spent it—on principle—always rather faster than it came in. The correspondence of the time is sufficient reminder that neither the affluence of American professors, nor the intense competition for their services between different universities, are a new phenomenon of the post–1945 period. Professor William G. Hale, of Yale, to Harper, September 10, 1891:

'You said to me that you felt sure that the salaries would be raised before long. How much more valuable the higher salaries would be

---

[39] For Rockefeller, see for instance Allan Nevins, *Study in Power: John D. Rockefeller, Industrialist and Philanthropist*, 2 vols. (New York, 1953); for Harper, see Thomas W. Goodspeed, *William Rainey Harper* (Chicago, 1928).

[40] Quoted in Richard J. Storr, *Harper's University, the Beginnings* (Chicago, 1966). p. 17. The official history of the University, of which this was an instalment, has unfortunately not yet been carried beyond Harper's death in 1906.

now, when you are endeavouring to get men to go to you! Your plan is to get the best men that can be found. Chicago trustees must be capable, as businessmen, of seeing that the best persons in any art are not easily to be dislodged from places where they have taken root.'[41]

Professor Hale himself consented to be uprooted when the Trustees raised the salary of head professors to $7,000. In real terms, today's Nobel prize-winners probably do not earn more. It was not easy, even then, to lure faculty from Harvard, but Harper's raid on Clark University, and his return with professorial booty by the carload, is still remembered in American academic folklore. (Of the PhD degrees held by the original Chicago faculty, German universities had granted fourteen, and American ones, twenty-one. The university opened at the moment when the international balance of academic trade had just been tipped in America's favour.) Equally remarkable, though less well known, were the beginnings of the University of Chicago's formidable library. Scholars, as the new universities in Britain have discovered, are reluctant to go where they cannot be assured of the books they are likely to want. Harper's response was characteristic. He went to Berlin and bought— without having the money at the time—the entire stock of a famous antiquarian bookshop, some 300,000 volumes (the exact number was later the subject of dispute and litigation). Impulsive as the purchase seemed at the time, the Special Collections Librarian of the University, Mr. Robert Rosenthal (to whom I am indebted for this information) is in no doubt that the collection, if it could be obtained today, would cost 'many, many times' what Harper paid for it, and some of these books are among the most-prized items on the shelves of the twenty million dollar Joseph Regenstein library that the Univeristy has recently built.

Rockefeller is dead, and though his Foundation lives on, not even this would today be enough to meet the cost of learning and education at the level the University of Chicago sets itself. Expenses have multiplied seven times since 1945 (total operation expenditure was $31,500,000 in 1947/8, $211,000,000 in 1967/8). Federal support, mostly for specific projects and specific professors, has in the same period multiplied fifteen times, from $2,620,000 to $40,450,000. Somewhat to its own relief, the university stands only 219th, with $1,360,000, in the latest list of universities and other not-for-profit institutions in receipt of Pentagon research and development grants. (The list is headed by the Massachusetts Institute of Technology with $119,000,000.) On the other hand between eighty and ninety million dollars goes into and out of the accounts for the Argonne Physical Laboratory, forty miles from Chicago, which the University manages on behalf of the Federal Government.

The size of the federal contribution makes Chicago, like other American private universities, private in a rather special sense. Yet the meaningful-

[41] Ibid., p. 74.

ness of the status is not in doubt, and if the Carnegie Commission on the Future of Higher Education, which is investigating the problem, recommends the 'federalisation' of the most distinguished but least financially secure private universities, the change of air in them would be drastic. The University of Chicago is what it is partly because even in the midst of plenty it has never quite known where the next million dollars was coming from. Its $360,000,000 ten-year fund-raising campaign launched in 1965 falls into perspective when it is realised that the University needs nearly $15,000,000 a year in gifts from corporations and individuals simply to stay in the black, and that many of the donors are the kind of people who are easily put off by a student sit-in—or by one of Dr. Huggins's 'Communist plots'. Nor does every dollar received weigh equally in the Treasurer's scale. He must always ask, for example, 'Will it attract a matching grant (from Washington, from the Ford Foundation, from anywhere)?', 'Is it restricted?' Michael Claffey, the young New York ex-journalist who directs the campaign, cheerfully remarked to me one morning that he had just turned down the offer of a million dollars from a man who wanted the University to build an old people's home with the money. If the Pritzker School of Medicine had happened to have a gerontologist who was longing for a living laboratory, and who was prepared to raise the rest of the money himself, the gift might have been welcome. Otherwise, the diversion of energy would be too great. 'Most donors prefer to ignore overhead costs,' writes Jacques Barzun, noting further that even reputable foundations are apt to strike out library items in a budget proposed for a research or instructional project, though it is known to cost today over ten dollars to put any book, however cheap, on the shelf of an American university library.[42]

Donors, however, are not quite as easy to find as they were a few years ago. Some of the reasons are national: after the first Russian sputnik went into orbit, universities in the United States only had to ask and it was given to them, but some donors' ardour was already beginning to cool by the time that student revolts doused it altogether. At the same time, the rapidly rising higher education budgets of state legislatures have driven state universities too into the hunt for private funds. Other reasons are more peculiar to Chicago, and the way Chicago men express them is itself illuminating. There is a feeling that the University is punished for its own seriousness: the high proportion of alumni who become professors themselves is little help, even in these days of academic affluence, when seven-figure contributions are being solicited; and there is also resentment of the New York-based media, which prefer to give news of eastern universities: 'When Pritzker gave $12½ million for a medical school here there were a couple of paragraphs in the *New York Times* but when some jerk with half a million endows a chair at Yale there's a picture and a two-column story.' At times like those Chicago fund-raisers feel comforted

[42] *The American University* (New York, 1968), pp. 158, 196.

that the chairman of the University's trustees is Fairfax Cone of the ultra-respectable Foote, Cone and Belding advertising agency, who lives in Chicago because he prefers it to New York, but will see to it that the word gets around.

Why then, if things are so difficult, remain private at all? It is difficult to imagine Harvard deigning to ask itself this question, but at Chicago it has been both asked and answered in an unpublished paper by Edward Shils, the sociologist, who divides his own time between his department at Chicago and King's College, Cambridge. Like his friend Edward Levi, Shils stayed in Chicago during the dark fifties and is protective about it, but his analysis of the virtues of privateness would apply elsewhere too. 'The important thing is that the university must keep its centre of gravity within itself and it must keep itself coherent.' This is partly a question of size: 'What is essential . . . is the sense—the deeply experienced sense—of being engaged in a common undertaking, with common standards applied to diverse intellectual topics and with a concern for the whole. A university which has become as large as some of our great American state universities or as large as the University of Paris or the University of Calcutta is treading on dangerous ground . . . When a university becomes disaggregated, its traditions become attenuated and its main functions are lost sight of; the junior members within the staff come into conflict with the senior members, the students become alienated from both and above all from the senior members. Numerous small sovereignties come into existence; the university becomes like the Holy Roman Empire, and particularistic interests grow at the expense of the main functions. Almost anything, however fantastic, appears to be compatible with being a university.'[43]

Clearly, privateness is no guarantee of modesty about numbers. Necessity or greed have driven many private universities in the US to expand beyond their resources, and in Japan private universities with 40,000 ill-taught students are not uncommon. But, says Shils, where a private university has—like Chicago—inherited a long tradition of concern for quality and innovation in undergraduate teaching, and is lucky enough to have leaders capable of seeing the institution whole, it is far better placed than a state university to weigh the needs of abstractions like 'science and scholarship', and of the voteless students yet unborn, against the pressing (and justified) demands of the education-hungry in the present generation.

It is a powerful argument, whose terms can readily be translated to fit the situations of other countries surveyed in this book. However, in

[43] See also the Report of the Committee on the Criteria of Academic Appointment (*University of Chicago Record*, December 17, 1970), whose chairman was Edward Shils. 'It is better for the University to allow a field to lie fallow than to allow it to be poorly cultivated. Appointments should not be made just because there is a list of candidates and funds to pay their salaries.'

Chicago during the spring of 1969, Shils's advocacy of institutional cen-
tripetalism, to preserve the quality of life and the quality of teaching,
would have been furiously rejected—if they had read it—by many
students in the undergraduate college. 'Quality and innovation' in undergraduate teaching was precisely what they missed. The necessary 'tight-
ness' of an institution with a history to revere and an intellectual mission
to protect had produced an 'uptightness', not merely among conventionally Left revolutionaries, but among good and potentially good students
who had come to Chicago looking for something or someone whom they
had failed to find. 'Some of them,' an administrator cruelly remarked,
'still expect to find Hutchins here waiting for them.' Whether this is true
or not, 'science and scholarship' on the German model were going sour on
them, and in Harper's temple of humane and Christian learning, they were
reading each other's palms and picking cards from the Tarot pack.
Another sociologist, Andrew Greeley, described it to me in this way:
'Even those who aren't engaged in Zen or drugs or witchcraft or astrology
or rice diets have a certain feeling towards it. It's not entirely new, and
it's not political radicalism (though related to it), but it's there'.

There were at the time obvious reasons for generalised unhappiness in
the student body: an unsuccessful, ill-motivated sit-in, followed by
traumatic disciplinary hearings and forty-two temporary or permanent
expulsions. But the malaise was prior. A year before the 1969 sit-in a
student journalist, commenting on the assassination of Martin Luther King,
had looked ahead and asked what white liberals would be saying 'when
the great mob of blacks charge out of Woodlawn across the Midway this
summer or the next summer or fifty summers from now, when they
knock out the leaded windows and throw in gasoline bombs, and when
the dean of the College can smell the books burning in Classics library'.
He was a good writer, and over and above his human indignation and
identification with the cause, the sense of relish was unmistakeable: when
that day dawned, science and learning would at last have received their
come-uppance, possibly for the first time since they burnt the library at
Alexandria. Private universities have yet to decide what to make of this
temper in their ever-more-carefully selected students, undergraduate and
graduate alike. In 1969, one Chicago dean subsequently told me, both
faculty and students were circulating among themselves photostat copies
of the other side's leaflets—without comment. The two positions were too
far apart for comment to be necessary: the joke, both sides thought, was
inherent in the text. But there were very few jokes at which both sides
could laugh, and a university without laughter is as much use as a
cyclotron without a drop of whatever cyclotrons use for oil.

CHAPTER TWO

Climatic conditions:
Tokyo and Berkeley

I UNIVERSITIES AND THEIR ENVIRONMENT

'You don't have to know how to lay an egg to tell when one is bad.'

Governor Reagan, to the author, on California politicians' qualifications for appointing faculty to the University of California.

'Je pense qu'aujourdhui, il est tout à fait concevable qu'un homme qui n'était pas socialiste à vingt ans le devienne à quarante, ou même plus tard. Ainsi arrive-t-il souvent que des hommes déjà âgés, mais qui ont dirigé des grands événements, traversé des lourdes épreuves et accumulé le méditation apportent aux souhaits confus de la jeunesse une comprehension profonde et lui proposent des réponses authentiques. Tel fut le cas des plus révolutionnaires du XXe siècle. Tel celui de général de Gaulle. Pourquoi ne pas citer aussi le nom de Herbert Marcuse?'

Edgar Faure, *L'âme du combat* (Paris 1970), p. 19

By describing Manchester and Chicago in some of their rich particularity, I intended to stress, after the past few years' carbon-copy accounts of student riots from Dacca to Dakar, that any university contains and occasionally helps individual human beings; and further, that universities are not—or at least, not yet,—as indistinguishable and historically null as airports. This microcosmic approach is liable to annoy the full-throated left wing social theorist, whose song and preferred habitat (Nanterre, Frankfurt, LSE, Milan . . .) are already familiar. It is odd, in a way, that those who complain loudly about the massification of universities are so often anxious to accelerate the process, by attributing to them more uniformity of intention and effect than is to be found, and by advocating mass institutions for places that have hitherto escaped them—for instance, a university-wide students' union for collegiate Oxford. However, the focus must now be broadened a little. Individual places have been allowed to give some human content to the state of being a student, a scholar, and a university. But beyond this inner ring of particularity, so to speak, there is a further concentric circle whose edges are much less well defined than the campus boundary. This is the social, political, or ideological climate within which a given university or university system operates.

This aspect of the matter has not been altogether neglected in the blanketing of higher education topics by the mass media during the sixties, especially where a symbiosis has developed between an individual university and an individual ogre-figure of high prestige or newsworthiness: Sorbonne/de Gaulle; Berkeley/Reagan; Tokyo/Sato. Nor have general theories been lacking to describe the interaction between politics and higher education in advanced industrial countries, especially where there has been a long-established Marxist tradition, as in Germany, Italy, and France; or a visible and fatal flaw in the society's use of its material and human resources, as in the US during the Vietnam War (and for that matter, before). On the other hand, academic explorations of the terrain, especially ones involving international comparisons, have been fewer than might be expected.[1] There are understandable reasons for this. The subject is vaguely demarcated, marginal to Sociology, Economics, and Political Science, marginal even to Education, which in all national bureaucracies and academic systems is the most domestic in its concerns, the least imperial in its ambitions, and the lowest in the budgetary pecking order. Again, no self-respecting academic would willingly venture far into the domestic affairs of a country whose language he does not understand. As for the jet-borne, conference-collecting professors of popular myth, they are often inquisitive and rewarding observers of other people's universities, but they go primarily for the advancement of their own disciplines, and a gathering of X-ray spectroscopists, or specialists in Hittite remains, normally yields a rather partial view of the problems.

But what are the problems? And is it possible to give some content to the phrase 'social and political climate', without falling back on the Marxist premise that western industrial capitalism, and the educational systems for which it is responsible, are essentially the same robber barons got up in a variety of national costumes, and that it is therefore superfluous to attempt more minute description?

My own conviction is that whatever may be the deficiencies of the nation-state as the unit of international political exchange, national characteristics and inherited national or local patterns of social organisation are still basic to an understanding of universities. True, the effect of learning itself has always been internationalist, drawing law students to Bologna and philosophers to Paris centuries before it drew Pakistani doctors to Britain and British physicists to the United States. But the academy itself, though officially dedicated to the pursuit of knowledge without distinction of national origins, has also, at most times and in most countries, expressed at once the cultural pride of a nation and the commercial interest of a locality. (Concepts of the *nation*'s commercial interest came

[1] A conspicuous exception is the quarterly *Minerva*, under Edward Shils's editorship. But see bibliography.

later.) Examples of both are not far to seek: John Harvard in 1636 founding his college for shame at the thought that the Puritan colonists of Massachusetts should find themselves with 'an unlettered Ministry' as a result of quitting the culturally rich soil of England;[2] the King of France in 1200, after the death of several students at the hands of the Paris police, granting the University of Paris its first and very favourable charter of privileges 'from fear, it is said, lest the master should withdraw from the city altogether'.[3]

The argument which emphasises the national particularity of universities also has the virtue of bypassing the other debate, now international in scope, over how far universities merely reflect their societies and how far they can be expected to challenge them. For whether they accept or whether they rebel, the chief influences upon their behaviour are deeply embedded national or group quirks and loyalties. There is no transnational, trans-temporal scholastic ideal which can be relied upon to resist the contingent presumptions of politicians. The ideal exists, but it is demonstrably more effective in securing the proper citation of a source than in preserving the job of a colleague who has become politically unpopular. At this point it would be natural for an Englishman to refer to the ease with which the German universities were 'captured' by Hitler, and American ones by McCarthy: let us notice, instead, that the Fellows of Trinity College, Cambridge, who purged Bertrand Russell from his lectureship in 1916, acted towards an atheist and war-resister not like the ecumenical scholars of academic myth, but like patriotic Englishmen and loyal members of the Church of England. (At least they did not try to pretend that Russell was not really up to his job as a philosopher.) It is perfectly possible that a similar conclusion would be reached from a detailed examination of the far more frequent occasions when an external attack on a university's integrity has been successfully resisted. Most such attacks are beaten back simply by the professional guild's instinct for collective security. In the rarer cases where something more is needed, the 'accidentals' of personality and institutional tradition generally determine which reeds are flattened by the wind and which spring back. Both between the wars and during the McCarthy period, for example, the University of Chicago was noticeably more successful than most American universities in repelling witch-hunts, and it attributes its success primarily to successive sets of trustees who had enough respect for the university's concept of itself to defend the institution and its president privately or publicly, sometimes no doubt against their own judgement. (Many trustees wanted Edward Levi to call in the police to dislodge the SDS sit-in of 1969, but the police were nevertheless not called.) Because bodies

[2] R. Hofstadter and W. Smith (ed.), *American Higher Education, a Documentary History* (Chicago, 1961), vol. i, p. 6.

[3] Hastings Rashdall, *The Universities of Europe in the Middle Ages* (ed. F. M. Powicke and A. B. Emden), (Oxford, 1936), vol. i, p. 295.

of trustees in private universities are self-perpetuating, traditions of this kind are perhaps more easily preserved than in state universities where appointments may be made by a state Governor or legislature. In Berkeley it would be thought absurd to refer to anything that anyone may have thought in 1895; in Chicago it is never irrelevant to remember the shape of the understanding originally reached by Harper and Rockefeller, both working from Biblical models of social organisation. Harper, though a doer rather than a philosopher of education, explicitly viewed the university as the 'prophet, priest, and sage' of democracy.[4] This was not a common American view at the time, nor since.

That is one example of the climate in which a particular university operates, and to which it is forced to respond. Other weather-indicators may be found in the books which political leaders responsible for education themselves write. M. Edgar Faure was Minister of Education in de Gaulle's Government after May 1968, and responsible for drafting and piloting the *Loi d'Orientation*[5] for the reform of French university education. Governor Reagan sits by right on the Board of Regents for the University of California, and also personally has the opportunity, as vacancies occur, to appoint the Board's new members—for sixteen-year terms. The contrast between the open-minded, even playful intellectuality of M. Faure's autobiographical introduction to his most recent book, and the populist, wise-cracking, smoothly bullying style adopted by Governor Reagan,[6] is unfair to both the nations they represent: France has no shortage of men who attempt to govern by rule and rote; several civilised Americans have had the honour of being elected governor by state electorates in the US. But it meant much to the University of Paris at a time of extreme crisis to have in charge of legislative reform a man who knew what education was about; and it means much to the University of California to be constantly looking over its shoulder at a man who has no such understanding.

This chapter is not concerned with the English 'climate' as it affects higher education, but the importance of intangibles to an understanding of probable English reactions and developments is notorious. There is a story that while Trotsky was living in London, Lenin paid him a visit to inquire why the Revolution was making such slow progress in England. For reply Trotsky took him to Sunday morning service at the London

---

[4] Storr, op. cit., p. 57.

[5] See Appendix B.

[6] See Reagan's autobiography, *Where's the Rest of Me?* written with Richard G. Hubler (New York, 1965), where a speech containing his political philosophy is re-printed: e.g., 'We need true tax reform that will at least make a start toward restoring for our children the American dream that wealth is denied to no one, that each individual has the right to fly as high as his strength and ability will take him. . . . But we cannot have such reform while our tax policy is engineered by people who view the tax as a means of achieving changes in our social structure.' (p. 310).

church of St. Martins in the Field's, where an earnest young clergyman was preaching radical social reform, with great vehemence. At the end, the well-dressed, middle-aged congregation filed out, and almost to a woman they shook the clergyman by the hand and said, 'Thank you very much, vicar. Such an interesting sermon.' Whereupon Trotsky turned to Lenin and said, 'Now do you understand?' Again, while engaged on this chapter I happened to listen to an English radio programme on conservation of the environment, in which various speakers discussed how derelict industrial land could be reclaimed for community use. Towards the end of the programme a professor from the University of Keele, in the Potteries of North Staffordshire, expressed the hope that if this were done, not all the picturesque ugliness of the landscape would be lost: 'Let them be sure,' he said, 'to keep us at least one spoil-heap.' England, that is to say, is a country which absorbs and tolerates enthusiasm to a maddening degree, and is reluctant to abandon either artefacts or procedures which served a previous generation well. It is a crowded country, concerned for the texture of life, and every innovator is born with a matching conservative. Change, if it takes place at all, is likely to proceed by minimal adjustments, preferably agreed between all parties in advance. And this, it turns out, is as good a key as can be found to all levels of the English educational system, which is otherwise so extremely puzzling to a foreigner, even if he has digested its sheer organisational complexity.

What I have described in the last few pages might perhaps be called the 'micro-climate' to which a university, because it is that kind of institution, is obliged to be exceptionally sensitive. A business has much less need than a university to pay attention to small shifts in the micro-climate, small changes in the mood of its constituency or in the personality and ideas of individuals external to its payroll. It employs specialist departments to study the whims of the market and to keep on good terms with labour force, but most of its major problems belong to what I shall call the 'macro-climate'. By this I mean the conditions under which in that particular nation the corporation plays the game that it plays, the laws which favour or hamper it against international competition, the size of its market, its elbow-room for expansion or product innovation, the relation between its own image and society's requirements ('Should we be switching from napalm to contraceptives?') and so on. But the university also has to operate within a macro-climate of this kind, though naturally the clouds in its sky are different ones. Its weather is made by, for example, the extent to which the university is independent of central government and administration, by the way scientific research is organised and funded, by the quality of preparation that incoming undergraduates have received at school and home, by the freedom which the university has to select the students it wants, by the status of academics in the community, by the state of the employment market for graduates, and — in certain circumstances most important of all — by the national economic and political situation (boom or bust? peace or war?).

All these are obviously factors which vary considerably between different countries: so much so, indeed, that not until 1968, that year of revolutions at once simultaneous and stereotyped, did it occur to most people that any true comparability existed in higher education. Since then, as I have suggested, the pendulum has swung too far the other way, and people—some with an ulterior motive and some in ignorance—have pictured to themselves or other people a uniformity of climate which did not in fact exist. In the sections which follow, I attempt to describe the effect which different social and political climates have had upon two national university systems which are structurally and statistically comparable with each other, even though sharply contrasted: the systems of Japan and California.

2 JAPAN—THE INFINITELY INFLATABLE CAMPUS

'There must be no reckless composition of Chinese prose and poetry satirically treating of contemporary events. It is unbecoming the student who wishes to prepare himself for useful service.'
                    Japanese Government code for students, 1866[7]

In Japan, western culture means American culture, beginning with the English-language newspapers, which faithfully reproduce the interpretative poverty and small-town gossip-and-gush of a hundred Middle Western counterparts, and with the visiting American professors, vigorously communicating in Tokyo's civilised and hospitable International House. In the United States, eastern culture often means Japanese culture: that is, not just Anglo-Saxon Zen addicts but Japanese Americans of the first, second, or third generation. Whether he is in Berkeley or in Cambridge, Massachusetts, the European visitor can easily satisfy a taste for tempura or sukiyaki, and American West Coast housing has long betrayed Japanese influences in its use of unpainted wood and deep, flared curves. It seemed only a logical conclusion to an historic process when, during **my** stay at Berkeley, a Chinese professor of engineering there, a self-confident yet innocent technical genius who had succeeded in supporting more weight with fewer struts than anyone else, delivered a hugely-applauded lecture on his idea for a 'peace bridge' across the Bering Straits between Russia and Alaska, linking the continents which water and war had so unnecessarily kept apart.

Even without the bridge, communication between Japan and California is getting closer all the time. At Sanrizuka, a little village just outside the market town of Narita, thirty-five miles north of Tokyo, I watched the collision of cultures. In a year or two's time, concrete will cover Sanrizuka's peanut and watermelon patches. American military charter planes, and tourists flying in for the 1972 Winter Olympics, will know the land only as Narita International Airport. The Japanese Left took up the cause of the about-to-be-displaced farmers. Many students stayed in the district for months, living with the peasants in what they hoped was the classical manner of Mao's Eighth Army, and making a film of the resistance to the

---

[7] Quoted in Ronald Dore, *Education in Tokugawa Japan* (London, 1965), p. 207.

contractors' men. In October 1969 about 5,000 students, with a supporting cast of citizens and railway workers, chartered a fleet of Mitsubishi buses and travelled out from Tokyo to beat the bounds of the site.

A casqued and bannered assembly of more than medieval magnificence began the day. The Japanese student's plastic helmet, painted and then scrawled with characters, is functional not only as a flimsy protection against the *kidotai* (the Japanese equivalent to the French *Gardes Mobiles*) but also as an indicator of the faction to which the wearer belongs. At Sanrizuka white was in the ascendant—white for Chukaku, the 'Core' Marxist sect which actually controls only thirty-five of Japan's 829 student unions, but has made a particular effort at Sanrizuka. After the assembly and the speeches, the students formed files and warmed up into a snake dance. Trotting and chanting in columns four abreast, eyed by wrinkled peasant women in conical straw hats and by riot police in full rig, they bobbed and weaved in Sanrizuka's tiny crossroads. From the press and television helicopters circling overhead the shivering dots of primary colour must have looked like an Op painting turned kinetic. After this warm-up, they set off on their long country tramp round the future air-port, accelerating occasionally into eldritch, targetless charges. Long after dark the columns returned to Sanrizuka, singing the 'Internationale', their banners in the short Japanese twilight reminiscent for a moment of the scenes before Agincourt in the film of *Henry V*. But an invited California observer had a grittier way of putting it. It sure was a good demonstration, said the Black Panthers' Minister of Information, a broad-shouldered, bearded Negro who preferred to be addressed just as 'Big Man'. But there was just one thing needful. 'If each of them had a gun it would really be something.'

Japanese students do not have guns. Even the members of the extreme but small 'Red Army' sect, who in 1970 hijacked a Japan Airlines Boeing and demanded to be taken to North Korea, had to wave samurai swords at the passengers—not just because of the sword's symbolic significance in the Japanese mind, but because of the extreme difficulty of obtaining handier weapons in Tokyo. Neither are all Japanese students Leftists. When I asked Hiroshi T—, a graduate student of Japanese language and literature at the University of Tokyo, what books had influenced him most, he astonished me by replying: 'Eliot's *Notes Towards the Definition of Culture*. That's the book for us.'

Naturally, Hiroshi is not a typical Japanese student. He comes from a Catholic family (only about one per cent of Japan's 160 million population are Christians) and reads Newman and Christopher Dawson as well as Eliot, though his beliefs, he said, are 'not the same as Newman's'. He was also an admirer, though not actually a member, of the novelist Yukio Mishima's Tate No Kai, a group of ultra right wing students from various universities whom Mishima drilled in person and clothed in uniforms at his own expense, for years before his extraordinary death in 1970 (by ceremonial suicide after invading an Army barracks, sword in hand, and addressing 2,000 soldiers on the theme of national corruption). Reading matter apart, Hiroshi is thoroughly Japanese. Like others, when he has a cold, he wears a white mask over his face all day so that he will not infect other people. Like others, he will not attempt to speak English, though he understands it quite well, partly no doubt because he cannot express complicated thoughts in it, but partly because he would consider it disgraceful or disrespectful to speak it badly. He is interested in the traditional religions of China and Japan, and thinks that it is hopeless to tinker with the rickety Japanese university system until fundamental questions about the philosophy of education appropriate to Japan have been faced. I set out these details about Hiroshi to emphasise the significance of the last remark he made to me—a remark which goes far to explain why there is resignation rather than resentment in Tokyo when Zengakuren (the generic term for the Japanese student movement) paralyses the city with an anti-American demonstration. He said, 'I belong to the New Right in Japan and I agree with the New Left on one thing—that what the Japanese were taught after the war about American peace and democracy was not true.'

There is here an important difference between Japan and Germany. In Central Europe after 1945, even after the Nazis' suppression of Social Democracy and the infamies of Hitler's 'German Christians', the ideas of democracy and Christianity were still lying about, waiting to be picked up again and combined in Adenauer's Christian Democratic Union (however approximate and even bogus the synthesis). But in Japan, the 'democratic' revolution after 1945, though sincere enough in its aspirations, was not really Japanese at all: it was a construct of the American Occupation. It was made visible by the towering figure of General MacArthur, photographed in shirtsleeves with the dark-suited Emperor, whose image had previously hung in every school lecture hall as a sign that a Japanese student's highest service was the service of the family and the State. It was by the same channel that the American higher education system entered Japan. While I was in the US, a Japanese professor at a famous Divinity School, a man whose affection for America had survived the highly unfriendly internment to which Japanese Americans were subjected during the 1939–45 war, talked to me about the educational reforms which had been imposed on Japan after the war by the civilian educationists who landed with General MacArthur's army of occupation (SCAP). It had in many ways, he said, been a stupendous and successful attempt to reorientate the whole culture, 'but only people who understood so little about the system as it was would have dared to change it so radically'.

This is a view widely shared in Japanese universities, especially in 'Todai', 'Kyodai' (the Universities of Tokyo and Kyoto) and the other five 'Imperial' universities which dominated the academic scene officially before the Americans came, and still dominate it unofficially today. But it is perfectly possible for a Japanese to express this criticism of the Americans with a faintly wistful air, as though he knows that it is no good, that Imperial Japan is dead and gone, and a good thing too—and at the same time to express in his living style and methods of work the sincerest flattery of American models. Michio Nagai, a Japanese sociologist whose own domestic style of life is most consciously un-American but whose knowledge of America is intimate, likes to argue that the similarities between the US and Japan are as interesting as the differences: both countries sense that they live on a 'borrowed' culture and suffer an inferiority complex because of it, both are adroit handlers of mechanical things, both have a flourishing mass culture. Both take sports with professional seriousness—and they are nowadays the same sports: golf for the *salariman*, as the Japanese white-collar worker is called, baseball as a spectator sport for a mass audience.[8]

When I suggested (p. 33) that the international history of universities should be seen as a persistent search for adaptable models, I had Japan especially in mind, for Japan, like the United States itself over a much longer period, has borrowed at different times not one model of university education, but two. The first, imported during the 1860s, was German, and to this day, Japan and Germany are the two countries where the tension between autocratic, immovable professors and the burgeoning demand for mass higher education can best be studied. Other Western influences percolated through during the nineteenth century. The English novelist Frank Tuohy, who taught for a time at Waseda, one of the leading private universities in Tokyo, noticed many visible embodiments of English Victorianism in the education system: 'frock coats, white gloves and calling cards, gold teeth, the study of Carlyle and Herbert Spencer at universities, the Imperial family's passion for marine biology'. But the latest educational model is essentially cut-price Californian, and now that it is out of guarantee, the design faults and indifferent workmanship are beginning to show. California, as is by now well known, has the world's first system of mass higher education. There, about eighty per cent of high school graduates go on to some form of college, day or residential, two year or four year, and though the drop-out rate is enormous, and though the situation of the twenty per cent who are left behind is even less enviable than it is elsewhere in the US, the 'climate' inevitably ripens two characteristics already rooted in the Californian temperament: social mobility and constantly rising expectations. (Most Californians are first or second generation immigrants into the state.) Japan has 845 colleges and universities, 379 of which are universities for students on four-year courses alone, and although the percentage of high school graduates who enter higher education is only a third of California's, between 1950 and

[8] See David Riesman, *Conversations in Japan* (New York and London, 1967), p. 186. Nagai is currently studying higher education in the United States at the invitation of the Carnegie Commission.

1968 the number of university students in Japan rose from 391,000 to 1,116,000, a faster rate of growth than in the United States as a whole.[9] Not surprisingly, the education business itself is booming: there are no fewer than 309 'research institutes' for education, governmental, prefectural, or private. This goes some way to explain why one English professor of education contemplating the launch of a new journal was advised, somewhat to his astonishment, that the success or failure of his pet plan would depend on the Japanese circulation. Another (hearsay) statistic that clings to the memory is that there are more Japanese students reading Old Norse in Hokkaido University than have been attracted to the subject in Oxford and Cambridge. But the director of one of the national research institutes—whose autonomy and external sources of support encouraged freedom of speech—told me that by any international standard of comparison, Japan still had only about fifty universities. Before 1939 there were forty-eight (three of them in Korea and Formosa), and seven of these were designated 'Imperial'. Below these elite institutions there had been 448 *semmongakkai*, modelled upon the German *technische hochschüle*. The United States Education Mission (working under the authority of SCAP) thought that this system, and the school system below it, was fundamentally elitist and undemocratic (which indeed it was), and worse, that it was responsible for people's failure to resist the official ideology of Japanese fascism in the Showa period. (That was more debatable.) They therefore substituted a version of the only system they themselves knew at first hand: a 6-3-3-4 year progression through primary school, junior high school, senior high school, and university with a two-year course in technical college or more recently junior college as an alternative to university. They also 'democratically' granted to all institutions of higher education, from proud Todai to the humblest college in Kyushu, the same title and autonomous rights: every place could call itself a university. Japanese academics at the time accepted the situation—they had to—and only became totally obdurate when the Americans tried to remove the university professor's inalienable right to take a cup of green tea on demand throughout the day. But the effect of the reform was that none of the hundreds of institutions could afford to sacrifice dignity and develop a function of their own, less exalted than but essentially different from the courses at Todai or Kyodai. Moreover, neither SCAP nor the Japanese government provided funds and an operational plan for their grand design, so 'education', as numerical expansion ran its course, deteriorated into stereotyped lectures delivered to classes of five hundred. Indeed the proportion of the educational budget devoted to higher education actually declined from 20·1 per cent in 1940 to 13·1 per cent in 1960.

The 'climate' which Japanese universities have to weather includes many more elements than this, and Californian experience is enough to

[9] Japan Statistical Yearbook, 1968.

demonstrate that sheer cash expenditure on higher education is no guarantee of student contentment, effective though it may be in securing an environment in which it is easy to win Nobel prizes. (Incidentally, it is some comment on the state of fundamental research, as opposed to advanced technology, in Japan that only two Nobel prizes have been awarded to Japanese scientists since 1945, both of them for work initiated before the war). But this structural background may help to render comprehensible an *Asahi Shimbun* survey (in November, 1968) of student and professional opinion in Japan which reveals, for example, that at Tokyo University ('Todai'—the highest ambition of an intelligent Japanese boy) sixty per cent of the student body were 'somewhat or completely disappointed with University life', and that three out of four professors suggested reforms which on most American campuses would still be regarded as unduly drastic: 'turn some universities into graduate schools', 'separate research and education', 'abolish General Education departments'. The authors of the survey add, 'There was strong support for the opinion that student participation in university administration should be the first step in the reformation of the universities; but neither professors nor students had any idea what form this participation should take'. A British Council lecturer at one of the Tokyo universities provided me with a gloss on this sentence by describing the difficulty which the Japanese language presents to anyone attempting to make an abstraction precise. He reported the following conversation with a group of students:

'We want more participation in allotting use of the university hall.'
'But you already control it: it was built for functions which students were to arrange.'
'We want more participation.'

Japan, as every visitor remarks, has the world's sharpest set of contrasts between tradition and modernity, private insulation and forced gregariousness. Not surprisingly, David Riesman's *The Lonely Crowd*, which uses the concepts of 'inner-direction' and 'other-direction' to describe men and societies, was a very popular book in Japan, which is, so to speak, an 'other' looking for an 'inner'. (However, Frank Tuohy suggests that the popularity of the book also has to do with the Wordsworthian resonance of the title in Japanese-English, which has such difficulty with 'l's and 'r's: 'I wandered lonely as a crowd . . . ') The crowd, of course, is the dominant, ceaselessly moving impression of Tokyo, including its universities, where an enrolment of 40,000 is not uncommon on a campus which might accommodate 10,000 westerners in conditions they would be prepared to tolerate. The city as a whole is on the verge of environmental collapse, saved only by the hygienic discipline of its inhabitants. One morning, I listened over breakfast in International House to an urban ecologist from Berkeley booming away to a Japanese colleague about

71

what the Apollo programme had done for human waste disposal: 'For a long interplanetary trip, some form of recycling from man to plants to animals to men would be necessary. Now if we could magnify that process up from a whole town in Thailand, let's say . . . ' If we could, the listener was surely thinking, we would have something very elegant, very Japanese, and much more urgently needed than it is in Thailand. The Japanese birthrate is still comparatively stable, but the population of Tokyo has grown from 3½ million to 11 million since the war, and 600,000 families in the city live with other families in unfit houses or 'non-dwellings' like shops and warehouses.[10] To this crush of humanity has been added the motor car, which (in theory) can only be licensed in Tokyo if the owner is prepared to provide it with parking space on his own exiguous house-plot.

For a child, once born, life in Japan is deceptively easy. Fed or at least comforted on demand, and carried in harness on mother's back, head lolling asleep, months later than a British or American child would be forced to toddle, he can have no inkling of the disciplined existence ahead of him. In the subway, if there is only one seat, he takes it, and mother or grandmother stands. But the prison-house shades cluster early and deep. Six is hardly too soon to embark on the meritocratic grind, which begins with learning two different syllabic alphabets and 2,000 *kanji* (Japanese characters). Young Ryo's 'education mama' may want for him a good job in the Civil Service or the Bank of Japan. For that he must gain entrance to the right university (only Todai or Kyodai will do for such employers), and for that he must go to the right high school and for that to the right junior school and even kindergarten, with if possible a few well-placed friends to help him on his way. There is room in Tokyo municipal senior high schools for less than half the age-group. The rest have to go to private schools, which are generally inferior, and cost three times as much as the municipal schools: ¥73,000 (£85) per annum against ¥22,700 (£26·25) per annum. Such a mother will occasionally attempt to bribe a professor whose personal attention she covets for her child. A box of sweetmeats with ¥200,000 (£232) at the bottom was delivered to one Japanese friend of mine. He returned it through official channels—a terrible humiliation for the donor—but not everyone would have resisted the temptation, for Japanese professors are so poorly paid that very many can only afford to give the university half of their time. 'In 1968 the Japanese government defined the meaning of "the middle range income group" for the purpose of taxation. According to this definition, those who belong to this income group received ¥1,500,000–¥4 million per annum ($5,000–$11,000 or a little less). Among college professors of both public and private institutions, only 28 per cent belonged to this group.

[10] William Robson, *Report on Tokyo Metropolitan Government* (TMG, Tokyo, 1967) and article in *New Society*, April 23, 1970.

In other words, most college professors belonged to the lower income strata.'[11] Before the war, many professors had private rickshaws.

Many of the students who achieve their parents' ambition for them are burnt out cases by the time they arrive at university. They pass through the 'examination hell' (*shiken jikoku*) which is a cliché of Japanese journalism at the point of entry to higher education, not at the point of exit. Graduation is virtually automatic, and since the quality of the teaching is a disappointment for most, the closure of several famous campuses for months at a time in face of student riots has not been uniformly disastrous even for the industrious, who have anyway often been able to meet professors in clandestine off-campus classes. Others, if their families could afford it, took the opportunity to travel abroad, which may yet, in the long run, do Japanese universities more good than normality would have done, by diminishing their isolation from the rest of the world. (Foreign travel, except for hard commercial purposes, is in Japan more often granted as a reward for long and dutiful service than as an incentive to the young and promising.)

For other students, though, closure of the university threatens a blighted career, or worse. Tokyo University admitted no freshmen in 1969, for fear of inability to control the student body after the previous year's prolonged and bitter battles. Seniors had other problems. Mumeomi, for example, a 22-year-old English literature student at Waseda, one of the top two or three private universities in Tokyo, had the offer of a highly coveted job—reporter for a television company. He had passed the company's examination (university exams by themselves are not enough for an employer like this) but the company was declining to take him unless he could present them with the piece of paper that certified him as a graduate. And if his university stayed shut, how could he graduate? And the chance, if he missed it, would not recur, for even in the communications industry there is very little mobility of labour. If he succeeded in joining his chosen company, and proved incompetent, he would be shunted into a siding rather than sacked. If he had to give up and join a different firm, he might well never be able to leave it. It was a typically Japanese bind. For some in situations of this kind the exit routes quickly narrow to suicide — in adolescence, Japan's suicide rate is one of the world's highest[12]—just as, at professorial level, conscientious scholars have committed hara-kari because they promised their students that police would under no circumstances be called into the university campus, and were proved wrong by events.

Quite apart from the harassment and closure of universities by student demonstrations, the climate in post-war Japan is in certain respects radically hostile to humane education and fundamental learning as the West

[11] Michio Nagai, *University Problems in Japan* (paper to conference of university administrators in Bellagio, Italy, 1969. Proceedings forthcoming).
[12] See World Health Statistics Annual.

has come to understand them. (This climate is, of course, part of what the student revolutionaries want to alter.) The causes are part political, part economic, part philosophical and temperamental.

Politically, Japan has been dominated since the war by the Liberal Democratic Party, a conservative administration which has forsworn all international adventures—including, critics would say, constructive aid to South East Asia—in order to build up, under the protection of the American alliance and inordinately high tariff walls, first a domestic and more recently an international economic miracle. The party's leaders have been unspectacular. There was a harsh truth in de Gaulle's reported remark, during the state visit to France of a former Japanese prime minister, 'Today I am going to have a little talk with a salesman of transistor radios.' The prime minister at the time of writing, Eisaku Sato, enjoys a reputation chiefly as a twister of businessmen's arms for party political funds, and indeed, though isolated corruption cases have not left either the party or the prime minister himself untouched, essentially the LDP has no need to be corrupt: it is too deeply penetrated by the philosophy and contributions of Japanese business. (The feel of its power games is well conveyed in Yukio Mishima's novel *After the Banquet*.)[13] Except in Tokyo municipal administration, where a powerful Socialist governor, Ryokichi Minobe, has impressed both the local electorate and international observers as an honest man and a far-sighted planner, there is no alternative to the LDP. The parties of the Left, the Japan Socialist Party and the Japan Communist Party, are often described as nineteenth century parties, whose Marxist stigmata give them the mentality of a permanent opposition, without constructive ideas for the solution of the huge domestic problems which the LDP has allowed to build up.

Some of these have already been touched upon. Japan, though in export performance and economic prosperity already one of the Great Powers, is socially an under-developed country. Her nine per cent rate of economic growth itself conceals very uneven development: two per cent in primary industries, twenty per cent in secondary, sixty per cent in electronics. In a curious way, all this has bypassed the universities. Companies have found it necessary to set up their own research units, and whereas before 1939 post-graduate engineers in the Imperial universities were apt to be told that they were learning procedures which industry had not yet caught up with, and warned that they might feel frustrated on entering employment, it is now common for the company's laboratory to be ahead of the university's. Companies, in fact, not content with the effects of their contributions towards the physical expansion of private universities like Waseda, are even beginning to found their own, and a campus like Kyoto Sangyo, with a board of businessmen and LDP politicians, and a faculty raided from Kyodai and other beleaguered

[13] Translated by Donald Keene (New York, 1963).

universities, has had enough money to bring in notable foreigners like Arnold Toynbee and Hermann Kahn to lecture. Whether it is possible to expect either innovation or independence from a university so constituted remains to be seen.

The root of the trouble[14] is that the Japanese government has willed— or has had willed for it—mass higher education without willing the means. The reasons for this apparently irrational policy lie deep in the past. After three centuries of xenophobic isolation, Japan rejoined the world at the Meiji Restoration in 1868. At that time, the country's leaders saw their supreme task in terms of catching up on Western development. Two brilliant young men were sent abroad to shop for an education system. Arinori Mori, who at the age of twenty-four was the first Japanese minister to the United States, admired the British system, but his colleague Ito, who had more influence, went to Europe and concluded that the Prussians had more to teach the Japanese than the English could about how a backward nation could catch up. He summoned Mori from London to a Paris hotel and persuaded him to visit Berlin. Soon after their return, Ito became Prime Minister and Mori, as Minister of Education, founded Tokyo Daigaku (University) in 1877. The adventurousness, both practical and intellectual, of Japanese leaders at that time seems astonishing in the gerontocratic milieu of contemporary Tokyo politics and academic affairs. Mori believed that for education to develop quickly, women as well as men should be sent abroad, and while in the US he arranged for five small girls aged ten or so to cross the Pacific—an adventure which Michio Nagai justly compares with the space flights of Soviet women in our own time. (In 1969, by contrast, after a new University Act had been rushed through the Japanese Diet, empowering the Government to close permanently universities that were paralysed by demonstrations for more than six months, the Education Minister, Mr. Sakata, appointed a thirteen-man committee of mediators, to cushion the impact of the measure on the institutions affected. The average age of the committee was sixty-five.)

The new Imperial universities, and the first private universities which arose in their wake, evidently had remarkable vitality. Ronald Dore has shown how they were able to take for granted, at the end of Japan's feudal period, a spread of elementary (*terakoya*) education and literacy which England herself did not achieve for the mass of the people until primary schooling became compulsory in 1870.[15] Book learning had also been incorporated, as a point of honour and utility, into the accomplishments of the samurai (warrior) class, many of whom became teachers when their martial traditions were no longer in demand. This too—as Sir

[14] The following analysis rests heavily on Michio Nagai, *Nihon no Daigaku* (Higher Education in Japan, Tokyo, 1965, American edition forthcoming) and on conversation with Professor Nagai.

[15] Op. cit.

Osbert Sitwell discovered when he joined the Guards—never happened to the British equivalent. But the liberal intellectual élan seemed to disappear in the early 1900s, soon after Japan's initial industrial revolution was complete. The government which enacted the University Ordinance of 1918 still thought it wise to concentrate on importing ideas and techniques from advanced nations, and on diffusing them through the primary and secondary schools. Basic research and advanced teaching were still seen as luxuries. State and municipal universities were somewhat expanded, but the brunt of training Japan's rising *salarimen* was left to private enterprise in private universities. The Americans after 1945, though they changed so much, could hardly be expected to abolish such a notable survival of laissez-faire capitalism as this, even in the educational sector of the economy.

No change in principle has been made since. Japan has acquired a mass system of higher education by yoking together the human ambitions of her people and her advancing economy's appetite for trained manpower, then leaving the two to make what they can of each other. Of the country's 1½ million students, seventy-five per cent are enrolled in private institutions, whose government subsidy has for the past decade remained below five per cent of their revenue. Per student, the Government subsidy to state universities is about £1,000, and to private ones about £10. The private universities could do only three things: keep raising the cost of tuition, use part-time professors, and cram more students in. They did all three, and are mostly bankrupt all the same. One technique, adopted when sudden, sharp increases in tuition fees provoked students into strikes and riots, was to charge a heavy matriculation fee at the time of entrance, when complaint was more difficult. In 1967 the average entrance fee for private universities was ¥200,000 (£232) and for one private medical college it was fifteen times as much. At Waseda, one of the best-supported private universities (at least until the 1969 riots, which left several buildings including a new students' union block uninhabitable) the charges are more modest: for Arts students, ¥100,000 as an initial contribution, and ¥80,000 for tuition (in scientific subjects, ¥150,000). In the faculty club, which overlooks a famous Japanese garden and is therefore a much coveted venue for marriage ceremonies, senior professors can lunch in a civilised manner for ¥500–¥1,000; but only senior ones, for teaching staff salaries begin at about ¥60,000 a month and stay there for a long time.

The university's 41,788 students (35,482 male and 3,747 female undergraduates; 2,360 male and 149 female graduates)[16] fare much worse. In 1967 a student survey, which appears to have been competently conducted, said that ¥7,000 a month for rent and ¥12,000 a month for food were necessary for a healthy life (prices of both have risen sharply since then).

[16] 1968/69 figures.

But forty-three per cent of students in lodgings spend under ¥250 a day (¥7,500 a month) on food.[17] The library, with nearly a million volumes, including 293,131 foreign books, is one of the largest in Japan outside the Imperial universities. But it is inadequate for the numbers involved and ¥1,500 a month is not considered enough for a student's expenditure on books. (The streets round Waseda are lined with cheap noodle shops and paperback bookstores.) The fault is not the university's, but it did not seem surprising that at the time of my own visit, a Zengakuren faction was occupying the administration building, and spending ¥200,000 a day on telephone calls from the University switchboard rallying sympathisers from distant parts of Japan. (They could not be prevented, since by a rare Japanese technical oversight this could not be done without cutting the cable, at a cost of several million yen.)

Waseda owns four digital and three analogue computers, as well as a Theatre Museum, the only one of its kind in the East, modelled both inside and out on the Elizabethan Fortune Theatre (though the creeping palm tree at the side of the portico gives the Tudor façade a distinct flavour of Japanese temple). The quality of the teaching and of the students is harder for a foreigner to fathom, even if he is on the staff. However, the accounts of English and Canadian Arts lecturers do suggest that apart from the overcrowded, under-financed environment, there are two substantial obstacles in the way of what the West would regard as academic excellence and creative teaching relationships. Neither problem is peculiar to Waseda. The first is the deliberate self-isolation of Japan from international influences. Academic tariff walls are as high as commercial ones. The most ludicrous example related to me concerned a Japanese English Literature scholar, a woman, who was considered good enough for a teaching post at Cambridge, England, but who on her return to Japan could find no university job other than a secretarial one. But the case is not isolated. Foreign qualifications do not count for credit in Japanese university common rooms. One of the very few Japanese professors of English Literature I met who actually moved with perfect ease in spoken English (a rare accomplishment throughout Japan, which is one of the main reasons for industry's growing discontent with the educational system) told me that his skill did him no good professionally, and that when he wrote an article for a scholarly journal he took care to restrict his vocabulary and breadth of reference, lest he seem to be showing off. Even in numerical subjects, similar taboos apply: a Japanese full professor in Mathematics at Princeton could not transfer his seniority when he wanted to return to Japan. However, this kind of thing is perhaps one of the reasons why Japan, in spite of dismal professorial conditions and salaries, has not so far suffered a damaging brain drain: the prospect of learning English is a severe discouragement to leaving the country, and

---

[17] *Waseda Guardian*, November 26, 1967.

loss of position as well as salary an equal discouragement to the exile's hope of ultimate return.

The second obstacle to university-level teaching is one whose shape and dimensions a foreigner is particularly likely to mistake. Japanese reserve must surely take less crippling forms when there are no language problems and no stranger present than it does in the kind of situation reported by a young North American English lecturer in Tokyo: 'They are afraid of you and also of their fellow classmates. You can't even get them to come to the front and read parts dramatically. I have had girls absolutely refuse, yet to say no to *sensei* (professor) is also absolutely impossible . . . ' But further elements in his indictment are harder to find excuses for: 'I am involved in setting exams. One of the questions I could not do myself, and all my colleagues were horrified that I should admit it. Everyone but maybe two per cent fails completely so you get no real range of achievement. Nor is there any curriculum. They seem to think it would limit a professor's freedom to tell him what he should teach. Theoretically a student could graduate after twenty-two courses on *Huckleberry Finn*, and English majors come quite without literary background: they don't know whether Milton or *Beowulf* came first.' The only European counterpart to this kind of situation is in Italy.

Naturally, very much of what goes on in the better Japanese universities is at a higher level of sophistication than is implied in this critique of English Literature, which in Japan is primarily a girls' subject. The Todai graduate student who admired T. S. Eliot's prose and talked to me intelligently about Lindsay Anderson's film *If* had a friend who preferred Daniel Bell's *The End of Ideology*, and both the Right and the Left among Japanese students could put many of their British and American counterparts to shame by the seriousness of their literary tastes.[18] Six Waseda students—none of them reading English Literature, but all members of the university's English Speaking Society—not only wrote but helped to translate into English a very useful account of the Japanese student movement since the war, recently published by a small Californian press.[19] At the same time, the 'massification' of Japanese universities has clearly done severe damage to the relationship, traditionally very close, between pupil and *sensei*—a word which itself used to indicate extreme respect and affection. Even today, though arrogant or absentee professors are common enough, a significant minority still feel the old sense of obligation to their pupils strongly enough to submit voluntarily to kangaroo courts and various public humiliations rather than lose contact with their students altogether in the university's time of crisis. This traditional relationship,

[18] Cf. the book lists recorded by Kazuko Tsurumi in her *Social Change and the Individual* (Princeton, 1970), pp. 356–7. (Today, the name of the brilliant young Japanese novelist Kenzaburo Oe would almost certainly be added to any Leftist student's list.)

[19] Stuart Dowsey (ed.), *Zengakuren: Japan's Revolutionary Students* (Berkeley, 1970—see bibliography).

even if it was a little *de haut en bas*, was probably the only one that could have made a Germanic academic system tolerable to twentieth century Japanese students as they began to break away from the bonds of filial and social obedience. The American system, with its less formal relationships constructed on the principle of free consumer choice, might have worked ultimately in Japan given resources and staff-student ratios of American lavishness. But as Junro Fukashiro of *Asahi* pointed out to me, the consumer society has arrived in Japan, and students are exercising their right to reject an inferior product.

Without American resources, the informal system only begins to show results in Japan at graduate level, where the problem of numbers and scale is less acute. The youngest member of the Education Ministry's Committee of Mediators referred to above, is Shumon Miura, a self-effacing novelist aged forty-three. He attracted attention to himself by resigning his job at Nihon University ('Nichidai'), one of the most bureaucratic and gerontocratic of all Tokyo universities, where two million pounds had recently been embezzled to provide—among other things—a mansion for the President (a close friend of the Prime Minister) and donations to the LDP. There are 100,000 students enrolled in what came to be called Nihon University Ltd. Miura, some said, should have stayed and fought the system, though if he was lucky enough to be able to live by his own and his wife's writing, it was hard to see why. 'I taught ten classes,' Miura told me, 'and if five had twenty students, the other five had to have two hundred, or the university would have gone bankrupt.'

That kind of problem is beyond a committee of mediators. A British-style University Grants Committee might help, if it were visibly independent both of the government and of the educational old guard, and if it were empowered to concentrate its resources on, say, seven experimental universities throughout Japan as a counter-attraction to the quondam Imperial ones. But any Japan hand could enumerate the political difficulties. For example, there is already a government-planned, Soviet-style academic city at Tsukuba, thirty-five miles north-east of Tokyo, which is intended to unite thirty-six universities and research institutes, and to attract a population of 160,000 by 1980. But construction, which started in 1965, has been slow, and staff are reluctant to move out of Tokyo to a city that would surely become a target for present or future student unrest.

On the other hand, Japan is one of the few advanced countries that are still capable, when the will is found, of abrupt conceptual departures from an existing pattern. She has already confounded Western orthodoxy—especially, for example, Harold Wilson's election speeches of 1963/4 vintage—by showing that it is possible for a country to dominate its competitors technically and economically even after half a century of comparatively low public investment in higher (as opposed to school) education. But now that the barriers against external goods and influences are being slowly lowered, the demands of prestige, the new national itch to be first in something other than adroit imitation, and the increasingly anxious search for unpolluted cultural springs from which to drink, will surely compel the Japanese to set a higher value on originality and excellence than they did while their attention was concentrated on practical utility and economic independence. If they do so, not only Japan will be the gainer. For from the world's point of view, the basic flaw in the Californian system of higher education is that only Californians—and now, they have begun to say in Reagan's Los Angeles, not even them—can hope to afford it. But if lately-backward Japan eventually contrives to provide for everyone higher education worth the name, how long will Western European countries be able to withhold it?

3 CALIFORNIA—THE LEMMINGS' LEAP

I said to my mama, I'm going down town
She said looky here son, Why do you put me down?
I'll send you to a place where they love you like me
Gonna send you to Berkeley, to the University.
Chorus: Where it's warm (pretty pretty, and oh so warm)
       People there love you like a mama would do
       And it's oooo, pretty pretty, it's a womb with a view.
                                            Berkeley song, 1964

I have heard some student friends say: 'We are living in a society of
murderers and to combat them we would be forced to kill them'. To
this, or something like this, I find myself replying: 'No, it is more true
to say that we are living next to a society of lemmings and it is our
moral duty to take away the sea.'
                              Tim Daly, *Jump, My Brothers, Jump,*
                              Freedom Press, London, 1970

It would be unrealistically hopeful to say that there will be no more
student disturbances in the future.
                              Berkeley Chief of Police in a written
                              report on the Great Panty Raid, 1956

Tim Daly, quoted above, is the young anarchist who in 1969 was
imprisoned for setting London's Imperial War Museum on fire, as a
pacifist protest. The University of California, whose academic mantle
has since World War II been spread over the physicists and the nuclear
engineers at the laboratories of Los Alamos, Berkeley, and Livermore, has
contributed more than any other single institution to the United States'
capacity to set the world on fire, if it so chooses. That would be one
reason, in itself rather specious, for conjoining the two. But it is Daly's
parable, not his action, which fits. Something of the Californian neurosis
or psychosis, expressed in its political volatility and in its restless search
for new pleasures, cults, and doctrines, derives from the ugly geographical
fact that this is the lemmings' leaping-off point, the terminus of the
American westward urge, where the rainbow ended and the crock of gold
was found; but long ago now, so that there is nothing left for the state to

81

become except economically richer and environmentally poorer. As every television viewer the world over knows, the future of humanity is being printed out in California, where the redwoods overlooking the Pacific pullulate with aseptic laboratories and translucent think-tanks. But the unemployment rate is the highest in the United States. It is not a state for great architecture, though it is entirely appropriate that just as Chicago has one of Frank Lloyd Wright's first buildings, northern California should have one of his last: the Marin County municipal offices, a mock-Moorish colonnade whose sea-blue sweep takes the driver's eye from the freeway more effectively than any billboard. More characteristic, though, is a refinery belonging to the oil company whose blown-out well lately fouled the sea off Santa Barbara: the huge cylindrical tanks painted in yellow, pink, and lavender pastel to give the (possibly unintentional) effect of giant toilet rolls. A euphemistic society, you conclude, but in a state where one out of every two marriages ends in divorce it was only a mild surprise to pass, later on, a motel with a more explicit message: 'Have your next affair here.'[20]

The air of liberality is deceptive—as any girl at Berkeley used to discover when she wanted an abortion and had to be hurried down to Mexico for it. A limited abortion law has since been passed, but no one who has followed the troubles at Berkeley over the past few years, during which the university administration has been pinched harder and harder between mutually hostile political extremes, can have missed the zest with which sexuality has been used by both sides as an ideological bludgeon. The Free Speech Movement of 1964 soon generated a by-product called the Filthy Speech Movement, and Governor Reagan could send shivers down the spine of San Francisco's Commonwealth Club in 1969 by telling them that in the Berkeley 'People's Park' the police had arrested a twenty-one-year-old man 'sitting, completely nude, in full view of park occupants and bypassers'.

On that occasion, most people in most countries (except possibly South Africa and Czechoslovakia) must have been quite unable to understand the deployment of massive force, including a helicopter spraying teargas, National Guardsmen with bayonets, and police firing volleys of buckshot, all to protect an urban parking lot from students and other members of the Berkeley youth culture who wanted to plant it with flowers. But before any attempt is made to describe the political and academic background to the Berkeley street battles of 1969 and 1970, or to explain how

---

[20] The significance of the motel to American student culture is probably fading, in the face of new rules archly described as '24-hour parietals' which allow girls to live full-time in men's dormitories if they choose. In straight-laced Indiana, the state legislature not long ago argued for hours over whether or not male and female students in the state university at Bloomington should be allowed to visit each other's rooms for a maximum of five hours a week. The student newspaper later discovered that opposition to the proposal was headed by local motel owners.

it is that a university system with an income of over $600,000,000 a year can be in danger of starving for want of public support, it is worth noting from an earlier episode one vital element in the Californian 'climate': the tendency to over-react.

Back in May, 1956, President Eisenhower was running America from the golf course and Ronald Reagan, a competent film actor clearly destined not to reach the front rank, was compéring factory shows for General Electric. ('These employees I was meeting were a cross-section of America . . . and they are moral. They thanked us because we had never embarrassed them in front of their children.')[21] Everywhere in the US, and in most other advanced nations except Japan, liberal professors were complaining that their students were only interested in their future careers, and were bored by social or political issues. At this time, the University of California at Berkeley suffered the wildest student demonstration it could remember: an outbreak of waterfighting on the streets after an unusually hot day, followed by a panty raid of which orgiastic but almost wholly false reports were published as far away as London and Beirut. After it was all over, 1,006 female undergarments were turned in to an ad hoc lost-and-found bureau, and $4,500 were paid in damages to the sorority houses from which they had been taken.

The girls apparently lost nothing else of moment during the evening, but there was nevertheless, as the court reports put it, a sequel. The Berkeley Chief of Police, Mr. John D. Holmstrom, printed his 'report and recommendations', and since few copies of this period document can exist outside the library of the University of California, it seems worth quoting extracts:

> 'Some officials of the University considered panty raids in Berkeley as unlikely. In any event, there was no discussion between the University and the Police Department of the limits of conduct which would or should be tolerated if women students encouraged the raids either by their behaviour or by telling boys how to get into their houses, or by telling them where to find undergarments in the houses, or by yelling from windows and balconies to boys gathered below . . .

> 'Many boys and girls were dressed in clothing suitable for the occasion. Some were in shorts or swimming suits. A few housemothers advised their girls to refrain from waterfighting. It was reported that some heeded this advice . . . At one stage, girls were being "dunked", not at all unwillingly, in the mud of Channing Circle. Others were carried about on the shoulders of boys. There is little doubt that this unusual relationship, beyond the bounds of ordinary restraint, and the physical contact between the male and female participants, engendered

[21] Ronald Reagan with Richard G. Hubler, *Where's the Rest of Me?* (New York, 1965), p. 259.

emotional excitement. This gave some impetus to the subsequent raids later in the evening . . .'

Mr. Holmstrom was not the only person from whom a written report was expected. Clark Kerr, later President of the University of California and chief author of the Master Plan for Higher Education in California,[22] later still Director of the Carnegie Commission on Higher Education, was in 1956 Chancellor of the Berkeley campus. In his account to the alumni, he described the panty raid as 'a juvenile and regrettable sort of game . . . We do not condone the water fight itself . . . But the subsequent acts of breaking and entering and stealing—for that is the accurate description—were far more serious . . . The shock and sober realisation which came to the students with the "morning after" was deep, and I am sure lasting.' However, 'in view of the distortions carried in the press, it is particularly important to stress what did not happen. No woman student was stripped of her clothing. No woman student was carried from a house.'

Kerr's eight pages of masterly analysis,[23] all devoted to a panty raid, may seem excessive, but Californian prudery demanded nothing less of its state university. One of his report's many ironies is that the devices he proposed for cooling student spring fevers—more athletic facilities, and more on-campus housing—themselves played an indirect part in causing the battle of People's Park. For the university has over the years entertained various ideas for the now notorious plot of land which it bought across Bancroft Way from the main Berkeley campus: first it was to be student housing, until the students made it clear that they did not like living in the administration's high rise concrete blocks, and preferred the pleasantly tumbledown wooden dwellings which the site originally carried. Later, an indoor gymnasium was proposed. This was a textbook response to 1956 assumptions about what keeps students quiet. (Compare the famous exchange early in 1968 between Daniel Cohn-Bendit and M. Misoffe, de Gaulle's Minister of Youth and Sport, who had come to Nanterre to open a new swimming pool: 'I have read your White Paper, M. Misoffe, and there is no mention of sexuality in it.' 'If you have that kind of problem, you should go and take a swim in the pool.') But in Berkeley, by this time, the constituency or a significant part of it preferred a 'people's park'. University administrations, like generals, are doomed to spend their lives fighting the last war but one.

But there is always a war, and in California it is generally on two fronts at once. Jacques Barzun, who described the university administrator's occupational disease as 'bends, or caisson disease, which comes from violent changes of pressure' is with some justice indignant about newspapers' personalisation of complex questions about educational policy,

[22] The Donahoe Act (Californian state legislature), 1960.
[23] Clark Kerr, *The Student Riots of May 16* (Berkeley, 1956).

but he is on less sure ground when he complains about the headline that Berkeley yielded in 1964: 'Clark Kerr versus Savio'.[24] At the time, the phrase covered the political realities of the situation rather well—or at least, neither more nor less accurately than the headline 'Johnson versus Ho' would have covered the realities of the Vietnam situation. The names would now be different, for Kerr and Savio, though both remained in Berkeley and Savio became a student again in 1970, are no longer in charge of events. But the main difference between then and now would be the introduction of a third name: that of Ronald Reagan, who has been Governor of California since the beginning of 1967. Savio, talking to me in the Berkeley bookstore where he was working in 1969 put it this way: 'We did not have to bother about the state in '64. Kerr had been so successful in building up the institution that its problems were treated as internal. Only when the argument was over did the state intervene. Now, the University's kicked around as a political football.'

It is a football worth kicking. The University of California received its charter in 1868. It rested on three props: the buildings and land of a fifteen-year-old denominational college in Oakland, State of California tax support, and a Federal land grant under the Morrill Act, 1862. This Act provided for the grant of state land, with its revenues, to agricultural and technical colleges. Its ultimate munificence, through the rise in land values, exceed the dreams of its framers, and the Morrill Act is the true source of the United States' most characteristic and original contribution to higher education: the state university, to whose tuition and practical advice all citizens are held to have a prescriptive right.

Now, the University is divided into nine campuses, spread across 600 miles from Davis in the north to San Diego in the south. Each has a separate Chancellor, and in 1970/71 student enrolments were 110,000. Berkeley itself had 28,525 students (18,425 men and 10,100 women; 18,822 undergraduates and 9,703 graduates). Nearly a quarter of them are married. Over three-quarters come from within California, and of the remainder (who have to pay $1,200 a year tuition fees on top of the $2,000 or so per annum which is the basic expense of any Berkeley student) 4,712 came from other states in the Union, and 1,963 from foreign countries (1968/9 figures). Of these last, 332 came from Hong-Kong, 226 from India, 103 from Japan, and 240 from China (which is the Berkeley statistician's name for Taiwan). France, Germany, Italy and Britain contributed only 350 students between them, although Berkeley's graduate faculty, including nine Nobel prize winners, may still be the best in the United States and hence in the world. It is evident that the university's

---

[24] Mario Savio, the Berkeley Philosophy student whose presence, eloquence, and fuzzy reddish hair made him the charismatic leader of the 1964 Free Speech Movement. A professor of poetry at the time called him 'beautiful and strong'. For Barzun's remarks, see *The American University* (op. cit.), pp. 164, 167.

pull across the Pacific is at least as great as its pull across the Atlantic and the United States land mass. In 1968/9 the University of California had a full time teaching and research staff of 8,530, of whom 2,450 were at Berkeley. The Berkeley Library had 3,475,000 volumes (note, in comparing American with European library sizes, that the former count as a 'volume' each copy of a book) and is bettered only by the Widener Library at Harvard and the Library of Congress. There are another two and a half million books at the library of the University's Los Angeles campus.

The structure within which Berkeley operates can be described in three ways. From California's point of view, the University is the apex of the state's public higher education system, as defined under the Master Plan. Below it are the nineteen state colleges, enrolling 200,000 students, of which San Francisco State is the best known because most turbulent example; and below them the ninety-three (two-year) community colleges, enrolling 800,000, of which Merritt in Oakland is the nearest to Berkeley, and one of the most enterprising in its attempt to instil an appetite for higher education into a clientele which by background, preparation, and formal attainments would in no other country in the world have a chance of being educated beyond the statutory school leaving age.[25]

This tripartite system is advised by a state co-ordinating council, which related the academic and physical plans of the three groups. This council includes representatives of the privately operated universities and colleges in the state, of which the best known is Stanford University at Palo Alto, south of San Francisco.

From the nation's point of view, Berkeley is unquestionably the leading state university in the US, in spite of New York State's efforts to catch up and in spite of the damage which seven years of trouble have done to Berkeley's magnetic attraction for top-grade faculty. (Student enrolments have increased steadily, but qualitative judgement would be difficult: students repelled by Berkeleys radical image are not necessarily the most intelligent.) But viewed from Washington, the importance of Berkeley is not just what Berkeley gives to the nation, but what the nation gives to Berkeley. In the fiscal year 1970/71, the University of California as a whole had an operating income of $602,452,000, of which about forty-five per cent came from the state, twenty-eight per cent from the federal government, nine per cent from the sales and services, four per cent from donations and endowments, eight per cent from student fees, and six per cent from auxiliary enterprises. Note the low proportion derived from student fees, and the twenty-eight per cent from federal sources—and

[25] Black enrolment at Merritt is about forty per cent, as opposed to two per cent in the University of California and three per cent in the state college system. A student revolt there in 1969 took an unusual form: students broke into the bookstore and distributed the books—a graphic reminder that twentieth century hunger for education may sometimes follow the lines of a French eighteenth century bread riot.

note, too, that the figures do not include $242,820,000 paid to the University by the Atomic Energy Commission for work done on the thermonuclear warheads and other hardware designed and dreamt up at Los Alamos, Livermore, and the 'Rad. Lab.' up on the hill above Berkeley. Almost two-thirds of the commission research done at Berkeley is paid for by the Federal Government, and if it were not for agricultural research, in which the State of California is acutely interested, the proportion would be much higher. Before World War II this source of income hardly existed. Berkeley as a great national university is essentially the creation of federal money and of the past twenty years. The humanities there have climbed to prominence on the backs of the sciences—the university did not even have a Sociology department until 1950.

From the point of view of those who work in it, Berkeley is the university which has been obliged for six years to be conscious of the method by which it is governed. No University administration can expect to be popular, but in normal times and in normal places it can at least expect to be anonymous and unobtrusive. Berkeley, as tends to occur with a campus of its size, wealth, and diversity of function, is at once bureaucratic and incoherent. It loses as well as gains from being the headquarters of the University of California as well as an independent campus. But since 1965, the Berkeley Chancellor and his attendant officials have only intermittently been in charge of events. Still less is the campus run by its faculty. The Academic Senate has power to determine standards for admission, establish curricula, set requirements for degrees, and 'advise the President and chancellors on academic affairs'. But it is not, as the Chicago faculty is and as Japanese faculties are, an executive body, and Mario Savio's characterisation of the Berkeley Senate's meetings, though confessedly second hand, is from other accounts[26] not too wide of the mark: 'There's a quorum of anything between 50 and 1,200 according to the crisis: it's like a demo. And when there *is* a crisis, Heyns[27] comes down and makes a speech and there's a palpable shrinking away of dissenters unless they've really thrown caution to the winds. It's nothing so crass as concern for the next salary rise: rather that they're afraid of being isolated from their colleagues.' In this atmosphere committees to reform this and report on that are very easily set up, for in a miniature town of 50,000 people there is always something that needs reform and someone who wants to reform it. But the community's powers of absorption are equally impressive. What usually happens is this: a committee of eminent and hard-pressed scholars labours long, at week-ends and in evenings, and produces a report, with a dissenting note by a maverick professor. It is generally admired, and printed in the *Daily Californian* or the *Los Angeles*

[26] For a masterpiece of bitchiness characterising the Berkeley faculty during the 1964 crisis, see Lewis Feuer, *The Conflict of Generations* (New York, 1969), pp. 452, 462–466.
[27] Roger Heyns, Chancellor of the Berkeley campus.

Times or both, and savagely attacked by the radicals on campus. Two months later, by the time the favourable notices from the foreign press have come in, everyone in Berkeley has forgotten about it.[28]

Real power now lies with the Regents, who in other American universities would be called trustees, with the same function of representing the constituency to the university and the university to the constituency. The situation has been admirably described by Professor Martin Trow of the Department of Sociology at Berkeley:

'California is in many ways a populist democracy: the Governor and the legislature discuss and revise the university's annual operating budget in an atmosphere increasingly directly political and responsive to popular sentiments and indignation; and the whole electorate votes directly on proposed bond issues that are required for capital expansion. The Board of Regents, a majority of whom are appointed [by the Governor—c.d.] to sixteen year terms, was conceived precisely as a buffer between the university and popular or political pressures, to protect the necessary freedom of the university to explore issues and engage in educational innovations that might not have popular support at any given moment. But as we are seeing, the board appears unable to perform that function; instead of defending the university to its external publics, it begins to function as a conduit of popular sentiment and pressure on the university.'[29]

In the past, according to Professor Trow, the trustees even of big state universities had to deal only with a small set of directly relevant 'publics': legislative committees, wealthy donors, alumni organisations, and other people like themselves. The University of California could imagine itself to be rather like a British civic university, as a self-governing institution living mainly on public funds. But expansion—the university has more than doubled in size and tripled in expense over the past dozen years—has enlarged the specific publics to the point where they become an undifferentiated mass public. Every parent or businessman in California thinks he has an interest in the state's 'multiversity', but a mass public of this kind does not have interests so much as fears and angers.[30] The Regents, who can no longer have extensive personal acquaintance with their constituents either outside or inside the University, begin to pay attention to the letters that come in—'Why can't you deal with those sex-crazed, drug-taking students? Why can't you sack Herbert Marcuse?' —and react with 'panic and rage' to developments which properly fall within the competence or incompetence of the University's faculty or administration.

[28] The Byrne Report, the Muscatine Report, the Foote Report: where are they now?
[29] 'Elite and popular Functions in American Higher Education', paper reprinted in W. R. Niblett (ed.), *Higher Education: Demand and Response* (London, 1969), pp. 181–201.
[30] See Appendix A for a sample of the Regents' incoming mail.

But even this situation was supportable as long as the Regents themselves were men who were appointed, and acted, under the old dispensation. Certainly, as was demonstrated even before the McCarthy period by a long and bitter controversy over the proposed administration of a 'loyalty oath' to the University faculty, the Regents could not be wholly relied upon to protect basic academic freedoms while the state legislature was demanding blood. Nor, in appointing Regents, did the former Democratic Governor of California, Pat Brown, omit to notice where their political loyalties lay, and what services they had rendered him. But the situation changed radically after the election, in 1966, of a Governor who expressed in his own person the 'fears and angers' of Californians, especially the southern Californians who now form a natural majority in the state. Moreover, Ronald Reagan's own natural medium, television, is supremely well adapted to populist government. Nothing that is done in committee (unless the hearings themselves are televised), nothing that requires close reasoning from figures or papers, can be expounded on American television, except perhaps with an hour of donated time and a sympathetic producer. From his office in Sacramento, Reagan pruned the University's budget and packed the Board of Regents, as places fell vacant, with his own sympathisers. On television he could rely on cameramen's sense of news values to do justice to the antics of Berkeley students and the Telegraph Avenue set, while he himself could speak directly to the mass public, first promising and then (by declaration of states of emergency) taking 'firm action'. One of his academic victims had this description of the technique:

'He made reference to a report of the district attorney for Alameda County about some orgy he claimed had taken place on the Berkeley campus. He would tell people on TV, "Look, I have this report", glance down as though it was in front of him, and say, 'It's so terrible that I can't tell you good people what's in it". But in fact there was no such report, and the district attorney later admitted it.'

Clark Kerr, who survived only seventeen days of Reagan's administration before failing to obtain a vote of confidence from the Regents, not surprisingly thinks that the University ought to have stood and fought at that juncture, when it was already apparent what Reagan wanted, and when the majority of the Regents were against Reagan politically, and favourably disposed to the University administration. Certainly the lines of future attack were in no way camouflaged. Before he was elected Governor Reagan had been told by political sympathisers on the Board of Regents about an administration proposal to raise the salary of an award-winning Mathematics professor who had also been involved in opposition to the Vietnam war. Reagan told the Regents and later the press that faculty members of the University of California were going to be appointed and promoted on the basis of their willingness to teach the morality of the surrounding community. 'It does not constitute political interference with intellectual freedom for the tax-paying citizens—who support the university and college system—to ask that, in addition to teaching, they build character on accepted moral and ethical standards.' (Reagan reported in *Oakland Tribune*, January 5, 1967) In his first budget as Governor, he cut the University's requested budget from $250,000,000 to $190,000,000. He consequently put $30,000,000 back, but at a time when state university appropriations were rising everywhere, this was fair warning that for the first time since the post-war expansion started, severe financial stringency lay ahead. Finally, and most revealingly, Reagan told the Regents and Clark Kerr himself that he saw the University of California's role as a residual one. Private universities and colleges in the state, he argued, ought to be looking after the top twelve and a half per cent of high school graduates in the state (this being the cream-off point in the University's selection and admission procedures) while the state university took the bottom twelve and a half per cent. 'Your job,' Reagan told Kerr, 'is to handle the Mexican Americans,' and in a speech to the Los Angeles Breakfast Club (July 26, 1967) he said, 'Many of the University of California campuses are available mainly to those from upper middle class white families. For example, last year fewer than a hundred Mexican American students attended the University of California, Los Angeles, and Negroes were represented not nearly in proportion to their percentage of the population. More than seventy-five per cent of University students come from families which earn more than $8,000 annually . . . '

The interest of this remark, and of similar sentiments expressed later to wider audiences, is twofold. In the first place, it ran somewhat athwart Reagan's other policies as Governor, and ex-officio member and President of the University Regents. (Reagan attends their meetings, but does not in fact preside.) For several years, he made persistent and finally successful attempts to persuade the University to charge California residents a fee for tuition, which had been free throughout the state's educational system since 1868. The case for a tuition fee for the affluent Californians of 1970 was, as the university administration itself admits, a strong one, but without an elaborate structure of scholarships and remissions (which Reagan was not simultaneously requesting) it could only act as a further barrier to California's black, poor white, Mexican American, and Indian minority groups. Similarly, under Reagan, state fiscal policy has required university extension work to be entirely self-supporting, with the inevitable result that, according to an official in charge, Extension's student clientele is 'even more affluent, even more middle class, even more white than their campus counterparts'.[31]

In the second place, Reagan's notion cut the ground from under the

[31] Charles J. Hitch (President, University of California) to All-University Faculty Conference, March 25, 1969.

Master Plan for Higher Education in California, whose chief architect was Clark Kerr. This plan, conceived and drawn up in fifteen months following Kerr's appointment to the presidency of the University in 1958, was itself—whether or not his colleagues realised it at the time—an ingenious balancing act between elitism and populism. Kerr could see that the demand for higher education in the state was about to run out of control, and that the University of California's own long-term planning depended on what was done at lowlier academic levels. If nothing was done, cut-throat competition for state funds and university status would develop between all the colleges in California, and it would thereafter be impossible to persuade them into a true diversity of function. The plan went through both the Regents and the State Legislature virtually on the nod, but it would hardly have accepted so easily if everyone had realised what was happening. Kerr had given the state colleges everything that they wanted at the time: power to design their own buildings, manage their own budgets, grant their own Masters' degrees. But the price was long-term recognition of the University of California as the permanent apex of the educational pyramid, to grant the Ph.D.s, carry the main load of research, and thereby keep its national position as an elite institution. The 'populist' pressure was to be kept off by the community colleges (eighty of them, distributed round the state), which are California's most original and internationally admired contribution to higher education, and the 'semi-populist' pressure was to be relieved by the state colleges. For both, a further safety valve was provided: easy transferability within the system for students who deserved or wanted it. It was precisely this type of long-term planning that Japan lacked in the same period, and in spite of mutterings from the junior partners in the system, California could hardly abandon it now. But it has proved vulnerable to two types of popular revolt which were not, and could hardly have been, foreseen in 1958. On the one hand, white students after 1964, and minority group students more recently, not only decided that they were being manipulated and reacted accordingly, but also began to question fundamentally a system whose exclusiveness was based upon the supreme value accorded to intellectual excellence as such. At the same time, a powerful figure arose on the right, anti-intellectual in a more traditional American manner, using similar populist arguments and tactics to rescue the ideology of competitive individualism from the evils he characterised as 'bureacracy, operation by computer morals and forced fiat, the submergence of man in statistics'.[32]

The effect of Reagan's control over the Regents is that the university administration is no longer its own master in negotiating with Berkeley students, or in deciding how it wishes to use university property. In 1969, even though the President of the University and the Chancellor of the

---

[32] Reagan and Hubler, op. cit., p. 298.

Berkeley campus wished to bow to community presures—at least temporarily—and allow 'People's Park' to be dedicated as a public open space rather than as a car park or gymnasium site, the Regents did not, and from their own highly politicised position could not, allow this 'surrender' to happen.[33] Polarisation and public disorder had gone—or been pushed —too far for the university's institutional autonomy to be protected; just as in Japan, public indignation over the prolonged closure of campuses by rioting students enabled the government to pass a law giving itself unprecedented powers over university administration.

The true nature of the 'climate' which the California Regents generate for their university can best be assessed in the comparative tranquillity that surrounds their dealings with faculty matters. In April 1969 the Regents, in their first major decision of principle since the Governor's appointments 'tipped' them to a permanent conservative Republican majority, took back from the university administration the previously delegated power to confirm or annul the appointment and promotion of faculty. The members (in 1969) of the body which took this decision, and which now holds the final power to decide which persons shall be allowed to teach and research in the University of California, are briefly listed in Appendix A, together with a summary illustration of the kinds of pressures to which they are subjected.

A list of this kind cannot impart the more informal information about the Regents that comes through channels other than the University's public relations department—for instance, that Dr. Max Rafferty, a noted scourge of homosexuals, wanted to review the political outlook of faculty before hiring them; that Mrs. Hearst represents (unofficially) an important family of university benefactors, and was once a showgirl in Atlanta; and that Allan Grant, the big California farmer, moved the motion to fire Clark Kerr at the first Regent's meeting which he attended. But the list of their business interests is enough to convey that, as a student radical pamphlet puts it, 'the Regents and their associates own and operate the state of California'.[34] Besides Allan Grant, Carter, Forbes, and Simon (who is best known to an international public as an art collector, and has since retired) have food-producing or retailing interests in the state. The University chose not to offer its support or services to the protracted grape-pickers' strike organised by Cesar Chavez, and now at last officially supported by the AFL-CIO, but set out to develop a grape-picking machine instead. Organised labour has not been represented on the Board of Regents since Reagan took office, possibly because in southern California at least, labour is as far as possible deliberately kept unorganised.

Perhaps the Regent who best personifies the 'idea' of a Californian

---

[33] *Los Angeles Times*, June 23, 1969.

[34] *The Uses of U. C., Berkeley: Research* (Radical Student Union, Berkeley, 1969). See also Ridgeway, op. cit., pp. 164–66.

university is Watkins, a conservative Republican appointed by Reagan, who began his career as an engineering professor at Stanford and 'span off' to add his own company to the 200 others that hover at the edges of Palo Alto. Watkins-Johnson 'engages mainly in the research and development of microwave electronic and solid state devices and related electronic systems and equipment used in the field of radar, instrumentation, communications, telemetry, electromagnetic reconnaissance, and electromagnetic counter-measures. National Defense and Space exploration provided 75 per cent of sales.'[35]

Politically, the Board of Regents by mid-1969 divided as follows. The conservative group consisted of Reagan, Reinecke, Rafferty, Grant, Pauley, Canaday, Campbell, Smith, Reynolds, Watkins, and Mrs. Hearst. As well as the ex-officio members, four of these were Reagan appointees: Campbell, Smith, Reynolds, and Watkins. On most issues the conservative group was also supported by Monagan, Moore, Boyd, Carter, and Witter. The liberals were down to four: Roth, Dutton, Coblentz, and Simon, with some support from Mrs. Heller, Higgs, and Forbes.[36] President Hitch, in this company, counts as a liberal.

The April 1969 meeting to assert Regental veto power over the appointments of tenured professors began with the introduction to the Regents of a trim blonde girl from Davis, who invited everybody to the annual picnic on her campus and gave obviously satisfactory evidence that she did not have a thought in her head and did not belong to the Women's Liberation Movement either. (Of Davis, she said, 'We have the honor system which we are very proud of and the majority of students don't cheat which is kinda unique'.)

The motion itself was proposed by Regent Smith, who said that the move was symbolic only, and that it would normally hold up appointments by not more than forty days. President Hitch asked the Regents whether they thought they could make better judgments about appointments than the Chancellors. He thought they could not. Or did they intend to apply 'different criteria' from those now used? If so, the university would be involved in 'a controversy of serious proportions'. Regent Smith said that he had no intention of changing the criteria for the promotion of tenured faculty. Under pressure, though, he agreed that his proposal was not wholly symbolic. 'It has a tiny tooth in it.' Several others spoke. Regent Pauley, who had started the hunt out of indignation at the reappointment of Herbert Marcuse to the University's San Diego campus, remained silent. A procedural vote was taken, from which it was clear that the liberals were going to lose. Regent Roth, salvaging what he could from the wreck, proposed an addendum, '. . . and provided that no political test shall be considered in the appointment of any faculty

[35] Standard and Poor's *Industrials*, p. 9049.
[36] *Los Angeles Times*, June 23, 1969.

employee'. Reagan, looking like a cat that had sighted a saucer of cream, quickly said 'aye'. It meant, as both men knew, very little. At the televised press conference afterwards, Reagan was asked what criteria other than political ones the Regents were competent to apply. He looked sharply at the questioner, hesitated a moment and then said, 'Well, it's an old line, but you don't have to be able to lay an egg to tell a bad one.'

The consensus among professors and administration afterwards was that you did not have to exercise a veto to enjoy its benefits. The University of California, as subsequent events have confirmed, was on the run. The Regents' 'symbolic' decision was hardly a resigning matter, but the President and the Chancellors knew that if they *had* resigned, their resignations might have been gladly accepted. In this atmosphere, confrontations between administration and Regents over an individual faculty member are liable to be rare. What is one among 10,000, when there are almost certain to be other equally qualified but less troublesome academics available elsewhere? Moreover, any academic freedom case is liable to be a bad one for liberals to defend. In the US, tough men and first rate scholars can usually put the opposition to flight by the edge of their tongues or the strength of their friends, but in California, the first significant Regental rejection of a faculty hiring decision after the meeting I have described was in the case of Angela Davis, a communist, black militant, and favourite pupil of Herbert Marcuse, who looks upon education as a branch of politics and was arraigned for complicity in a Black Panther gun battle shortly after she lost her job as a UCLA philosophy professor.[37]

Nor will it be known for some time whether or not Regental pressure on the Berkeley faculty has had the effect of lowering the standing of the university outside California. Even an attempt (by Robert Reinhold in the *New York Times*) to show that the disturbances of the past few years had led to an unprecedented exodus of 'Berkeley refugees' to supposedly 'safe' East Coast colleges—like Harvard—ran into the sands of statistical dispute.[38] It is only once in every generation or so that a genuinely authoritative grading of different universities, and of different departments within universities, can be made:[39] all else is popularity rating or folklore. The budgetary effect of Reagan is more susceptible of exact description: at the end of 1969, $40 million or so short of the sum requested from the California Legislature, the University decided to cut back sharply on graduate student enrolment. (In 1970, the state legislature cut the University's budget by $5 million, and

[37] See *Soledad Brother: The Prison Letters of George Jackson* (London, 1971).
[38] *New York Times*, March 2, 1970; *San Francisco Examiner*, March 23, 1969 (Berkeley's reply, tabulating the faculty 'brain-drain' over the past decade). Cf. also the anonymous situation report from Berkeley in *Encounter*, December 1970.
[39] Allan Cartter, An Assessment (op. cit.).

rejected a five per cent salary increase for academic staff.) But since the 1966 growth plan envisaged that by the year 2000, forty-five per cent of students in the University of California would be graduates, and since in 1966 Allan Cartter was already predicting in some fields the surplus of Ph.D.s, that by 1970 had already occurred, retrenchment may be no disaster either for Berkeley or for America.[40] An unemployed B.A. problem is formidable enough, as numerous under-developed countries have discovered. An unemployed Ph.D. problem, considering the tedious and humiliating hoops through which the pilgrims are put on their way to the Promised Land, might bring on the revolution sooner than expected.

All this naturally begs the larger question of whether the Berkeley faculty—Naval Biological Laboratory, agribusiness research, and all— is too politicised in its soul to be *worth* protecting against explicit political interference. But it is clear that if a serious attack on the place were mounted in the seventies, it would be the Arts and Social Science subjects that would stand in the firing line. In the forties and fifties, American conservatives anticipated treason primarily from scientists: it was the physicists who had a novel, terrible, and incomprehensible power, and were preparing to give it away to America's external enemies. Today the perceived threat is within America, and the treason anticipated is within the mind: what matters is not so much behaviour but thinking dangerous thoughts, and teaching social disruption to the young. That is a problem as old as Socrates. However, Socrates did not have the protection of a trade union—the American Association of University Professors—and of a Washington research contract, transferable at will to another university, to keep body and soul together. Berkeley may fall a place or two in the academic ratings, and a few assistant professors in the University of California may be thrown to the Governor's wolf pack, but the faculties' personal and collective positions are mostly assured. No wonder Reagan, with his uncanny eye for an issue, began in his 1970 gubernatorial campaign to protest at the injustice of the professorial tenure system, arguing that if a business executive can be fired, so too should a university teacher put his job at risk. The beauty of this is that several progressive academics, not to mention students, in America have in recent years come round to a similar view—but for somewhat different reasons.

[40] Just to indicate the scale of the industry: Berkeley alone conferred 727 Ph.D.s in 1968/69, seventy-nine of them to women. The figure for Masters's degrees (2,234) is only just under the total number of graduate students in the entire United States in 1890 (2,382).

4 CODA—TROUBLE: 'WHY US? WHY NOW?'

These detailed examinations of the social and political climate, within which two national higher education systems live and breathe, will hopefully have been worth undertaking even if it proves impossible to draw any global conclusions from them. However, in Japan during the fifties and sixties, hindsight permits one to identify many of the probable preconditions for acute generational discord, focused upon university institutions. On the one hand, there was the de-authoritisation which Lewis Feuer identifies as the prime cause of generational strife.[41] The post-Hiroshima babies, and their immediate elders, had no cause to respect the generation to which their parents, teachers, and political leaders belonged. Again, the students in this age-group were becoming for the first time a mass society within the larger mass society, instead of an elite and privileged minority. This destroyed most of the remnants of samurai-style obligations and dignities, which Japanese students were able to experience up till 1939, and which can be traced far back into the country's social history.[42] They found themselves in institutions which had not adapted themselves either to society's requirements or to students' expectations. Finally, the government, which had failed to plan with sufficient realism for mass higher education, had a political complexion and social record which made it peculiarly vulnerable to the analysis of Marxist fundamentalists. It is often said in the West that the Marxist political and economic critique has lost its force because the problems have changed utterly since Engels wrote *The Condition of the Working Class*. This is also true in Japan, but not uniformly true, and the lineaments of mid-Victorian capitalism can still be discerned in contemporary Tokyo. The LDP in Japan has been saved from overthrow, and the universities subjected to unprecedented measures of governmental control, through the 'unrealistic' perfectionism

[41] *The Conflict of Generations* (op. cit.), p. 154, etc.

[42] Saito Setsudo (1797–1865), emphasising to his noble pupils on an evening walk the duty for 'intellectual labour' in government, pointed out to them a group of farmers industriously working well into the dusk to take in the harvest. He remarked that it took ten or twenty households of farmers working night and day to support a single samurai. A samurai who did not live up to this deserved—and could expect—'divine punishment'. (Quoted in Dore, op. cit., p. 43). Post war-Japanese students have felt their position to be more analogous to that of the farmers.

of its Marxist opponents. Unfortunately, the Marxist export models available to Japanese adolescent buyers were, in the mid-twentieth century, designed for geo-political, anti-imperial use rather than for domestic economic application. What the Japanese needed, but have never yet found, was a concept of Marxist gradualism.

The radically different Californian background has produced, for the university, a similar result. The Free Speech Movement of 1964 arose in an environment where higher education had been more elaborately planned and richly endowed than anywhere else on earth, and at a time when the process of 'de-authoritisation' initiated by a disastrous war had scarcely begun. It is for this reason that to this day conservative politicians and their supporters in the state have such a strong sense of unfairness that this should have happened to them, and remain unshakeably convinced that 'if only' someone had cracked down on the few dissenters at the outset, Berkeley would be at peace. In that temper, it was and is natural for the mass public to demand the heads of university administrators.

This analysis ignores too many inconvenient facts to be remotely convincing. In particular, there was the history of radical pacifism in the Bay Area (there were campus strikes at Berkeley against 'war and fascism' every year from 1935 to 1941, and in 1934 at UCLA, about 2,000 students met to protest at the suspension of five students who had held an illegal (*sic*) meeting to discuss the state election campaign).[43] Again, Berkeley was not—though it would be difficult to convince any Californian of this— the starting-point of American radical student protest in the 60s: students at the University of Chicago had got in first a few weeks previously, by sitting in the president's office to protest against alleged racial discrimination in university employment policy. A more accurate conclusion might be that although any student revolt in the US was bound to touch an institution of Berkeley's size and sensitivity, and possibly be magnified there, Berkeley's emergence as the movement's first and most enduring symbol owed much to sheer historical accident.

For example, Clark Kerr, looking back, identifies one serious mistake of his own and one almost wholly fortuitous disaster that set the Free Speech Movement of 1964 and its successors inexorably on their way. His first mistake, he thinks, was made when he returned from a visit to Tokyo on September 16 and learnt that his Berkeley Chancellor, Edward Strong, had two days before withdrawn the campus's tradition of Hyde Park style free speech. (This right was originally exercised at Sather Gate, and then, when the Sather Gate ceased to be the boundary between campus and community, on the pavement at the top of Telegraph Avenue.) Kerr knew that this was a terrible thing to have done, and at that stage his own prestige with the Regents as the architect of the university's

[43] Seymour Martin Lipset and Sheldon S. Wolin (eds.), *The Berkeley Student Revolt* (New York, 1965), pp. 12–14.

national prestige probably stood high enough for him to have overruled his Chancellor and won. But he confined himself to 'advice', which was rejected.

The inadvertent disaster which followed had overtones of broad comedy. On December 7, some 16,000 students, faculty members and staff gathered in Berkeley's open-air Greek theatre (a gift of the Hearst family) to hear a proposed settlement, which entailed washing out the sit-ins and mass arrests of the previous three months, and making new rules for campus advocacy of social and political action. No police were to be allowed near the theatre. Kerr, on the platform, accepted the settlement subject to the Regents' approval and sat down to a standing ovation. As the meeting adjourned, Mario Savio strode to the microphone. He intended, apparently, only to announce a Free Speech Movement rally in Sproul Plaza. But neither he nor Kerr knew that earlier in the morning, Chancellor Strong's deputy had been warned that violence was threatened in the Greek theatre. It was a threat that Kerr—a member of the Society of Friends—would probably have discounted. But there was no way of consulting him. The Vice-Chancellor rescinded the ban on police, and stationed a few in the wings. When Savio strode towards the platform party, Berkeley's Keystone Cops thought that their cue had come, and rushed on stage, somewhat disarranging Kerr's gracious exit. The spectators were treated to a *peripateia* worthy of any Greek tragedy, as Savio was seized and dragged away; and at the FSM rally later, 10,000 people rejected the settlement by acclamation.

Even this ludicrous episode, like the panty raid eight years previously, enables one to define the Californian 'fatal flaw' as a propensity to over-react. For at the same period, Kerr's critics among the Regents and in the community were furious with him for not calling more police earlier. Yet this temper, in turn, arose from the structural, political, and geographical factors which have been described in this chapter. The point in common between the Bay Area and Tokyo was and is the presence of a 'critical mass' of students, quasi-students, and permanent students. 'Like a vast factory', writes Professor Lipset, a large campus brings together great numbers of people in similar life situations, a close proximity to each other, who can acquire a sense of solidarity and wield real power . . . It is relatively easy to reach students; leaflets handed out at the campus gates will usually do the job. These conditions facilitate quick communication, foster solidarity, and help to arouse melodramatic action.[44]

In 1964, the critical mass of non-students on Telegraph Avenue, inter-penetrating with and visually indistinguishable from the Berkeley mass itself, was not as important as it has subsequently become—thanks to the free nationwide television advertisements provided by the extravagance of Californian dissent and Californian repression. By April 1970, the Uni-

[44] Ibid., p. 6.

versity administration was close to despair. After a moderate student had been killed by a sniper during the Bank of America battle at Santa Barbara, a University official admitted to a local reporter that they had lost control of the issues. 'Riots are planned weeks, perhaps months in advance. There are no concessions we can make any more to avoid them . . . The cadre of militants at Berkeley, for instance, knows now that all they have to do is start throwing rocks to get the authorities to come out in force. The reaction in any university community to police wearing helmets and gas masks and carrying clubs is predictable. The result is destruction.'[45] A few days later, the militants, tired of throwing their own rocks, constructed a giant catapult. Governor Reagan's predictions had turned out to be self-fulfilling, as demagogues' predictions often are. The 'society of lemmings' was about to take its jump, and nothing short of the long-expected north California earthquake could take away the sea.

[45] The *Guardian* (Manchester and London), April 21, 1970.

CHAPTER THREE

An idea and its inheritors

1 MEDIEVAL BOLOGNA: UNIVERSITY FOR STUDENTS

'Item, pro malvasia libras III. Item, pro vitris fractis . . . '
(Item, for Malmsey, £3. Item, for broken windows . . .)
Bologna student guild accounts, 1292

' . . . the sound of the English aristocracy baying for broken
glass'
Evelyn Waugh, *Decline and Fall* (London, 1928)

'*Om svasti,*' said the University of Bologna in 1958, greeting the University of Allahabad on the latter's seventieth birthday. '*Prayapuristharicvavidyalayasya saptatisamvatsarikamahotsave Bononyanagaristhavicvavidyalayasyadhisthata,*' it went on in rolling Sanskrit, thoughtfully supplying an Italian translation which can be found in the *Acta Universitatis studiorum Bononiensis* if one cares to look. '*O pace, pace, pace* . . . ' I was unable in Bologna to discover who it is that spends his time composing Sanskrit salutes to oriental universities, but the paternal feeling which the custom expresses are understandable. For Bologna has an earlier claim than Paris and Oxford to be the source of the university idea, and neither its tourist office nor its official historians allow the visitor to forget it. A.D. 1088 is the city's admittedly fictional date for the moment when isolated groups of European law students, living and learning in Bologna without civic rights, coalesced to form a self-governing institution which could be recognised, after the lapse of a century or two, as the Western world's first real university. No one seems yet to have noticed that the medieval jurist Irnerius, whose teaching is popularly supposed to have raised Bologna to European status in the first place, has a modern counterpart who might be regarded as the father of the twentieth century 'idea' of an 'open' university:[1] Guglielmo Marconi, who passed his youth '*nell' austera e ispiratrice atmosfera*' of the University of Bologna, and conducted his early experiments with radio in the Villa Grifone, ten miles away.

A pilgrimage to Bologna offers pleasures, intellectual and sensual, which are entirely contemporary. But for the moment, I am concerned with what Bologna was, not what Bologna is (part of the most ramshackle university system in Western Europe). Similarly, in the third section of this chapter, with the Oxford college I have chosen to describe. Some

[1] See pp. 254-5.

defence of this procedure is probably necessary. We live in an age which believes that the past is best left to professionals, and that only present reality or future probability can affect the nature of institutions. However, so much in universities is only comprehensible in terms of the past, and so many of the earliest academic themes and patterns are being energetically re-created by contemporary students, that it is worth knowing what happened and why, eight centuries ago. In Japan in 1969, a book purporting to show how the students of Bologna in the twelfth century had anticipated the thoughts of Mao in the twentieth sold half a million copies in a month. The culture of our time may indeed be set on an entirely new tack, but it is of the nature of tacks that the helmsman spends much of his time looking back the way he has come. Nothing could be newer, or more rebarbative to conventionally-trained ears, than much contemporary music, with its ideogram scores, aleatoric performance, and obsession with timbres both natural and electronic; but it is noticeable that in their anxiety to avoid almost all the patterns of musical argument that have been devised since Monteverdi's time, composers and performers in this genre are often happy to relax with the crum horns, sackbuts and innocently complex rhythms of Renaissance composers, from whom their parents thought they had nothing to learn. As with music, so with ideas about social organisation, for which the contemporary world can provide new techniques but seldom—kibbutzim notwithstanding—new models. Here, too, once revolutionaries conclude that almost every development since the invention of printing and the rise of the Protestant ethic has been either misguided or superseded, the chief landmark still discernible astern is the Middle Ages. Perhaps there is more to be found in this particular pond than either our revolutionaries or our social engineers have as yet thought of dragging for. At the outset of his great history of the medieval universities—a work on which anyone who dips but a toe in these waters is bound to rely—Hastings Rashdall threw out a characteristic aphorism: 'Ideals pass into great historic forces by embodying themselves in institutions. The power of embodying its ideals in institutions was the peculiar genius of the medieval mind, as its most conspicuous defect lay in the corresponding tendency to materialise them.'[2] Perhaps only a world which is finally shaking itself free of the most massive and obstinate of these defective materialisations—that is, the Roman Catholic Church as it was before Vatican II—could begin to look with fresh respect at the peculiar genius of the Middle Ages.

Rashdall, however, discussing the origin of the term 'university', warns off unwary trespassers. 'The notion that a university means a *universitas facultatum*—a school in which all faculties or branches of knowledge are represented—has, indeed, long since disappeared from the page of professed historians; but it is still persistently foisted upon the public by

[2] *The Universities of Europe in the Middle Ages* (1895), ed. F. M. Powicke and A. B. Emden (Oxford, 1936), vol. i, p. 43.

writers with whom history is subordinate to what may be called intellectual edification.'³ We will not make this mistake over *universitas*, which may be translated 'community' (of scholars, or masters, or both) and which at the head of a letter—*universitas vestra*—means something close to the Southern American phrase "you-all". (The thirteenth century phrase for what we now know as a university was *studium generale*, meaning not a place where all subjects are studied, but a place where students from all parts are received.) However, 'what may be called intellectual edification' is not altogether avoided in this section. There can, of course, be no intellectual edification where history is actually played false, but all historians, even professional ones, make their own selection of the available facts; and as every journalist knows, it is the choice of matter to omit or compress that often determines the reliability of any newspaper report. I am content to follow J. H. Plumb's distinction between 'the past' and 'history' and select one of the purposes for which, in his view, man has characteristically used the past: 'to vivify his cultural and educational processes'.⁴

Three springs—Salerno, Bologna, and Paris—form the headwaters of the European university, a stream which changed its course somewhat with the foundation of Oxford and Cambridge, but which was not significantly augmented until the nineteenth century, when Wilhelm von Humboldt, planning the University of Berlin, gave a new seriousness to the pursuit of fundamental knowledge, and the Morrill Act in America defined, or at least made room for, the concept of a university as a community service station. Salerno I can with good conscience omit, for though the oldest, it was a medical school, and medical education is only incidental to my purpose. Paris is Paris, and the most influential spring of all. Nevertheless, it is really only in Oxford and Cambridge that there is a true continuity between the medieval Parisian 'university of Masters' and any contemporary organism. Oxford was founded by migrants from Paris, and though it was by no means a carbon copy its collegiate structure preserved the medieval form better. Nor did it suffer, as Paris did, an administrative break comparable with the Code Napoléon, which centralised French universities under the authority of the State itself. (Had those Parisian migrants settled in London instead, the story might have been very different. It is only in recent times that politicians' desire to rearrange higher education has outpaced their reluctance to stir from their capital cities. Oxford survived by its provincialism.)

Bologna, the other source, was a 'university of scholars'. There, students held the power partially from the begining, at a later period wholly but, now no longer. This is the only reason why students (and professors) from Santa Barbara to Addis Ababa are likely to be interested in Bolognese history today. But it was also a university founded on the study of juris-

³ Ibid., p. 4.
⁴ J. H. Plumb, *The Death of the Past* (London, 1969), p. 11.

prudence, and on the literary and grammatical curriculum that was necessarily associated with the study of law in an age when not only briefs and
bulls but all business transactions of any importance were conducted in a
dead language. This aspect of medieval Bologna is less calculated to
entrance the trashers and bomb-throwers of contemporary universities,
who consider that they have little reason to love the law, even the
Pandects of Justinian and the Decretum[5] of Gratian, on which Bologna's
legal curriculum was based (and apparently still is, in spirit if not in letter).
But the reason why Bologna grew to maturity as a university of jurists
cannot be separated from the reason why it came to be governed by its
students. The Dark Ages were not wholly dark in the cities of northern
Italy. The great texts of Roman jurisprudence had never been quite
forgotten, nor had all education—as in France during the same period—
been confined to cathedral and monastic schools. The Lombard nobility—
like the Japanese samurai of the Tokugawa period—gave their sons a
literary education while the knights of Germany, France, and England
looked upon reading and writing as unmanly. The Lombard cities themselves, by playing off the Holy Roman Emperor against the Pope, had
achieved by the end of the twelfth century an autonomy and a civic
political life which Rashdall feels able to compare with that of the ancient
Greeks. Just as the University of Paris was founded on a thirst for speculative knowledge, unrelated to social life—a thirst eventually slaked by the
rediscovery of the forgotten Aristotle—so in the Italian 'climate' of
commercial and political freedom there arose a demand for the more
mundane but civilising and socially practical science of law. 'It is only in
such communities that so democratic, so unhierarchical an institution as
an autonomous university of students could have sprung into existence.'[6]

They were, of course, rather special students. In the German 'nation'
(or college) at Bologna about half the students were beneficed clerics,
though by canon law, a boy of fourteen could be canon of a cathedral, and
the majority of such students were probably no older than modern undergraduates. But many of them were considerably older than that, and their
professor was, strictly speaking, merely a private-enterprise lecturer,
whom a group of gentlemen between the ages of fifteen and forty had
hired to instruct them in legal reasoning. The relationship, that is to say,
was commercial rather than hierarchical. But the master's superior scholastic attainment was not his only significant difference from his students.
The master, typically, was a Bolognese citizen, while the students,
typically, were not. Irnerius, the commentator on Justinian who summed
up rather than initiated the rise of the Bolognese law school, was himself a
citizen, a protegé of the Pope's ally Countess Matilda (though by 1118 he

---

[5] The *Decretum*, published in Bologna about 1140, was an instantly successful textbook,
reviewing and where possible reconciling conflicting ecclesiastical canons.

[6] Rashdall, op. cit., vol. i, p. 97.

took part in the Imperialist campaign to elect an anti-Pope, which must have helped to recommend the Bologna *studium* to students from Germany). Citizenship, in medieval Bologna or Padua or Ravenna, mattered enormously. There were no reciprocal rights between cities, unless by express negotiation, and the immigrant student, however good his family, lived under harsh alien law. University statutes elsewhere in Italy frequently mention a privilege exempting scholars from torture except in the presence of and with the sanction of the Rectors. The student communities were therefore obliged to create for themselves an artificial citizenship, which the visible commercial advantages of their presence eventually forced the municipality to grant. The foreign students and masters acquired the immense powers and privileges that were enjoyed by the members of any other medieval trade or professional guild. They had an intrinsic right to elect their own rector and enact their own statutes. In Bologna, the only objectors were, not surprisingly, the professors of law, who claimed that the students were merely pupils, with no more right to form their own *collegium* than the apprentices of the smiths or the skinners. But then as now in academic communities, dollars counted for more than doctorates. 'Townsmen and professors alike stood in awe of a body which by the simple expedient of migration could destroy the trade of the former and the incomes of the latter.'[7]

This did not mean that trouble was at an end. Although the student statutes claimed to overrule all contradictory provisions in the statutes of the doctoral colleges, the town statutes enacted the opposite. Professors were involved in town and gown disputes, especially in 1321, when a scholar who had attempted to abduct a notary's daughter was executed by the city, and half the university seceded to Siena. Nor will any American academic reader be surprised to learn that extraordinary precautions had to be taken to prevent the high-rated Bolognese professors from migrating elsewhere on receiving offers of more liberal remuneration. When oaths proved ineffective, the death penalty was decreed (in 1432) against any citizen doctor over the age of fifty who took a visiting lectureship elsewhere without permission of the city magistrate. (A younger professor, in those days less valuable, was subject to a fine of 200 ducats.)

But the discipline which the city imposed on the professors was mild by comparison with that imposed by the students. The professor was obliged to swear obedience to the Rector of the student university, in whose Congregation he had no voting rights. If he wanted a day off he was obliged to ask permission first from his own students and then from the Rector's office, and if he wanted to leave the town he had to deposit a sum of money against his return. If he failed to begin his lecture when the bells of St. Peter's rang for mass, he was fined twenty *soldi* for each offence, and the

[7] Ibid., vol. i, p. 165.

end of the hour was regulated with more devilish ingenuity: the student could be fined ten *soldi* if they failed to get up and go when the bell rang for tierce. Even in the actual conduct of his lectures, Rashdall pleasantly observes, 'the doctor is regulated with the precision of a soldier on parade or a reader in a French public library.'[8] He was fined if he skipped a chapter and forbidden to postpone a difficulty to the end of the lecture in case he should 'forget' to tackle it. Precautions were also taken to discourage the habit—which teachers have had since the dawn of academic time—of spending so many hours on the early pages of a book that none were left for the rest. The law-texts were divided into *puncta*, or portions, and at the beginning of each academic year the professor had to deposit ten Bologna pounds with a banker. For every day that he lagged behind time, a sum was deducted from the deposit.

The modern reader is likely to wonder whether—as happens under a vaguely similar system of student control in Latin American universities —the oppression of the professors resulted in a catalysmic decline of academic standards. On the whole, this seems not to have happened, at least during the period in which students' rights were being most vociferously asserted. Bologna was not inferior to Paris: it was simply different. Bologna was absorbed with questions about the relations of papacy and Empire, Church and State, feudalism and civic liberty, while the schools of France were investigating the unity of intellect, transubstantiation, and the reality of universals. The Englishman John of Salisbury, one of the very few who has left any contemporary record comparing the two centres, reports that Alberic, his teacher on the 'Mount' of Ste. Genevieve outside the walls of Paris, went to Bologna and unlearnt the dialectic he had been teaching, then returned to Paris and 'untaught' (*dedocuit*) the new style to his old pupils.[9] During the thirteenth century, rhetoric and grammar, and the professional study of law for which these subjects were the preparation, were better taught in Italy than anywhere else in Europe, and at this time the teacher was absolutely dependent on his *collecta*, the fees he negotiated with his pupils. The process was, to say the least, undignified. Here is the famous jurist Odofredus, who is the source of the information that there were 10,000 students at Bologna towards the end of the thirteenth century, dismissing his pupils at the end of a year:

'And I am telling you that next year I propose to give ordinary courses properly and according to the law, as I have always done; but I do not think I shall give extra-curricular lectures, because students are not good payers. They want knowledge, but not the bill: as the verse has it, "everyone wants to learn, nobody wants to pay". That is all I have to say to you: go with the Lord's blessing.'[10]

---

[8] Ibid., vol. i, p. 197.
[9] Ibid., vol. i, p. 109.
[10] Ibid., vol. i, p. 209 (where the quotation is given in Latin).

Gradually, as the university's importance to the city was more and more clearly recognised, first the payment and later the nomination of professors was taken over from the students by the State. A century later, in 1381, twenty-three salaried doctors of law were receiving amounts varying from 100 to 620 *librae*. (Note the differential—and also that at the beginning of the thirteenth century a famous surgeon, Hugh of Lucca, was induced by an offer of 600 *librae* to come to Bologna. The legal system mattered, but health and healing of wounds mattered more.) It is tempting to blame this 'nationalisation' of the school for the decline in its standards after the middle of the thirteenth century, especially as the professoriate at about the same time became largely hereditary. In 1259 the doctors were compelled to swear—probably under student pressure— that they would not prevent external doctors duly elected by the universities from filling a chair at Bologna, but the joint interest of both doctors and city in securing a Bolognese monopoly of the emoluments deriving from the *studium* in the end proved too strong. However, there were also intellectual reasons for the loss of verve. The besetting fault of medieval learning, as of modern American high schools, was its reverence for the text book. As long as the text book was itself the original authority, this hardly mattered, but when the same reverence was extended to the glosses, originality was stifled. Rashdall, noticing before McLuhan the effect of the medium on the message, accounts for some of the 'vast amount of unnecessary commentation' that has survived by pointing out that in the Middle Ages, 'when it was possible to produce a dozen copies of a book at the same proportionate cost as to produce a hundred or a thousand, the temptation to the publication of lectures was greater.'[11]

Only one inconvenient fact prevents the advocate of student power from claiming medieval Bologna as a successful example of his own utopia. Even the Bolognese student guild left to the masters the right to examine the qualifications of candidates for admission to the profession. This was done in two stages. The serious part was in private, where the candidate was in the morning assigned two passages in civil or canon law to study at his house and expound before the doctors in the afternoon, answering any further questions they cared to put. (The student statutes, mindful of the ordeal, required the examiner to treat the examinee 'as his own son'.) The successful candidate then became a licentiate, and could proceed at will to the formal *conventus* or public examination in the cathedral, where the medieval love of ceremony and display was given free reign. The candidate defended a legal thesis, but this time against opponents selected from among his fellow students, not the doctors. He was then seated in his chair with a ring on his finger, a biretta on his head and the kiss of peace on his forehead. Finally he was carried in triumph through the town, preceded by the three university pipers and the four

[11] Ibid., vol. i, p. 257.

university trumpeters, and there followed what to the candidate himself was by far the most expensive part of the ritual: the banquet he was expected to provide for his new colleagues. (At some of the Spanish universities, where parts of the medieval ceremonial of inception survive to this day, the incepting doctors were required to provide a bull-fight for the amusement of the university.) Anyone who has ever remarked on the affection for feasts which is a feature of most academic communities— and its is not uncommon nowadays for both students and professors to suggest that the money would be better spent on scholarships or secretarial assistance—should perhaps pause to consider how much of the historical life and soul of the institution is invested in its banquets.

The student democracy of the University of Bologna as a whole was reflected in the internal organisation of the colleges. The chief of these is the College of Spain, founded in 1367 under the will of Cardinal Albernoz, for poor Spanish students. The College still survives on the same site in Bologna, in sumptuously adorned sixteenth century buildings, though it is administered by the Spanish Government and its students are no longer poor. Its original statutes survive too,[12] and from them it can be seen that even the stiff hierarchical assumptions of a Spanish cardinal's executors could be reconciled with the Bolognese style: the scholars selected their officers from their own ranks by secret ballot. By setting up the house, the Cardinal intended to obviate 'the ignorance of the Spaniards among whom the knowledge of letters and the number of trained men have been much reduced because of the crises of wars and innumerable disasters which befell this province in his own time' (Statute III). In spite of the 'democratic' constitution, measures for the physical, intellectual, moral, and spiritual welfare of the students were carefully laid down in the statutes: 'a pound of mutton or veal of ordinary quality every day, to be served with some suitable dish at the rector's decision'; tuition outside the college for boys who arrive from Spain insufficiently prepared; mass at least once a day; and 'because woman is the head of sin, the devil's weapon, the expulsion from Paradise, and the corruption of the ancient law, and therefore all commerce with her should be shunned carefully, we expressly prohibit and forbid anyone, in any manner whatever, to dare to introduce any woman, however respectable, into the said college'.[13]

Women's liberation in Bologna, astonishingly, flourished even in the century in which that sentence was written. So did astrology, which was so to speak, the reverse side of the university's preoccupation with jurisprudence. The subject arrived through the medical faculty (which like the arts faculty was organised separately from the study of law) towards the end of the thirteenth century, when Bologna was beginning to take over Salerno's medical reputation, and when the influence of Arab

[12] Berthe M. Marti (ed. amd transl.), *The Spanish College at Bologna in the Fourteenth Century* (Philadelphia, 1966).
[13] Statute XXIX. A chaplain who stayed out all night lost half a year's salary.

medical writers was at its height. But it also proved to be the route by which the counterpart of Parisian philosophic speculation flourished at Bologna. There was a salaried professor of astrology in the university in the fourteenth century, one of whose duties was to supply opinions free for inquiring students. The chair was, however, in the most literal sense a hot seat, and the occupant highly vulnerable to a twist of politics or the suspicion of necromancy. Cecco d'Ascoli, one of the most distinguished Bologna astrologers, was burnt by the Inquisition at Florence in 1327.

Astrology did not do the progress of medical science much good. In other fields, it was more beneficial. As soon as the new humanism began to replace the old scholasticism, an interest in the movement of the heavens took on a scientific aspect. It was at Bologna that Copernicus— a student of canon law—began the calculations which launched modern astronomy. Altogether, academic deans of West Coast universities faced with student demands for an astrology minor might do worse than respond, straight-faced, with the Bolognese curriculum (for which credits in Mathematics and Latin would naturally be prerequisite):

(1) A work on arithmetic styled *Algorismi de minutis et integris*.
(2) Euclid, with the Commentary of the 13th century geometrician, Johannes Campanus of Novara.
(3) The tables of Alfonso I, King of Castile, with the Canons of John of Saxony.
(4) The *Theorica Planetarum*.
(5) The *Canones super tabulis de lineriis*, i.e. rules for the use of astronomical tables to determine the motions of the heavenly bodies, by John of Lignierès of Amiens (fl. 1330).
(6) The *Tractatus astrolabii* of Messahala or Maschallah, a Jewish astrologer of the ninth century.
(7) Alcabitius, fl. c. 850; probably his *Isagoge* to judicial astrology, translated by Gerard of Cremona.
(8) The Quadripartitum and the Centiloquium of Ptolemy with the Commentary of Haly, which were works upon judicial astrology.
(9) A certain *Tractatus Quadrantis*, on the use of the quadrant.
(10) A work on astrological medicine or medical astrology, which bore the title, very characteristic of the Arabs and their followers, *de urina non visa*, by William of England, written in 1219.
(11) Portions of the Canon of Avicenna.'[14]

All this, and the Averroist philosophy that also arrived at Bologna with the Arabs, was part of the culture imbibed by the university's most celebrated medieval alumni: Dante, a student in 1287, and Petrarch, a student in 1322. (They disagreed about the virtues of Arabism, Dante paying tribute to Averroes in the *Inferno*, and Petrarch declining even to be treated by drugs with Arabic names.)

[14] Rashdall, op. cit., vol. i, pp. 248-9.

Renaissance humanism itself bypassed the universities of Italy, or rather entered them from outside, in some cases as late as the seventeenth century. Rashdall, with justice, notes in this connection the extreme tenacity of educational traditions: 'A philosophy, a mode of thought, a habit of mind, may live on in the lecture rooms of professors for a century after it has been abandoned by the thinkers, the men of letters, and the men of the world.'[15] (That was certainly true of the French universities at the time of the *philosophes*, and it is a serious question for contemporary universities whether or not the same is beginning to happen again.)

However, in one respect which today seems not unimportant the University of Bologna anticipated the humanists. From the earliest years of the thirteenth century Bologna seems to have accepted women students, and from time to time allowed them to teach. The most famous of these women were Novella and Bettina Calderini, whose parents both held doctorates, and who both when need arose took their fathers' or later their husbands' place at the lectern. Of Novella it is recorded—though the tale is calculated to make the modern reader sceptical—that her beauty compelled her to veil her face on the rostrum to avoid distracting her hearers; and also that when Urban V offered to make her husband Giovanni de Legnuno a Cardinal and Novella herself a nun, they refused the honour, preferring to continue living together. This tradition of feminine emancipation survived to Bologna's second golden age, at the turn of the seventeenth century, when the names of Malpighi and Galvani, and the experimental resources given to the Institute of Sciences in 1714 by Count Marsili, ensured that the line of internationally significant Italian science did not peter out between Galico and Fermi. Laura Bassi (1711–78), philosopher and physicist, was just over 20 when she was crowned with the 'laurea dottorale' in Philosophy, after a public interrogation by five professors. This was only a beginning. She wrote verse, experimented in physics, and was proficient in Latin and Greek. She published two dissertations on hydraulics and mechanics, married a Dr. Veratti, bore twelve children, and educated them herself. The evening before her death she spent a long time in discussion at the Academia Benedettina, and was given a civic funeral. A contemporary, Anna Morandi (1716–74), studied drawing and modelling, and married an anatomical modellist whose professional partner she also became. She lectured on the structure of the human body, declining lucrative offers of posts in London and St. Petersburg because she preferred to remain in her native city.[16]

Much has been omitted in my description of medieval Bologna. More-

[15] Ibid., vol. i, p. 265.

[16] For these accounts, I am indebted to Edith Coulson James, *Bologna, its History, Antiquities, and Art* (London, 1909), pp. 177–183. It should be remembered, though, that for most of the eighteenth and nineteenth centuries, the University had two to three hundred students only.

over, even the reader who scans every page on the subject in Rashdall and other authorities, even the reader fluent in Latin and Italian, and conversant with the history of Italian medieval thought and culture, would still have to draw upon his own imagination to live the life and breathe the atmosphere of the place. By its very nature, a university is an exceedingly complex institution, and relatively speaking this is no less true of thirteenth century Bologna than twentieth century Chicago: indeed, the former expressed the total culture of its time, with all its nuances and variations, more completely than the richest and most various university can express our own. But in selecting out those aspects of Bologna that are most likely to amuse, edify, or disconcert a white Anglo-Saxon Protestant academic or student, I seek only to show that there does exist a model of the university which is radically different from the one which he has himself inherited in Oxford or Ohio. There is a powerful tendency in all men to regard the educational systems in which they have themselves been brought up as 'given' and unalterable. Even reverence for more distant historical precedent does not necessarily abate this tendency. When the University of London, after being empowered by royal charter (1836) to do everything that a university does, wanted to admit women to degrees, it was legally advised that it could not do so without a fresh charter, because no university had ever done so.[17] (Rashdall, who was later able to discuss the point with the counsel concerned, reports that better information about the Bolognese background would have modified the legal opinion, but it would not necessarily have modified academic opinion. Until the 1969/70 affrays on the Senate House lawn and in the Garden House hotel, the most recent violent demonstration in the University of Cambridge was a mob assault on the gates of Newnham College in 1928, protesting against the admission of women to higher degrees.)

Bologna, then, shows that there is much less that is 'necessary' about the form which a university takes than deans of students and other custodians of youth are apt to pretend. The university was able to become and for a couple of centuries remain one of the most vital institutions in Europe under the government of students who had by no means—as the current phrase has it—'earned their right' to participate in the selection and judgement of academic personnel. The most striking quality of the University which emerges from its early history is its adulthood, and this by comparison not only with the universities of later centuries (corporal punishment was applied to students up to the age of twenty in Cardinal Wolsey's Christ Church) but with its contemporary French and German universities, whose student numbers were—Paris excepted—rather smaller, but whose collective adolescent culture was more assertive. On the other side, one must emphasise the extraordinary high motivation of the medieval Bolognese student, who had travelled half way across Europe, in conditions as perilous as any encountered by the explorers of

[17] Rashdall, op. cit., vol. iii, pp. 460–1.

the American West, to study for years in a hostile community. Whether he made the journey for love of learning or of advancement, this fact undoubtedly conditioned his response to the minor irritations of university life, and gave the student body a sense of coherence and purpose. The modern university's need to re-create something of this atmosphere is urgent.[18]

Finally, before leaving thirteenth century for twentieth century Bologna, the influence on the university of Italian city-state democracy and cultural sophistication must again be stressed. The pattern of a great university, or indeed of any great institution, cannot arise from a social void. The conditions must be right, as they must be for the creation of new life of any kind. All the intellectual and spiritual force that went into the creation of medieval universities might have spent itself in a generation if the first wave of troops had not been able to entrench themselves in their own version of the medieval guild system. The twentieth century, in criticising the institutions which it has inherited from the past—the Church, the University, Parliament and Judiciary— should occasionally pause to consider what comparable, if embryonic, institutions have been created in our own time, and how much they reveal about the societies which conceive them. To go no further than the university milieu, this century has so far yielded twin extremes of academic diffusion and concentration: public broadcasting systems and the Open University on the one hand; the research institute and 'think-tank' on the other. It is sobering to realise that history may choose to adopt both, or one, or neither; gratifying to realise that history can sometimes be reversed, and that after living for centuries with a university of masters, we are concluding that there is at least something to be said for a university of students.

[18] See Chapter seven, section 2.

'The organised official teaching of Italy remained mediaeval and
barbarous long after her great writers and artists had launched their
country, and Europe along with her, on the line of modern ideas and
modern civilisation.'

Matthew Arnold, *Schools and Universities on the Continent* (*1865–67*)
(ed. R. H. Super, Ann Arbor, 1964, p. 143.)

The beginnings of humanism, according to Hastings Rashdall, were
in palaces rather than universities, in Tuscany rather than Lombardy, in
'artistic, dreamy, Platonic Florence' rather than in 'stately, scientific,
scholastic Bologna'.[19] Contemporary Italian tradition has three rather
different epithets for Bologna: *dotta*, *rossa*, and *grassa*. *Dotta* is a bow in the
direction of the University. *Rossa* is earned by the Communists who rule
the city. As for *grassa*, there has probably never been a time since the
invention of *pasta* when the Bolognese failed to merit the description,
which is hardly translatable in English. 'Fat' or 'greedy' would not do,
for Bolognese actually eat rather less than Romans and Neapolitans, and
people who prefer mussels to mortadella may think that Genoans and
Venetians eat better. The connotation is of rich materials lustily enjoyed,
and the visual image is that of a plump *signora* glimpsed through a shop-
window early one morning, bent over a vast sheet of yellow paste,
dabbing ravioli down on to the marked squares at a rate of two per
second. It was no surprise to take lunch for five shillings or so in the
University *mensa*, about which the students naturally complain, and find
an American lecturer declaring that it was the best in Europe, and that he
wished they had a restaurant like it back in Minneapolis.

Academically, whether for students or professors, life is much easier in
Minneapolis than it is anywhere in Italy, under a university system which
is paralysed partly by its own feudal traditions, and partly by the centralisation of all political and administrative decisions in Rome, where very
few decisions of any kind have been taken in recent years. The University
of Bologna's problems are not primarily of its own making, and the 850-
year-old symbiosis of university and city can only alleviate them a little.
But Bologna, with its leaning towers, red-ochre pedestrian colonnades,

[19] Op. cit., vol. i, p. 268.

An idea and its inheritors

and astonishing basilicas, has one of the most alluring townscapes in all
Italy. This forms a medieval and Renaissance core to an industrial city of
half a million people. All Italian railway journeys tend to pass through
Bologna, which has been a junction of travel routes since Roman times.

Railway apart, the industrial base consists of small firms, feeder factories
to the great plants of Turin and Milan, and even Bologna's Communism,
which strikes terror into the hearts of American political scientists, rests
more firmly on Emilian anti-clericalism than on geo-political militancy.
As late as 1956, the Communist candidate for Mayor could argue successfully to the electorate that the victory of his opponent, an extreme left-
wing Christian Democrat, would return Bologna to the control of Pope
and Cardinals. Yet Catholicism itself in Bologna, under Cardinal Lercaro,
became more radical than anywhere else in Italy. Relations between city
and university, though strained by the student revolts from 1967 onwards,
are good. The Communist Mayor of the city and the 'left liberal' Rector
of the University knew each other in the Resistance during the war, and
this matters in Bologna, which displays outside the Town Hall to this day
the names and photographs of its fallen or executed Resistance heroes and
heroines. The city endowed the university's department of Political
Science, which betrays not the least sign of the fact, and the Mayor, by
leaning gently on the appropriate Communist cells, did much to ensure
that the 1969 student occupation of the university administration ended
ignominiously.

This conservative alliance naturally distresses young revolutionaries in
Bologna, who include at least one member of the Mayor's own family. A
local leader of *Potere Operaio* ('Workers' Power'), a syndicalist movement
which encourages students out of the universities to agitate in factories,
complained to me with a perfectly serious expression: 'You cannot make
a revolution in Bologna: the Communist Party is too strong.' Its strength
is hardly at all reflected in the university itself, though the Italian Communist Party has long courted intellectuals, especially academic ones. No
statistics, naturally, are published, but an informed guess was five Party
members out of 150 tenured professors. Among assistant professors and
students the proportion is certainly higher, but perhaps not inordinately
so. The Leftist minority has moved far to the left of the PCI, and for the
rest, the bourgeois business and pleasures of this deeply-rooted city
dominate life. 'We have a patron saint,' said one State official, 'San
Paganino—St. Pay-day.' The bookshops—among the best in Italy—were
in 1970 selling *La baby aerodinamica color caramella*, *La legge del Signor
Parkinson* and *Lamento di Portnoy*; and at the week-end, if you were too
old or conservative for alien pop groups ('*Gran Gala di Biologia con The
Only Men*', '*Tradizionale veglione di lettere e filosofia con The Primitives*')
there was always the Italian national sport, opera, for Rossini's *Moses* was
playing to a crowded house in the resonant Teatro Communale, which
Bibiena built in 1756 on the ruins of Bentivoglio's palazzo.

The University's first permanent home in Bologna was Terribilia's Archiginnasio, built in 1563, and now—with at least some of its armorial decorations happily preserved from Italian Republicans of the 1790s and Allied airmen of the 1940s—it is Bologna's public library, much used by students in preference to their own. By 1802, the medieval *Studio* needed more room, and was united with the Institute of Sciences in the Palazzo Poggi, in Via Zamboni, where there were 1,500 students by the time the octocentenary was celebrated in 1888. The scientific departments were moved to newer buildings between the wars, and there is talk of moving them again, either to an entirely new campus ten miles away, or to land purchased from the municipality three miles from the centre of Bologna: a cheaper solution, since no new roads and fewer dormitories would have to be built. The humanities, it is felt, belong in the middle of town. At present, town is where everyone is. The University of Bologna, which in the middle of the last century had 300 students, had 19,000 in 1965/6, 30,000 in 1969/70, and is soon to have 50,000. The University has four dormitories, with residential accommodation for 400 students, and a dozen or so Spanish graduate students study in flunkeyed ease at the College of Spain. Of the remainder, most of whom have to take a job in order to support themselves, about 20,000 attend the University for a couple of months in the year only. About 10,000 have to find rooms in the town, for which the university counts as a major industry.

This situation is reproduced in most universities all over Italy. Bologna is one of the better ones, since even though two-thirds of the students, through idleness, penury, or politicisation, seldom attend the university, about half the tenured professors actually reside in Bologna and teach regularly. In an Italian university, this is a high proportion. In the South, or in an out-of-the-way town like Urbino, the university is likely to be served by a 'travelling faculty', whom students may not see for months. Some of the most conspicuous absentees are eminent Italian politicians, who pick up their professorial salaries from the State and pass their time in Rome, forming and re-forming Cabinets. The tenured professors (*professori di ruolo*) are in Italy popularly styled *barone*. They are a self-perpetuating body, owing allegiance to no one, and in this respect may justly be regarded as the heirs of the hereditary professors of Bologna in the fifteenth century. Of the 156 full professors listed in Bologna's 1965/6 quinquennial year-book, three were women. The age-structure, with forty born after 1920 and thirteen before 1900, was conventional enough, but for the junior faculty (*professori incaricati*, or *assistenti*) the *ruolo* is a tight circle indeed, only possible to penetrate, if at all, with luck, good connections, or extraordinary ability; or alternatively by years of lobbying and half-paid academic devillings for an individual professor. If the professor moves, the *assistente* and his hopes must accompany him. Not surprisingly, both political radicals and women are quite numerous among the *assistenti*.

Thus, the not altogether unfavourable student-teacher ratio in Italian universities (1:13) is strictly meaningless, on the one hand because the students are not there to be taught, on the other hand because the staff are not there to teach them. Nor would the situation be greatly eased by the university reform Bill (*Legge Sullo*, or '2314') which was on its way through Parliament during the Cabinet crises of 1970. In this it was proposed to enlarge the number of tenured professors in Italian universities from some 3,000 to 10,000, simply by granting tenure to 7,000 *assistenti*. The total number of teachers, and probably their attitude to the job, would have remained unchanged, but the discontent of one generation of teachers would have been bought off at the price of denying the unlucky generation immediately below any promotion for a decade or two. A very Italian solution.

The Italians, however, could fairly blame part of their academic misfortunes on the French, who, when they retreated from Italy after the Napoleonic wars, left the administrative structure of the Code Napoléon behind them. The erection of a centralised bureaucratic structure on a base of social and political disunity served the purposes of an occupying power but jarred horribly on the Italian temperament, which is localised and individualistic in essence. 'Culturally,' said one Bolognese professor ruefully, 'we are still a province of France.' The effect of this cultural imperalism on Italian attitudes to law and administration goes beyond the scope of this inquiry, but the full consequences of the constitutional structure have only struck home to higher education in the past few years. Indeed, the French system, in its pure and unreformed state, could until the end of 1969 be better studied in Italy than in France.

By far the most important provision of the system is open access to university for any boy or girl who has passed the *maturità* (the Italian equivalent of the French *baccalauréat*). The post-war expansion of high-school education, and the extension of university entrance rights to certain categories of technical high-school graduates, coupled with the demands of the rapidly-advancing Italian economy, doubled the number of university students in Italy within a decade (1957/8: 220,175; 1966/7: 460,193). It is moreover clear that this process has much further to go. The proportion of working class students at university (thirteen per cent) has remained comparatively low, and the social disparities between the North of Italy and the Mezzogiorno (which in per capita income is ten to fifteen years behind the national average) are well known. Half of Italy, in fact, is still an under-developed country, whose population as a whole reads fewer newspapers per head than the population of peasant Turkey.

When he has passed his *maturita*, the Italian student is entirely free to register at the university of his choice. Although in recent years several new universities have been built in the South, no regionalisation is enforced, nor is there any direction of enrolments within a given region. A professor of physics at Bologna may have 500 students on his books, while a scarcely inferior professor at Modena five miles away may have fifty. The Bolognese professor knows that half of his 500 will not stay to get a degree, for which year-round residence in the city is in laboratory subjects virtually essential. This enables him, if he chooses, to keep some personal acquaintance with the 100–150 students who regularly attend his lectures. The others, unless they can find well-paid and not too exhausting work locally, or have the good fortune to obtain one of the very few scholarships available, inevitably drift away. Tuition is cheap: not more than L35,000 a year even in expensive subjects like industrial chemistry, and six years medical schooling at Rome could in 1967 be had for a grand total of L45,000. The cost to the State of a student in physics is estimated to be about L2,500,000; but this subsidy is indiscriminate.[20] The cost of maintenance—say, L70,000 a month for a young man in Rome—bears pretty hard on a family in the Mezzogiorno, where the average per capita income is still short of L448,000 a year. At graduation, the proportion of working class students is down from thirteen per cent to six per cent— about the same as in West Germany.

At the end of the university course, the situation is hardly more satisfactory. As in the Middle Ages, the only degree which Italian universities bestow is the *laurea*, or doctorate, which is in value somewhere between an American first and second degree. This has a legal value in Italy. A *laurea* in Jurisprudence is an essential qualification for the majority of administrative-class posts in Government service, and an engineer with his doctorate needs no further professional qualification to design a building —though if he has it from an unreliable university, an industrial firm will test him before hiring him. On the whole, however, the standard of the degree itself has been kept up. Had it not been, Italy could hardly have made the technical and economic progress that has startled Europe since the war. 'I went to MIT after I graduated,' said one Bologna scientist, 'and I was not in trouble. We had very good engineering during the war. Now in America they are working on integrated circuits, cryogenics, and so on, and we are following with perhaps a ten or fifteen year delay. We have a good general background, and a strong mathematical tradition.'

But there is at present no way of distinguishing different levels and types of achievement, except by the marks awarded for the *laurea*. Of a hundred engineering students at Bologna, fifty will go without a degree, twenty-five will go into industry, and twenty-five will teach. It might be argued that the number of high school teachers with doctorates has something to do with Italian technical proficiency but 'they are horrible teachers, because they are frustrated'. Similarly, lawyers frustrated of Civil Service jobs may enter schools and teach subjects of which they know nothing for higher wages than specialist teachers receive. Two

[20] Figures taken from Eduardo Volterra, 'La Riforma dell' Università Italiana', in *Il Foro Amministrativo*, March 1968 (Milan).

alternatives have been discussed. The first, preferred by industry and reformist professors, would set up a more refined degree structure, with new levels of qualification both below and above the *laurea* level. This is bitterly opposed by the student movement as an attempt to preserve 'the system' by streamlining it. (The *Movimento Studentesco* would, in fact, make the same criticism of any attempt to make the system more just, for example by giving scholarships to working class boys.) The other idea which more than one Italian Prime Minister has played with is to remove legal value from the *laurea*. This would be tantamount to handing over part of the higher education problem to private enterprise, since industry would be forced to set up its own examination system—at considerable profit to the professors whom it would have to hire as consultants.

So much for admission and graduation. In between, what happens? An American professor at the Johns Hopkins Center in Bologna—a degree-granting institution that takes graduate students from European countries as well as from the parent university in Maryland—wished that he could bring all American radical students on a short tour of Italian universities, and explained why:

'You go to a university—if you can get yourself registered, which is another problem. You won't be able to find out what courses there are or when or where, but anyway you're better not going because you might get discouraged. But you read some books in the hope of finding something that interests you, and at the end you will be examined orally on something that bears no relation to the courses but which you may happen quite by chance to know. Or you may know the professor which matters more. Success qualifies you to become an *assistente*, which means you work for an absentee professor at a fifth of starvation wage, meeting students, doing his research for him, and all the other things that he doesn't want to do. This goes on for several years and at the end, if you are lucky or someone dies, you may become a professor and do the same to other people.'

An Italian physicist put it more temperately:

'We can produce very good carbon copies of ourselves, but industrialists tell us that our graduates are only capable of routine work—they are not creative. The way to produce creative intellectuals is to let them do research on their own, but *assistente* are not encouraged to do that. Partly the problem is money, and professors' "baronial" attitude, but also we do not have the English ability to separate friendship from objective judgement. We cannot say to colleagues, "This research is good, and that research is not." Similarly with the Consiglio Nazionale delle Ricerche. Until a few years ago it had no national programmes: just a rain of small amounts of money on everybody.'

Objective and—since nothing has substantially changed in the past twenty years—up-to-date confirmation of these opinions about Bologna comes from an inquiry conducted in 1962 into the verdict of recent alumni on the teaching they received at university.[21] Over a quarter of the 1949–59 graduates sampled said that their university education had not been useful in the profession they had entered, and over a half reported difficulty—chiefly arising from inadequate preparation—in entering employment. Asked to evaluate what they received at the university, twenty-nine per cent expressed themselves satisfied, while sixty-nine per cent expressed varying degrees of dissatisfaction. Asked what characteristics of their own faculties they would like to see kept for succeeding generations of students, and what innovations or modifications they would like to see introduced, almost all respondents desired innovations, and a substantial minority in each faculty (in Economics and Commerce a majority) wanted none of the system's existing characteristics to be preserved. (At Bologna there are eleven faculties: Medicine, Engineering, Letters, Law, Sciences, Pharmacy, Veterinary Medicine, Agriculture, Industrial Chemistry, Education, Economics and Commerce.)

All this is but the academic aspect of what Luigi Barzini calls 'the perennial baroque' in the Italian conduct of affairs; a single symptom among others which one Bologna professor has lately listed: 'A Parliament apparently unable to legislate, an inept central and local bureaucracy, a judiciary still thinking of Italy as a basically agrarian society, the most expensive and least efficient social security system in the Common Market area, a shameful health and welfare system, a wretched school fabric—briefly, a decrepit social and administrative structure which does not allow a more equitable distribution of the benefits accruing from the tremendous economic and technical progress of the last decade.'[22]

The state of Italian universities alone would have been enough to produce a revolutionary student movement, but it may have needed the other symptoms as well to ensure that it arrived earlier than the French, more Marxist than the German, more violent than any except the Japanese.

Long before the Movement, Italian students were fully politicised along adult lines, with rigged elections and occasional violent clashes between the left wing UGI and the neo-Fascist FUAN. Similar clashes in 1970 on the streets of Milan and Rome thus represent a reversion to type rather than an altogether new development. But in the autumn of 1967, the new consciousness at last found expression in the slogan 'Keep political parties

[21] Achille Ardigo, 'L'Università Italiana e la Società in Transformazione', in L. Bertin, *Scuola e Società in Italia* (Bari, 1964), pp. 181–194.

[22] Federico Mancini, 'A Letter from Italy', in *Dissent*, XVI (Sept.–Oct. 1969), pp. 479–491.

out of the university.'[23] The university, in other words, was going to generate its own politics. In November, the Turin Arts Faculty was occupied, and the centralisation of Italian universities helped to ensure an instant spread of technique and reaction: student conditions of life and instruction were everywhere the same. On March 1, 1968—six weeks before Columbia and the German students' attack on Axel Springer's newspapers, two months before the Paris barricades—3,000 students fought police, with hundreds of casualties on both sides, at Valle Giulia in Rome. For the rest of that year, the moral fervour of the Movement, and the sense subsequently familiar from other universities and other countries that everything had suddenly become discussable, created a degree of political unity. A core of left-wing Communist was surrounded by fringe groups of Maoists, Trotskyists, radical Catholics and liberal reformists.

In Italy, of all countries, the unity could not and did not last—though the indiscriminate violence of the police did much to prolong it—and if there ever was a moment when the university itself could have used the Movement to secure practical reforms otherwise impossible, that moment has passed. In the winter of 1968/9 the strategists of the Movement, think-ing that the revolution was at hand, tried to turn the universities into 'red bases', and when it became clear that there was going to be no revolution for the time being, because the PCI did not want one, they left the universities altogether to warm up the industrial 'hot autumn' of 1969, at the time when various groups of workers were re-negotiating their contracts with companies and with the Government. Their success in fomenting 'wildcat' industrial trouble, and in goading the unions into raising their demands, went beyond the American student movement's fondest dreams, and it is noteworthy that this success was achieved in spite of the irredeemably bourgeois background possessed by the great majority of the students involved. But it was not the revolution proper, and at the end of 1969 a piece of legislation (*la leggina*, or 'little law', the first and so far the only instalment of a larger measure of university reform to reach the statute book) brought some political activists back into the universities.

The *leggina* was little in length and scope, but not in impact. It provided for 'liberalisation of study plans'. Liberalisation of any kind would have been a major reform in a system of unbelievable rigidity: in law, for example, or political science, 18 out of the 21 courses required for a degree were compulsory, and this curriculum had remained unchanged since the Fascist 1930s. But the *leggina* solved the curricular problem by virtually abolishing curriculum. From December 28, 1969 each individual has been free to plan his own course of study, provided he can persuade his faculty

[23] For a fuller account, see Mancini's essay, cited above, which also refers to several Italian sources; and cf. also Ady Mineo in Julian Nagel (ed.), *Student Power* (London, 1969), pp. 112–124.

council that his programme accords with his 'cultural and professional needs'. From the Rome Government's cynical point of view it was a delightful measure, which would lure students back from the industrial world into the universities, and direct their rage from Italian politicians to the professors who vetoed their study programmes. For theoretically, there was nothing to prevent a medical or engineering student from leaving out anatomy or hydraulics in order to take courses on sociology and fine art. Still less do there exist in Italian universities tutors or course advisers who might help him. The system had taken a 180-degree turn from Napoleonic authoritarianism to the 'free elective' systems which softened the backbone of American higher education between the wars— except that American students had some ideas about how to use freedom of this kind, and most Italians do not. Indeed, the reform was in many ways analogous to Italy's post-war switch from a corporate fascist model of the state to a democratic model which few people knew how to operate. 'If you know your way round the bureaucracy you will be able to learn what you like. If not, you will learn nothing,' remarked one exceptionally intelligent left-wing student in Bologna, who was too pre-occupied with teasing out the political philosophy implicit in the fourth book of *Gulliver's Travels* to have much time left for the Movement. In January 1970 the *aulae* of the palatial slum which the University of Bologna occupies rang with the angry or puzzled voices of those who did not know what it all meant, and relied on Movement wall-posters (*dazibai*: an Italian borrowing from the Chinese) to tell them.

The *aula*—in the Sorbonne it would be *amphi*—is the only place where a large group of students can meet. It is not totally impersonal. High up on the wall, above the loudspeaker, and above the blackboard chalked with the slogan 'Viva Mao', is a little glinting crucifix, mandatory in public buildings under the Vatican Concordat of 1929. 'No Italian sees it,' explained a professor. 'It is part of the furniture.' The argument of the morning was between the *Maoisti* and the Communists, to decide on the correct line to be taken in the face of the system's sudden attempt to reform itself. Two well-matched champions deployed their easy, musical rhetoric. The Maoist, who happened to be an Italian Albanian, from a pocket of Albanians left behind in the Abruzzi after their country was conquered by the Turks, was in a quandary. He wanted to oppose re-formism, but would lose support if he suggested that students should enslave themselves to a curriculum from which the Government had set them free. The Communist made fun of him, calling him a 'moderate subversive'.

The major reform which hangs over the heads of Italian universities is called by its Parliamentary number—2314—since no one knows who will be Minister of Education when, and if, it is passed. As well as creating a three-tier degree structure and enlarging the professoriate, it is designed to cut down uncontrolled industrial consultancies, and force professors to spend a set number of hours every week in 'contact' with students. It also threatens a version of the German *drittelparität*—a third share for students in university decision-making bodies. The effects of this—and of the particular ways in which its provisions would be evaded—cannot be foreseen, though even the 'little law' may eventually change more than it purports to do, by breaking down some of the barriers between Italian faculties, with whom it is almost a point of honour not to tell each other what they are doing, and what courses they are offering, and why.

The Student Movement, however, has long since lost interest in all this. The Bologna survey cited above shows that long before 1967, a substantial proportion of Italian alumni, looking back in calm after an interval of several years, found nothing to praise in their university education, and their more activist successors, almost from the beginning, have declined to be 'co-opted' into helping to run the 'pig-sty'. By 1970, the extent of their interest in the teaching process was a demand for *voto unico garantito*: all degree work, that is, to be done in study groups, not individually, with an equal grade for all participants, that grade to be guaranteed in advance.

This does not mean, however, that Italian Marxists are uninterested in the politics of university expansion. Indeed, they are far readier than English or American intellectuals to apply strict Marxist analyses to the interaction of technocratic and academic growth, partly perhaps because the Gramscian revolutionary tradition inclines them that way, partly because in Italy the achievement and rapacity of the technocrats, on the one hand, and the expansion of student numbers on the other, have together been two of the most sudden and spectacular social developments over the past decade, in a country more accustomed to social stagnation. Neither of these categories of growth are expected to slow down. Common Market agricultural policy will compel a further large-scale evacuation of the countryside (as a proportion of the labour force, agricultural workers dropped from 34·3 per cent to 24·3 per cent between 1959 and 1967, but the latter figure was still easily the largest in the EEC countries). University students now number 500,000, though the annual output of graduates has only in 1969/70 reached 50,000. Student numbers are expected to reach one million by 1980. In a country where, as we have seen, university education comes without the graces that are attached to it in Britain and America, the Centro K. Marx at Pisa, in a serious and well-documented paperback,[24] has no doubt about what is happening:

'The fundamental contradiction between productive forces (in this case, the intellectual labour-force) and the system of production (hierarchical organisation of salaries and jobs and the consequent under-

---

[24] *Sviluppo capitalistico e forza lavoro intellettuale* (Jaca Book Edizioni, Milan, 1970). Centro K. Marx 'lascia libera riproduzione di parti del libro ai fini di un utile lavoro politico'. Uncertain if I meet this criterion, I have nevertheless taken the liberty of translating and reprinting these passages.

utilisation of intellectual capital) entails a permanent conflict in the intellectual labour force to which capital can find only two solutions: either *numerus clausus*, with authoritarian planning of the labour market and its levels of qualification (and this is the solution now practised in state-capitalist countries like the USSR), or a fluid selection mechanism before, during, and after a person's scholastic career (and this is the solution adopted by western capitalist countries with market economies) . . . (p. 6)

'It is clear enough that an improvement in the qualifications of the labour force is not and will not be matched by a parallel and equivalent improvement in salary levels. In other words, workers with high school certificates are simply substituted for workers with elementary school certificates. From this derives a substantial change in the value of degrees, in the sense that the levels of formal qualification required for a particular professional job all slide upwards . . . ' (p. 36)

The (anonymous) writer goes on to argue that in Italy the true cost of this *'scolarizzazione di massa'*, which the economy is not yet ready to absorb, is paid by the working class and by the peasants who are driven out of the countryside. Another hidden cost of 'scholarisation' is the Italian brain-drain: between 1945 and 1964, nearly 13,000 Italians with professional or technical qualifications took American citizenship or immigrated into the US. If nothing is done to relieve the extreme frustrations of men who want rather more from the intellectual life than a university barony or an industrial consultancy, Italy's annual total of about a quarter of a million emigrants will themselves include a higher and higher proportion of *laureati*. (As in Japan, a considerable unintended obstacle to the emigration of intellectuals is the parlous level of English teaching at school.)

In Italy it is always easy to believe in a conspiracy. After all, there very often *is* a conspiracy, sometimes conscious, sometimes so deeply rooted in national styles of conduct that conspiracy seems too harsh a word. For example, there is intense pressure for *razionalizzazione* of the university system from a huge firm like FIAT, whose international competitors do not have to spend, as FIAT does, one per cent of their turnover on education and training. The Marxist critique of this 'capitalist reformism' is reinforced by a much more deeply rooted Italian resistance to merito-cratic individualism, even among people who are fully alive to the vices of the social system which meritocracy replaces. Any approximation to social justice in the Italian higher education system would imply, if only for a transitional period, various devices for selecting the most able from the mass of the qualified, and allowing for the economic and cultural handicaps of young people from the Mezzogiorno. But, said the Bolognese scientist whom I have already quoted:

'There is a subconscious campaign against this kind of thing, among professors as well as among radical students. Meritocracy selects, and partly because there were so many injustices in the past, there is a fight against the idea that whoever is good may study, and whoever is not may not. Every nation has its own character. We are trying to improve. There is no possibility of our behaving like the English or the Swedes, but on the other hand there is no really important corruption, and more effort goes into work here than in India or Greece or Spain. It is hard to invent a university . . . '

The idea that every nation—even every university—has its own character does not appeal to the student Left in Europe, which is dedicated to discovering in its own cultural terrain, however unsuitable, the Yenan or the Sierra Maestra where revolution, international-style, can be made. It was not an intellectual but a comfortably placed young manager at FIAT in Turin who reminded me that the Risorgimento had been started by students, and that the present generation could be no less influential if they did not surrender their personalities to romantic Marxist globalism, and if they concentrated for a while on 'Italian things, Italian philosophy'. From an Italian student, that would be likely to receive the reply, 'Well, Mussolini did that.' But there is something in it, all the same. In 1834 Mazzini, who had enjoyed his first arrest as a student of sixteen for organising a disturbance in his university church, tried to found Young Europe, an international organisation of youth extending to the rest of the continent the emotional fervour of Young Italy. It failed: the generational tinder was dry all over Europe, but each nation's youth wanted to do revolution in its own way.[25]

In Italy, students' perception of their task is heavily influenced, as one might expect, by their own most distinguished Marxist intellectual, Gramsci, especially perhaps by a famous passage in the *Notes on Machiavelli*:

'Ilici [Lenin, in Gramsci's prison vocabulary] realised that the war of movement victoriously conducted in the East in 1917 did not suit the conditions of the West, where only a war of attrition was possible . . . In the East the state was everything and the civil society was primordial and gelatinous; in the West there was a balanced relation between state and civil society and when the state trembled the robust structure of the civil society immediately emerged.'[26]

Nothing better demonstrates the accuracy of this analysis than what happened in France after May 1968, when the 'trembling' of the state was absorbed by the society's padding of bourgeois conservatism and agricultural stolidity. But in Italy, the extreme Left managed to convince itself that the contradictions of galloping industrial growth and socio-

[25] Feuer, op. cit., p. 34.
[26] *Note sul Machiavelli* (Turin, 1949), p. 68. I owe the reference and translation to Professor Mancini.

political stagnation had in fact rendered the civil society 'gelatinous', and that the time for a 'war of movement' had come. When it became obvious that there was not going to be an Italian revolution, disillusionment set in. 'They want to make revolution,' said one professor of his students, 'but they also want to ski.'

In Rome and Venice, Milan and Bologna, the works of Lenin and Gramsci cram the university bookshops, and it is even possible to buy long-playing records of the noise in the streets at famous demonstrations, which presumably have the same effect on *aficionados* as a record of the Flying Scotsman at speed has on a certain kind of Anglican clergyman. But a more subtle and pervasive influence is the very conditions under which a young Italian acquires the culture and ideas that shape his response to the world. Family, for any Italian, is the prime source of cultural influence, but most students, especially revolutionary ones, are having trouble with their families. A peer-group culture, based on coffee bars and fashionable intellectual reading, is the only alternative for young men whose formal higher education is limited to buying the professor's lecture-notes for an artificially high price. The period in which the *Movimento Studentesco* saw the university as a potential ally in the shaking of the Italian foundations was necessarily short. Subsequently, students have oscillated between thinking of the university as a quaint survival, conceivably a weak point in the system; and as an instrument of advanced capitalism's attempt to tighten its grip on the world. Hence their resistance to university reform, for at present the instrument is gratifyingly ineffective. One *Potere Operaio* leader in Bologna put it this way:

> 'We have a university which meets the needs of landowners and small industrialists, but which does not meet the needs of advanced capitalism. The university is going to create a bureaucratised mass of highly qualified technicians. In Italy we have discovered a new thing, a welfare state which can swallow up large numbers of unproductive people . . .
>
> 'The basic need of students is to know. The basic need of workers is not to be exploited. The intellectual must be aware of himself as a new proletariat. We cannot offer the same education to everyone, but we *can* offer the knowledge of what reality is.'

It is not easy, under present circumstances, for an Italian student to acquire knowledge of other types of reality as well as of the political realities of his own condition. Nor is the situation likely to alter soon. In 1969 Professor Adriano Buzzati-Traverso of the University of Pavia, then Director of the International Laboratory of Genetics and Biophysics in Naples, now Unesco's Assistant-Director-General for Science, published a collection of articles about the difficulties of scientific research in Italy. Some of the articles were twelve years old, but this did not matter, for as the author wrote, 'In the course of twelve years the conditions described have deteriorated, even though public investment has notably increased, especially in recent years'. When the book went to press it was calculated that in 1970 there would be 437,900 students (excluding extramural students) in Italy, at a cost to the State of L218,921 million (average cost per student, L500,000). The estimate, like most such estimates, was about ten per cent too low. 'To improve universities to acceptable standard with existing numbers,' Professor Buzzati-Traverso writes, 'would take the estimate up to about L300,000 million. Real reform—including not only grants to students but compensation to families for loss of their sons' labour, would probably cost L1,000,000 million, and compel a complete reassessment of economic and political policy.' In the meanwhile, 'our educational system is a powerful brake on change in the social structure'.[27]

[27] *Un fossile denutrito: l'università italiana* (Milan, 1969—o.p.), p. 261.

'Then is Oxford the University of heresies, if she will not allow orthodox truths to be published.'

Archbishop Courtenay in 1382, after the University had refused to circulate the official condemnation of Wyclif's theses.

In May 1970, when they declined to allow Her Majesty's Foreign Secretary to speak in the Oxford Union, radical undergraduates were probably unaware of the ancient Wycliffian example to which they could have appealed. But the episode is a reminder, if a reminder is necessary, of the historical fact that universities as the Western world knows them were conceived and born in struggle, both intellectual and institutional.

Affrays on the streets between town and gown, like the bloody shooting match in Oxford on St. Scholastica's Day, 1355, are the most notorious of these struggles, for the state of mind involved is intelligible to anyone, even if he knows nothing of a university's purpose or constitution. Often, indeed, riots of this kind expressed, or gave rise to, a more deep-seated antipathy between a university and a community of which it was a valued but awkward guest. But something had had to happen in the intellectual world for the students to be there at all. The happening took place not in Oxford but in Paris, and not in the fourteenth century but the twelfth. It was symbolised by a single individual, Peter Abelard. The University of Paris did not exist formally until long after Abelard was dead, and it is open to anyone to argue that its birth would not have been long delayed even if Abelard had never lived. Nevertheless, it was Abelard who took the philosophical orthodoxy of his time and tossed it, as a dog tosses a bone, and then turned his speculative mind, even more daringly, to the meatier subject of theology. Intellectually, his offence in the estimation of his tireless enemy St. Bernard was, as Rashdall expresses it, 'not this or that particular error but the whole tone, spirit and method of his theological teaching. He had presumed to endeavour to understand, to explain the mystery of the Trinity: he had dared to bring all things in heaven and earth to the test of reason.'[28] Institutionally, Abelard grew up in a time

[28] Op. cit., vol. i, p. 57.

and place when all learning and all education was confined to monasteries and cathedrals. Abelard, too, both learnt and taught at the Cathedral School of Paris, which was the institutional chrysalis out of which the young university later emerged. But he also showed—when he was forced to migrate to a haven provided by a chapter of secular canons at the 'Mount' of Ste. Geneviève south of the Seine—that even in an ecclesiastical milieu a freelance intellectual could attract a crowd and criticise orthodoxy with impunity. (Abelard was in the end terribly punished, for untheological offences, but by then the point had been made.)

A further contribution of Abelard's to the history of intellectual institutions should not be overlooked by the Parisian advocates of '*pluridisciplinarité*' 850 years later. Abelard made his name by picking the 'nominalist' side in the great medieval controversy between nominalism and realism, and by defending it successfully against his teacher, the realist William of Champeaux. (The controversy, whose bitterness and amplitude partially derived from its explosive theological implications, cannot be summed up in a sentence. But briefly, realists maintained that reality belonged only to 'ideas' or 'universals': the particulars were mere phantasms. Nominalists declared that universals are 'empty sounds' and that only the individual thing or person was real. The problem is itself too 'unreal' to have interest for contemporary philosophers, but perhaps the modern difference between thinkers who believe in the possibility of metaphysics and thinkers who do not vaguely corresponds to the lines of the controversy and the heat it engendered.) By the time Abelard left Ste. Geneviève, he was supreme in his own field of dialectic (i.e. logic) and grammar (i.e. Latin), and decided to conquer theology as well. He went to Anselm of Laon, who was regarded as the best man, and was thoroughly bored. Talking to fellow students, he said he found it astonishing that educated men should not be able to study the Bible for themselves with no more help than the text and the gloss. They jokingly challenged him to make the attempt, and he promised, if they provided him with one of the usual commentaries, to start lecturing next day on the most difficult book of the Bible that they cared to choose. They offered him Ezekiel, and he delivered the lecture, which was followed by several more, with the audience getting bigger every time. Not for the first time in the history of the Church, but for the first time in several centuries, a major philosopher had applied both his method and his conclusions to the theological teaching of his day, and by sweeping away the accumulated written rubbish, and reinstating original texts (classical, incidentally, as well as Biblical) had left the way clear for the Thomist synthesis a century later.

Abelard had gathered the audience, but the meeting had not yet been called to order. By early in the twelfth century there were hordes of students in Paris, and the teachers themselves were too numerous to be accommodated within the cathedral cloister, or even in the island on which Notre Dame is built. The students were much younger than Bologna's. These were not beneficed clergymen of thirty, congregating round the men who could teach them canon law. Rather, they were adolescents wanting quick recognition as qualified philosphical disputants. 'Yesterday boys, today masters,' was John of Salisbury's comment. The masters (of arts) then very often continued as students in higher faculties. In the circumstances, the formation of a guild of masters was inevitable, and it seems to have taken place by about 1170. Various immunities were granted to the scholars quite quickly but their first charter of privileges resulted—as already noted[29]—from a 'police riot' in 1200, during which several students were killed, including the bishop-elect of Liège.

The next struggle which defined the nature of the university was that with the Chancellor of the Cathedral Church of Paris. The Chancellor was not an officer of the University, but his powers as a judge in the ecclesiastical court and as head of the schools were formidable. However, the masters found a way of limiting them. Although the masters could not force the Chancellor to grant one of their number a licence to teach, neither could he compel the masters to admit to their society someone who had not complied with their regulations. In other words, they had the power of boycott which is used by professional associations to this day. In this way, public inception as a master became as essential to the aspiring university teacher as was the Chancellor's licence. It is true that the university had two powers in reserve. The first was to withdraw labour and cease lecturing, the second was an appeal to the Pope. But both these powers had to be used sparingly, the first because of the inconvenience involved, the second because every appeal to the Pope implied a diminution of the university's own autonomy.

Cessation of lectures, followed by large-scale dispersion, was tried after the death of several students in the Carnival Riot of 1229, to the great gain of Oxford, Cambridge, and several French universities such as Angers. This time it was the King himself who suffered defeat, and the university's show of nerve was rewarded with the Papal Bull *Parens Scientiarum*, which codified many of the rights to which the scholars had laid claim against the Chancellor. But the next struggle was not against superior authority, but against rival scholars. Here, organisational and intellectual issues interacted. At about the same time as Arabised versions of Aristotle arrived from the East to tickle the fancies of Parisian scholars, the Mendicant orders—Franciscans and Dominicans—arrived to re-Christianise the backsliders. The culmination of that process was the *Summa Theologiae* of St. Thomas Aquinas, whose influence on the thought of the West is still palpable. But the friars, though competent philosophers and theologians, were awkward colleagues. Their right to teach was

[29] P. 62.

unquestionable, but in 1252-3, after another town and gown riot, the university declared a cessation of lectures, or lock-out, which two Dominican doctors and a Franciscan refused to join. After that the university enacted that an oath of loyalty to the statutes and decisions of the university be extracted from all masters, and the blackleg Black friars were expelled.

But this time, the university had picked a fight that it could not win. The friars were well placed at the French court, and more important, 1254 produced a Pope, Alexander IV, who supported them all down the line in the Bull *Quasi lignum vitae.* The masters then ingeniously issued a proclamation renouncing all Papal privileges and dissolving their own voluntary society, reserving their right to lecture in hired premises—and also, though they naturally did not say this, to boycott and harass the friars, who were granting degrees themselves under armed guard. (Aquinas himself was admitted to his degree in this way.) In 1261 a new Pope reversed the policy and the university, in its turn, got most of what it had been hanging out for, including less foreseeable consequences in its own social organisation: a binding together of the faculty of theology, hitherto independent, with the other faculties; a system for raising money, necessitated by law suits in Rome; and not least, an anti-Papal, nationalistic feeling in the University which lasts, some think, to this day.

It may be well, before going further, to summarise what seem to have been the main achievements of the medieval university in its formative first two centuries, and at the same time notice what it conspicuously failed to achieve. Naturally, both achievements and failures were properties of the medieval mind itself rather than simply of the institutions in which medieval ideas were embodied. Nevertheless, the models have proved to be uncommonly durable.

Above all, then, the universities quickly became the intellectual foci of their age, in spite of its being an age in which the penalties for having the 'wrong' idea could be severe and immediate. Their scholasticism, which later earned them a bad name for disputatious irrelevance, was not irrelevant at the time. Nothing but a niggling concern for intellectual structure could have made much of the confused remnants of classical civilisation which had survived the (so-called) Dark Ages. Nor did they neglect social issues. The numerous professors whom Harvard has seconded—not always with the happiest results—to Washington have their predecessor in Stephen Langton, who in his lectures at Paris at the beginning of the thirteenth century discussed the theoretical justification for opposing tyrants, and several years later, as Archbishop of Canterbury, found himself confronted with Bad King John.

Their second achievement, the professionalisation of learning through the craft guild system, was more ambiguous. It was a condition of their survival, and the utility of the model is apparent from its survival to this day in the concepts of academic apprenticeship and qualification, as well

E

as in the rituals of examinations, degree days, and robes of office. But professional bodies which combine for their own protection seldom subsequently run the risk of innovation, and whereas even the Church carried within its structure the seeds of its own reformation, the University, if for any reason the intellectual curiosity of its members guttered low, could not easily be refuelled from outside. There was to come a time when the Academy itself needed its St. Francis or St. Dominic, its Luther or Calvin. But instead, Paris had to wait for Napoleon, and Oxford for a Royal Commission.

Thirdly, they began, and for some time remained, international institutions. This in itself was a source of protection, for when the municipality began to wonder whether students were worth the money they brought in, and started breaking heads, appeal to Crown or Pope, or migration to another country, were among the possible sanctions open to the university. Internationalism of this kind could hardly survive the Reformation and the rise of the nation state, and as Dr. Marjorie Reeves points out,[30] migration became impossible as soon as universities ceased to meet in hired classrooms and became large-scale property-owners.[31] But though universities to this day are organised on what to an outsider observer seems a surprisingly parochial basis, it means something that their origins lie in centuries when internationalism was possible. If the Western model of a university were a sixteenth century one, its contemporary marque would be different in ways that we cannot easily imagine.

Nor is it easy to imagine the errors of omission for which the medieval university is responsible, for its products have so shaped our minds that alternatives are almost impossible to envisage. But it is easy to list a few of the intellectual developments which the world has found necessary, but for which it had to look outside the university. The most serious deficiency was scientific investigation, for which an appropriate institutional form was not discovered until the sixteenth century. In medieval universities the only modern-sounding scientific subject studied, apart from medicine, was astronomy—perhaps the international subject *par excellence*, to which an observer in a different country has always been able to add something new, and in which strange intellectual continuities are found: Western science reached Japan in the seventeenth century through the Dutch Astronomy Office, and in the mid-twentieth century, there is still no pure science to which Japanese scholars have contributed more. There is no need here to go into the reasons for the medieval academic's contempt for the practical and the manual, without which neither physical nor medical research could be started. The idea of a national scientific research institute may well be dated from a plan which Sir Humphrey Gilbert drew up for Queen Elizabeth in 1570. In a special academy, the natural philosopher and physician were to practise together continually:

[30] 'The European University from Mediaeval Times', in Niblett, op. cit., pp. 68-9.
[31] Cp. the University of Chicago's problem, p. 51.

'to try owt the secreates of nature, as many waies as they possibly may. And shalbe sworne once every yeare to deliver unto the Tresorer his office faire and plaine written in Parchment, withoute Equivocacion or Enigmaticall phrases, under their handes, all those proofes and trialles made within the forepassed yeare.'[32]

Professional education which kept pace with the needs of society was another gap in the medieval university's map of learning. The British academics of 1970 who look with suspicion at the rise in their universities of business studies and industrially-financed operational research may or may not be justified in their suspicions, but their attitude is indubitably, though unconsciously, influenced by the fact that European universities of the Paris and Oxford pattern drove professional education to the gates of their academic paradise, whereas their American successors did not. Common Law in England had to be organised by the Inns of Court, and surgical practice and teaching by the Company of Barber-Surgeons. Both, of course, were constructed on the guild model, with the appropriate restrictive practices, no less tenacious than those of the universities. (Indeed, if one compares the contemporary attitudes of the British Bar and the American Medical Association, it is hard to see much difference in the ultimate effect of professional education conducted within a university setting, and that conducted outside.[33]) Dr. Reeves, in a striking image, sums up the matter by saying that the medieval university's concept of knowledge limited its intellectual growth, like a pot-bound plant:

'The concentration of resources within the "pot" had been essential in the first stages and a plant of great strength had been grown. Its chief fruit was a sharp, precise mind, trained in logical distinctions and methods of verification. As a system of education, however, it did not foster curiosity or experiment nor produce qualities of imagination or perception, though these, of course, were not lacking in individuals. Concentration on methodology finally tended to make it barren.'[34]

John Gerard, the barber-surgeon whose *Herball* (1547) fertilised modern botany, would have appreciated that conceit.

[32] Quoted in Armytage, op. cit., p. 78. It is a pity that this early concern for agreeable reading and easy information retrieval subsequently lapsed in the scientific community.

[33] Most leading British lawyers will have taken a first degree at a university, usually in law, before reading for the Bar elsewhere.

[34] Op. cit., p. 71.

However, images of the garden and the plant-nursery come more naturally to the pen of people who contemplate an invention of the medieval university whose significance is human rather than strictly intellectual: the college. Of Robert Abbott, Master of Balliol 1610–16, his biographer says:

> 'As a careful and skilfull Gardiner he set his nurseries with the best plants, making alwayes choyce of the towardliest young men in all elections, and when he had set them, he tooke such care to water and prune them that in no plat or knot in the famous nurserie of the University of Oxford there appeared more beautiful flowers, or grew sweeter fruit, than in Baliol Colledge whilst he was Master.'[35]

The origins of the college system, which is still being imitated and adapted in institutions as new as the Santa Cruz campus of the University of California and the University of Lancaster in England, lie—as we have already seen in the Bologna section—in the medieval undergraduate's need for some protection from the rigour and expense of twelfth century town life. The earliest Paris colleges were charitable hostels, though the Sorbonne itself (chartered 1267) was a college for graduate students who might otherwise have been tempted away from secular theology to the security of a Dominican house or the prosperity of a canonist's post. All these, however, were swept away at the Revolution, while 'of all the secular foundations which medieval piety bequeathed to Oxford she has lost not one'.[36] In spite of the Royalist occupation of Oxford during the Civil War no college ever fell victim to bankruptcy, though in the late 1660s Balliol had to be bailed out by Christ Church—a circumstance seldom mentioned by Balliol men. The English institutions contrived to adapt themselves, sometimes after a disgraceful time-lag, to altered circumstances: the French ones did not.

Anyone who knows either Oxford or Cambridge, whether as student, teacher, researcher, or rubberneck, will know that no college in either place is exactly similar to another one, and that between the largest and the smallest, the richest and the poorest, the oldest and the youngest, the

---

[35] Daniel Featley in T. Fuller, *Abel Redivivus* (1651), p. 543.
[36] Rashdall, op. cit., vol. i, p. 533.

liveliest and the dullest there are wide gulfs of style and practice. Similarly, the dweller in Oxford (or Cambridge) has in recent years had it impressed upon him more and more often that there is also in the city an entity called the University, whose heart is hard to find and whose policy is hard to fathom, but which pays part of people's salaries, finds space for men and books, negotiates with the University Grants Committee, and employs, now, a permanent as opposed to a rotating chief executive, known as the Vice-Chancellor. In Oxford in 1970 he was Alan Bullock, historian, and Master of St. Catherine's. The Chancellor (at present Mr. Harold Macmillan, who was elected by the M.A.s of Oxford while still Prime Minister) has been an absentee head since the fifteenth century, when the university needed a representative at court, and a mere ornament since he lost the power to appoint Vice-Chancellors.

Some apology is therefore needed in this book for virtually ignoring, within the University of Oxford, the university itself, except in its bearing upon the lives of college tutors and students; and for treating of but a single college. Three things may be said. First, books about Oxford are beyond man's numbering, and several of them are good, recent, and accessible. Second, the time when Oxford as an institution could be successfully imitated is several centuries gone. (Harvard in the seventeenth century is probably the last example.) Third, I cannot myself view the place with even a pretence of objectivity. None of these considerations applies with the same force to a single college, not my own, and for singling out Balliol in particular, even less excuse is needed. It has some claim to be the oldest college, founded (unlike Merton, its rival in antiquity) on a Parisian pattern. Its powers of adaptation to altered circumstances and educational demands are unrivalled, and in the nineteenth century, particularly under the Masterships of Jenkyns and Jowett, it symbolised the new seriousness of learning in English universities. Throughout the twentieth century, it has undoubtedly given more professors to other universities, in Britain and abroad, than any other undergraduate institution of its size in the world. (Between 1919 and 1939, 250). Much more recently, it has acquired a rather spurious notoriety as the headquarters of Oxford student radicalism. Finally, the college possesses, as well as a competent college history,[37] a carefully compiled series of college registers, of which the most recent was published in 1969.

The present study can do no more than toy with these materials, but it is much to be hoped that some sociologist of education with time on his hands will address himself to them before long. Once, the English Prime Minister Arthur Balfour paid a visit to Jowett, and was found wandering vaguely in the Back Quad. Asked what he was doing, the statesman replied, 'I am trying to find out the secret of Balliol.' It was well hidden

[37] H. W. C. Davis, *Balliol College* (revised edn.), Oxford, 1963.

then, and it is well hidden now, but most of the virtues and some of the faults of English higher education lie concealed with it.

Balliol too began in struggle, though it was a struggle unconnected with the university. In about 1260 Sir John de Balliol, lord of Barnard Castle on the Scottish Border, 'unjustly vexed and enormously damnified the Church of Tynemouth and the Church of Durham'. No one knows how, but it was a rash man who tangled with a thirteenth century prince-bishop. Not long afterwards, Sir John knelt at the door of Durham Abbey, where he was publicly scourged by the bishop, and undertook to provide perpetual maintenance for certain poor arts scholars at the university. They were allowed eightpence a week, and governed by a pair of external procurators, a Franciscan friar and a secular master of arts. In 1282 Dervorguilla, Sir John's widow, gave the college its first statutes. This remote history would be worth mentioning if only as a means of illustrating the zany continuities that Oxford affords, and the curious sources of the wealth on which British higher education was until very recently built. Balliol's first exhibitions in modern history and natural science were endowed in the 1860s by Miss Hannah Brackenbury, who had inherited a railway fortune from her brother, a Manchester solicitor. She gave the money to Balliol because she was convinced that she was the last lineal descendant to Perse Brackenbury of Sellabye near Barnard Castle, who married in 1086 a daughter of Hugh Ballyeul, an ancester of John Balliol. In 1931 one of the Brackenbury scholars was Christopher Hill, a young man of Yorkshire Methodist parentage, who became expert in the history of Puritanism and the English seventeenth century revolution, joined the Communist Party (and left it in 1956) and is at the time of writing Master of Balliol, where he was responsible for administering the proceeds of the one million pounds raised for the college from alumni and other benefactors in the 1960s.

Oxford as a university dates from about 1167, though its first written statutes do not appear until 1253. Its constitutional development, and the local tensions that accompanied the rise of the university, follow in broad outline the pattern of Paris, and cannot concern us here, except to note that the enormous power which the university had and indeed still has in the affairs of the town is extensively owed to the townsmen's savage and sacrilegious slaughter of scholars on February 10-11, 1355, after a quarrel between students and landlords in the Tavern called Swyndlestock. (It was not until 1825 that the Mayor and burghers were allowed to omit the annual penance and offertory in St. Mary's Church which was enjoined by the bishop of the time.) Oxford's most significant difference from Paris lay in the role of the Bishop's Chancellor, who in Oxford became an officer of the university, endowed with immense personal power, academic and ecclesiastical, civil and criminal. This happened very largely because Oxford was neither the capital city of England nor the see-town of the bishop. Its independence and greatness as a university—and sometimes also its slackness—derive from its enjoyment of what scholars generally regard as the precondition of good mental work: it was left to itself.

Balliol was in one very important respect not the type of an Oxford and Cambridge college. The most genuinely English article, as well as by most criteria the oldest, is Merton (1264). The scholars whom Walter de Merton endowed with college buildings, deans of students, fellows, a warden, a visitor (the Archbishop of Canterbury), and other functions and titles familiar in Oxbridge to this day, were not pensioners receiving an endowment administered by others, but corporate landowners. This is an aspect of the English college system which foreign imitators have been less anxious to adopt. It appears to have been Walter de Merton's intention that as many fellows should be elected as the resources would maintain. History, as Rashdall drily records, decided differently:

'A provision for a similar increase in the number of fellows proportionate to their increasing wealth is found in many college statutes even where the original and normal number is prescribed. It is probable that these provisions have very seldom been observed. Already in 1284 Archbishop Pecham complains of the excessive and unstatutable salary which the Merton fellows had assigned to the brewer and the cook and of the increase which they had voted to their own allowance of 50s. a year to defray the cost of "delicate living" . . . The history of the English colleges is one of increasing wealth and increasing luxury secured by unearned increments and some perjury. Such a result is due largely to that freedom from external financial control of which Walter de Merton set the example. On the other hand, the interest of English fellows in their property has perhaps prevented the waste, dissipation, and loss of college reserves of which the history of Paris supplies so many examples.'[38]

There is really no more to be said about that, especially by a writer who attended a sumptuous Oxford college Gaudy[39] while engaged on writing this book. The Japanese teacher's reminder that it takes ten hard-working farmers to keep one samurai in the style to which he is accustomed,[40] and that privileges entail corresponding responsibilities, has not been acceptable in British universities for the greater part of their history.[41]

Balliol, though actually or nearly the oldest, is not the richest of Oxford colleges. In the table of endowment incomes published in Rose and Ziman's *Camford Observed*[42]—the soundest and wittiest recent book on the two ancient universities as educational institutions—it stood eighth on the

[38] Op. cit., vol. iii, pp. 198–9.
[39] Feast for alumni.
[40] See p. 96.
[41] See, for instance, David Caute's attack on his own college, All Souls, for under-utilisation of its revenues (*Encounter*, March 1966, pp. 3 ff) and replies in later issues.
[42] London, 1964.

Oxford list, with £57,779.[43] Christ Church had more than twice as much, Hertford less than a tenth as much. But the time is long past when the Fellows, who in 1970 numbered sixty-seven, could be paid out of endowment. Most of them, like their counterparts in other colleges and the Other Place, and like the numerous lecturers and research students in both universities who have not yet landed or never will land a Fellowship of a college, receive the bulk of their salaries from the University. Probably only an American politician, used to a federal structure in which Washington provides money and exercises certain powers, while individual states of varying wealth spend the money and exercise other powers, has much hope of understanding from outside the relation of the University to the colleges in Oxbridge. The curious may discover how it works in Oxford from the two thick volumes of the report of the Franks Commission, and from such Acts of Convocation as have since been passed to put the Commission's recommendations into effect.

But some glimpse of the system must be given here. The organisation of education in the University requires, and has required from the beginning, that lectures be given, which all members of the University are free to attend. Rather younger, but still venerable enough, is the notion that each undergraduate should have these lectures supplemented by private teaching from his college tutor (the tutorial system). Younger still—dating only from the middle of the nineteenth century—is the idea that quite apart from whatever private interests college Fellows care to pursue, the University and beyond it the State has a responsibility or interest to foster and maintain original research, especially in the sciences. All this, it is thought, is what a university is about, and for these tasks, as well as for innumerable minor administrative offices of a medieval flavour (Proctorships, Syndicships, Esquire Bedellships), men and occasionally women have to be hired. Similar jobs have to be done by somebody in other universities. Much of Oxford's particular flavour is due to its insistence that though there may be diversities of gifts, there is only one calling. The ideal, now rarely discovered, Oxford don is a man who is prepared to do a little bit of teaching, counselling, research, administration, and ceremonial entertaining, and who is capable of doing them all well. Therefore, each hiring represents the outcome of a compromise, or horse-trading, between the interests of the parties involved.

The university, through the appropriate faculty board or department head, offers a lectureship—in Hellenistic Studies, let us say. The college does not have many students who are interested in Hellenistic studies as such, but it does need someone to teach its undergraduates how to read and write classical Greek prose, and if the candidate also happens to be capable of taking pupils doing History of Science to A.D. 500, and looks as if he would get on well enough with undergraduates to be a potential

[43] But see p. 150.

Junior Dean, and plays a passable game of croquet, it may be prepared to elect the man to a Fellowship.[44] More often, the initiative in the appointment comes from the college, not the University. The successful candidate is then paid a stipend, like any other British university lecturer, by the University, which gets its money *en bloc*, but wrapped up with hints, from the University Grants Committee, which in turn gets its money, subject to financial crises, from the Government. (In 1970, British university lecturers were being remunerated on a scale of £1,355–£3,650.) The college then tops this sum up by anything from £200 to £500 a year, according to the wealth of the college and the teaching or administrative load the tutor is carrying, and throws in the fringe benefits of free meals, rooms in college, and rights to the Fellows' garden which to some young dons are worth almost more than their salary, and to some—especially if they are married with young children and living in north Oxford—may be worth nothing.

It is claimed for the system, as for most things in Oxford, that although it sounds idiotic, it 'works', or at least, that the greater good of preserving the college system, with its intimate acquaintance of teacher and taught, outweighs any waste and injustice. As A. C. Tait remarked in his Journal for 1835, 'There is no good to be done in Oxford unless one is intimate with undergraduates', and many of contemporary Oxford's contrivances are designed to make intimacy possible in spite of student numbers and the fissiparous nature of modern scholarship.

One injustice took a generation to solve. The post-war expansion of Oxford and Cambridge created a large class, running into hundreds at both places, of sometimes very eminent non-Fellows, especially in subjects which colleges considered to be too obscure to be worth one of their own precious places, or which they secretly or openly despised. Failure to get 'tenure' is an agonising experience for scholars thousands of miles from Oxford, but in a university where the colleges are the centre of all social life, and where there is not even a Faculty Club, exclusion from college privileges and mysteries—exclusion which often implied a criticism either of one's person or one's subject—was especially hard to bear. Eventually, the colleges were each persuaded to take their share of such 'wandering scholars' who had been without a collegiate home for more than five years, but their dilemma is an illuminating example of two characteristic Oxford retarding mechanisms: reluctance to solve a problem until it has been notorious for about 25 years, and oblique resistance to academic diversification (the barriers which first economics, then sociology, found erected against them in Oxford were built of other materials beside collegiate self-interest, but colleges' feeling that the subject was marginal and the practitioners very likely unclubbable was certainly a major factor).

[44] A recent advertisement for an Oxford lectureship in the Politics of Latin America said that 'the lectureship is open to persons who have not so far specialised in the Politics of Latin America'.

But back to Balliol, which as the prime intellectual source of the Oxford Politics, Philosophy and Economics school '(Modern Greats', now normally known as PPE) is less vulnerable to the last criticism than any other college. Balliol, in fact, has a fair claim to be the cradle of the modern English university. Since about 1808 it has gathered first-class honours in armfuls. These were, of course, the honours of the traditional, primarily classical curriculum, but from the middle of the nineteenth century onwards the college began to make up lost ground in the natural sciences. Jowett's Mastership (1870–93) is so firmly associated in people's minds with philosophy and the mental preparation of British imperial and domestic administrators that his perceptiveness about science and technology (in his introduction to Plato's *Republic*) comes as a surprise:

'The resources of the natural sciences are not half developed as yet; the soil of the earth, instead of growing more barren, may become many times more fertile than hitherto; the use of machinery far greater, and also more minute than at present. New secrets of physiology may be revealed, deeply affecting human nature in its innermost recesses. The standard of health may be raised and the lives of men prolonged by sanitary and medical knowledge . . . The ever-increasing power of locomotion may join the extremes of the earth.'[45]

The flavour of Balliol between the accension of Jowett and the resignation of Lindsay in 1949 has been rolled on the tongues of many memoir-writers. The essential point is that this was one of the rare periods and places in the history of higher education where individuals' notion of what they wanted for themselves as persons, and a State's ill-formulated, possibly misjudged, but still unmistakable demand for a certain type of recruit to the governing elite, coincided with the existence of an institution capable of meeting both demands at once. Both sides of the equation could be illustrated a dozen times over: not just by the monopoly which Balliol held over Liberal Cabinets and Regius Professorships of Modern History, but, for instance, by the advice of Edward Caird (Master 1893–1907) to the future Lord Beveridge: 'While you are at University, your first duty is self-culture, not politics or philanthropy. Then go and find out how poverty can be cured.'

Was this unique conjunction of demand and supply 'the secret of Balliol' which Balfour sought in the Back Quad? Perhaps, but there were also the expectations which each year's intake of freshmen knew they aroused. By Beveridge's time Balliol had enjoyed a century of intellectual pre-eminence. True, it accommodated peers and playboys as well as paupers and pedagogical *pupae* (my own grandfather-in-law, who was up in the 1880s, was not an arrogant man, but he was destined for an academic career and therefore, it was said by his family, associated with no one who

[45] Benjamin Jowett, *The Dialogues of Plato* (translated and introduced), Oxford, 1892, vol. 3 (*The Republic*), clxxix.

was not 'reading for a First'). But this did not detract from the aura of the place, and A. L. Smith, who more than any other man was responsible for the college's grip on Modern History professorships, once said at a college meeting that Balliol ought to sprinkle its incense on the altar of the god Momentum, for it was *he* who kept it going.

The point of considering this period is not to rehearse yet again the plentiful anecdotal material about Hilaire Belloc, Ronald Knox and other quintessentially Oxford figures of the time, but to provide some yard-stick of comparison for the Balliol of today, whose students, dons, and—if the word is permissible—customers are rather less sure that they are finding or providing precisely what is wanted. Not that the golden age itself lacked critics. Long before Flexner wrote his critique of Oxford, a lesser-known American, who was at Balliol in 1896, assessed his own experience:

'In all social aspects the colleges are as nearly perfect as human institutions are capable of becoming, and they are the foundation of an unequalled athletic life. Educationally, their qualities are mixed. For the purpose of common or garden English gentlemen, nothing could be better than a happy combination of tutorial instruction and university examining. For the purposes of scholarly instruction in general, and of instruction in the modern sciences and mechanic arts in particular, few things could be worse than the system as at present construed.[46]

'Though the English undergraduate is not taught to read manuscripts and decipher inscriptions—to trace out knowledge in its sources—the examination system gives him the breadth of view and mental grasp which are the only safe foundations of scholarship. If he contributes to science, he usually does so after he has left the university. The qualities which then distinguish him are rare among scholars—sound common sense and catholicity of judgement. Such qualities, for instance, enabled an Oxford classical first to recognize Schliemann's greatness while yet the German universities could only see that he was not an orthodox researcher according to their standards. If a man were bent on obtaining the best possible scholarly training, he probably could not do better than to take an English B.A. and then a German or an American Ph.D. As for the world of deeds and of men, the knowledge which is power is that which is combined with address and pluck; and the English system seems based on practical sense, in that it lays chief stress on producing this rare combination . . .

'The Oxford honor first knows what he knows and sometimes he knows more. Few things are as distressing as the sciolism of a second-rate English editor of a classic. The mint sauce quite forgets that it is not Lamb. The English minor reviewer exhibits the pride of intellect in its purest form.'[47]

[46] John Corbin, *An American at Oxford* (Boston, 1902), pp. 243–4.
[47] Ibid., pp. 193–4, 198.

The passage of seventy-five years has modified but not dimmed these opinions, which may be compared with the more recent critique of Oxford on pp. 312–18, and perhaps also with what a young German modern historian at Balliol told me about his attempts to introduce pupils to systematic historical research as it is carried on in his own country's universities, where students are, he said, given a good grounding in the handling of documents and then expected to find their own books. 'I tried it with students here. All they could do was to write nice essays. None of them could analyse a document, which would mean for instance writing down the names and looking them up in the Dictionary of National Biography, then asking for what purpose the document had been written, and so on. They read a document as though it were a book.'

But who are 'they'? Even elaborate resources for sociological investigation could only produce a partial answer to this question. The collective politics of students are comparatively simple to ascertain, and their individual attitudes, hopes and fears are generally not kept secret from a serious inquirer. (See, for instance, Zweig's 1962 study already quoted.[48]) But with students, and perhaps more especially with Balliol students, curiosity about who a man is extends to the man he may become. Social researchers naturally make no claim to prophetic powers: however, in Britain it is certainly the case that more could be known than is known about the relation of people's higher education and their early professional experience to their judgments of value and their concepts of themselves. American universities, whose dependence on their alumni is more directly economic, have a more powerful incentive to conduct such inquiries, but it is probable that the present generation of student revolutionaries will, in Britain as elsewhere, provoke the asking of numerous previously unconsidered questions.

However, in the present context it is worth remembering that in British universities, and even more so in Oxford, the social and educational sub-structure of the student and teaching bodies change much more slowly than the cultural and political moods of the place. The former are taken for granted, the latter are constantly being picked up and sniffed by the brightest intelligences in the country. So at a time when Balliol and bolshevism are inextricably entangled in the public mind, it may do no harm to set out a few indications of where Balliol men have come from, and where they tend to go to. As has already been mentioned, Balliol's 700th birthday appeal raised well over one million pounds. The difference between Oxbridge and other English universities is that the alumni, when they are touched, pay up; and bolshevism is not exactly the word that comes to mind when one contemplates the pages of the *Balliol Register*.[49]

The Prime Minister, Mr. Edward Heath, entered Balliol, along with

[48] P. 31.

[49] Elsie Lemon (ed.), *The Balliol College Register, 1916–67* (Oxford, 1969).

89 other people, in 1935. Out of this intake, 17 had fathers who had also been to Balliol, and 10 were students from foreign countries (mainly as Rhodes Scholars from the United States) or the Commonwealth. Of the schools from which they came, only Eton and Harrow are mentioned more than twice, and there are only two schools listed which signal themselves as neither public schools nor grammar schools. Perhaps significantly, one of these two schools contributed one of the 19 Balliol men of this year who subsequently became university professors or lecturers, in Britain or abroad. A further 8 became schoolmasters, so the academic profession absorbed almost a third of Balliol's entire intake for the year. The old professions (the Law, Medicine, and the Church) absorbed another 12. Business and industry took 10, and the Civil Service 13. The 62 men whose age at (first) marriage is disclosed in the Register have an average of 2·3 children each and their average age at marriage was 31·5. There are of course considerable variations within these figures. The largest family was 6, just as the figure for the books the men have written —66—is considerably swollen by the Canadian who has published 18.

Fifteen years later, in 1950, the intake of undergraduates was only slightly larger: 92. Only nine had Balliol fathers, and the number of foreign students, 19, was nearly doubled. But the general pattern of their schooling was hardly changed, except that Winchester (5) and Rugby (4) replaced Eton (1) and Harrow (0) as the chief sources. Well over a third of the whole (37) were—whether they knew it or not—destined for university or college teaching, and that is before counting the six school-masters. It could, I think, be demonstrated from closer examination that the intellectual calibre and achievement of the schoolmasters produced by Balliol after 1945 is considerably lower than it was between the wars. An academically-inclined British child's chances of coming into contact with a first-class mind before his own intellectual habits have been formed may even be diminishing with time. The technical academic qualifications of teachers are of course constantly being bettered, but that is not quite the same thing. Eleven men went into the old professions, twelve into business or industry, and only five into the Civil Service. At marriage, the average age of the alumni was 28, three years lower than their predecessors' average marrying age (which was in many cases postponed by the 1939–45 war). The average number of children born to them (2·4) remained almost the same, though one Old Rugbeian solicitor headed the table with eight.

For 1960, the last year whose Balliol intake I have selected for analysis, the story is necessarily incomplete. Most of this year's undergraduates were only beginning to form families when the Register closed in 1968. On the other hand, 49 of the 116 students who entered Balliol in 1960 were by then already married, and their average age at marriage was 25·0. One of them, who took a first in English and became a university lecturer, married a girl (from his home town, not from Oxford apparently) during his second year at Balliol, at the age of 19. There is also a perceptible trend towards marriage with foreign girls (6 already in this year, against 6 for the 1950 entry and 2 for the 1935 one). Again, the pattern of schooling is not substantially changed. Eton is back in the lead with four entrants, but Poole Grammar School (one of Balliol's traditional forcing-houses) also has four. Shrewsbury (3) has overtaken Rugby and Winchester. A glance at the most recent years for which lists are available does not suggest any further change: the anarchists mayhave taken over Balliol, as Mr. Heath is said to have told Lord Derby (*Sunday Times*, March 10, 1970), but the secondary moderns and comprehensives have not.

For the 1960 intake, it is early yet to draw conclusions about subsequent careers, for not all those still doing research degrees at the time information was collected necessarily ended up in the academic profession. But if they did, 1960 produced 39 academic researchers and teachers, with a further 11 schoolmasters. The shift in the emphasis of studies in Oxford as a whole can be seen from the fact that 37 men in this year were reading 'numerical' subjects (mathematical or scientific), as against 16 in 1950 and 13 in 1935. Outside the academic world, the Church, the Law, and the Civil Service still recruit in Balliol, but occupations that would have been strange to the 1950 generation (TV, computers, and the space industry) begin to appear. However, more traditional occupations remain: a Scandinavian Prince and a church organist are both listed. The budding academics in the entry have hardly yet begun to publish, but others have been less shy, notably perhaps the man who took a Fourth in Oriental Studies and published four years later a book entitled *The Aryanisation of the Jewish State: a polemic*.

In the fifties, as the Master of Balliol put it to me, undergraduates at Oxford 'wore natty suitings and thought about their pensions'. My own recollection, as an undergraduate of the time, accords with this. The 1960 Balliol entry whose educational background and subsequent careers I have noted can be explored further through Zweig's survey, conducted in 1962, of most third-year Oxford students. The continuities and discontinuities appear with surprising clarity.

In a number of respects, the early nineteen-sixties already seem a distant period in Oxford life. Students, for instance, would be less likely now to tell a researcher that 'sex is a great force which needs controlling by self-discipline or sublimation', and the researcher himself would be unlikely to say of his inquiry about sexual experience, 'This question was never addressed to girl students.'[50] Nor would nearly a third of the students questioned say they wanted families 'as large as economically and biologically possible'. On the other hand, the Campaign for Nuclear Disarmament had by 1962 come and almost gone, leaving behind it a deposit of political pessimism and classless generational discontent. 'Some of the

[50] Op. cit., p. 62.

basic ills of British society,' say Zweig, 'were ascribed to an archaic and unfair system of education long overdue for reform,' and 'commercialism, especially commercialism in culture, entertainment and leisure activities . . . stands in the forefront of students' preoccupation with the ills of present-day society.'[51] At the same time, the 1960 entrant who chose for his first job on going down a clerkship at Oxfam rather than a traineeship at ICI was something of an odd man out.

[Before passing on, it may be of interest to compare results from a 1968 survey of Harvard alumni. In the classes of 1930–39, 26 per cent had fathers who also went to Harvard. In the 60s, the proportion is 18 per cent. Just under half the entire alumni body went to private high school but, says the survey, 'there is no significant difference between the public and private school groups in what they say about their attitudes at the time they were in college'. (A similar finding about Oxford undergraduates would be highly improbable.) One man in 12 married a Radcliffe girl, though two-thirds of all wives themselves went to college. Nearly one in ten reports two or more marriages. Of the 80 per cent who are in the labour force, over half (46 per cent) are in one of the professions, with education (13 per cent) just topping law and medicine/dentistry. The same proportion (13 per cent) ticked 'college or university' as an employer, so it may be doubted whether there are many Harvard men 'teaching school'—especially as the median earned income for all alumni is $16,189, and 55 per cent of members of the classes of 1950–59 are earning over $15,000.][52]

Fashions change, and the vocal minority of contemporary Oxford undergraduates who could not be less concerned with their future professional security undoubtedly represent a much larger subterranean shift of attitude.[53] That this movement should find its epicentre in Balliol is not surprising—nor can it all be attributed to the mythical machinations of a Marxist Master. Balliol, which educated Wyclif and saw Latimer and Ridley burnt in the Broad outside its gates, is no stranger to ideological conflict. The last Master but one, A. D. (later Lord) Lindsay, stood as an Independent candidate in the famous Oxford by-election of 1938, in opposition to the appeasement policy of the Prime Minister Nevile Chamberlain, which was supported in Oxford by the Conservative candidate, Mr. Quintin Hogg, now Lord Chancellor. (Mr. Heath, as a Conservative undergraduate, supported Lindsay.)

It is also 70 years or so since complaint was first made about the disrup-

[51] Ibid., p. 77.

[52] The Harvard Alumni Survey, published in *Harvard Alumni Bulletin* (October 21), November 11, December 2, December 23, 1968; January 13, 1969). For comparative purposes, note that in the US 'Class of '70' means the graduation class of a man who actually entered college three or four years earlier.

[53] Also at Harvard, where 'only members of the classes that have graduated in the 1960s vote strongly that the college is too conservative'. (ibid., October 21, 1968, p. 33).

tive behaviour of Old Etonian Socialists in the college, and it was said then that 'the Master forgives them because they are Socialists, and the Dean because they are old Etonians.' The present Master, when this was quoted to him, laughed heartily and agreed that some would say the same today. For from Balliol in the spring of 1970 there marched (taking good care not to tread on the crocuses) an undergraduate expeditionary force to lay siege to the University Proctors in the Clarendon building, on the presumption that their files might contain material as embarrassing as had recently been discovered by students in the files of the University Registry at Warwick. (The Proctors replied, in the best Oxford manner, that indeed they had files, 'some of them going back to the seventeenth century.')

In Balliol the Left has for some time controlled the Junior Common Room. In 1970 the president, a birthright member of the Communist Party in the sense that people are birthright members of the Society of Friends, was constantly being outflanked from the Left, so Mr. Heath's reported observation that the anarchists had taken over Balliol had some superficial justification. JCR meetings to define a political line have been known to last all day, reconvening after dinner. Argument, as one would expect in Balliol, is subtle, well-turned, and on the whole amiable. One characteristic radical stance is worth recording. In 1970 Congregation at Oxford voted to abandon its high-minded but almost solitary defiance of a Labour Minister of Education's 1968 decision to raise sharply the fees charged to overseas students at British universities. There was every incentive for the university to abandon its opposition, since it was having to pay the increases itself, and the recent introduction of a postal vote into the constitutional procedure of Congregation (which enables hard-hearted scientists to defeat the soft-headed artists without actually turning up) ensured that realism would win over liberal protest in the end. Quite right too, argued a Maoist in Balliol JCR: most of the overseas students in Oxford came from the United States anyway, he said, and those who came from 'Third World' countries were very often refugees from people's regimes which very properly would not tolerate them at home. It all sounded very like the inter-War Oxford epoch described by the cartoonist and architectural critic Osbert Lancaster:

> 'In the years following my departure Oxford underwent some profound and to me depressing changes. Aesthetics were out and politics were in, and sensibility was replaced by social awareness ... In the more influential JCRs Party members proselytised with a zeal that had formerly been the monopoly of Campion Hall, and everywhere the poets hymned the dictatorship of a proletariat of whom they only knew by hearsay.'[54]

Not that the older Balliol, or the older Oxford, is by any means dead.

[54] *With an Eye to the Future* (London, 1968), p. 94.

The Oxford societies to which Balliol contributed officers in Hilary Term 1970 included the Monday Club,[55] the Christian Science Organisation, the P.G. Wodehouse Society (which claims to serve unlimited quantities of free vintage claret at all meetings) and the Choolant Society, which meets termly to eat choolant, 'one of Oxford's rare educational delights'. The Boat Club, which symbolises everything that the JCR Left hates, is not far from the Head of the River. And college historical continuity is well taken care of by one of the present generation of undergraduate classicists, Richard Jenkyns, who is descended from two famous Masters: in the nineteenth century, Richard Jenkyns, who was, according to Dean Church, 'an unfailing judge of a clever man, as a jockey might be of a horse'; and in the eighteenth century, Theophilus Leigh, who was not only Master but Jane Austen's great-uncle as well.

But it is, not unnaturally, the activist left which is observed most closely —and sometimes sardonically—by the Senior Common Room. 'I have actually heard the phrase "running dog" used in this college,' said one conservative young don. 'When that young man goes down I expect he will be dragged kicking and screaming into a bank.' (Students, of course are even more merciless observers of each other. 'There are revolutionaries here who dine at the Grid,'[56] said one, naming a well known Maoist.) A rather more charitable view was taken by the classicist Robert Ogilvie, then Senior Tutor, now Headmaster of Tonbridge School, who was himself president of the college JCR in 1954, and in 1968/9 was a member of the Hart Committee on Relations with Junior Members.[57] 'A very large number of people in Balliol suffer from over-developed social consciences,' he told me, 'and at the same time feel helpless. The only thing they can do is take it out on whatever lies to hand. One can shrug it off, or try to canalise it, but the dangerous thing is the Cohn-Bendit doctrine that activity is its own justification—that it doesn't matter what you do if it's active and violent. I remember a senior member saying at a recent student meeting, "I haven't the slightest idea what you are demonstrating about but I wish you every success" . . .

'It's the lack of a sense of humour that I like least. There's much less desire than there used to be to get fun out of university—though there are exceptions, like the man who told his tutor: "I'm terribly sorry that I can't come to my tutorial, but I'm writing an essay and if you care to come to the Delegates' Room [where a sit-in was at the time taking place] on Tuesday morning at ten I'll read it to you." '

[55] 'Americans for Goldwater' would be a rough transatlantic equivalent for this Conservative political organisation.

[56] An exclusive Oxford club.

[57] University of Oxford, 1969. Though much of this admirable report is necessarily of local interest only, Appendix A (pp. 154–160) offers a succinct, accurate, and well-written characterisation of student radicalism in Oxford—and elsewhere.

Overdeveloped social consciences also sour the traditional, mostly easy, relationship between students and college servants. 'There's a lot of resentment at having a man cleaning your rooms,' Ogilvie said. 'But colleges are still geared to servants rather than self-service.'

Gripes about the 'scout' system—in Balliol, several scouts have served the college for thirty years or more—may seem a far cry from the National Guard's volleys at Kent, Ohio, and the Japanese 'Red Army's' hijacked Boeing. Certainly, British students are everywhere anxious for bigger game when they can find it, and revelled in their discovery of the University of Warwick's dossiers on students and staff, and over-intimate connections with local business.[58] In Oxford, at the same period, this kind of preoccupation relieved the dons by diverting radical interest from the colleges, which are the genuinely sensitive and vulnerable points in the university, to the university itself, which is so elusive that even Senior Members cannot always find it when they want it.

But the global significance of Oxford is that it is a place where inter-group relations are still held, sometimes with difficulty, on a human scale. An embattled university administrator from New York, Berlin, or Tokyo might conclude that this makes them less complex and demanding. He would be mistaken. On the contrary, they demand closer 'reading', in the Leavisite sense, with attention paid to 'tone' and 'texture'. Oxford is a place where serious moral problems are raised—or dismissed—not only in terms of Vietnam but also in terms of actions performed within the sheepfold. The tone, not just of 'Oxford philosophy', but of Oxford itself, was well caught in an Oxford Radical Students Society pamphlet that was objecting to both:

'*The Language of Morals* [by R. M. Hare, a Balliol philosopher] is full of painstaking analysis of what constitutes a good car, a good egg, even good sewage-effluent; J. O. Urmson has graded apples for us; the late Professor J. L. Austin [in his presidential address to the Aristotelian Society, 1956] confessed to total moral bankruptcy: "I am very partial to ice cream, and a *bombe* is served divided into segments corresponding one to one with the persons at High Table: I am tempted to help myself to two segments and do so, thus succumbing to temptation . . . But do I lose control of myself? . . . Not a bit of it. We often succumb to temptation with calm and even with finesse." What is needed instead of the forced digestion of the after-dinner concoctions of the declining gentry is a study of those writers who have put forward worked out ethical ideals, and who have discussed ethical questions of the sort which actually arise in the world, as opposed to at the High Table of an Oxford college, and in the context in which they arise. Sartre is essential

[58] See E. P. Thompson (ed.), *Warwick University Ltd.* (London, 1970); and Lord Radcliffe's two reports to the University on the same events (University of Warwick, 1970).

reading for students in this respect, so are many novelists and theologians
—e.g. Brecht and Kierkegaard.'[59]

One of the problems for radical students in Oxford is that the college
servants themselves—who in a properly politicised world should be the
first to object to this kind of thing—are in fact the most passionate pre-
servationists of the *bombe* culture. In Balliol over the past decade, gowns
have gone out and women have come in, or so nearly so that a formal
governing body vote for coeducation would entail few changes in the
rules, though several in the plumbing. Both changes have been demanded
by undergraduates and resisted by scouts, though some of the latter are
also probably relieved to be no longer under the obligation (often dis-
regarded in practice) to inform the Dean about a man whose female
dinner guest stayed till morning tea. I suggested to one young Fellow that
a civilised solution to this problem might be the imposition of a fairly
stiff charge for keeping a guest, male or female, overnight in college. Fine,
he replied, except that this would render the college liable to prosecution
as a disorderly house. Balliol settles instead for a rule that women may not
remain in college overnight—with no definition of what constitutes a
night. If there is a 'do not disturb' notice on the door, the scout is only
supposed to invade a room if he has reason to suppose that the man may
be committing suicide. If he finds himself mistaken, he should withdraw.
Almost everyone—scouts, tutors, undergraduates—likes to tell inquirers
that what happens now between the sexes is what happened always, except
that it is now over-exposed and over-discussed. Statistically that may be
true, but 'over-exposed' gives the game away: on the scale of an Oxford
college the difference between private 'vice' and public assumption that
vice is virtue becomes a difference indeed. An affectation of exuberant
sexuality fits in naturally with the rest of the 'noble savage' style that
keeps undergraduates' clothes assertively casual and the JCR itself,
in spite of luxurious furniture, ill-administered and physically squalid.

No one really knows how men and women choose to behave in private.
The only possibly demonstrable change is that Balliol bedrooms are
warmer than they used to be. The lobby for the formal introduction of
coeducation into the college—a lobby which means most of the JCR and
probably well under half the SCR—has for different reasons hesitated to
force the issue. The JCR, in imitation of students at other universities,
prefers to attack what it believes to be the central power in Oxford, and
use that as a surrogate for the central power in the country, the world,
the universe. It has not seriously demanded representation on the Governing Body, which would have to be approved by the Privy Council. The
SCR has been equally reluctant to tackle the issue, for though it is
arguable that coeducation would actually reduce sexual tension and

[59] Trevor Pateman, *The Poverty of Philosophy, Politics and Economics* (Part I) (Oxford,
1968, duplicated).

competitiveness in the college, it could not be introduced without a fight, and the fight would swallow precious research time, and perhaps damage the spider-web of personal relationships on the Governing Body—which means the Fellows, all sixty-seven of them, for even a college of this size has not yet taken refuge in 'cabinet government', and for many a junior Fellow, the taste of corporate democracy he gets at Oxford is itself sufficient discouragement to taking a job with a lower teaching load at a more hierarchical university. Most people in Oxford seem to expect the distaff dam to break sooner or later (in Cambridge, King's, Churchill, and Clare Colleges have already decided to admit women) but not many want their own college to be first. Some of the strongest opponents are the heads of the under-endowed women's colleges, which would lose some of their most promising students to Balliol and New College, and to which few men would be anxious to be admitted. (The Presidents of Black colleges in the American South will know how they feel.) The 7:1 ratio of men to women in Oxford will alter slowly, if at all.

However, Balliol has already altered it, in a small way and a different context. It became the first Oxford college to house one graduate for every two undergraduates (the proportion recommended by the Franks Commission). At Holywell Manor, opposite the English Faculty building and library (also new: the very *introduction* of English Language and Literature as a subject into Oxford still lies within living memory), graduate members of both Balliol and St. Anne's live in cosy, gas-ring domesticity on alternate floors, with—so far—at least one marriage to relieve all those dissertations. The Balliol graduates have already used their voting power to cool down the college JCR, which found itself, somewhat to its dismay, saddled with a graduate for president in 1970/1. Balliol's move into the graduate market was originally proposed by Ogilvie, in a memorandum written twelve years ago. Coeducation was then casually proposed by someone else at a college meeting, and carried against the vigorous opposition of the previous Master, Sir David Keir. Ogilvie then found himself negotiating academic details with his own mother, who was at the time Principal of St. Anne's. Balliol built the necessary extension, to standards which the University Grants Committee would have regarded as unduly sumptuous if it had had any control over the matter, out of its birthday appeal fund.

The 'cooling' effect of the Balliol graduate student vote is significant. The lot of an English graduate student is somewhat less miserable than it used to be, but higher degrees still require high motivation, and the discontented, draft-evading graduate student familiar from American campuses is strange to Oxford (except that, of course, a few Americans of this type find their way to Britain to lead student revolts). In Oxford, as in Chicago, there is now some pressure to make the university whose pride was the liberal education of undergraduates a preserve of graduates. This, too, would be resisted fiercely by people more concerned with educational values than budgetary tidiness—and that still goes for most people in Oxford. But the external pressures to become a graduate institution are more serious. Any politician or administrator can see that Oxford and Cambridge are very expensive places in which to conduct undergraduate teaching, and that their 'plant'—the Bodleian, the Ashmolean, the Taylorian, and all the other libraries and institutes in the city —exist primarily for serious scholarly work.

Rationalisation, professionalisation: these must, in some degree be the enemies of Oxford. Balliol itself probably feels that it has temporarily done its duty by the *zeitgeist*. There have been too many changes for comfort, already. The Fellows, who in 1961 numbered thirty-five, in 1970 number sixty-seven. They are, of course, much less predictable in their views than the undergraduates, for it takes a deep trawl and a catholic skipper to assemble a good catch of dons for an Oxford common room: Professors of Sanskrit and of Numerical Analysis: degrees from Valparaiso, Tasmania, Hamburg . . . (The last belongs to the Junior Dean,[60] a young twentieth century historian whose splendidly Junkerish name— Hartmut Johann Otto Pogge von Strandmann—is rationalised by the Balliol porters as 'Mr. Poggy'. The college duties of a junior dean are perhaps best captured in this reminiscence of a former holder of the office: 'I remember late one night telling, with some irritation, a man who was engaged in some noisy horseplay that he was nothing like as drunk as he was pretending to be. This made him really cross. The Dean then arrived and in his greater wisdom assured him that he *was* extremely intoxicated, upon which the man contentedly went to bed with great good nature.')

The teaching load which some of these men carry during term (Oxbridge terms admittedly only last eight weeks each) would be regarded as inordinate by any comparable scholar in a comparable American college. 'If I am teaching no more than twelve hours a week,' said one philosopher, 'I enjoy it. But if, as often happens, I am teaching sixteen to twenty hours the enjoyment goes out of the other twelve. It is not just the hours, but the spread of subjects. In the US you can prepare both lecture and tutorial by reading the same books and notes. But in Oxford you give lectures for the university and tutorials for your college. Each college tries to be a university in miniature. This term I am lecturing on Aristotle's *Ethics* and giving tutorials in medieval philosophy, epistemology, modern philosophy, Wittgenstein, and Descartes. This is connected with the difficulty of changing the syllabus, because of the Oxford principle that you cannot be examined by the people who taught you. That is good. It's no use feeding back tutorials to the man who gave them to you. But it means that one can't put something in the syllabus unless there is someone in each college capable of teaching it. Colleges get unhappy if too high a proportion of their men have to be sent out to other colleges for

---

[60] At the time of my visit: he has since migrated to Sussex.

tutorials. Then of course, committee work takes more and more time because of the general desire to have everything in writing.'

The Governing Body has delegated what it can. Warburg's, the London merchant bank, handles Balliol's investments, but the time which that saved the Estates Bursar is gradually being filled up by the demands of 'participation'—which sounds fine until you have to find room in the diary for the committee. The investments themselves look healthier after the Birthday Appeal, to which seventy per cent of alumni contributed.[61] This enabled the trustees to go to outside benefactors and say, 'Look how much they've done for themselves.' Even this did not gain the ear of the big foundations, which might be accused of favouritism if they gave money to a single college. If funds of this kind are to be found for Oxford in future, the University itself will have to do the begging. The increase in the number of Fellows is also partly due to the appeal proceeds. Each new job could have been justified several times over, but the cumulative effect has clearly raised the size of the Balliol SCR close to the point of no return where human communication has to be institutionalised and government by sub-committee begins. Then, too, it may no longer be possible for dons to point out amiably to students that college files could be exposed for public gaze with no more elaborate equipment than a brick and a tin-opener.

Student numbers themselves have not risen nearly as fast as staff numbers. (In 1949 there were 350; in 1965 415.) By the set policy of both the University and the colleges, numbers have been kept low enough for everyone to spend at least his first year in residence, and a substantial chunk of the Appeal money was spent on slotting new sets of rooms and an SCR block into the Back Quad without ruining the effect unduly. Balliol is not a beautiful college, though time has reconciled people to Butterfield's marzipan chapel (1857) which was its last major building experiment. More remarkable, however, than the limitation on size, which in Oxford is common prudence, is the self-limitation of the intake. The founding of new universities in Britain over the past decade was intended to take some of the numerical pressure off Oxford and Cambridge, and at the same time to provide elbow-room for academic innovation. Few people seriously expected them to relieve the pressure in a qualitative sense. But the 'Plateglass' formula has proved so much more successful than the 'Redbrick' formula of the previous century that in Britain, for the first time since the Middle Ages, young men and women financially and intellectually capable of conventionally brilliant Oxbridge careers have sometimes chosen to go elsewhere. Financially, it makes no difference, for the local education authority grant which almost all British university students receive in whole or in part is increased to cover the higher incidental expenses of Oxford. (In 1970, a student on full grant at

---

[61] Statutory endowment income in 1968/9 was £110,839.

Oxford was receiving £420 p.a. to cover everything except maintenance during vacations, which remains the responsibility of the student himself and of his parents.) In these circumstances, that Balliol should on occasion have been short of candidates to read Modern History—of all subjects in all colleges in all universities—would astonish an academic in any other country that I visited, yet it has happened. No less surprising, perhaps, is that neither Oxford as a whole nor, till recently, Balliol itself have had anything that could fairly be described as a policy on admissions; nor have radical students yet bothered to press for one. The reason goes to the heart of the problem posed by almost any educational issue in Britain: that is, social class, as expressed not just in the responses of living people, but in the structures devised by generations long dead for the education of a governing elite on the one hand, and a labouring mass on the other.[62]

The general problem posed to universities by the egalitarian instincts of our civilisation—or perhaps better, the problem posed to egalitarians by the existence of universities—must await another chapter. In Balliol, rather ironically, the Admissions Tutor who inherits both the general problem and the particular English history is an American, Bill Weinstein, who came to Balliol via Brooklyn and Columbia. In brief outline, this is a summary of the structure within which he has to operate.

Since the Robbins Report (1963), British national policy on access to higher education has been fairly clear. Every man or woman who has passed the 'A level' examination (taken at secondary school at the age of seventeen plus) in two subjects has a chance of entry if he can convince a particular university that he is capable of profiting by higher education. In fact, the pressure on places has pushed academic standards higher than that for the majority of entrants. But Oxbridge colleges, even if they are as dedicated to intellectual values as Balliol, have no desire to become meritocracies in miniature. No longer can a monumentally stupid boy get a place at Oxford solely by virtue of being a competent oarsman or the son of a noble alumnus. But grades alone never decide the matter, especially now that the educational sociologists have confirmed what Oxford dons have always believed on hunch: that as predictors of academic performance at final examination (let alone of mental agility or profundity in later life) 'A level' successes leave much to be desired. So the dons do as they always have done. They try to select a human salad whose ingredients will react upon each other in an interesting manner, and if possible taste better than the previous year's. They sniff, they nibble; they add a pinch of musician to a slice of second-row forward, and hope that the outcome will be a community. It usually is, and Balliol still usually gets more first-class degrees than any other men's college. But the dons have now themselves

---

[62] For a concise and perceptive—though not neutral—account of what happened and why in English education since the Industrial Revolution, see Raymond Williams, *The Long Revolution* (London, 1961), pp. 155–165.

fallen victim to the terror and inverted snobbery which the whole process inspires in the prospective students, their parents, and their teachers. Certain schools, often certain masters in those schools, traditionally supply Oxford entrants, either at ordinary or scholarship level, or both. They are not only, or even mostly, fee-paying public schools. Balliol itself, in 1965/6, admitted 43 men from independent schools, 18 from Direct Grant schools (these are mainly the older, well-established grammar schools, supported financially by the State, but constitutionally independent and possessed of a strong academic tradition), and 36 from Maintained schools (grammar, secondary modern, and comprehensive) which the vast majority of English children attend.[63] The first two categories of school now have other universities in Britain to which they feel they can steer promising pupils. The last category includes hundreds of schools whose teachers themselves do not have university degrees, let alone Oxbridge ones, and whose pupils' parents will in most cases have left school at the age of fifteen. Since recent research in England, and the experience of other countries with mass higher education systems, shows that innate intelligence is no respecter of social class, though measured intelligence can often be depressed by environmental factors, Mr. Weinstein has had every incentive to follow the practice of Admissions Deans in the US, and go looking for promising students in schools that were, in some cases, actively discouraging boys from applying to Oxford. There was no need to make the search an explicit hunt for 'working class boys': in England, concentration on certain types of school in certain areas has the same effect. Nor is there any question of lowering academic admission standards for 'disadvantaged' students: as Mr. Weinstein put it, 'It's not clear how a "brand snatched from the burning" would be helped in his career if standards at the university itself remained the same. Even the students themselves might object.' However, in one respect Balliol has gone further than any other Oxford college. At the prompting of President Kingman Brewster of Yale, who visited Balliol in 1967, it has conducted what in the US would be known as an 'Upward Bound' programme at a summer school for thirty fifteen-year-old boys whose potential for a university career was, on their headmasters' judgment, better than their prospects of achieving it. No commitment was implied on either side, but dons (including the Master) had to give up three weeks' research or holiday time for the project, and ten headmasters, Weinstein hopes, discovered that Balliol meant business.

The radical left in Balliol would see no more virtue in this kind of thing than in other conscience-stricken overtures by the bourgeoisie to the working class, from the university settlement movement onwards.

---

[63] As long ago as 1955, thirteen per cent of Oxford entrants had fathers in manual occupations, as compared with nine per cent at Cambridge and thirty-one per cent at other English universities (Robbins Report, Appendix Two (B), Annex C).

They would argue, no doubt correctly, that the socialising force of Balliol is so powerful that wherever its undergraduates were drawn from, they would end up as 'oppressors' just the same. The hold of Oxford and Cambridge over the leadership of both political parties in Britain is well known: less familiar, perhaps, is the recent finding that of the 359 judges named in the Law List for 1968, 292 attended fee-paying schools, and 273 went to either Oxford or Cambridge.[64] The average age of British judges (who are appointed by the Crown from the ranks of senior lawyers) varies from sixty-one to sixty-nine according to category, so their Oxford is the Oxford of *Decline and Fall* and *Brideshead Revisited* rather than of modern Balliol, where half the dons were themselves students in the post-1945 period, and where undergraduates complain to the college library that there is nothing there on linear programming 'although it is now in the Maths. syllabus', and nothing by Camus, 'in particular *Le Mythe de Sisyphe* which is more valuable than fifty per cent of the moral philosophy we have at the moment'. But in Oxford, if one keeps one's ears open in the bookshops and restaurants, it is equally easy to conclude that the men who will be appointed to the Bench in A.D. 2000 are still being socialised in the old way:

> 'It's going to be a real swinging party. The whole Blue boat's coming and the whole Wadham Boat Club. Roger's supplying the amplifier and I hope I've invited all the chemists . . .'
> 'I have nice parents so I'm still in Oxford . . . .'
> 'The thing I like about Barton is that he can drink such a huge amount without anyone noticing it.'
> 'Please compliment the chef on that wonderfully hot curry. I have sweated away all my impurities.'

In 1355, in the tavern called Swyndlestock, conversation must have run on very similar lines. Six centuries hence, who can tell?

[64] *New Society*, May 14, 1970.

CHAPTER FOUR

The making of a university

1 STYLE FRANÇAIS: VINCENNES

'For all Parisians our wood of Vincennes has become more than ever an absolute necessity. It is our duty to preserve it intact, jealously guarding it from being deprived of the smallest particle.'
(Guidebook to the Château and Bois of Vincennes)

'*M. Victor Golvan (UDR):* You are against selection, and whether you like it or not, selection is a law of nature. Man has to be adapted for his task in the community.
'*M. Edgar Faure (Minister of Education):* That is where we reach the nub of the debate. For me, the laws of society are not the same as the laws of nature. The law of the jungle is not a law of society. ("Hear, hear")'
(Debate in the French Senate on the law to reform
higher education, October 24, 1968)

In the last chapter, I tried to show how the idea of a university was fledged; how in England, thanks to an extraordinary set of social and political continuities, it was able to keep most of its feathers intact down the centuries, whereas in Italy, the vicissitudes of domestic discord and foreign conquest affected its evolution so severely that to this day models of student self-government are more clearly visible in the universities of Scotland and Scandinavia than in the original Bolognese nest. The system by which the students of Aberdeen elect their Rector is as well-defined a medieval survival as any in Oxford or Cambridge. The same university was also the first in the British Isles, possibly in Europe, to have a mixed hall of residence. In the mid-twentieth century, that seemed like a revolution, but at the back of the Scottish mind, the assumption is made that university students are adults not children. The Oxford tradition, uninfluenced by Bologna, assumed the opposite.

Even the newest university, its concrete freshly poured, cannot cut itself wholly free from this organic relationship with the past. Its founders, if they are trying to make a clean break with an educational system they deplore, will themselves have been shaped by that system willy-nilly, and if in their search for imitable models they are driven abroad, as the Americans and the Japanese were in the nineteenth century, they are merely obliged to borrow, and re-interpret in the light of their own culture, fragments of another people's past. Nevertheless, the style of their innovation will also incorporate the assumptions of their own time and place. For twentieth-century men, the creation of a new university, or the grand reform of a higher education system, has something of the significance which the Middle Ages attached to the building of a cathedral. It is a temple—built not with hands but with pre-fabricated breeze blocks—to the only god they recognise. There is still room, as the edifice rises, for national character to put its stamp on the whole—through the gut reactions of human architects, through political neccesity, bizarre coincidence, and plain skullduggery. Nowhere are all these elements better exemplified than in the University (originally 'Experimental Centre') of Vincennes, on the eastern edge of Paris. By comparison, the manner in which the new generation of British universities was launched necessarily sounds tame. Peace-loving academics in search of a global model for new universities are attracted more often by Britain than by France. Michio Nagai, for example, has recently published a book in Japan recommending to his countrymen (amongst other things) the organisational and architectural principles of the new British universities.[1] For this reason alone, there is point in exploring the background and evolution of the University of Lancaster against that of the University of Vincennes. But the difference is also most expressive of the difference between two separate national attitudes to education and social organisation. *Vive la différence*—but let us at least notice now it works.

The public history of Vincennes (now called 'Paris VIII') begins with *les événements de Mai, 1968*, which in France are still referred to simply as *les événements*. What the Paris students' anarcho-syndicalist revolution did to the Government of France at the time, and ultimately to General de Gaulle's prestige, is known to everyone. Less well known outside France is what has since happened to the structure of French higher education, whose worm-eaten joists and grossly overloaded floors allowed political and generational discontent to focus upon a real, hard grievance. After May, and the General Strike that the Sorbonne revolutionaries were able to touch off, the conservative backlash at the elections of June 1968 allowed the country as a whole to slip more than half-way back into contentment with the status quo, which looked far less expensive to the taxpayer than the emotional purities of either the extreme Right or the extreme Left. When de Gaulle finally went, the electors chose in his place M. Pompidou, a conservative banker brought up in the Massif Central, who had as Prime Minister kept his head better than anyone else during May. Then they relaxed.

But long before that, in the summer of 1968, something had to be done about the French universities. They were, as M. Raymond Aron has not neglected to point out, better than the Italian ones, and though this defence is significantly modest, the discredit heaped upon French Aca-

[1] See bibliography.

demia during the revolution was—as is generally the case in revolutions—
not invariably deserved. At several points within the loose federation of
faculties that was called the University of Paris outstanding work was
being done. The Nobel Prize list is adequate testimony to the achievement
of young French biologists since 1945, especially in experimental embryo-
logy, and the names associated with the Ecole Pratique des Hautes Etudes,
such as Claude Lévi-Strauss and M. Aron himself, need no gloss anywhere in the world. Outside the university system itself the *grandes écoles*—
the *Polytechnique, Sciences Po*, the *Ecole Nationale d'Administration*—
have turned out men who, on top of the narrow brilliance that one
associates with this type of education, have proved adaptable enough to
preside over the technical and planning revolutions which have revitalised
the French economy in the past decade. The Collège de France, a 400
year-old institution where the most eminent men in their fields teach the
results of their research, itself has a kind of mobility built into its structure.
There are fifty-two professors (not exclusively scientific) and nearly 1,000
researchers and technicians, but chairs are awarded to individuals, not
disciplines. When a man dies or leaves, the place may be offered to someone who is doing exciting work in a quite different subject.

The trouble is that when this happens, the surviving members of the
late professor's team (*équipe*) have nowhere else to go. This is itself a
symptom of a fundamental weakness in the structure of the higher learning
in France. Historically, the weakness goes back even beyond 1789. Before
the Revolution the universities were under the influence of the Church,
and innovators who needed elbow room and academic freedom for secular
experiments had to found their own institutions. The intellectuals who
set out to break the power of Church and aristocracy over French research
and education in the universities considered it necessary to transfer that
power intact to the new secular State, as a guarantee against the counter-
revolutionary tendencies which survived—and survive to this day—
among people who had never genuinely accepted the Revolution. The
effect was to replace ecclesiastical by secular inflexibility. New institutions
to meet new needs still had to be founded outside the university system,
because any reform within it automatically entailed a political battle at
the centre, whose outcome often depended on strictly non-academic
factors. Once founded, for some particular purpose, these institutions in
their turn became unreformable. In the universities themselves, no
administrator on the spot had any real power. Budgets and staff appointments were controlled from Paris, by the Minister of Education in the
Rue de la Grenelle. Students and teachers were equally powerless to
improve their own conditions by the Anglo-Saxon process of negotiation
and piecemeal reform. Hence the Nanterre psychodrama in 1968.

In material terms, the psychodrama could be simply explained: too
many students, too quickly. In France, as in Italy, access to university was
and is free to anyone who can pass his *baccalauréat*. Society's demand for

trained, quality-guaranteed manpower, parents' ambitions for their children, and the officially stimulated demographic boom did the rest. Enrolments increased from 123,000 in 1946 to 232,610 in 1961-2 and 514,000 in 1966-7.[2] State expenditure on education increased six-fold between 1950 and 1965, and education's share of the French gross national product grew from twelve per cent to seventeen per cent between 1960 and 1969.[3] M. Pompidou was able to claim in his 1969 campaign for the Presidency that his party had built more universities than it had found when it took office eleven years previously, and reforms introduced in 1966 by the then Minister of Education, M. Christian Fouchet, created 12,000 places in new technological universities to satisfy the demands of French industrialists, and sought to provide an intermediate alternative qualification for the students—between a third and a half of the entire university entry—who failed to graduate. But the construction of raw education factories up and down France—especially in Paris itself, where 130,000 students were allowed to congregate—did not constitute a reform. The introduction of selective entry to the university system was politically impossible, and all power was still concentrated in the hands of the Paris bureaucracy. Selection took place eventually, of course, but as M. Alain Peyrefitte put it in 1967, when he was Minister of Education: 'It is as if we organised a shipwreck in order to pick out the best swimmers.'[4] On the bureaucrats, here is the personal testimony of M. Aron, who resigned his Sorbonne sociology professorship in January 1968 'because the organisation of the university depressed me':

> 'In the university as it was, the teachers had no power to arrange study curricula, to select their students, or to maintain a reasonable balance between the number of students and the available resources (facilities, funds, teaching staff). The Sorbonne, with all its assemblies and sections, did not for practical purposes administer anything. Where there is no administration how can there be co-administration? At the Sociological Centre of the Sorbonne I had (from 1966-7) an annual credit of some F.10,000. What use would a *commission paritaire* have been for scattering this chicken-feed?'[5]

[2] *Le Monde* (April 16, 1969) published the following table:

(Students inscribed)		France	Germany	Italy
	1961/2	232,610	224,167	287,000
	1965/6	413,756	270,674	404,938
	1966/7	514,000	272,038	425,466
(increase)		121%	21·3%	48%

The French figures exclude the numbers (67,000 in 1966/7) of students in the *grandes écoles*.

[3] *Le Monde*, November 14, 1969.

[4] Quoted in Patrick Seale and Maureen McConville, *French Revolution, 1968* (London, 1968), p. 23 (Penguin edition).

[5] *Encounter*, August 1968, p. 23.

Even if M. Peyrefitte had behaved with more discretion than he did during the May events, he would have had to go. In a system as over-centralised as the French, if something goes badly wrong with the universities, the Minister of Education carries the can. De Gaulle appointed in his place Edgar Faure.

Faure is an old friend of Mendès-France, and he held numerous political offices under the Fourth Republic, from Prime Minister down. His membership of the Radical Party did not prevent him from accepting office under de Gaulle, whom he warmly admired. He comes from a family of small landowners in the Aude, on the edge of the Pyrenees. 'Most Frenchmen,' he says in an autobiographical essay at the beginning of his latest book, 'come of peasant stock, and their pride in it is unaffected by the number of others who can make the same claim.'[6] But his father and one of his grandfathers were doctors, and another grandfather a teacher. The family had been well and truly professionalised by the time Faure himself emerged from the Sorbonne as *agregé* in the Faculté de Droit, and started specialising as an advocate in two subjects which appealed at once to his internationalist enthusiasms and his flair for publicity: the oil industry and the cinema. He appeared for Edwige Feuillère and against Danielle Darrieux, and after President Cardenas' nationalisation of Mexican oil deposits, defended against an oil company boycott the right of nations to do what they pleased with their own mineral resources. He spent the latter part of the war with the Liberation Committee in Algiers, represented France at the Nuremberg Tribunal, and embarked on his political career.

Intellectually, Faure was undoubtedly the most impressive Minister of Education that any European country had had for generations. He has a lawyer's quick absorption of detail allied with the conceptual grasp of a philosopher, the sensibility of a writer, and the experience of a much-travelled man of affairs. These may seem large claims, and there is no shortage of Frenchmen who will tell you that Faure is above all a demagogue in love with novelty. But the details support the claims. Faure's diplomal dissertation was written on Turgenev's *Fathers and Sons*. He says, 'I re-read the book during the May events and I was surprised to discover how tame it seemed today. Yet it is there that one finds Bazarov's striking remark: "First, let us destroy: we shall see afterwards how to build." '[7] This early interest in Russian and German revolutionary ideas made him a shrewd observer of Mao's China when he went there in 1956,[8] and *L'âme du combat* is an attempt to engage French left-wing sociologists in an argument about the nature of consumer society, and continental Marxists generally in debate about the proper form for a new *contrat social*.

[6] *L'âme du combat* (Paris, 1970), p. 9.
[7] Ibid, p. 21.
[8] See *The Serpent and the Tortoise* (translated by Lovett F. Edwards, London, 1958), where at one point he describes China as 'a vast humming evening class'.

In June 1968, as Minister, his problems were at once more formidable and more mundane. He set himself the task of reforming the French educational system, at both school and university level, as thoroughly as the conservatism of the interested parties would allow. At the same time, he had to make preparations of a kind for an event that would have been inescapable with or without the May events: the *effluxe des bachots*, the appearance in Paris, at the *rentrée* in October, of 30,000 more new students than had turned up at the Faculty gates the previous year. If the conditions they found were no better, or rather worse, than those that had been so colourfully described by their immediate elders during May there would, all Frenchmen hoped or feared, be more trouble.

This meant new campuses, as M. Faure told the National Assembly. Where? Understandably, in view of the act of piracy his Ministry was at that moment committing, he did not trouble the Assembly with 'purely geographical details'. Instead, citing the Nanterre mistake and the British example, he insisted that the new universities should each have a personality of their own, and be built on a human scale, 'that is, to receive ten to twelve thousand students'. (The history of the assumption that this figure is the maximum consistent with humanity would bear investigation. Certainly, the assumption is common in England, and the expansion of Oxford and Cambridge is restricted accordingly. Chicago with 10,000 regards itself as more human than Berkeley with 30,000 or Waseda with 40,000. But Oxford and Cambridge were regarded by their inmates as ideal universities when they were hardly more than half the size they are now. More probably, ten to twelve thousand is an administrator's figure, denoting a size at which economic use can be made of specialised teaching and expensive scientific equipment, but which does not call for a large corps of professional administrators.)

The environs of Paris are no richer in empty spaces for new universities than London or Rome would be. The process of acquiring academic sites at Villetaneuse and Verrières had already taken seven and four years respectively. The solution adopted by Faure and Michel Alliot, his Chef de Cabinet, was—from men who were assuring everyone that the Napoleonic conception of a centralised and authoritarian university was finished—unreformed Napoleonism. They discovered an old artillery range in the Bois de Vincennes, a favourite Parisian recreation ground, commanded by a famous royal château. The land unquestionably belonged to the City of Paris, but it was by then late July, and all the councillors were sunning themselves at La Baule or Sables d'Olonne. On August 8, the Minister ordered GEEP, a firm specialising in industrial building, to go to work. The master-plan was finished by the 15th, and on the 21st, work began. On November 18, the contractors were able to hand over to the Ministry a group of nine buildings for 7,000 students, including seminar rooms, restaurants, large halls, offices, library and—a last minute addition—crèche. The pace suggested that whatever else might

be wrong with French higher education, there were some pretty competent civil engineers about. By the delivery date the Paris councillors were
back from their holidays, and as angry collectively as any one of them
would have been individually if he had discovered that his neighbour had
annexed a piece of his garden for a new summerhouse. M. Faure owned
up. 'I know very well that we're in the wrong,' he said. 'Let's make the
best of it.' He eventually consented to renounce his claim to another plot
of the Bois, which was earmarked for a lycée, and honour was more or
less satisfied.

But the physical planners of Vincennes were not the only ones to
practise what Alliot called 'a politique de fait accompli'. Someone had to
decide what kind of university was to be put into GEEP's shell; what was
to be taught, and who was to teach it. This time, it was the Minister of
Education himself who was bypassed, and there can be few stranger
stories in the long and chequered history of the University of Paris.
Academic responsibility for the experimental centre at Vincennes was
vested in the Dean of the Sorbonne, Raymond Las Vergnas. (The original
intention was that Vincennes would simply be an annexe of the Sorbonne,
with about 1,500 students, all in the Arts faculty.) Las Vergnas, however,
was a heavily beset man that summer, and indeed for years he had carried
more than his share of the strains of overcrowding. He had presided over
the Institut d'Anglais at a period when it had seven teachers to 2,000
students. (In English universities, the student-staff ratio is normally about
8:1.) He looked round for someone to whom to delegate the detailed
planning of Vincennes.

Two people with a thorough dislike of the existing academic system in
France, and well-devised ideas for its reform, were particularly close to
Las Vergnas. One was Pierre Dommergues, a stocky, vigorous *maître
assistant* in his English department at the Sorbonne, an American Studies
specialist, and author of a book on Saul Bellow. The other was Hélène
Cixous, an avant-garde novelist, literary theorist, and Medici Prize
winner, who was lecturing at Nanterre. As a combination, they were
formidable. Hélène Cixous, in particular, is a woman such as no culture
except the French seems to produce. Of Algerian Jewish parentage, she is
formidably intelligent, but far from sexless, and ruthless in getting her
own way. She was closer to the student left than either of the others were,
and by January 1968 she knew what was going to happen. After May, she
knew through Las Vergnas that the Ministry of Education, at its wits' end
to know how it could open the university year in the autumn without
another revolution, was in a mood to hand out more money and more
freedom than usual. 'I thought,' she told me, 'that we university people,
students and teachers, should try with all our strength and cunning to
play the game. The students thought they were going to be "recuperated".
That could be used two ways. The Ministry and the university staff were
both ignorant and terrified. "Let's use it." They were ready for anything.

I thought we had a chance of making a revolutionary university by abolishing the examination system and—because I was disgusted with the way studies were developed—with entirely new teaching staff. They commissioned me to work it all out. There was to be a small nucleus, an "egg' of thirty-six persons, drawn from each department, who would appoint all the other staff. I hired those thirty-six. I knew many of them, especially psychoanalysts and philosophers—people like Lacan and Derrida. Many of them were teaching outside the universities. They were excluded because they were leftists, though the political criteria were never made explicit. They were delighted to be offered an audience. Michel Foucault,[9] for instance, I stopped on his way to America. We made new departments: for instance, psychoanalysis of the Lacan school, and Mathematics in a university of Letters, which had never been done on that scale. All these departments had something besides politics in common. They had read what is being published *now*.'

Not all the players of the game were on speaking terms by the time the university actually opened its doors, and the Dommergues *équipe*'s hindsight is slightly different. But at the crucial planning stage they were all in in each other's pockets. The essential document on which the university was built, after it had been talked up from a 1,500-strong extension of the Sorbonne to a 7,000-strong independent university, was Dommergues' *rapport pédagogique*, written in forty-eight hours, which insisted upon the need to break the yearly examination system and substitute *unités de valeur*, UVs for short;[10] and to concentrate on contemporary studies, with particular attention to living languages, taught by language laboratory methods hitherto hardly known in France. (French university builders work to a set ratio for the cost of buildings and of their equipment. The Vincennes planners calmly tripled the proportion for equipment, and installed 340 language cabins, which are used intensively, and TV equipment, which so far is not.) Architecturally, the most significant decision was to keep the rooms in the university down to seminar size, so that except in the three large halls, *cours magistraux* in the Sorbonne style would for ever be impossible. On the whole, though rooms which hold fifteen comfortably and thirty uncomfortably now sometimes have forty-five packed in, this ruse has worked. Knowingly or not, the authors of Vincennes were riding the crest of a revolution in French teaching methods. One Oxford philosopher who has also taught both in France and in French Canada told me what happened when he took a seminar in Montreal in 1968 and behaved as an Oxford don is supposed to—chatting

[9] Author of *Histoire de la Folie* and *Les Mots et les Choses*, translated into English as *Madness and Civilization* (London, 1967), and *The Order of Things* (London, 1970).

[10] Each UV or 'course credit' is supposed to represent up to fifteen hours of teaching, and is normally attainable in one semester (university half-year). The *licence* or its equivalent is granted to the possessor of thirty UVs, with continuous assessment substituted for a final examination.

over the table, discussing papers with students individually, and so on. 'They were astonished that a professor should behave like that, and expose himself to being wrong. But since then, others have done the same; and in France itself, I hear, the present generation is entirely different, and the really significant thing is that in such a short time they have accepted this method as a matter of course.'

But in October 1968, with the university half built, Vincennes' troubles were only beginning. The Ministry of Finance began to grumble about the high cost of the electronic equipment, but was overruled by Faure himself. Pierre Dommergues and Hélène Cixous broke, just as the all-important *noyau co-optant* of professors was being appointed. There ensued a savage struggle for the Ministry's ear, with Las Vergnas as the ear trumpet, snatched at alternately by both sides. In the end, the Dommergues *équipe* influenced Modern Languages, History, and Political Economy (Economics); while Hélène Cixous influenced Psychology, Philosophy, Sociology, Linguistics, and French Literature. A further impasse then developed. The university had no administration to speak of until well after it opened. It was obliged to open in January 1969, for the Minister's prestige depended on it. But if too few people knew about it, and too few students were enrolled, only half the 240 teachers whom the *noyau co-optant* was co-opting could be appointed. Dommergues and his colleagues spent the Christmas holiday ringing up the newspapers. The effects of this last minute campaign to sell the infant university to French adolescents are clearly visible in French press cuttings, and enrolments quickly jumped to 5,000. Vincennes was in business—if that is a word that can be properly used about an institution where from the very first, political passion has always won over administrative order.

Vincennes is successful because it exists. Teaching is secondary, and research, if its hard-pressed professors are able to do any, must be carried out elsewhere. Even a Fleet Street journalist—or M. Faure himself, who attributes his '*extrême tolérance à la sonorisation*' to hours spent doing homework while his pianist elder sister practised—would find it difficult to work in such a hectic atmosphere, with rare periods of calm punctuating the strikes and demonstrations. Cynics, at the time and since, have supposed that part of M. Faure's purpose in founding Vincennes was to create a 'leech' to draw off *gauchiste* blood from other places. Inevitably, by the character of its teachers and courses, and by its burgeoning press reputation, it had this effect. At the opening in mid-January, *comités d'action* called participation at Vincennes '*une vaste supercherie*' and proposed to debunk the 'myth of the miraculous faculty'. A week later, the first practice grenade was thrown, and after a battle with the CRS (riot police) in which several hundred pounds worth of damage was done to the new buildings, the *comités d'action* went on strike for more construction, and education was temporarily suspended. When students were arraigned, Michel Foucault and other teachers demanded to be arraigned too, and

Faure warned the *contestataires*, both students and teachers, that expelled students could not qualify, and that if Vincennes could not operate to the formula laid down for it, another way would be found. But worse was to come, as the time approached for the elections to the *commission paritaire*, the joint participatory committee for university government, provided for in M. Faure's *Loi d'Orientation*. One of Vincennes' few Right wing students was stripped by his fellows at the end of a lecture, beaten, painted, and dragged naked down the corridors; a Communist professor of German, Alain Gisselbrecht, who had attacked the *gauchistes* in *Nouvelle Critique*, was menaced by Maoists and defended by what the Maoists described as 'young revisionists armed with chair legs'; and when election day arrived on June 18, the Vincennes administration put sixty-eight unguarded and vulnerable voting urns all round the buildings and looked surprised when *gauchistes*, both local and visiting, destroyed them. The elections eventually took place under Communist protection, and battles royal between Communists and *gauchistes* became, as elsewhere in France, common form, the Communists accusing the *gauchistes* of kidnapping their women, and the *gauchistes* accusing Communist professional bully boys of torture sessions in the woods. In the middle of all this, the Vincennes council of management succeeded in meeting, at the third attempt; eight teachers called a press conference to defend Vincennes as an educational experience; in July M. Pompidou's new Minister of Education, M. Olivier Guichard, validated the centre's degrees and confirmed its experimental character.

With variations, and rather longer periods of calm, this pattern was repeated during the 1969/70 academic year. Vincennes has taken its place among the faculties of France, but to visit it remains something of an adventure. Vincennes is where the Metro ends and the bourgeoisie begins. It has a famous racecourse where you may put your francs on Uranus II and Jean Santeuil for the 2-30, but if you walk through the Bois, keeping an eye open for ancient trees, *Juglans nigra*, *Gingko biloba*, and *Quercus sessiliflora*, and an ear open for *bruits sauvages* from the local zoo, you may come across the new campus of Vincennes, whose 7,000 students have a F.250,000 crèche but no car park, and wander round the buildings. I was there during the *journées du sang*. That did not mean fulfilment of the wish expressed in the wall scribble, '*Patrons, flics et collabos vous aurez des comptes à rendre*'—but merely that the local hospital was collecting blood. It was also Black Panther Week, and a (white) American girl from Berkeley was talking about the movement in halting French to the other members of her class, whose young French teacher had prepared a brief based on her experience of teaching in Chicago the previous year. The lavatories had been sexually liberated, and the standard of the graffiti maintained something of the May, 1968, élan. '*Que chaque étudiante Maoiste mette sa libido au service des travailleurs et des immigrants*' was greeted with '*C'est ça, la ligne de masse*'; and another, more intellectual writer announced, '*Quand je vais au chiotte je pense à Weber.*' In one of the amphis, modern language teachers were meeting to protest against the Minister's decision to make the learning of a second foreign language optional instead of compulsory. Any attack on 'living languages' is taken to heart at Vincennes, which regards them as its own preserve, but some of the listeners were sceptical of the stand being made by the teachers. Russian Italian, German, and the other languages count as 'second' simply because most French people choose to learn them only *after* learning English. 'These chaps,' a cynic said, 'are just defending their beefsteak. Fewer enrolments for the second language means fewer jobs.'

Another ministerial 'attack' on Vincennes took the form of a refusal to grant a *licence* (to teach in a *lycée*: the fundamental qualification for a professional career in education) to graduates of Vincennes Philosophy department. Already in October 1969 a commission had reported that the 'pedagogical philosophy' of the Philosophy department made its UVs impossible to validate. The syllabus printed as an appendix to this section certainly reads rather unusually beside the sedate programme of Aristotle, Kant and Wittgenstein which would be its counterpart in England.[11] Anthony Sampson, author of *The Anatomy of Britain* and *The New Europeans*,[12] who taught a fortnightly course for the Anglo-American department at Vincennes in 1969/70, remembers receiving an essay from a student, 'a brilliant analysis of the bourgeois effect of English parliamentary institutions, except that it was signed "Trotsky". When I said that it ought to be her own work she replied, "He said it much better and besides it's true."' The Vincennes Philo teachers are not so naïve, but they argue with perfect self-consistency that until the revolution is achieved it is pointless to talk philosophy. Therefore philosophy begins with Marx, not Plato. An American graduate student whom I encountered in a Vincennes class took the view that if you wanted to learn Marxism it was best to learn it from Marxists, and that was why he was there, even though some of the students in the same class were quite startlingly ignorant—like the young man from North Africa who maintained with perfect seriousness and against all criticism that there were still slaves in the US.

To gauge the distance that separates Vincennes seminars from the *cours magistraux* of the Sorbonne and the *grandes écoles* it is only necessary to taste a few examples. Attend a class at *Sciences Po* (the national school in the Latin Quarter which prepares men and women, mostly postgraduates, for the administrative class of the French public service) and the competitive atmosphere rises from the group like steam from a casserole. They stand up when the professor—a senior man at the *Ecole Pratique des Hautes Etudes*—enters the room, and listen respectfully as he tells them how to pass examinations:

[11] See John Birtwhistle's critique of Oxford philosophy, pp. 312–18.

[12] (London, 1962 and London, 1969). See also his description of early-period Vincennes in the *Observer*, August 3, 1969.

'You may irritate examiners if you don't put accents in . . . Don't write thirty-five pages like this young lady. You dispute a great deal, made-moiselle, your essay is very dialectical. There used to be a great philo-sopher and metaphysician here who would put a subject very clearly and then have a critical paragraph in precisely the opposite sense. On the other hand you mustn't be like the pre-war Radical Socialist Party under Herriot, with everything muddled and grey, and no decision . . .'

'One must sometimes contradict the depth of your ignorance with the eternal verities. It would be wrong to suppose that before the eighteenth century man lived on grass and had no economic problems.'

And so on. The brilliance and knowledgeability of the intellectual machine-tools turned out by this system are undoubted, and a *Sciences Po* pupil expressed to me succinctly the difference between the school and the university law faculty from which he had previously obtained his *licence*: 'At the faculty one learns what theoretically ought to be the case. At *Sciences Po* one learns what is.' At Vincennes, to carry the antithesis a little further, one learns what might be if only . . . Neither Britain nor America—nor Italy nor Germany, to go no further than the Continent of Europe—yield such sharp divergences of style and character between educational institutions at tertiary level as France does; and this is why the Vincennes teachers, ruthlessly raided from other French universities by the *noyau co-optant*, were so enthusiastic about their experience, even though they realised that their Centre existed mainly by grace and by God. 'I have never in fifteen years worked in such a pleasant environment, except perhaps in American universities,' one French Literature lecturer told *Le Monde*, and a lecturer in Russian added that Vincennes had proved that bettering relations between teachers and students could transform both the quality of teaching and the returns from it.[13] Bernard Cassen, a mass-media specialist in the Anglo-American department, pointed out from his own knowledge three ways in which Vincennes had broken obstinate log jams in French higher education. First, it had questioned the dominance of literature over life in university teaching, especially of languages: this was the importance of the language laboratories, and also of the parity between English and American studies at which his depart-ment aimed. Second, the number of visiting professors—one third of all staff in his own department—was unprecedented in France, where acade-mics 'don't want foreigners because they speak English better than we do'. But it was not easy even for the snootiest *maître de conference* to disparage the names of the visitors: Leslie Fiedler, Christine Brooke-Rose, John Wain . . . Third, and most generally important, Vincennes was open to *non-bacheliers* (or as the British system would put it, mature students without O and A Level certificates). 'It was very difficult because though the *Loi d'Orientation* made provision for people already in the labour force, whether or not they had university qualifications, it never said that they should follow the same courses and take the same degree. But we did it. Other universities could, but do not.' The *non-bacheliers* are supposed to be tested at entry, but inquiry suggests that most departments simply sign the form and let them in, only for them to drop out again when they fail on the 'continuous assessment' method which the university uses, or is supposed to use, for awarding its *unités de valeur*.

Of course, hopes have been disappointed as well as fulfilled at Vincennes, quite apart from the political struggles that have persistently racked the place. There was never enough space or money to create the fine art department that might, given the highly contemporary cultural concerns of other allied disciplines in the university, have produced interesting work. Information theory (*informatique*) is the nearest to a scientific subject in the institution, and that only got in because one of Hélène Cixous's appointees insisted upon it. Still in the balance, too, is not just individual successes and failures at Vincennes and the other experimental universities, but whether or not they are to remain 'sports' in a fundamentally unaltered system. The implications of the admission of *non-bacheliers* and the 'softening' of the examination system raise fascinating questions, both political and administrative, about the future of French universities. To frame these correctly, it is as important to understand what Vincennes *is* as to understand what the *Loi d'Orientation* says.[14] Yet without any doubt, the *Loi d'Orientation* is the most important attempt which any country has made in this century to reform its higher education system by act of Parliament. It is distinguished, for example, by its intellectual coherence from the laws imposed on the Japanese by the Americans after 1945, and from the laws still under discussion in Italy; it is distinguished from the Master Plan for Higher Education in California by the fact that the one took a strong pre-existent system by the shoulders and faced it about, whereas the other merely 'nationalised' and codified a free-market system that was already moving in the same general direction.

However, although the full consequences in France are not yet clear, and will not be for some time, it is already possible to notice some of the respects in which acts of Parliament do not and cannot of themselves alter university systems.

According to Professor André Lichnerowicz of the Collège de France, president of the *Association d'étude pour l'expansion de la recherche scientifique*, France has never really had a university, only 'isolated and mutually jealous faculties'. Like M. Faure, he insisted on the need for new interdisciplinary structures, for more and more contacts were needed between disciplines formerly considered distant: music with mathematics, medicine with sociology and psychology. 'The barriers kept up by existing faculties are anti-cultural.'[15] The parallel evolution in M. Faure's thought may be

[14] See Appendix C.
[15] *Le Monde*, February 26, 1969.

studied from several sources, but soon after his appointment, on July 24, 1968, he told the National Assembly (speaking of secondary education) that the time had come to abolish at this level 'the traditional, almost sacramental divorce between the literary and the scientific.' Article 6 of the finished law (passed November 12, 1968) states simply: 'The universities are inter-disciplinary and should link arts and letters with science and technology as closely as possible. They may nevertheless have a dominant emphasis.' In *L'âme du Combat*, published in February 1970, M. Faure further connects the idea of inter-disciplinarity with his search for a way to 'de-alienate' man:

> 'La pluridisciplinarité n'est pas la reconstitution d'un humanisme adapté au goût du jour. Elle ne désigne pas une somme monstrueuse de connaissances disparates. Seulement affirme-t-elle un choix: l'homme moderne, si spécialisée que soit son activité professionelle, n'est pas celui d'une discipline. Et elle indique une tendance: une discipline dominantes'enrichit et se renouvelle au contact d'autres disciplines... Le but recherché n'est pas tant de donner des connaissances que des instruments, de transmettre un savoir que de discerner et développer des aptitudes. Désaliener l'homme, c'est refuser de l'enfermer dans une connaissance, dans 'sa' connaissance, empêcher cette étreinte suffocante où l'homme est détruit par son savoir, et le détruit.'[16]

The method chosen for securing inter-disciplinary institutions on the projected 'human scale' of 6,000–18,000 students was, in the French context, an extremely drastic one. The old faculty empires were to be broken down into six times as many *'unités d'enseignement et de recherche'* (UERs), corresponding to a group of departments in an American or British university, each with its own statutes, participatory government, teaching methods, and examination procedures. At the same time, these UER atoms were to form university-size molecules by a process of attraction and repulsion, with the proviso that the Ministry would only approve the creation of each university when it was convinced that a sufficient variety of UERs had gone to make it up. In other words, 10,000 medical students, or sociologists, or chemists, did not make a university. The universities thus formed (and at the time of writing, still being formed) then became the legal corporation, under the direction of the national Council for Education and Research, for the distribution of money and jobs between the various UERs. M. Faure, in a long interview with *Le Monde*, admitted that 'to a considerable extent, the reform will stand or fall on the creation of the new universities: if they are nothing more than a juxtaposition of the different departments out of which they

[16] Op. cit., pp. 223–4. Cp. the Anglo-American recipes for general education discussed on pp. 233–47.

are composed, people will be able to accuse us justly of balkanising higher education.'[17]

It is too early to pass judgment on this aspect of the *Loi d'Orientation*. It is anyway hard for a British or American observer, used to universities that are residential as well as intellectual communities, to visualise this breaking-up and reforming of physically separate institutions in a large city. But it is no less hard for French academics to respond to an intention which—as some of them have been quick to point out—failed to take account of all the complexities of the situation. The degree of turmoil and inter-departmental dispute has of course varied with the history and habits of particular places: Bordeaux was especially obstinate. Difficulties of this kind may be temporary. Less easy to resolve, in the long run, are the structural conflicts of interest between different disciplines. In Paris, where there are, now thirteen universities (see Appendix D) the doctors are particularly unhappy. They belong to a discipline in which the training of a student in the minimum necessary technical qualification is long and expensive, and must be carefully verified (French doctors are deeply suspicious of Italian medical qualifications which they suppose to have been diluted by maladministration). In medicine there is also a strong, and in some senses not at all illiberal, tradition of guild hostility to state interference. Doctors are hard to convince that their students would benefit by contact with a 'soft', highly politicised discipline like sociology, imported for the sake of 'inter-disciplinary folklore'—as one doctor put it to me—at the expense of more directly related UERs such as Pharmacology or Biomathematics.

The bargaining positions taken up by the UERs have already resulted in some strange alliances—in Strasbourg, for example, between Jewish theology and a dental school.[18] In the process of negotiation between academic imperial fiefs, normal French modes of political self-expression inevitably swam to the top, and one eminent French sociologist compared the process with cabinet-making under the Fourth Republic. 'The law,' he told me, 'did not define the university in relation to its goals. It did not ask "What sort of training is needed to produce a good doctor or a good sociologist?" Instead of looking at the building-up process in terms of intellectual formation the framers took the formal approach, and devised the university from a kind of sociogram in which people choose partners. In a sociogram it works, because you don't have to fit everyone into the scheme, and the partnership is not for life. With universities it is different. I am afraid that the dualistic structure in France—the *grandes écoles* over against the universities—will only be intensified.'

[17] *Le Monde*, March 23/4, 1969.

[18] See also Tony Mockler's description (*The Guardian*, August 8, 1970) of the infant Paris universities: 'Probably the most interesting, certainly the only truly pluridisciplinary university, is Paris VII. Here linguists, ethnologists, paediatricians, and pure mathematicians are combining to work out new courses and new teaching methods.'

There are certainly other pressures in precisely the same direction, as can be readily deduced from the account I have given of the Vincennes experiment. Before 1968, the entire French educational system from kindergarten to university was predicated upon quality guarantees—the intellectual equivalent of *appellation controlée* on a bottle of French wine. Every French boy—to adapt Napoleon—was supposed to carry a doctor's ermine in his satchel. At every successive stage—*baccalauréat, licence,* CAPES (*certificat d'aptitude pour l'enseignement secondaire*), and for the really formidable minds, *agrégation* and eventually *doctorat d'Etat*—the aspirant was scrutinised more and more closely in more and more difficult tests, until he emerged triumphant, to inflict the same system on the next generation. (Faure's notion of abolishing both the *agrégation* and compulsory Latin is known to have horrified M. Pompidou, himself an *agrégé*.) The mental set which a century or two of this process has fixed in the French intelligentsia and political elite is ineradicable by ministerial fiat, and everywhere one now hears anxieties expressed about the *dévalorisation* of degrees. Part of this anxiety is common to most advanced nations, as we have already seen in the case of Italy. Even in Britain, where the absolute standard of all university degrees is probably kept up more rigorously than anywhere else in the world, people are beginning to reflect—in the words of W. S. Gilbert's song—'When everyone is somebody then no one's anybody'. But in France there are two further exacerbating factors: a particularly sudden increase in the *effluxe des bacheliers,* and an equally sudden exposure to unfamiliar examination methods. 'Continuous assessment is the theory,' one law student said, 'but in practice, one assistant had to decide the fates of fifty students in 2½ hours, so the professors instituted mini-examinations, and both the extreme Left and the extreme Right protested. The *licence en droit* is being devalued. With it, you used to be able to enter a bank as *redacteur.* But the Credit Lyonnais now demands not just the *licence* but the *concours* as well—and it's a state bank, rejecting the qualification conferred by the state.' To revert to the vinous analogy, it is beginning to matter in France, not merely what your degree is, but what vintage it is: 1966 has a better 'nose' than 1970.

All this has merely intensified the pressure on the institutions such as Sciences Po and the Polytechnique, whose qualifications are beyond academic reproach. This aspect of the Faure reform is an interesting illustration of the truth—which defenders of the British public school system have successfully resisted for so long—that a country's educational system can seldom be effectively reformed if any single part of it disposes of so much political power that it cannot easily be taken in hand at the same time. 'How', I asked the librarian of Sciences Po, 'will you find room for your collection to expand, in this cramped part of the Latin Quarter?' '*Nos élèves,*' he replied with a hint of a smile, '*sont bien placés.*'

One further subterranean development in French higher education after the Faure reforms requires mention. This is the long term strategy of the French Communist Party. In France it is always important to remember that government is far less firmly based on consent than it is in Britain, and even in the United States. Significantly, when M. Faure presented the *Loi d'Orientation* to the National Assembly, he was obliged to defend—presumably against potential critics in his own party—his 'liberal procedure' in receiving, during his preparation of the Bill, 'all the groups, organisations, and delegations' that express the desire to see him. (A British Minister in charge of a Bill who failed to do this would be bitterly attacked.) Everything that has happened since 1968 has testified to the Communist Party's determination to secure by legal, reformist means what before May seemed quite beyond its grasp: an effective, if indirect, share in the political and administrative control of France. As Seale and McConville's book on the May events reminds us, the CPF is profoundly nostalgic for the power that it briefly enjoyed in the Ramadier government after 1945, and as anyone who has met a few of them will agree, French Communist voters (between a fifth and a quarter of the whole electorate) are 'reformist, not revolutionary . . . integrated into society, not alienated underdogs'.[19]

The CPF has never been forgiven, and never will be forgiven, by the Trotskyist, Maoist, or Rousseau-esque Left in France for sitting tight during the May revolution. But though the CPF Central Committee declined to be drawn in, it learnt the appropriate lesson—that the educational system had unsuspected possibilities as a source of social and political leverage, and that the inevitable numerical decline of the heavy industrial labour force made it the more urgent to capture the developing mass institutions of the new intellectual proletariat. The CPF's concern was graphically expressed in the slogan under which it campaigned at Vincennes—'The University for the sons of the workers'. Entirely new opportunities were opened up by the *Loi d'Orientation*, which provided for democratic participation by parents in school government and by students and young teachers in university government, and not only preserved the principle of open access to the universities, but extended it to *non-bacheliers* already employed in the industrial labour force. The student organisation corresponding to the CPF, UNEF-Renouveau, dominated the university elections in the spring of 1969, the first to be held after the passing of the *Loi d'Orientation*.

The *gauchistes*, who boycotted the elections, were embittered and isolated by this development, and in an institution such as Vincennes—for which as individuals they had considerable respect and affection—their attitudes became positively schizophrenic. The violence that later broke out, and is still endemic among Paris students, need surprise no one.

It remains to be seen what the workers and their sons will do with the

[19] Op. cit., p. 182.

power that the reform of French education is opening up to them. Perhaps, as in other countries, it will depend on the length of their memories. In the past in France, it has generally taken two generations to produce a *fonctionnaire*. The *petit bourgeois* dreams of professional qualifications for his children; the working class family, deterred in part by the length and—in the absence of effective scholarship support—expense of a career in medicine or law, hopes for nothing more than a teacher in the family. If the leap from a dockside in Marseilles or a bench at Renault to the *Ecole Nationale d'Administration* could be more often accomplished without that intervening generation, French educational institutions would be put under a new—but this time a salutary—strain.

Appendix to French section
University of Vincennes: department of Philosophy
List of *unités de valeur* available, 1969/70

UV	Topic	Lecturer
1728	La 3ème étape du marxisme-léninisme: le maoïsme	(Judith Miller)
1729	Problèmes concernant l'idéologie I.	(Judith Miller)
1730	Problèmes concernant l'idéologie II	(Jacques Rancière)
1731	Théorie de la 2ème étape du marxisme léninisme: le concept de stalinisme	(Jacques Rancière)

Introduction aux marxistes du XXème siècle:

1732	(1) Lenine, Trotsky, et le courant bolchévique	(Henri Weber)
1733	(2) Les écrits de Mao Tsé Toung	(Henri Weber)
1734	La dialectique marxiste	(Alain Badiou)
1735	La science dans la lutte des classes	(Alain Badiou)
1736	Problèmes de la pratique révolutionnaire	(Jeannette Colombel)
1737	L'idéologie pédagogique	(René Scherrer)

1738	Logique	(Houria Sinaceur)
1739	Epistémologie des sciences exactes et des mathématiques	(Houria Sinaceur)
1740	Epistémologie des sciences de la vie	(Michel Foucault)
1741	Pb. épistemologiques des sciences historiques	(François Chatelet)
1742	Critique de la pensée spéculative grecque	(François Chatelet)
1743	Nietzsche (histoire et généalogie)	(Michel Foucault)
1744	Les idéologies morales d'aujourd'hui	(Françoise Regnault)
1745	A propos de la littérature et del'art	(François Regnault)
1746	Le signe chez Nietsche	(François Rey)

'The essence of our submission is that the City of Lancaster is eminently suitable and well qualified as a University town. Briefly stated the grounds of our case are that:

(1) We believe that the national need for additional University places can only be met satisfactorily by the foundation of new Universities;

(2) a University in the City of Lancaster, the ancient capital of the County Palatine, would fit into the national pattern of distribution of Universities and would fulfil a longstanding need for a further seat of learning in the North-West;

(3) all sections of the Community, including industry, are deeply interested and enthusiastic in their support for the project and are ready generously to demonstrate this in financial terms;

(4) notwithstanding the antiquity of the City and its colourful history in matters civil, ecclesiastical, and military, Lancaster is a progressive, prosperous and well-balanced community, supported by agriculture and industry alike;

(5) Lancaster enjoys and fosters a cultural heritage and background which would befit a University town, and situated in one of the Country's outstanding areas of natural beauty, it provides all the amenities and social facilities which could be desired;

(6) Lancaster is strategically situated in relation to the developing motorway system and to the main line railway from Scotland to London, and to the North-East. Communications are therefore excellent.

(7) a pre-eminently suitable and attractive site of 200 acres or so is immediately available for a University within two miles of the City centre, the land having been offered as a gift by the City Council.'

Submission to the University Grants Committee by the Council for the Promotion of a University in North-West Lancashire, May 1961

'Whereas an humble Petition has been presented unto Us by the Executive Council for the Establishment of a University at Lancaster praying that We should constitute and found a University within Our

City and County Palatine and Duchy of Lancaster for the advancement and diffusion of learning and knowledge and to grant a Charter with such provisions in that behalf as shall seem to Us right and suitable:

AND WHEREAS We have taken the said Petition into Our Royal Consideration and are minded to accede thereto:

NOW THEREFORE KNOW YE that We by virtue of Our Prerogative Royal and of Our especial grace, certain knowledge and mere motion have willed and ordained and by these Presents for Us, Our Heirs and Successors do will and ordain as follows:

There shall be and there is hereby constituted in Our said City and County Palatine and Duchy of Lancaster a University . . . '

Royal Charter of the University of Lancaster, July 1964

Only in England, the reader may feel, is the bourgeois political strategy which Marxists call 'mystification' raised to the status of an art. Here are extracts from two documents, both significant to a university which is one of the youngest and most successful in Britain. If one visits Lancaster, and inquires about the origins of the university, copies of this Charter, and of the original Submission by the university's local sponsors, are courteously furnished. Neither document is merely a blind; neither belongs wholly to the dignified rather than to the efficient part of the British constitution. In Britain, the attitude of a local authority and local people is of genuine importance in determining that a new university will be built here rather than there. (The town of Blackpool also put in for the North-West's new university, but lost its chance when it became clear that the house of learning was to be accommodated next door to a fun fair, and that the decisive voice in its residential policy would belong to seaside landladies.) The Royal Charter, likewise, is a document just as vital to a modern British university as it was in the Middle Ages, for it grants freedom from external political interference. (The BBC, to take an internationally familiar British institution, operates under such a Charter, which however has to be periodically renewed by Parliament. Broadcasters become very jumpy as the renewal date approaches, and so would academics if the same rule applied to them.) The difference in Britain between places for research and higher education which have Charters and are called universities, and those which owe constitutional allegiance to local educational authorities and are called polytechnics, is very marked, and would be even if there were no difference in academic standards and physical facilities. The difference is above all one of confidence. Spokesmen for British universities always sound not merely outraged, but actually astonished, when the Government of the day exercises the only substantial power that it has over them: the power to withhold funds expected or promised. No other educational institution in Britain, save only the fee-paying public boarding schools, can command this astonished tone, which is heard at its most resonant in the correspondence columns of *The Times*.

In similar circumstances, schools, colleges of education, and polytechnics only succeed in sounding aggrieved. They have been through too much to sound surprised.

Somewhere at the heart of most educational debates in England (Scotland, thanks to national pride and continental influences, developed rather differently) this issue of confidence is to be found. At its lowest and most personal level, it appears when a couple of industrialists agree over the Liebfraumilch at a country club that graduates of public schools and Oxbridge are superior to graduates of grammar school and Redbrick because though they may be technically inferior, they have more 'confidence'. But the same is true at the level of institutional history and sociology. Each new agency for the distribution of the higher learning has, as it evolved, at once resented and coveted the enormous privileges that were originally wrested from Church and Crown by the universities of Oxford and Cambridge; and for this reason, no genuinely popular form of higher education has been able to stay popular once the people involved realised that they had a chance of entering the same club. (Symbolically, one of London's famous clubs is called the 'United Universities'. There are now forty-four universities in Britain, but the club is still officially confined to graduates of Oxford and Cambridge.)

Of the two documents to which I have referred, the Charter is the more important. It is even important enough for the University, at the time of writing, to be seeking to revise it, in order to regularise the degree of student participation it has conceded. But examination of this and other relevant documents only reveals the elusiveness of power in the organisation of British higher education. The only name which appears in both the Charter and the Submission is 'Our right trusty and right well-beloved Cousin John Earl of Derby', educated at Eton and Oxford, who was President of the Promotion Council, and became the university's Pro-Chancellor, hence chairman of its Court of Governors. The Earls of Derby are still political forces to be reckoned with in the north-west, and the present Earl's grandfather, a Conservative Minister during the 1914–18 War, controlled Lancashire almost as a personal fief. But neither Lord Derby nor anyone else on the Promotion Council, separately or collectively, would have stood any chance of being listened to by the Government if the first item in their Submission, 'We believe that the national need for additional University places can only be met satisfactorily by the foundation of new Universities', had not already been accepted. Back in 1947, a local committee had been formed to pursue with the University Grants Committee (which in Britain is the buffer or hyphen between the universities and Government) the possibility of a university in Lancaster, 'but as finance was not available at the time for university building, the proposal lapsed'.

At that time, two years after an emotionally and economically exhausting war, it was not surprising that finance was not available, and only

mildly surprising that even with a reforming, modestly socialist government in power the will to 'popularise' British higher education was not
available either. Most of the members of the 1945 Labour Government
had themselves been educated at either Oxford or Cambridge. The most
influential Left-wing thinker on education in Britain between the wars—
R. H. Tawney—was himself educated at Rugby and Balliol, but left his
deepest mark on the state schools and on middle class attitudes to them.
British reformers of educational institutions seldom begin with their own,
but attempt to improve ones that will be used by other people. An exception to this rule was A. D. Lindsay, Master of Balliol (1924–49), a Labour
peer. In 1946 Lindsay with the help of Tawney himself and Sir Walter
Moberly—the one by then a member, the other Chairman, of the UGC—
overcame the UGC's hesitations and pushed through his plan for an
experimental university at Keele, in the Staffordshire Potteries. Lindsay
became its first Principal himself.

So nervous were the members of the UGC, almost all Oxbridge men,
of curricular experiment in an institution granting its own autonomous
degrees that they kept the size of Keele down to a starting figure of 600,
which has since risen slowly to 2,000 or so. Such modesty, in an advanced
nation which in 1949/50 had only 85,000 university students in a population of 45 million, was still possible politically because the mass of the
people had been socially trained not to expect full time education beyond
the age of sixteen, unless they were either demonstrably brilliant or
unpleasantly rich. In 1952, only 6·6 per cent of the age group were still
at school at the age of seventeen. The real educational revolution in
Britain since 1945 is the change in public sensibility which has transformed
this figure to 16 per cent in 1967 and a projected 22–27 per cent in 1980.
(The lower of these last two figures is the estimate in the Robbins Report.
The higher is more probable.)[20] In educationalese, this tendency among
British parents and their children to stretch the period of full-time education is cryptically called 'the trend'. The factors affecting it are common
to several countries, and they are summed up for Britain by Layard,
King, and Moser as 'the employment prospects for those who stay on,
which represent the monetary benefits from doing so; the financial terms
on which education is available, which affect the costs; parental income,
which determines the ability to finance a period of study and also influences the 'consumption' demand for education; and a whole host of
social factors which affect the values attached to education'.[21] Of these
last, the most important appears to be the educational level of parents,
which ought to entail a further surge in demand during the 1980s. But
together with the post-war demographic bulge in the British birth-rate,
which then remained higher than expectation for reasons that go beyond

[20] Richard Layard, John King and Claus Moser, *The Impact of Robbins* (London, 1969)
p. 33.
[21] Ibid., p. 13.

the scope of this chapter and the knowledge of demographers, the 'trend' accounts for the fact that, in the words of the same authors, 'apart from electronics and natural gas, higher education has grown faster than any major national enterprise in the 1960s'.

All this was still hidden in the mid-fifties, when fundamental planning had to be done if Britain was not to be caught short, as France was, by the onrush of the qualified. The Robbins Commission, on whose Report and statistical projections British higher education policy has since been based, was not appointed until 1961. The elision of historical time in people's memories has by now indelibly associated the publication of the Robbins Report with the creation of new universities in Britain, but in fact the projects for the Universities of Sussex, York and East Anglia were all approved by the UGC before the Commission was even appointed, and before there could be said to be a national *system* of higher education at all. In 1955, however, it was still possible for academic speakers, including an eminent economist presumably capable of doing sums, to tell a Home Universities Conference that a stable figure of 90,000 students would be enough, with a temporary peak of 105,000 in the critical years of 1964–67. The conference knew better, and Lord Simon of Wythenshawe, a Labour industrialist, Chairman of the Council of Manchester University, and a fervent supporter of public education, called the proposed numbers 'totally and almost fantastically inadequate'. Britain had a desperate shortage of scientists and technologists, and a smaller proportion of university students in the age group than any other civilised country. University places would have to be doubled by 1965. They were. It was the final explosion of a long but mostly private struggle for expansion. Even then, though Sussex and the other new universities quickly caught the public fancy, the scale of the changes contemplated was not appreciated until Robbins reported.

Indeed, the existence of a 'public opinion' about higher education in Britain cannot itself be dated further back than the early sixties. When Professor Harold Perkin, on whose account[22] the foregoing paragraph rests, suggested to Lord Murray, chairman of the UGC during the critical period, that considerations other than mere expansion of numbers had weighed heavily with the committee in considering whether to form new universities rather than expand old ones, the reply was, 'It was one-third numbers and two-thirds new ideas'. British universities, that is, needed to be shaken out of their insular departments, specialised single subject honours courses, and insensitivity to the needs of graduates destined for non-academic but nevertheless intellectually demanding careers. But these were not topics on which the UGC at the time sought or desired public debate. There are, after all, numerous graduates of Oxford

[22] *New Universities in the United Kingdom* (OECD, 1969), Ch. 3. This report, already cited, contains a mass of detailed information on the subject though the lack of an index makes extraction difficult.

and Cambridge in both Houses of Parliament, but not many of them could safely be let loose in a debate about either research or teaching. To the secretive British academics of the 1950s, it was second nature to keep the argument in the family. The Treasury accepted the UGC's recommendation that there should be built with Government money eight new universities, reformist in design and concept, and costing collectively over twelve million pounds a year (in 1971/2) on top of a basic stock of buildings and equipment worth about sixty millions. Parliament was at no stage consulted about the matter. (Neither had it been consulted about the Attlee Government's decision to build a British H-Bomb, but that cost less money.) The power which publicly unknown men enjoy to take important decisions in private about the future of Britain remains undiminished. But it is not a power which is any longer available to those who decide the future of universities. There are technical administrative stimulants to disclosure: the Comptroller-General's new power to inspect university accounts, the presence of a Minister responsible for the universities within the Department of Education and Science, and, still in the future, the proposed substitution of a Higher Education Commission, covering the whole field, for the University Grants Committee, whose responsibility is limited to universities. But the strongest stimulant to disclosure is political: during the 1960s, too many people had their interest, or self-interest, in university education aroused for grand debates to be concealed any more.

The decision in principle to build new universities was taken in Britain, not by a Minister, but by the Civil Service on the advice of a non-governmental body. We have seen how in France a Minister's decision to build a new university at Vincennes produced, thanks to French academic disorganisation and the rather special circumstances of June–September 1968, one kind of result. In Britain a similar task, lacking only the extreme urgency, was tackled in the following way. The details are peculiar to the example (Lancaster) I have chosen, but substantially the pattern is true to the method by which British universities have lately been launched, and for the next generation of universities, which seem likely to be created before 1980, no alternative method has yet been canvassed.

Once the struggle between Lancashire and Cheshire County Councils for the award of the North-West's new university had been decided in favour of Lancaster, the UGC set up an Academic Planning Board. This administrative device had been invented three years earlier for the new University of Sussex—the first to be built since Keele. The Board, to which eminent academics from other universities were appointed as individuals, was to consider the range of subjects to be studied at Lancaster and the arrangements by which academic standards were to be maintained in the degrees awarded; to prepare a draft Charter and to select the first governing body; and to nominate the first Vice-Chancellor and, on his advice, the nucleus of professors. This Board was entirely independent of the locally-based Executive Council, whose role in preparing a constitution for the University was consultative only. Unlike the similar committee of academic elder statesmen which was supposed to supervise the grand plan and initial appointments at Vincennes, Lancaster's Board exerted in practice fundamental influence on the shape of the new university. When Lancaster opened its doors in 1964, the Planning Board converted itself into an Advisory Committee, responsible for 'keeping under review the standard of education and research in the university, including the standard of degrees awarded'. It was finally dissolved in 1969, on the grounds that the University no longer needed a formal outside witness to its standards, other than the system of externally supervised degree examinations which Lancaster has in common with other British universities.

The original members of the Academic Planning Board were: Sir Noel Hall (Chairman); Dr. F. S. Dainton; Sir Malcolm Knox; Miss Kathleen Major; Professor R. J. Pumphrey; Dr. J. A. Ratcliffe; Professor B. R. Williams; and on his appointment, the Vice-Chancellor, Mr. Charles Carter. In the Britain of 1961, the current of ideas which has recently given the founding committee for the new German University of Bremen a proportion of six professors, three junior teachers, and three students would have been not only abhorrent but unimaginable. Yet certain members of Lancaster's Board, in spite of their collectively advanced age and academic probity, came to it determined on changes in the Oxbridge and Redbrick patterns which they had themselves known. Sir Noel Hall, though he had just become Principal of Brasenose College, Oxford, was a teacher of management, formerly head of the Staff College at Henley. His contacts belonged to the industrial rather than to the academic world. Like Lancaster's eventual Vice-Chancellor, he was also a member of the Planning Board for the University of Kent. Dr. F. S. Dainton, now Vice-Chancellor of Nottingham University, is in British educational circles chiefly identified with the report of the (Dainton) Committee on the Flow of Candidates in Science and Technology into Higher Education,[23] which recommended compulsory mathematics teaching at sixth-form level in British schools to correct the 'drift from science'. This type of concern may also have been reflected in the Board's choice of Mr. Carter as Vice-Chancellor, for he himself takes the view that not only sixth formers but also university vice-chancellors need to be numerate. Dr. Ratcliffe, who was head of the Radio Research Station at Cambridge, had there fathered a scheme for special science courses to be given to arts students. It had come to grief in the Fens, but he hoped to revive it in the more bracing air of the Ribble. Another significant Board member was Professor Bruce Williams, now Vice-Chancellor of Sydney University. He had collaborated with Mr. Carter on two economics books and therefore knew him well. Besides, both men belonged to the University

[23] Cmnd. 3541 (1968).

of Manchester, and had been impressed by the failures of its academic
and social life, symptomised by a student body which had as little as
possible to do with the university outside its studies, and autonomous
departments which took as little notice as possible of neighbouring disciplines. It was not surprising that this group decided to adopt for Lancaster a collegiate structure, without a strong central students' union, and
to look for more breadth of studies than the single honours degree course
could provide.

But unquestionably, the Board's most important decision was its
choice of Charles Carter as Vice-Chancellor, at the age of forty-two. A
Quaker, educated at Rugby and St. John's College, Cambridge, with a
spell in the Friends Relief Service, he possesses—like many Quakers—a
religious zeal for the economic use of resources, human and material.
This was expressed in his academic career as a business economist (one of
his books is *The Science of Wealth*) and in his membership of official
committees like the British Association Committee on the Metric System
and the Heyworth Committee on Social Studies, but the University of
Lancaster gave him *lebensraum*. Unlike the Planning Board for the new
University of Kent, which had spent some time discussing what sort of
university to create before it appointed a Vice-Chancellor, the Lancaster
Board had done nothing for six months but look for their man. There
were 'no papers, no blueprints'. Consequently one can be fairly sure that
everything at the university, from the constitution to the colours ('Lancaster red and Quaker grey') has a touch of Carter. Pink of cheek and
precise of speech in an almost military manner, he is not a flamboyant
leader, and few people have seen him angry. One of the few told me that
the occasion was a trip Carter had made to ask a very well-known British
motor manufacturer for a donation to a research project of great potential
usefulness to industry: the man responded with a cheque for one hundred
pounds. Not many of his colleagues feel they know him, but few fail
to respect him as an administrator and—though he might not care for
the description—as a politician. 'He is Oliver Cromwell,' said one early
appointee, 'conscience and efficiency.' Several of Lancaster's most admired
and imitated achievements are in areas close to Carter's own interests: the
Department of Operational Research, which makes fifty thousand pounds
a year for the university from industrial research contracts; the construction of student accommodation to normal standards through commercial
loans instead of Government subsidy, at just over half the usual cost per
room; and the achievement—for obvious reasons less publicised—of
running a tolerably contented university on a staff-student ratio twenty-
five per cent worse than the British norm of 1:8.

Politically, Carter seems to favour a technique often used by industrial
wage negotiators, and in university administration by Kingman Brewster
at Yale: that of buying peace by offering rather more than was expected.
Lancaster was the first new British university to offer its students places

on all three governing bodies of the University: Court, Council, and Senate. (These three bodies correspond closely to Manchester's, already described. Court has no executive power, and exists primarily to provide contact with the local community; Council governs everything that is not assigned to Senate, which means finance, buildings, equipment, and university policy generally; Senate is responsible for academic affairs, and for student living conditions and discipline.) However, the future inclusion of students in the Senate will entail reserving problems of academic hiring and firing to a small committee under the Vice-Chancellor's chairmanship, whose decisions will then be ratified by the full Senate. The notion, already accepted or seriously discussed in parts of Germany and the US, that academics may become dependent for their obs on committees which include students is still almost wholly repugnant to British dons. At Lancaster, however, one of the professors noted that the solution adopted will in fact give the Vice-Chancellor more autocratic power than he had previously possessed. Significantly, perhaps, he went on to wonder, not what Mr. Carter might do with it, but what a future Vice-Chancellor might do with it.

Mr. Carter himself will never have as much power to make or unmake the university by hiring and firing as he did with the first dozen or so professors appointed. The courses offered at the opening of the university were: Biology, Chemistry, Classical Background, Economics, English, Environmental Studies, French Studies, History, Mathematics, Philosophy, Physics, and Politics, taken in pairs either as major and minor or as combined majors, together with—in each case—an obligatory distant minor unrelated to the major subject. The original intention to have a professor of German Studies, frustrated at the time by Mr. Carter's inability to find the right man, has never been fulfilled, but other departments have germinated: Engineering (established against resistance from the UGC, which regarded it as one of the many subjects for which there was already adequate provision at other universities and technological institutions); Religious Studies; Computer Studies, Operational Research; Systems Engineering (paid for by ICI); and Financial Control (paid for by the Wolfson Foundation). The last three of these were the first of their kind in Britain, and have now been joined by a fourth, Behaviour in Organisations: 'In recent years developments in theory and research have made it possible to consider behaviour in organisations as occurring within a system of independent forces, each of which can be analysed and set in the perspective of other forces. The basic analytic framework evolved from this idea is appropriate for analysing behaviour in any kind of organisational setting, be it business, government, hospitals, or educational institutions. . . . Basic disciplines from which the study is derived are psychology, sociology and anthropology. . . . Courses are still under consideration . . .'.[24]

[24] University of Lancaster Prospectus, 1970/71, p. 70.

One of the subjects which arrived after the first wave is Religious Studies, whose professor is Ninian Smart. His account (in conversation with the author) of how one man got a job and one innovation was achieved in a new British university has a certain exemplary interest, different though the details would be in other cases. Ninian Smart was formerly Professor of Comparative Religion at Birmingham. One night an Egyptologist friend left a copy of the *Universities Quarterly* in his house. He picked it up and read an essay by Alec Whitehouse (Professor of Theology at the University of Kent) on 'Theology as a discipline'. He sat down and wrote a reply called 'Religion as a discipline'—arguing in effect that in today's pluralistic society, the comparative approach was the only one possible for a university. Three years later he was asked to be an assessor for the proposed Chair of Religious Studies at Lancaster, and the Vice-Chancellor asked him to say in advance what he thought the department should teach, since they needed to know their own mind about this before hiring a man—a principle, as we have seen, that was not observed by the Academic Planning Board in founding the university itself. Smart circulated his *Universities Quarterly* paper, which still represented, he said, 'what I roughly think'. The assessors met and talked about names. In the car on the way to lunch the Vice-Chancellor quietly observed to Smart, 'People should practise what they preach', and pointed out that if Smart withdrew from the election he could apply for the job himself. Afterwards Carter drafted and showed to Smart the advertisement for a Professor of Religious Studies, including the phrase which became notorious in British ecclesiastical circles, opening the job to a man 'of any faith or none'. (The vast majority of British professors of theology are ordained members of the Established Churches, Anglican in England, Presbyterian in Scotland.) When he saw it, the Anglican Bishop of Blackburn, a member of the university's Council, telephoned Smart in Birmingham to say 'surely we can't have this?' Smart replied that he thought this was what a secular university was about, and the bishop subsided. Smart was then appointed. The sixties were depressing years for institutional Christianity in Britain and most of his friends thought he would be lucky to get more than half a dozen students. What actually happened was that the department became one of the most popular choices among incoming students, with the happy result (for Smart) that the intellectual calibre of those admitted could be kept high, and more staff hired. One can only guess at the reasons, and some of the students may originally have been looking for what they supposed to be a soft option. However, they are expected at Part I level to study in four different areas: modern religious and atheistic thought in the West, modern scientific approaches to religion (including the sociology of religion), New Testament studies, and the history of Indian religion in the modern period, with reference to both Islam and Hinduism. Neither Barth nor Sartre is easy reading. Essentially, the success of the department was a matter of timing. Students in the late sixties were developing an open, eclectic attitude to religion which the organised churches and established university departments of theology could not possibly satisfy. The promise, implied by Lancaster's initial advertisement, that here at least none of the interesting questions would be prejudged, and the prospectus's promise of courses ranging from the phenomenology of religion to Japanese Buddhism and the Marxist-Christian dialogue, could hardly fail to attract people. Smart himself—a stocky, bow-tied, genial man—has also turned out to be as powerful an influence as any in forcing the university to make room for more of the innovatory spirit with which it began.

However, before mentioning the criticisms that were being made in 1970, six years after the university opened, it is necessary to set down what both students and staff, and also the general public, have come to take for granted about the University of Lancaster. First of all, it is physically there, a campus university for—eventually—7,000 students on the rolling rural outskirts of an ancient county town. Every building is accessible on foot and under cover from its central plaza and pedestrian spinal cord. The university is collegiate, not in the sense that Oxbridge is collegiate, with each college enjoying financial and academic autonomy, but in the sense that all undergraduates and dons, whether actually in residence or not, are members of one of the six colleges, whose buildings include, as well as all the necessary social facilities for both junior and senior members, the teaching and office rooms for departments in non-laboratory subjects. Every student has access to a personal 'college tutor' to consult as distinct from a departmental supervisor in his own subject area. Students are free to live as they choose in their own quarters: indeed, the university's first sexual row was enjoyed (by the newspapers) long before there were any students there at all, in the course of a theoretical debate in Senate on the extent to which accommodation should be mixed: buildings, floors, corridors, rooms, beds. . . . Student drug-taking has now almost replaced student sex as the British public bogy, and just as the Dean of Balliol claimed to have been able to tell the first wave of pot-smokers by their clothes, one of the Lancaster professors pointed to the Bowland Tower (the only tall building in the university) and said that the trouble was concentrated on one particular floor. Socially, the percentage of Lancaster students with working class parents (twenty-seven per cent) is the highest in the new universities, though not higher than the percentage among British university students as a whole.[25] The figure for Lancaster may be somewhat affected by the university's liberality (for Britain) in admitting promising students without A level qualifications, and sometimes at a comparatively advanced age. One such student, during my visit, was taking his final examination in the sick bay while recovering from a

[25] Perkin, op. cit., p. 107.

prostatectomy. 'Fancy,' said his professor, 'a student with prostate trouble'.

Academically, Lancaster's first, admittedly rather crude, attempt to bridge the 'Snow line' between literary and numerical subjects has undergone several modifications. There was not time at the outset to find professors for the new university who were all equally enthusiastic about the Planning Board's determination to enshrine 'flexibility', 'breadth' and other concepts hitherto unfamiliar to British higher education in the Lancaster course-structure. Physicists, in particular, have even been known to complain about the time they were expected to spend in their college as opposed to their department, let alone about the suggestion that their students should spend a ninth of their time on, say, French Studies, or History of Art. Yet the most important principles—that a student should not have to take a final decision about his main specialism until the end of his first year, and that he should have to spend at least a portion of his time on a subject whose way of looking at the world is unfamiliar to him—have survived, and in some instances have been expanded. The head of the Mathematics Department, Emlyn Lloyd, not himself an enthusiast about the original 'distant minor' requirement, says that the creation of the Engineering Department revealed a pool of people who needed maths as a tool for engineering but had been badly taught at school. A research project was put up to the Department of Education and Science and a first rate teacher from a mathematically-minded public school appointed. The researchers needed 'guinea pigs', and discovered that there was already in the university an 'undergrowth' of students in other subjects who needed mathematics and were picking it up somehow. So there are now about 120 people doing elementary maths courses specially devised for specialists in other subjects. Elsewhere, the 'breadth' requirements have worked best where the concept has been coherent and the departments concerned co-operative. It is little use doing a joint honours degree in French and English if neither department knows or cares what the other is doing, but a combined four-year major (most courses in Lancaster, as in other British universities except Keele, last only three years) in French and Latin studies is regarded as particularly successful. On the French side it works by tracing the transmission of ideas, institutions, and literature of Greece and Rome through French civilisation. This approach has even been extended to a scientific subject, and Professor T. E. Lawrenson, who like Professor Lloyd was one of the group of professors originally appointed, has borrowed twenty teaching hours from Biology in order to tackle evolutionary theory as it is expressed in the quarrel between Cuvier and Lamarck. At the same time, someone has to pay in terms of work-load for the complexities involved, and as at Vincennes, it is chiefly the professors. Few of them except the most single-minded can do much research during term, and when Professor Lawrenson himself added up his working hours for the inquiry which was in 1969 circulated by the Committee of Vice-Chancellors, he found himself averaging about sixty per week. There is no reason to suppose this figure exceptional. The Vice-Chancellor, in describing to the University Court the intense involvement with students, individually and in small groups, which the Lancaster and other similar systems demanded, went on:

'It is a mistake to suppose that room for all this work with students is readily to be found by means of a generous staffing ratio. The student-staff ratio of British universities is often quoted as about eight to one, and is contrasted with much higher ratios in other countries. But this ratio is greatly affected by some special cases, notably medicine and agriculture. For arts and science faculties, ten to one is more normal. . . . Nor do the international comparisons mean quite what is usually assumed. In industrial terms, the student-staff is a ratio of "work in progress" to skilled staff. This is a very odd thing to measure; one would expect to relate the desired output of the system, graduates, to the number of staff. When one does so, the much higher drop-out rates in many countries make the British ratio appear normal rather than luxurious.'[26]

It is always difficult to make this kind of international comparison, because there are different degrees of what an economist might call production wastage. A German student who spends three years at a German university, but drops out aged twenty-three before his first *staatsexamen*, might even resemble a finished article almost as closely as a British student who takes his first, comparatively undemanding degree at the age of twenty-one. However, Mr. Carter's main point stands: Lancaster dons are not under-worked. Nor is a heavy teaching load the only penalty which the pleasure of life in a new university carries with it. Like their counterparts in Oxbridge colleges, Lancaster teachers are likely to have to familiarise themselves with what an American professor would regard as an unacceptable range of subjects or periods; unlike Oxbridge men, when they do find time for research, they may find their university's library resources wholly inadequate to their needs. Six years after opening, Lancaster still has only half its library (work on the other half was delayed by the Government's 1968 cuts in capital expenditure) with some 200,000 volumes. Even when the other 221,000 can be bought and accommodated, the university (in the words of one professor) 'can only hope to have a good undergraduate teaching library'—at least by transatlantic standards. (It is constant use, not spot checks, that reveal the strength and weakness of a library, but for curiosity I turned up Lawrence Wylie's name in the catalogue: his earlier *Village in the Vaucluse* book was there, but *Chanzeaux* was not[27]—this in a university which is strong in French studies.) Library

[26] University of Lancaster, Fifth Annual Report (1969), p. 8.
[27] See pp. 257–265.

resources, quite apart from the difference they make to the working lives of resident academic staff, are also important deciding factors in the minds of visiting foreign scholars when they are deciding whether to go here rather than there. Lancaster does not do too badly, with (in 1969) seventy-seven foreign graduate students, out of 363; and five visiting professors, out of a teaching staff of 261. But with a run of *Hansard* to 1899 now costing £7,660 from the reprint houses, and the typical price of a scholarly book edging closer and closer to £5. Lancaster's annual book purchase figure of about £50,000 looks pretty small. Not many new American universities would be content with the notion that they might, if they were lucky, possess a million books in half a century or so.

In what sense were these new universities new, and is their capacity for innovation now at an end? What influence will Vincennes and Lancaster exert upon their successors, wherever and whenever they are built?

British and French educationists may puzzle over these questions for some time. Americans, who create universities often enough to be unselfconscious about it, may be surprised that the questions are even raised, but in Europe the pattern of higher education in each country has until very recently been set and regular. An optical break in it is remarkably visible, and the most iconoclastic step taken by Vincennes and by the group of new British universities was simply to open their doors and offer something different from what had gone before. What they taught, and how they chose to teach it, was certainly important, but it was secondary to the affront of their existence. Not everyone in either France or England wanted these awkward academic children to be born. In France, only haste, secrecy, and the extraordinary circumstances of 1968 could have worsted the academic and political forces represented by the Société des Agrégés and the conservative wing of the Gaullist governing party. In Britain, the academic changes introduced by the new institutions were real but not radical. The difficult victory was won at a much earlier stage, when academic and Civil Service opinion had to be convinced that British interests as well as natural justice demanded the provision of university places for those judged fit to occupy them. Even then, the criteria of fitness were not set any lower than before. To do so would have been politically impossible while the argument that 'more means worse' was—not for the first time in the history of British universities— being forcefully put.

The proponents of campuses in a string of Shakespearean-sounding towns (York, Lancaster, Canterbury, Norwich . . .) had a secondary fight to win against the party, including influential scientists like Blackett and Chain, who agreed that many more graduates were needed, but considered that the cultures ought to be grown in urban 'centres of excellence' rather than in 'cottage universities'. But for the urban Redbrick universities' failure in previous generations to break the stranglehold which Oxford and Cambridge had over the entire system, this last argument might well have been accepted. Today, with the stranglehold relaxed, the decision would almost certainly go the other way. The practical argument for siting a new university at Lancaster, for example, rested heavily on the availability of hundreds of seaside lodging houses at Morecambe, a few miles away, where students could live during term time. But in the event, the university has provided most of its own accommodation, student *moeurs* have diverged further and further from those of seaside landladies, and the burghers of Morecambe are rather cross about the forgotten promise. Students themselves are much more reluctant than they were in 1960 to accept their elders' 'paternalist' notion that university work requires a retreat into a secluded, preferably pastoral environment, and there are staff as well as students at Lancaster who would much rather live in reconditioned old buildings in the middle of town, and who sigh for the days when the university opened—on the Vice-Chancellor's insistence—in a temporarily converted furniture warehouse, two years ahead of schedule.

Some time ago a Plateglass professor suggested that a new university's potential for innovation fades after about three years. If its most significant innovation is its very existence, this matters less than it might seem, and there are other factors to take into account. At Lancaster, as we have seen, the fundamental pattern was laid down by the Vice-Chancellor and his twelve professorial disciples at opening day, and is unlikely to alter much. On the other hand, innovation is still possible, perhaps even likely, while the university is growing physically and numerically towards a target that will not be reached before the mid-seventies, and while new subjects with new professors keep arriving to criticise the assumptions of the founding fathers.

At Vincennes, the hostile political climate in which the university is wrapped makes the outlook grimmer. A traditionalist Minister of Education, and a President of the Republic who is an agrégé with a strong belief in compulsory Latin, are unlikely to bail Vincennes out of any trouble which it attracts by its educational iconoclasm or its uproarious *gauchisme*. Its staff, when it is time for them to move on, will have trouble finding jobs in other French universities whose methods they are known to despise. Therefore, people in other universities, unless politically attracted by the Vincennes way of life, will think twice about coming. (The French system allows a professor with a job at Amiens or Besançon to live in Paris if he chooses and commute to his lectures, so the advantages of a job in the Paris *banlieue* are not as great as they would otherwise be.)

In sum, though, the influence of these new institutions upon their successors is bound to be great, whether by action or reaction. It is also unforeseeable, since so much will depend on the political imponderables of that country at that time. If universities' growth and decay were ever unrelated to what was happening in political society, they will never be so again. The best illustration of this is perhaps the turbulent history of the 'phantom' university of Bremen, in north Germany. West Germany has built a few new universities in the past decade as well as inflating old ones to bursting point, and Bochum in the Ruhr is more technocratic and proletarian in concept than the traditionally hierarchical German model. But fundamental constitutional change was harder to achieve, and between 1960 and 1970 three different committees of German academics have tried to found the University of Bremen. The first two failed because as German political society found its balance and the ideological freeze of the Occupation and Adenauer periods gave way to democratic disputatiousness, the occasion of a university's founding became a struggle between old and young, conservative and socialist, professor and junior teacher, over the control of the future. Bremen had to wait for its university. The issue may have been resolved in 1970 by the Bremen Parliament's appointment of a third academic committee to found the university: a committee which was in theory equally divided between the academic and political sides, but which in fact had been decisively tipped to the left because one member of the professorial caucus was himself a New Left man. Once that point was reached, the founding committee could elect a chief executive and start work.[28]

Bremen's experience suggests that the next French and British new universities will be harder to establish than either Lancaster or Vincennes were. The opponents of the British Plateglass universities were negligible forces compared with the body of opinion supporting them, and though some people criticised the new institutions as prestige projects for an elite minority (which was true), no one criticised the manner in which their courses and constitution were laid down by a committee of ageing, undemocratically appointed professors. In France, opposition to Vincennes would have been fierce if anyone had known what was going on, because there existed no social or educational consensus on which such a radical experiment could have been based. But the political and academic structure of the country allowed both authority and the subverters of authority to work away in peace, uninterrupted by interdictory raids from the academic Right, or by formal demands for 'participation' from the political Left.

Perhaps the most important service which these new institutions have rendered to their successors has been to clarify and at the same time broaden the issues which the next generation of founding fathers will have to tackle. In Britain, now that Oxford and Cambridge are no longer regarded by students or even by all university staff as the pinnacle of ambition, people can attend to the differences, if any, which need to be preserved between universities—town or country—and other places which admit students and do at least some research, but are not called universities, governed as universities, or equipped as universities. The

[28] For details of the Bremen struggle see for instance Nina Grunenberg in *Die Zeit* (July 11, 1969, p. 19); Jörg Richter in *Deutsches Allgemeines Sonntagsblatt* (July 13, 1969, April 26, 1970).

nature of the obstacle to further innovation is also clearer. The British school system, as the 1964–70 Labour Government found, is almost unreformable by external administrative fiat. It has gone some way to reform itself at the primary (first to seventh grade) level, where there is a common school for almost all children in a district, and where teachers have been free to apply, even in degraded buildings, what Piaget and many other educational researchers have told them about the learning processes of young children. But at the secondary (eighth to thirteenth grade) stage both social commonalty and educational flexibility are frustrated by three factors: the universities' admission or rejection of children by specialised examinations set at the age of seventeen or so; the nation's inheritance of three separate types of secondary school, two state and one private, distinguished from each other by social esteem and financial resources as well as by academic quality, and offering hardly any opportunity for transfer within the system; and parental ambition's anxious response to these alternatives, which is expressed in ritual battles over education between the two main political parties, both locally and nationally.

In Britain, the importance of the decisions that must over the next decade be made about the tertiary education system, and in particular the decision whether to allocate new resources to universities or to polytechnics, thus lies partly outside the realm of tertiary education itself. Soon, between a quarter and half of the British age group will be receiving full-time tertiary education of some kind. The Department of Education and Science estimates that in 1981 there will be 727,000 students in full-time higher education in England and Wales. The National Union of Students, and academic expansionists generally, recommend up to twice this figure, which should be compared with the present (1969/70) figure of 443,000 students, and with the Robbins Report's own prediction for 1980 of 500,000. If by the end of this decade it appears that the primary school that one attends is determined chiefly by geography, and the university or college that one attends chiefly by personal inclination, a secondary school system in which choice is determined partly by intelligence, partly by purse-length, and partly by political leverage will speedily become intolerable. Already, most people in Britain now want secondary schools to be comprehensive—to include, that is, all levels of ability except for children whose handicaps or praeternatural intelligence require special provision.[29] No one would claim that the new universities and polytechnics founded in the 1960s of themselves brought this particular issue to a head. But without them, it would still be hard to see the British educational system as a whole, and the issue would today be much more confused than it is.

Viewed in terms of organisation and institutions, the prospect in

[29] See the survey introduced by D. V. Donnison in *New Society*, June 25, 1970.

France is utterly different, though there is a link to be discerned in the ineradicable elitism of the two countries' political and intellectual leadership. However, but for the sharp differences of emphasis between the state secular schools and the surviving Catholic ones,[30] and the difference between the countryside and the towns in the level of demand for secondary education, French schoolchildren can be said to have access to a common education, whether (like the majority) they leave school at fourteen, or whether they go on to *collegè* and *baccalauréat*. After the *bac*, though, real social divergence is sharpened, whereas in Britain it is now becoming blunted. The *grandes écoles* were left out of M. Faure's *Loi d'Orientation* because, like the fee-paying 'public schools' in Britain, they were too powerful to be attacked. In the event, their status has been enhanced by their omission, because their qualifications remained irreproachable while the qualifications conferred by universities were suffering, in the eyes of French employers, a devaluation consequent upon an excess of popular democracy. In a country where esteem for certification is so deeply rooted, it is hard to envisage any diminution in the power of the *grandes écoles*. On the other hand, their size is finite, and their curriculum and teaching methods are conservative. At any point in the next twenty-five years, some abrupt technological or social change could leave France as seriously short of appropriately-educated manpower as her previous slowness to create middle-level technological institutions left her short of design engineers. Nor have French universities even begun to satisfy, as the British ones have done, industry's interest in novel academic approaches to problems of management and control. In a crisis of this kind a place like Vincennes, which now appears an academic squib without either a past or a future, might be used as a model for a more convinced and convincing assault on the stratified fortress of French tertiary education. But next time, that fortress will not easily fall to an unsupported boarding party of Structuralist literary critics, eyebrows plucked and daggers between their teeth.

[30] The difference between religious and secular schools in France extends to history textbooks. Joan of Arc and Louis XVII are hardly recognisable as the same people in Catholic and public-school texts.

PART II

Mainly Reflections

CHAPTER FIVE

The governance of universities: models and myths

(incorporating a case-study of the 'political' model
for the reform of West German universities)

I FIVE MODELS: MONASTERY, SCHOOL, CLUB, CORPORATION, BODY POLITIC

'In order that these statutes be preserved with due reverence and observed duly both by the head and by the members, if not for love of virtue, at least for fear of penalty, we decree and command that if the rector himself (which God forbid) fails to observe these statutes or to cause them to be observed by others; or if he presumes to do anything contrary to the regulations of these statutes, or attempts to do so, or even gives his consent to it; or if he mismanages college properties, he shall straight away be admonished secretly by two of the senior scholars, in accordance with the true teaching of the Gospel, to put an end to what he has undertaken. If he should refuse, they shall admonish him in the presence of two chaplains or of other members of the college. If, scorning these admonitions, he fails to put an end to the actions thus undertaken, the aforementioned scholars shall be required to call upon some one of the visitators and humbly to urge him to cause the statutes to be observed. By Jesus Christ's bowels, we request this visitator to bring the rector to the observance of the statutes and, if he refuses, even to compel him by chiding and by punishing him. First, however, he shall investigate the truth of the charge against the rector.'

The Spanish College at Bologna in the Fourteenth Century,
statutes edited and translated by Berthe M. Marti
(Philadelphia, 1966), p. 342–3

'We cannot understand why discipline is so bad. With about one master to ten students at Keele it ought to be enough to ensure that students keep their trousers on.'

Local council spokesman in 1970, withdrawing financial
support from the University of Keele after a group of
students had stripped during a heatwave.

(*The Guardian*, June 27, 1970)

How shall twentieth-century universities be governed? Until the disturbances of the past few years, not many people either in the academic or in the lay world thought this question was worth bothering about. Universities governed themselves, referring occasionally to a rule-book which bore little relation to the constitutional practices of their host country, and were not infrequently in Latin. This, at least, was how it looked in Europe as late as 1964, half a century after it had first become obvious that the difference in efficiency between one country's educational system and another's could mean the difference between winning and losing a major war. In America, whose scientific and mass educational achievement had by 1914 already surpassed that of individual European countries, university constitutions less often lapsed into Latin and the resemblance between the president of a university and the president of a great corporation was more easily discernible. After all, they even bore the same title. But the connection between academic and business organisation in America was not in fact as close as this coincidence of nomenclature implies. Even in the United States, and even in the nineteenth century, it was to the Protestant denominations rather than to commerce that the University looked for a model by which to govern itself. As for the connections between types of university government and levels of academic efficiency, they are little explored, for reasons that can be expressed syllogistically: (1) most countries are familiar with only one type of university government; (2) only twentieth-century social science has possessed even approximately reliable tools for measuring academic efficiency, and as Charles Carter of Lancaster points out (p. 184) the tools are sometimes foolishly used; (3) therefore only a multi-lingual social scientist from an academically 'neutral' country, who also happened to be interested in higher education, would be likely to reach illuminating conclusions. (This, as it happens, is a formula which points pretty clearly at Professor Joseph Ben-David of the Hebrew University in Jerusalem.) But the 1960s have made an issue out of university government in almost every industrial nation. Totalitarian countries have not been exempt. Russia and China have both had problems with students, and the chief exception to the rule, presumably because of the external pressures upon her, is Israel. In many instances academic structures which had stood for centuries crumbled into dust at the touch of a student's impudent finger. Heads of German universities were replaced by junior lecturers, who disdained the title of *Rector Magnificus*; at Oxford the Proctors retracted a decision on the steps of the Clarendon in the face of a noisy but not especially belligerent crowd. From Waseda to Wisconsin, the riot policeman became as common a sight as the football coach. America popped like corn with the sound of university presidents being fired, after their anonymous mass public had deemed them to have failed in a mission that had never been defined; and in the new British University of Warwick, already a magnet for pure mathematicians from all over the world, dons and students together settled down to a campaign of attrition in the hope of forcing the Vice-Chancellor and a few of the university's lay governors into resignation. All these events and others of their kind are taken by some to mean that the academic idea is dying, and by others to mean that it is generating a new form of life. This chapter does not assume that constitutional organisation or reorganisation can by itself save the university from destruction or preserve it for a yet more brilliant future. But it does assume that in any country, troubled or peaceful, the question is worth discussing. My premises are that with all their faults, inherited and acquired, universities that can be made to work are better than universities which cannot; and that independent of the end product—whether defined as graduates, scholarly monographs, or discoveries in fundamental science—the existence of a university capable of governing itself by the consent of its members is some pointer, even if not a sufficient one, to the present or future capacity of a whole people to govern itself by a similar form of consent. To illustrate this last point a little: much can be learnt about the stability of British society by examining the *microcosmographia academica* of an Oxford or Cambridge college; and the depth of the roots which democracy has grown in West Germany since 1945 can more accurately be gauged by listening to German scholars, students, and parliamentarians dividing power between interest groups in a new university law for their own *Land* than by following the course of a West German Federal election campaign. The converse is also true. A people's inability to govern itself quickly shows in its universities. In Belgium, Flemings and Walloons have become unable to trust each other. For the famous medieval University of Louvain, this held out the prospect of partition. How do you divide a 600 year-old university? In 1970, feeling was running so high that the university library seemed likely to be divided by each side taking alternate floors, or alternate numbers in the catalogue. That still left the problem of the wine cellar. . . .

In recent years, many changes have been made or proposed in the internal and external government of universities in the countries surveyed by this book. But very few of the changes have been fundamental. It is always easier to give a new interest group—students or junior teachers— a share in government than to alter the structure of government itself, and only in a highly centralised system like the French is it possible to secure simultaneous change in the way a university governs itself, and in the way it is governed by the State. The argument of this chapter is that most changes, and most resistances to change, can be best understood by referring to the models of university organisation which are, or have been, available to their law-makers. As with all models for political organisation, the myth or image of human society on which they are based is also relevant.

For instance, the two passages printed at the head of this chapter present or imply two different models of communal organisation which have at different periods been adopted by universities. Although it was founded by a Spanish Cardinal, the College of Spain in medieval Bologna was run on lines to which the closest modern counterpart would be the universities of Sweden or Finland, with their student-run buildings and businesses. The rector, who held great disciplinary, administrative, and financial responsibilities, had to be a student, and was elected by secret ballot from the scholars' own ranks, with four councillors, also elected by secret ballot, to advise him. But the checks on the rector's behaviour, specified in the passage quoted, reveal that the model for the constitution was the self-governing community of the medieval monastery. The same statutes also reveal that the model of a university as a student-run community, hiring its own goods and services (including teaching) as it thinks fit, is one that has from the earliest times been available for imitation, though it has only lately been revived.

The second passage I quoted is no less eloquent of the model to which it appeals. The university, in the minds of English local councillors, is neither more nor less than a school, whose scholars must be whipped if they are disobedient, and whose 'masters' are directly responsible for passing on, along with a little learning, the moral attitudes and social customs of the surrounding community. Related to the history of English universities, this attitude is not as absurd as it now seems. To be *in statu pupillari*, in Tudor Oxford, did in fact mean that you were not safe from a whipping if you displeased your tutor (see p. 110); and in our own time, Governor Reagan of California has not hesitated to assert a local community's rights over the moral education of university students in its midst (p. 90). This position is not incompatible with the possession of quite sophisticated knowledge about the detailed workings of a higher education system: Reagan knows how to scrutinise and slash the University of California's budget, and the council spokesman who thought Keele students should be made to keep their trousers on evidently knew that the student-teacher ratio in British universities stood at 8 or 10 : 1, even if he had forgotten that in Britain, people are now legally adult at the age of eighteen.

These, then, are two probably irreconcilable models for university government and administration: the monastery and the school. Yet both, in one sense, rest upon the same myth of human behaviour, which is now more suspect among the young than any particular type of academic organisation: the myth of original sin. The Spanish Cardinal assumed that sooner or later, a Rector of his College would commit some of the sins which it was his duty to discourage, and would have to be disciplined and prevented from doing the same thing again. Scholars, even if endowed with democratic privileges, were still considered subject to the temptations appropriate to their age. (Statute LII: 'Moreover, since we understand that scholars often enter the cellar and kitchen without necessary or just cause, which at times gives rise to scandals and consequent harm to the college, we decree that no one among the scholars shall enter the cellar or kitchen without legitimate reason.' The motive given for this enactment is interesting. In Balliol in 1970, I heard tutors expressing anxiety at what a city magistrate might say about the college if students won the right to drink when they pleased in the college bar and then went out drunk to kill or be killed on the Oxford bypass.) The model of a university as a school also assumes original, though not necessarily total, depravity. Most of the rules in the schools which English municipal councillors in their youth attended were framed on the assumption that pupils would take their own or each other's trousers off unless they were specifically forbidden to.

It has not yet been proved that the myth of original sin is a worse guide to the framing of university constitutions than the myth of original virtue. However, it is obvious that neither of the two models which I have just described, and which depended on that myth, will do for a modern university. That has been obvious to the discerning for many years, and to that extent the crises of the 1960s could have been predicted. The monastic model could not stand once the values and desires of the secular world invaded the cloister. In the past, the masters concentrated on training doctors, lawyers, and clergymen to live and act by a life-pattern which the university had itself originally devised. But then they began to make and distribute original discoveries in science, which were intended to be exploited and modified for profit or national aggrandisement by people who shared none of the cloister's assumptions. Eventually it became necessary to pay scholars at the rate of a new 'leisure class', in order to dissuade them from leaving university for secular employment. (To bring the monastic analogy up to date, it is demoralising enough for his colleagues when a Catholic priest drops his vows and marries, but it would be a good deal more demoralising if an elaborate system of sabbaticals and fringe benefits had to be devised and offered to discourage others from following his example.)

The school model, though its artificial prolongation of adolescence had substantial material and intellectual advantages whichever side of the lectern you sat, only ever really thrived in Protestant cultures, and not even in all of those. In England and in the United States, where it had a long innings, it has been very suddenly dismissed. The fairytale flavour of Berkeley's Great Panty Raid in 1956 (see pp. 83–4) is one illustration of this, but there are plenty more. On both sides of the Atlantic professors and tutors, who a decade ago would have fought vigorously to confine student fornication to motels or vacations, now amiably tolerate whatever the boys and girls like to do on university premises during term-time, so long as it does not bring the cops in or frighten the donors. In Oxford in 1970, one scholar on the point of retirement told me gently and soberly that the style of the place had changed more in the two years just past than in the preceding forty, and in particular that college loyalties, societies, and daily social observances (like dining in hall) were losing strength so rapidly that it was a question for some colleges how long they could continue as self-contained social institutions. No one any longer wants an extension of school.

The decline of these hierarchical models led to the enunciation of a new one, based on the principle of voluntarism. One British Vice-Chancellor of a technological university has even suggested publicly that a university is like a golf-club whose rules students should expect to obey if they care to join it. (Jews and Negroes presumably excluded.) But this attempt to revive the model of the voluntary society, in a more explicitly secular form than the notion of a semi-sacred 'community of scholars', is doomed to failure in an advanced industrial country where most young people have no effective choice whether or not to attend a university: if they can, they do, and increase their earning power thereby; if they cannot, for want of intelligence or parental encouragement, they make do with the jobs the graduates leave.

Far more powerful, in a world community which traces most of its successes (and a few of its failures) to large-scale organisation, is the managerial or bureaucratic model of a university. The United States has been accustomed to this model for some time. Its evolution followed quite closely the evolution of the American business corporation from the dictatorship of the entrepreneur to the rise of the managers. Clark Kerr in his classic *The Uses of the University* dates the change from autocracy to bureaucracy in American universities somewhere in the decade 1935–45, and suggests that Robert Hutchins of Chicago (who is still alive and living in Santa Barbara) was the last of the giants 'in the sense that he was the last of the university presidents who really tried to change his institution in any fundamental way'. Kerr goes on to describe his own job in the Californian 'multiversity', which at the time of writing in 1963 employed 40,000 people (more than IBM) in over a hundred locations:

'There are several "nations" of students, of faculty, of alumni, of trustees, of public groups. Each has its territory, its jurisdiction, its form of government. Each can declare war on the others; some have the power of veto. Each can settle its own problems by a majority vote, but altogether they form no single constituency. It is a pluralistic society with multiple cultures. Coexistence is more likely than unity. Peace is one priority item, progress another.

'The president in the multiversity is leader, educator, creator, initiator, wielder of power, pump; he is *also* officeholder, caretaker, inheritor, consensus-seeker, persuader, bottleneck. But he is mostly a mediator.'[1]

[1] Kerr, op. cit., p. 36. But this concept of the presidential office and the university bureaucracy as a mere holder of the ring for faculty research entrepreneurs has lately been criticised. The administration 'failed to grasp the full impact which sponsored

The managerial revolution in universities took a surprisingly long time to cross the Atlantic. The British University Grants Committee was formed in 1919 to distribute Government money to the universities, but at the receiving end the Vice-Chancellorship of Oxford was until the 1960s rotated among heads of colleges on the principle of Buggins's turn. It was a testimony, partly to British conservatism, partly to the smooth operation of the system which Sir Eric Ashby has called 'government by consent and after consultation'. It took the Robbins Report (1963) to show the nation, and the Franks Report (1964) to show Oxford, that higher education could no longer be directed by gentleman's agreement; and the new universities, founded at about the same time, also brought forward a breed of executive head who was openly or secretly flattered to be described by the Sunday papers in the language formerly kept for the City pages, as 'abrasive', 'dynamic', 'spectacular'. The meaning of all this did not begin to dawn on the British public, nor on students, until during the agitated years 1967–70 relationships began to go sour at one or two of the new institutions. The 1965 edition of Anthony Sampson's *Anatomy of Britain* reports that 'the University of Warwick, largely promoted by the late Lord Rootes, plans to be a huge, cosmopolitan technological place, and a bluff dynamo-don, Jack Butterworth, is its Vice-Chancellor' (p. 237). By 1970 one of Lord Roote's successors, a member of the University Council, had sent an industrial spy to bring back a report of a meeting addressed by a visiting American political scientist,[2] and the Assembly of academic staff had carried a motion asking Mr. Butterworth to resign.[3] But of the documents discovered and circulated during the student sit-in at Warwick, the most germane to my present point was the 1968 report of a firm of management consultants on the running of the university (the Tyzack Report), which concluded:

'Taken as a whole, the University is certainly inefficient by normal commercial or industrial standards; it is inefficient in its decision-making processes, in its administrative structure, and in many of its administrative practices. . . .

'Roughly half the University's annual expenditure on income account is devoted to paying the salaries of the academic staff. It is difficult to envisage economies in this sphere which do not involve

---

research would have on the full round of activities of the university. Until recently, it failed to understand that sponsored research would make the university much larger and would enlarge its graduate educational activities.' (Frederick Betz and Carlos Kruytbosch, 'Sponsored Research and University Budgets', in *Minerva* VIII, 4 (October, 1970), pp. 492–519.

[2] E. P. Thompson (ed.), *Warwick University Ltd.* (London, 1970), p. 107.

[3] *The Guardian*, June 1970.

an increase in the ratio of students to academic staff, or an increase in the proportion of lower-paid senior staff. Clearly only marginal changes in teaching costs can be expected, unless there is a country-wide change of view in universities, for no university alone could embark on revolutionary changes in academic structure. Nevertheless, marginal improvements are possible and should be actively sought at Warwick in the long term interests of the University, which for many reasons demands expansion far beyond its present size. . . .

'The Vice-Chancellor . . . has to represent his University in the outside world, fostering its interests in the highest circles, attracting financial support, and enhancing its status by playing a part in the public life of the University world at large both inside and outside the United Kingdom. His image is its image . . .

'Sooner or later, the University of Warwick will have to come to terms with the age-old conflict between democratic principles and effective government. In its early days, the policy of allowing everybody to have his say in nearly every cause and problem was workable. At its present size, the resulting system of committees and debating forums is a source of inefficiency.'[4]

I do not cite these paragraphs to show that the managerial model of a university is by its nature, or by the nature of its exponents, biased against any particular group of people within a university. This may be true; on the other hand the authors of this report told the Vice-Chancellor that his students, for example, suffered from many grievances, both 'objective' and 'subjective'. The point to notice is rather the number of challenges quite casually posed to normal British academic assumptions about the style of life appropriate to the pursuit of learning. The doctrine of efficiency dictates that direct democracy—'the policy of allowing everybody to have his say in nearly every cause and problem'—is unworkable. The doctrine of uniformity and technical compatibility dictates that 'no university alone could embark on revolutionary changes in academic structure'. The paragraph in the *Tyzack Report* about the functions of the Vice-Chancellor is particularly interesting to anyone who knows the history of this curiously-named office. The Chancellor of the University of Oxford—an office now so formal that the Oxford MAs could trust Harold Macmillan with it while he was still Prime Minister, and later listen to him telling them that it was one of the few offices from which he could not possibly be ejected—was originally the Bishop of Lincoln's private eye on the unreliable scholars of distant Oxenford. A century or two passed, and the scholars managed to co-opt the Chancellor; another century or two, and he was representing their interests at Court, so that executive power in the university (such as it

---

[4] Reports reprinted in Thompson, op. cit., pp. 136–143.

then was) passed to his deputy. Now it is for the deputy—in Warwick, the 'bluff dynamo don'—to represent his University in the outside world, 'fostering its interests in the highest circles'. Behind him he leaves, not a deputy, but a bureaucracy.

It is important to realise that this development does not only affect university administration. If it did, there would be no struggles. In Britain today, as in America yesterday and Germany tomorrow, the problem is that the old, enjoyable, vertical distinctions between institutions—for example, the custom that Oxford men pole a punt from the opposite end to Cambridge men—are now cut across by interest groups which have much more in common with like-minded people elsewhere than they have with anyone they meet in quad or refectory. The visible symbols of this are the itinerant student agitator, and the microbiologist or econometrist whose face is more familiar to colleagues in Turin or Toronto than it is to his own pupils. But the less visible symbols may be more important. In every British university now, there have to be people at or near the top who know how to play the Government Research Councils, draw up a rolling decennial plan, manage the outflow of news, and anticipate the questions of the Public Accounts Committee. That is what the British have willed by acquiring, in the course of a single decade, the resolve to hold universities answerable for the public money they spend, and the expectation that academics will by some alchemical process transmute advanced knowledge into economic growth. But it is then no surprise if the people entrusted with tasks of this nature have more to say to officials of the Ford Foundation or the managing directors of large companies than to labour historians and literary critics in their own universities. This often happens even if the chief executive concerned starts out in the job as a scholar among scholars. One of the very few criticisms I heard voiced—by an academic—of Charles Carter at Lancaster (see p. 180) was that he tended to neglect his own powers of academic *leadership* in favour of building up the university's academic *enterprises*, which improved its financial position and public reputation. This may or may not have been a fair criticism, but it serves to underline the point that the outstanding characteristic of the managerial model for a university is its strength. It pulls people along in its wake, whatever their initial desires were, and it does so because, on one level, it works. Europeans, C. P. Snow once wrote, are sometimes surprised to learn that about eighty per cent of the pure science being done in the entire West is being done in the United States, and most of us were surprised to learn from Robert Oppenheimer than of all the scientists who had ever lived, ninety-three per cent were alive in 1960. But even Europeans who have digested these statements sometimes remain under the misapprehension that it is all because Americans are rich. Much more probably, it is because, long before the Federal Government needed big science and needed it quickly, American universities had taken the managerial model into their systems.[5] In nineteenth-century Europe, research and higher education were regarded by the individual as a *beruf*, or calling, and by the nation as a luxury of which only a little could be afforded. By the turn of the century, the managerial university in the US made both into a business. Professor Ben-David thus describes the change:

> 'The fact that the United States universities were to a large extent non-governmental bodies made it necessary for them to develop an enterprising leadership and efficient administration. For the European civil servant in charge of the matter the problem of financing universities posed itself in the form of how to spend as little as possible given an established set of objectives and a scale of priorities. The American university president, however, had to ask himself how to increase income by convincing a variety of donors about the importance of the university and by finding new markets and extending existing ones for its services. For the university president the range of objectives and the scale of priorities were not regarded as given.'[6]

This is how the American university and segments of American industry came to look—as Clark Kerr confesses—more and more alike. Professor Ben-David adds that 'the vice-chancellor in English universities has somewhat similar functions, but his scope of enterprise and powers are more limited'. As in several other respects, British universities are in this sense half-way between those of the United States and those of Western Europe. But they are edging closer to the US all the time, not least because their professors in all disciplines now trip to and fro very easily across the Atlantic, and can see for themselves that in American universities today, the professors have themselves largely displaced the president as the institution's chief fund-raisers and go-getters.

Given the power of the managerial model, and given the sums of money involved (in the US, about a billion and a half dollars a year, mostly from the Federal Government, for basic research in the sciences) it is rather surprising that not just the social sciences, which have pretensions to 'usefulness', but the humanities too, have prospered as much as they have. If there is a 'crisis in the humanities'[7] in the US, it is intellectual rather than merely financial. The balance in the minds of presidents and vice-chancellors is much better preserved than one would expect from the head of a large business who knew that—as a British Conservative

---

[5] According to Lord Bowden (in a letter to the author), 'before 1939 the Americans took it for granted that the best research would be done in Europe and that they would exploit it. The whole university scene was transformed by Vannevar Bush's reports called *Science—the Endless Frontier*, which he wrote for President Roosevelt at the end of the War.'

[6] Joseph Ben-David, *Fundamental Research and the Universities* (OECD, 1968), p. 36.

[7] J. H. Plumb (ed.), *The Crisis in the Humanities* (London, 1964). See also *Daedalus* ('Future of the Humanities' issues, Summer, 1969).

Minister once remarked—'you can buy a professor of Greek for three thousand pounds a year and a Liddell and Scott, but a professor of science may cost a million pounds of equipment.'[8] Arts men grumble, of course, about the gleaming new laboratories, complete with reception desks for visiting dignitaries, which seem to go up overnight on their campuses, but in Britain and America they do not—like their overloaded counterparts in French or German universities—murmur bloody revolution. There are several possible reasons for this. It cannot be fear of student uproar, for that has only entered into people's calculations since 1964, and it cannot be a sense of cultural and political solidarity across the Snow line, for in most universities none exists. However, any President or Vice-Chancellor who wants peace in his own house has to reckon with the mentality of the professorial 'guild', and the political pressures it is capable of mounting within and without the institution without distinction of disciples. It is also relevant that the line between 'purity' and 'utility' is not drawn conveniently between the sciences and the humanities. The professor of astro-physics with his million-pound machine may be as 'pointlessly' obsessed with the question of how much hydrogen there is in the outer layer of a blue star as his colleague with the Liddell and Scott is obsessed with a fragment of a lost play by Sophocles. Both are spending tax-payers' money without hope of an economic return, so why should they be treated unequally?

However, there is here a prior question: why should either of them be spending tax-payers' money without hope of an economic return? There is also a subsequent question: if professors like these are to be hired for activities whose return can only be measured—or rhetorically justified —in social or even quasi-spiritual terms, how are we to assess the Californian professor of Agricultural Automation whose return may be economic but anti-social, or the Defence Department micro-biologist whose return may be anti-social without even being economic? And what price is to be put on the heads of the managerial university's most conspicuous, though only partly-finished, product; educated men and women? The formulation of each question is associated in the public mind with student revolts. But it does not have to be. Neutrally stated, the change which the questions, and all the turbulence of the past six years, represent is the appearance on the world screen of a new model for the structure of academic organisms: a political one. Not the monastery, not the school, not the voluntary society, and not the corporation; but the internal and external relations of the city-state, the town meeting, or the village soviet are the precedents to which unconscious appeal is now made. There are several points of interest, and also of extreme difficulty, in this development.

For one thing, it represents a shift, not only of model, but also of

[8] Sampson, op. cit., p. 243.

underlying myth. I have already argued that both the monastic and the pedagogical models of university organisation assumed the depravity of some or all of the people by whom the model was meant to be operated. The voluntarist and the managerial models, by contrast, assumed not depravity, nor yet perfectibility, but rationality. People who pay their own money to join a golf-club may or may not pick up their balls in the rough when no one is looking, or seek to escape standing their round in the bar, but they are unlikely to drive a plough across the greens. People whose services are retained by a great corporation, or who consume its products, are not expected to question its goals, though they are permitted and even encouraged to make it more efficient, whether through the force of market choice and rejection, or through the company suggestions box. Even from the humbler levels of the work-force rationality of a kind is expected. The lads, that is, may push their luck in industrial bargaining, but will agree that something has gone wrong if the effect of their militancy is to close the plant and throw themselves out of work. (That happens, of course, especially in the British and American newspaper-printing industry, but people never quite believe that it is going to happen until it is too late.) Universities in different countries vary considerably in the room they allow for the free play of market forces in their own structure. Freedom for both students and professors to shop around for better conditions of research, teaching, salary, climate, or instruction is greater in the United States than it has ever been anywhere else. German university students traditionally enjoyed, though now less often make use of, freedom to migrate from one campus to another during their student careers. In England, until very recently, not only students but even professors had little chance—and seemingly little desire—to migrate from campus to campus.[9] In Japan the entire higher education system is frozen and stratified by prestige to a degree which a foreigner, especially an American, does not easily understand.

But almost universally in the free world, universities have been administered as an 'open' system, in which engagement was voluntary, and wrecking parties correspondingly rare. In this sense the title of James Ridgeway's book on the military and industrial involvements of American universities, *The Closed Corporation*, is a misnomer. As long as the model of American university operation really was 'corporate' or managerial, its activities were open. The practices, some odious and some innocent, that Ridgeway describes signified—though this was for some time not realised—a politicisation of the entire model, complete with Official

[9] I am indebted to Mr. Frank Heller for the suggestion that the comparative immobility of European academics derives from the steep pyramidal structure of their profession, which is also divided, especially in Britain, into numerous grades. In the US the proportion of full or associate professors is higher, and even assistant professors have considerable powers and responsibilities within a department. The structure is simpler and, as it were, flattened. It encourages lateral movement.

Secrets Act. And with politicisation of the model arrived a new revision of the underlying myth. No longer could rationality and at least conditional goodwill be safely attributed to all participants in the enterprise, for the university was becoming a paradigm of the larger society in which, notoriously, these qualities cannot be relied upon. On the other hand, it was impossible to return to the monastic model's assumption that all members of the institution were in equal need of being recalled to the Rule by prayer and occasional scourging. As for the pedagogical model's assumption that all masters were virtuous and all pupils depraved, this was difficult to operate in practice, because it was obviously untrue—and besides, where did you put graduate students? The conditions were right for depravity and unreliability to be defined, as in the wider society, not by absolute criteria but by the group which happened to be dominant. As long as the permeation of the entire academic system by politics could be concealed from the system's constituents, this meant that the university's faculty and administration could, in their own eyes and also in other people's, do no serious wrong. Quite unconsciously, they simply enlarged their concept of the mission of a university to include whatever society proposed, from Project Manhattan and Project Camelot to the humblest research contract from the Education Office or the Milk Marketing Board, and it would have been a rash student or perilously isolated professor who objected, even if he knew about it. It is always in the interests of the conservative element in society to conceal as long as possible the political component in any decision, because once people pick up the sound of political gears engaging, they begin to ask themselves in a wider frame of reference where their own interest lies.

Sooner or later, of course, an opposition had to arise. It was precipitated in different countries by different external phenomena which nevertheless posed similar challenges to similar kinds of people: in the US the Left and the young were aroused by Civil Rights, in Britain by nuclear weapons, in France and Germany by the Algerian War, in Japan by an Occupation which was artificially prolonged by the Korean War. For a long time, the University's unique combination of managerialism and mystification preserved its own structure intact, but by the time its internal politicisation was made explicit, the positions which the parties took up were too fixed for political adjustments to be made. The attackers saw vicious depravity, the defenders foolish utopianism: each side was convinced that the other had no place in a university; and since the defenders called in aid the 'rationality' of the managerial model from which they were gradually being dislodged, the attackers were forced to argue, in some cases, that rationality had no place in a university either.

There are several difficulties, not yet resolved and possibly irresoluble, about the political model for a university community. The most important is that its predecessor, the managerial model, is not only far from dead, but in several countries has yet to evolve. To be more precise: in Britain it is approaching adulthood, in France and Germany it is infant, in Italy and Japan it is unheard of. Only in the United States, of the countries under review, might it be described as senescent, and this hesitantly, for if under pressure from without the American university's golden age is ending, its strength and variety is such that it can still, like Father William, kick its juniors downstairs. Other countries will find it no easier than Britain has done to forgo its benefits. Yet by its very success, as we can now see, it drags the political model in its train. The university becomes all-inclusive. The margins between campus and society blur. Soon, all the conflicts of interest already familiar from political life are repeated in the academic microcosm, which is unprepared for them because, according to its own theory of itself, they should not occur.

The fascination of higher education today, considered internationally, consists largely in the spectacle of university administrations and Ministries of Education squirming to achieve systems of American managerial efficiency without either abandoning their cultural history, touching off their students again, or incurring expense of an American order of magnitude. In most countries, success is still in doubt. Britain is by far the most comfortably placed, with a stable domestic political situation (to which Ulster is regarded as a peripheral annoyance), an immensely strong tradition of academic organisation, and no serious backlog of material investment to make up at the tertiary level (schools are another matter). Imminent politicisation of Britain's peacefully adopted managerial model is showing at three points; parliamentary insistence on greater control over university budgets, symbolised by a faster growth rate in the public sector of higher education ('polytechnics') than in the semi-private, privileged sector ('universities'); restiveness at all levels in both sectors at the prospect of the class divisions that have bedevilled British education at the primary and secondary levels being repeated at tertiary level; and within institutions, collisions between politicised students and unreformed academic decision-makers, who apply, on the whole, a monastic model in universities and a pedagogic model in polytechnics.

Japan, on present form, will be capable of incurring the expense of bringing her universities up to a civilised standard as soon as she chooses to do so, and there is no cultural tradition involved in her Germano-American, century-old, higher education system that she is not capable of re-inventing. No country in the world is so adept at rapid social change. Her students, however, are deeply alienated from the mainstream of political society, and even if they could be persuaded to participate in the direction of new model universities, the risks involved might well seem too great for the country's timidly conservative, businessman's administration.

Italy has neither money nor managerial competence in her higher education system, and in a heartlessly long perspective, it might be better for her universities to remain substantially unreformed until the job can be done under conditions of political stability. The universities of themselves cannot contribute much to the achievement of that stability, and under present conditions, interference with them seems certain to disrupt what cultural tradition they retain without achieving anything but pockets of technocratic efficiency in a wilderness of political despair.

France is of all countries the least likely voluntarily to create a discontinuity between her remodelled institutions and her cultural inheritance, and judgment must be suspended while the system is digesting the uniquely French paradox of a centrally-imposed decentralisation and an officially-sponsored politicisation. Like Italy, however, France has not yet faced squarely the question whether she can continue to admit to higher education all qualified applicants in whatever subject and district they care to apply. Economically she probably cannot sustain the expense of a true mass system of higher education, but schisms which lie close to the surface of her social and political structure make it difficult for her administrators to get away with saying yes to some and no to others.

Western Germany is a still more interesting case, for there the self-government of minorities, and the relations of universities to their public sources of money and legitimation, are at the present time developing in unforeseen and original ways. Essentially, what seems to be happening is the simultaneous imposition of both the managerial and the political models of a university on to an existing model which has elements of both monasticism and voluntarism. But since no German university has yet been discussed in these pages, some preliminary detail is needed before the argument can be resumed.

The German idea of a university, as the visitor to Tokyo, Chicago, and Manchester well knows, has during the last century and a half been the most powerful in the world. It dates from 1809/10, when a Prussian gentleman-scholar, Wilhelm von Humboldt, founded the University of Berlin to express his conception of a university as a place where culture, education, and original research (*Kultur, Bildung, Forschung*) are inextricably linked.[10] At that time, Oxford and Cambridge were finishing schools for gentlemen in which a few scholars of world reputation happened to live and work; Yale and Harvard were teaching a set classical and theological curriculum to the sons of the newly-independent colonists; and scientific discovery, whether in Paris, London, or north Italy, was only casually associated with the historic universities and the education of the young. Examples could be multiplied of important intellectual innovations which under these conditions were stored away on the innovator's death. Mathematical statistics, as practised by Pascal and Laplace, had to wait for the twentieth century and the computer to be fully exploited. But within half a century of von Humboldt's foundation, German scholarship was an international byword—a rude word, indeed, in Oxford and Cambridge, but the procession of Americans travelling to Germany in search of Ph.Ds told its own tale. In the sciences, the success of the new method of academic organisation was dramatic. Professor Ben-David accounts for it in this way:

> 'Due to the introduction of laboratory training in the German universities, the span of time and space between the inception of ideas and the working out of their implications in experimental research was decreased radically. What used to be accomplished by the undirected efforts of scientists working over decades or centuries, singly or with one or two disciples far away from each other, became now the co-operative task of relatively large groups of advanced students concentrated round one or several teachers.'[11]

[10] See von Humboldt's 1809/10 memorandum, *Uber die innere und aüssere Organisation der höheren wissenschaftlichen Anstalter zu Berlin* (Berlin, 1903), translated by Edward Shils in *Minerva*, April 1970, pp. 242–50. Also a recent paperback in German: Peter Berglar, *Wilhelm von Humboldt* (Rowohlt, Hamburg, 1970).

[11] Op. cit., p. 29.

By these methods was developed the now-familiar cycle of idea →
co-ordinated research → fundamental discovery → applied research and
development → useful or profitable exploitation. The development of
aniline dyes, and the demonstration that numerous diseases are bacterially
caused, were early examples, and the two separate fields came together
with Ehrlich's discovery that chemical weapons borrowed from dyestuffs
could be used against the spirochaete that causes syphilis.

The expense of these developments was considerable, and could only
be provided by the State. The Hegelianism dominant in early nineteenth-
century Prussia made this easy to arrange, and the same philosophy's
elitist implications made it correspondingly easy to decide who should
rule the system at institutional level. It was, and in most respects still is,
the professor (Ordinarius) who decides what courses to offer to undergraduates, what shall be the emphasis of his own research team, and (in
committee with his colleagues at faculty and university level) what
appointments shall be made, expenditures passed, and reforms admitted.
The freedom of the professor to teach what he pleased how he pleased
(*Lehrfreiheit*) and the freedom of the student to seek education and choose
courses where he pleased and at his own pace (*Lernfreiheit*) were absolute.
The conservative stranglehold exerted by most faculties of most German
universities was not inherent in the system, but was the product of the
nineteenth century German social structure and political assumptions.

The system was ruined by its own spectacular success, which disguised
from Germans the flaws, both intellectual and administrative, that it
contained. It was difficult to quarrel with a system that produced for
German nationals between 1901 and 1950 more Nobel prizes than went
to any other country (39 out of a total of 164). But in the period 1951–66
the United States had 44 (out of a total of 88) and Germany had 7; nor
does the detailed evidence support the natural conclusion that it could
all be blamed on the Nazi catastrophe. The cross-over point on the graph
occurred between the wars. Intellectually, the difficulty was of the professors' own making. The knowledge explosion was not accompanied
by departmental reorganisation and 'trade-offs' to take account of the
new maps of learning. The professor was supposed to be master of his
'discipline', even when the discipline had become impossible to master.
(One sociological polymath from this tradition, though by now firmly
entrenched in American university culture, lamented to me in 1969 that
whereas until about 1950 he had been able to keep abreast of all the
important literature in his subject, in several languages, this was no longer
possible.) But if the German professor could no longer master his discipline intellectually, he could still master it hierarchically, by subordinat-
ing the newer research institutes to the interests of university professors,
and by preserving the fiction that his ever-enlarging team of *privatdozenten*
and research students were bound together in the same intimate, familial,
discipular nexus that had been the basic unit of the original system.

When German history recommenced after 1945, this form of peda-gogical and hierarchical organisation was not, as it was in Japan, reformed by the Western occupying powers, in spite of the ease with which it had been 'captured' by National Socialism during the 1930s. It seemed more important to provide higher education quickly for returning veterans, and to preserve continuity with a system whose historical excellence most English and American educators recognized. A new departure was made only in Berlin, where it was necessary to create a 'free' institution as a counter to the old Wilhelm Humboldt University (included in the East Zone). The Free University, built with Ford Foundation money, pro-vided for token student representation on faculty committees and the Senate, but by the 1960s it was obvious that—as one student put it to me—you could not make a radical university with reactionary professors. As at Berkeley, political discussions in university buildings were pro-hibited, and an assistant lecturer lost his job for revealing in a newspaper article the political background of a decision taken by the Academic Senate. Meanwhile, the SPD and the CDU between them saw to it that ideological stagnation prevailed in Bonn; and everywhere in Germany, the multiplication of qualified school-leavers (*abiturienten*), together with the migration of able young people from the East Zone, began to produce the constituents of mass higher education, without the human, material, or administrative resources for shaping it into a system. Student numbers doubled to 280,000 between 1958 and 1968, and in several faculties—especially those which traditionally led to teaching posts—the ratio of students to staff declined to about 40 : 1. Libraries and seminar rooms be-came intolerably over-crowded, and between a third and a half of arts students left university without a final degree. Although the proportion of the staff possessing professorial rank had declined from seventy per cent in 1890 to fifteen per cent in the 1960s, their influence on university decisions was unchanged, and they remained the only people entitled to act as examiners, so students often met 'their' professor for the first time in the final, often decisive, oral exams.[12] (This, a commonplace in British universities which have external examiners, is a traumatic experience for a German student. In theory, the student tells his professor when he is ready to take his exam. His professor asks him a few questions, and shakes him by the hand, or alternatively tells him to go away and do a little more preparation. This civilised, if sometimes invidious, procedure is hardly possible if the professor has never set eyes on the student before.)

The student revolution of the 1960s began earlier in Berlin than any-where else in Europe. The Free University's first large scale strike on a free speech issue took place in May 1965, a year after Berkeley's, and in general, Berlin's uncomfortable geo-political situation seems to make it an initiator of trends which are taken up elsewhere. (This is an ill omen

[12] The analysis in this paragraph draws on an essay by Eva Weller and Wilfried van der Will in Julian Nagel (ed.), *Student Power* (London, 1969), pp. 45–58.

for the structural reforms of German universities at the present time, which have reduced Berlin, but so far nowhere else, to unmanageable chaos.) Besides, the German student movement has a kind of adulthood seldom found in other countries. The reasons are simple: Germans do not take their *abitur* exam until they are twenty, and then after military service they spend at least five years (nine to ten semesters) at university before they take their first *staatsexamen*. At the same time, the historical academic situation described above brought about a particularly close alliance between students and *assistenten*, who are now paid junior teachers, but were until recently unsalaried. The student movement also derived a certain philosophical and political seriousness from the Central European Marxist tradition and its longest-surviving curators, of whom Herbert Marcuse and the late T. W. Adorno are examples. German students were therefore far more likely than French or Italian ones to seek reform of the university system itself, which many of them did not expect to leave until they were thirty or so; nor did the German political situation, indignant though they were about it, present the Gramscian 'gelatinous-ness' that could tempt them to pursue for very long a programme of revolutionary adventurism in streets and factories. Consequently, through much of the period in which the *Bund*, the *Länder*, industrial leaders, and the *Wissenschaftsrat* [13] have been tabling proposals for managerial reform and updating of German universities, the Left has been prepared with a political model for the same purpose.

By 'model' I had better make clear that I do not mean 'programme'. It is of the essence of the political model that it begins with the issue of power and control, and leaves the issue of content to be decided by the winners. The official reformers are above all anxious to reduce the length of time which German students are obliged to take over a degree, which would entail introducing an intermediate qualification for those who do not intend to proceed to academic research; to slow down or at least control the rate of growth in student enrolments, by *numerus clausus* or other means; and to make the internal organisation of universities and their academic programmes more responsive to national manpower needs, without abandoning the traditionally close German association between education, professional training, and exact scholarship. However, these aims—which are only the German version of what preoccupies Ministers responsible for higher education the world over—are in Germany provisional and tentative, for in educational questions, though Bonn has the money, it does not yet have much power. Education remains the res-

[13] The *Wissenschaftsrat* (Council for Science and Learning), founded in 1957, is a joint body whose members are nominated by the Federal and Land governments, and by the University Rectors' Conference. Its reports and inquiries are usually adopted as official policy. See for instance the 1966 report on university reform translated in *Minerva*, April 1970 (pp. 250–267). The *Wissenschaftsrat* is now responsible for preparing an overall plan for research and higher education in Germany.

ponsibility of the *Land* governments, and since it is their last major sphere of control, they will not easily surrender it. However, in 1969 the Federal Chancellor, Willy Brandt, felt strong enough to establish a joint *Bund* and *Länder* group for educational planning, and initiated the drafting of a skeleton Federal law for higher education, on which negotiations proceed.

This regional structure provided the radical reformers with their opportunity. A centralised system, like those of France, Italy, and Japan, would have confronted them with the embattled conservatism of a national Civil Service and the anxious resistances of a mass electorate. But in Germany there is still an internal, invisible frontier which divides the Protestant, Social Democratic north from the Catholic, Christian Democratic south, and north of that line, once the attention of the SPD's left wing was focussed upon the university question, one SPD *Land* after another passed an *universitätsgesetz* (university law) restructuring the university more or less on the lines that the reasonable section of the Left requested.

The most spectacular result of the new laws has been the election, in Berlin and Hamburg by the time of writing, of an *assistent* to the office whose title was formerly *Rector Magnificus* and is now simply *Präsident*. The enormity of this change can only be comprehended if one has tasted the social flavour of a German professorial team. At one north German university I called upon an arts professor, politically a liberal, and a scholar of international renown who seemed to have been a visiting professor at most of the universities mentioned in this book. His *assistent* was present, and during the conversation we discussed the impact of the reforms that had taken place, and their effect upon the lives of people in the university. In the course of the hour, the *assistent* opened his mouth, I think, twice. His true function was to pour the tea, hand round the chocolate biscuits, and listen to what his professor had to say. If a generous man with an international outlook could maintain this style, it was easy to believe reports of other professors whose *assistenten* used to be expected to baby-sit, do the washing, and in the intervals, contribute unacknowledged research to the professor's current book.

These elections of *assistenten* to the presidency were the predictable result of the system known as *drittelparität*, which the law enforces. *Drittelparität* has (as yet) no exact equivalent in English. It means the sharing of voting strength between the three main interest groups which constitute the university: professors, *dozenten* and *assistenten*, and students. Once this principle was admitted into the bodies—Council and academic Senate—by which German universities are governed, the post of chief executive was almost bound to go to a member of the middle group, as the only candidate upon whom professors and students were able to compromise. So it was in Berlin, where a thirty-one year-old sociologist, Rolf Kreibich, was elected president after a poll in which four-fifths of the *assistenten* and only one-fifth of the students voted. In Hamburg, similarly, the job went to a thirty-seven year-old theologian from Bonn,

Peter Fischer-Appelt, whose power base and qualifications for administrative office was his chairmanship of the all-German Conference of Assistants.

The system is well exemplified in Hamburg. Neither the city nor the university is readily associated with extremism. Hamburg has been an international port for five centuries, and in protesting against the merciless bombing to which it was subjected in 1943 Bishop Bell of Chichester was able to tell the House of Lords that it had been a centre of German democratic opposition to Hitler. (Max Liebermann, whose painting of the *Hamburgerische Professorenkonvent* in the City Art Gallery gives a splendid impression of German scholarship, all full beards and drooping moustaches, is said to have muttered when the Nazis came to power: '*Man kann nicht so viel fressen wie man kotzen mochte*'—'You can't swallow as much as you'd like to vomit'.) The university, a large one, with 20,000 students, an extensive campus, and numerous new buildings just outside the old city wall by Dammtor station—was founded in 1919. It has traditional strengths in medicine, physics, overseas economics, and evangelical theology, but no obvious weaknesses. In 1968/9 it was subjected, like other German universities, to sustained attacks by student radicals, who wisely concentrated on the least defensible aspects of the professorial system, and campaigned under banners like '*Unter den Talaren Moff von tausend Jahren*' ('Under the moss of centuries') and—referring to the particularly well-entrenched medical faculty—'Every tenth private bed makes the Herr Professor fat' (*bett* and *fett* rhyming). The university was closed altogether by the police for a fortnight in 1969. The result of the agitation was that the Left obtained from the City and Land of Hamburg a university law on *drittelparität* lines.

From the legislature's point of view the law was undoubtedly framed, not merely out of sympathy with moderate students' case against the university, but out of a desire to be rid of the institution as a daily creator of problems. The University of Hamburg, though still dependent on the *Land* for money, now has an autonomy closer to that enjoyed by the British civic universities. However, only time will show how real this autonomy is. The old Rectors, though the office was circulated among the professors every three years, could afford—such was their intellectual and social status—to behave as though the state legislature and budget did not exist. The new President, although elected for a seven-year period and obliged by the law to have had some administrative experience beforehand, may in spite of his 'democratic' support within the university be easier for outside interests to capture.

It is too early, also, to judge the effect of *drittelparität* at university level. The Hamburg branch of the VDS[14] boycotted the first university

---

[14] The German students' organisation, *Verband Deutscher Studentenschaft* has 250,000 members nationally. Its politicisation was recognised in 1969 by the withdrawal of Government financial support. The SDS, which launched the revolts of 1967–68, was by 1970 a comparatively negligible force, with 2,500 members.

elections, so the student members of Senate and Council were in 1970 moderates. Herr Fischer-Appelt, who appears for interview flanked by professional administrators, is still feeling his way, though he talks confidently of getting even the medical schools under social and financial control eventually. (That problem, however, cannot easily be solved by one university alone. In Germany, even top men in academic medicine only make about half what they can earn in private practice. The earnings of a private consultant may reach DM130,000 a year, less thirty-five per cent for running expenses. Hence the system of private beds in the excellently equipped university clinics, which allow the medical professor to have the best of both worlds. Reform at a single university would merely drive the best men elsewhere.)

More immediately painful are the effects of the law at departmental level. The old faculties have been swept away and replaced with perhaps six times as many *fachbereiche*, or subject committees, all with their own form of *drittelparität*. The *fachbereich* elects, from its own midst, the administrative chief of the department, who need no longer be the professor, and it also makes academic appointments at junior level. There is also provision for a departmental general assembly (*vollversammlung*), but the number of students who bother to attend is very low. The real fights take place in the *fachbereich*, where the law does not insist, as it does for the University Council and Senate, on full *drittelparität*. For example, in the Hamburg History department, the parity consisted of up to twelve professors, three *dozenten*, three *assistenten*, and six students, giving a built-in professorial majority. At the time of my visit the Left, led by one of the *dozenten* whose personal and professional friendship with one of the professors gave the struggle an extra piquancy, was arguing for a parity of nine professors, six *dozenten*, six *assistenten*, and nine students.[15] This is a balance which in any critical decision would force one or two members of any one group to 'cross the floor' and vote on the questions' merits. 'And besides,' the Left argues with assumed innocence, 'three fewer professors on the committee means that three more professors have time for their research.'

For in fact, the exorbitant demands on time which the new system makes are its most serious drawback. True, some professors have tried to claim that several of the new university laws contravene the German constitution's provision for academic freedom in teaching and research—the freedom, that is, to do as an individual something which the *fachbereich* committee might consider inexpedient—and the history of extremism among German student movements in this century makes the fear understandable. (German students were, in fact, Nazi before the Nazis. They demanded academic self-government in the twenties as a slogan

[15] The same man, Dr. Imanuel Geiss, has acted as the political catalyst on the founding committee for the University of Bremen (see pp. 187–8 ff.).

against liberal professors, and when their chance came in 1933, they stormed classrooms, assaulted Jewish and Socialist students, and contributed to the banishment, over a four-year period, of 1,600 professors from universities and *Hochschulen*.) However, democracy has its own terrors. One *dozent* in the Overseas Economics Department, which has eighteen professors and twenty *dozenten* to 4,500 students—a ratio considerably worse than 1 : 100, lightened only by the part-time grading and invigilating work of *assistenten*—described the position:

'You can fight off the radical students and the law's interference with freedom of research, but when the end of term brings 160 exam scripts, you just don't have the time left for anything. In this department the chances of outside earnings are good—usually about twenty per cent on top of academic salary—but it's going down because the reputation of the university in business circles has suffered. It's no longer thought useful to have a professor put his name to a company document just because he is a professor. In fact it is being said that if you are at the university it is because you did not have a better offer from elsewhere: from industry, from government.'

A professor of German Literature also spoke of 'the intolerable time spent on discussion without real results', and went on sadly:

'I have done no serious work for two years. We are being punished for past failures, and it's hard because most of us lost much time during the war. Now, when we are in a position to work, we are faced with this. But the radicals are not soft-hearted. I was in a concentration camp for the last eighteen months of the war but they tried to make a Nazi of me.'

Leftist *dozenten* have more stomach for the fight, and argue further that the interminable discussion is a phase that has to be passed through before the new system can run as smoothly as the old one superficially appeared to. But everyone is wondering whether the next few years' intake of students will be as radical as the intakes of the sixties. For in Germany the post-war baby boom started much later than in France, Britain, and the United States, so that the agitations of 1967/8 did not coincide with the peak in student numbers. Had it done, there might have been much more serious trouble. Trouble may arrive anyway, for in Germany, as elsewhere, political missionaries have taken radical tactics into the schools. 'In Hamburg,' said one professor, 'the schools are seriously upset. Scholars attend when they like—and this is Germany!' On the other hand, the newest generation of students is behaving more calmly. It is this generation which will decide whether a democratic university can also be an efficient one.

Few Germans at the present time would claim to have discovered yet how a university should be governed in an industrial or 'post-industrial' society. All the same, the history of the world of learning over the past five years does suggest that of the five models discussed here, only the political one stands much chance of ultimate acceptance by all the parties concerned. To review the reasons:

(1) The monastic model, within which all members of a hierarchically organised institution obey a set of rules metaphysically prescribed, was the matrix out of which universities in the West and the East were shaped. The physical lay-out of Cambridge in the English Fens, or of Buddhist Koyasan in the pine-clad mountains above Osaka, testifies to the cultural fertility of the model and also to its survival power. But there is little hope of transplanting it, nor even of preserving it unaltered in its original setting. A time and a society whose governing principle is pluralism has put out of the question any general or lasting agreement on a single source of external authority.

(2) The pedagogic model, which overlaps at several points with the first, has become obsolete through demographic and sociological changes which are probably irreversible. It will be no easier in the twenty-first century than it was in the Middle Ages to treat twenty year-olds—still less, as in German universities and American graduate schools, twenty-five year-olds—as a separate race of elderly children. The prolongation of middle-class childhood within the walls of an institution can now be recognised as a nineteenth century conception. The conception owed something to protective evangelical theology, but more to the educational expediency of the 'sheltered workshop', which prepared a person's intellect and emotions to last him for the whole of his pre-determined, single-track career. The art of government, in the British Empire, was conformity to expectation under stress, and the creation of a close-knit British 'colony' in an unfamiliar environment. Victorian Oxford was perfectly fitted to supply this quality.

(3) The voluntaristic model regards the university as a convenient canopy beneath which professors, students, and the rest pursue, as they might in a club, their private interests: on the one side research leavened with a little teaching; on the other side qualifications leavened with a

little education. There is clearly an element of this model in any modern university. In North America, especially, professors are often able to use the institution that nominally employs them as a roof for projects which are as readily transported as they are themselves. There, too, the rich variety of academic institutions encourages the growth of self-selected, experimental academic communities. Black Mountain College, anarchic in structure and creative in curriculum, was a good example while it lasted. So are the 'Free Universities' which sprang up on the West Coast in the late sixties, and which the indifferent, privatised professors of a place like Berkeley have willingly clasped to their own bosoms. But as a model for most of the world's universities and colleges voluntarism is unreal, for it assumes that students have exercised a real choice to be students, and to attend this institution rather than that one. Unfortunately, under the normal conditions of life in a technocracy, this is not the case.

(4) This last objection is equally applicable to the managerial model of a university, which has however proved too successful to be easily dismissed. It is of course possible to criticise, say, the University of California by asking how much its Radiation or Naval Biological Laboratories have contributed to the sum of human happiness, and whether its graduates emerge any better prepared intellectually to comprehend the known world than the astrology majors of medieval Bologna. But the criticism may be beside the point. Very probably, if there were no universities to run tertiary education with their own kind of managerial efficiency, business and government—the 'military-industrial complex'—would be providing by now a much less likeable substitute to fulfil their basic requirements, without bothering about the cultural graces of Academe. FIAT'S response, in Turin's technological university, to the shortcomings of Italian higher education is a good example of what would have happened on a terryifying scale in the United States, but for the success of a university system which cast itself in the role of entrepreneur. Just as modern industry tends to be organised, not round a single or multiple 'product' like shoes or books, but around vaguer concepts, more inviting to innovators, like 'footwear' or 'information', so a company producing information retrieval systems might well, in the absence of a managerially successful university, organise itself to produce the information to be retrieved, and the kind of men who would want to retrieve it. The alternative to the university as a not-for-profit corporation doing well by doing good may be the university as a profit-making corporation unconcerned with questions of value. In other words, if the University of Chicago did not own a bit of the *Encyclopaedia Britannica*, the *Encyclopaedia Britannica* might one day have a controlling interest in the University of Chicago, Inc.

But there remain serious limitations to the managerial model of a university. The most obvious is one section of the community's refusal to be managed—immortalised in the phrase borrowed from the IBM cards: 'This is a human being. Do not fold, spindle, or mutilate.' (The University of Chicago, jealous for its personality, declined to simplify its own administrative records by giving each student a coding number instead of a name.) This practical obstacle to the onward march of managerialism revealed the fundamental clashes of interest within the institution, which the managerial model has to deny. To this day, because they were never encouraged to learn the political facts of life, both students and faculty at Berkeley are able to convince themselves that their university really belongs to them, not to Governor Reagan and the Californian voters out there in the warm boulevards of the nirvana state.

It is worth comparing another type of institution which admits human beings after examination for long or short stays, and discharges them, suitably modified, on to the labour market—an institution, moreover, which is also centrally or peripherally involved in the advancement of knowledge. I am thinking of hospitals, where there are also strong, though not always recognised, conflicts of interest between different parties. Patients wish to get well and get out. Doctors want this too but also want to make money and meet interesting problems. Nurses sympathise with both but also want a routine that runs smoothly, with no need to think about exceptions. Each of these groups has or should have political rights in the institution, but the model for the whole can properly be a managerial one, because as a hospital defines health, all can agree on what a healthy person is. If hospitals were too much afflicted with chaplains of the kind who went about saying, 'Ah, you may think you're getting well, but in reality you're *sick*', the managerial model could not survive.

A university also contains within itself the disparate interests of teachers, researchers, students, administrators, and ancillary staff. Most people who have studied the problem seem to agree that this heterogeneity is necessary to the function which a university sets out to perform—that teaching decays into instruction when it is severed from the advancement of knowledge; that research workers lose a little of their edge when they are shut up in think-tanks and no longer under constant pressure to communicate their methods and results in a form comprehensible to the generation rising; and that in a constantly expanding intellectual universe, where disciplines form, break, and re-form bonds with other disciplines, the human agglomerations gathered for mutual help and comfort are apt to be so large that professional or semi-professional administrators are needed if scholars are to be able to do their own thing. (Of course, the necessity of administration is sometimes disputed. I was once present while a group of professors in a large American state university were discussing what might be going on in a meeting, then in session, of campus deans and other high administrators. 'If a bomb fell on that room,' said one man, 'this place would come to a grinding halt—for five minutes.' Laughter and applause.)

But though a university contains disparate interests it parts company from a hospital when it tries to define its end product. There cannot be agreement in a university on what constitutes an educated man or woman, and even originality is an elusive concept sometimes. I do not just mean that agreement is difficult, and that when it is reached, a solemn stillness descends. I mean instead that as soon as agreement is reached, there has ceased to be a university, for a university, like a political situation, is auto-destructive. The people involved in it are always trying to unmake what they know in favour of what has only been glimpsed. For example, if government or society tells them that more scientists and technologists are needed, academics may agree—for have they not been saying the same thing for years? But after thought, they may then reply that the guidance received is itself misguided, and that what society really needs is artists, to do something not originally envisaged in the brief. To the manager—and professors and students too are usually managers with part of their minds—this canker in the apple of academic certitude is distressing. All of them can and do take refuge in what Theodore Roszak calls the 'myth of objective consciousness' which the twentieth century has substituted for God. (Consider, for instance, the use of the word 'competence' in the academic appointments system. Competence is a quality which is judged, from published work and performance at the dinner table, by an applicant's fallible peers, but it readily comes to be thought of as something measurable, suitable to be shown in the university's intellectual accounts and audited by the Great Polymath Up There.)

Even from this point of view, the university as multi-million-dollar business has many virtues. It can keep innumerable options open against an uncertain intellectual future. Nor has any more flexible academic system yet been devised. The games American academics play—Hunt the Federal Dollar, and What Has He Published Lately?—see to that. Some would criticise the waste—all those Ph.D. theses ejaculated, and only one or maybe two fertile conceptions. But the real flaw is that the system is bound to repress, not the person who wants to do or say some new thing for his own honour and glory, but the person who wants the institution as such to alter course. This is because no one but the manager—and usually not even he—can see the operation whole, and the manager, by Clark Kerr's own confession, is primarily interested in preserving the peace. It is all right to add to Professor X, but not if it means taking away from Professor Y—unless it can be done without his noticing. Actual redistribution of power or income can only be achieved, if at all, by political decision. Or as Lenin put it, 'who whom?'

(5) The political model for a university, as exposition of the German situation has shown, is open to many objections. So is the rest of life. The point to grasp is that a modern university is not—like a company, a club, or even a medieval university—a body corporate within society. It *is* society—'in microcosm' would be the cliché, but an inaccurate one, for only certain groups and classes are represented. Rather, it is society organ-

ised into committee for the reinterpretation of the past and the invention of the future. It depends on experts, but need not be ruled by them. If the university fails to reproduce, in whatever forms are most appropriate to academic life in a particular place, the political pressures which arise from social life, it will still be in the business of conferring and transferring power, and hence a political institution. For learning in the last hundred years or so has become power, and power abhors a vacuum. If an institution formerly vacuum-tight is unsealed to admit the pressures of the outside world, but maintains the fiction that the inrushing air is politically sanitised on entry, civic life within that institution will remain in Hobbes's state of nature, however 'civilising' the enterprises it has in hand.

A recent exchange in Britain casts light on the fictive powers of the academic mind. Mr. Enoch Powell, as an ex-professor of Greek, a politician, and a demagogue of no mean talent, understands enough about the role of power within a university to be sure that students ought not to be given any, and made a speech saying so. Sir Eric Ashby, formerly Vice-Chancellor of Cambridge, who understands more than most men about universities, does not seem to understand as much as Mr. Powell about power, for he replied from the Institute of Advanced Studies at Princeton to the effect that students have power already: 'In the [British] civil universities students are not only statutory members of the corporation, they are, with the approval of Parliament, represented on the governing bodies (courts) and have been so for sixty-seven years. All that is happening now is a long overdue reform of this principle.'[16] This represents a failure to take account of the distinction, already referred to in these pages, between the 'dignified' and the 'efficient' principles of university constitutions. In Britain, university Courts represent the dignified. Councils and Senates, or the committees of those bodies, represent the efficient.

To be fair, Sir Eric discusses the issue much more satisfactorily in his recent book, *The Rise of the Student Estate in Britain*.[17] Students, he there says, tend to be disappointed with their experience of consultative 'participation' or 'minority representation' in university business, and would in fact be equally disappointed with parity representation or even majority control, because they misapprehend what power in universities is, and where it lies:

'The power to make the decisions upon which universities really

---

[16] *The Guardian* (Manchester and London), June 15, 1970; ibid., July 3, 1970.

[17] (with Mary Anderson). London, 1970. See also Edward Shil's review in *Minerva* VIII 4 (October 1970). Professor Shils rejects arguments for the formal participation of students in university business, partly on the grounds that the condition of being a student is too temporary to be called an 'estate'. If, as I suggest in Chapter Seven (pp. 291–295), 'recurrent education' were made part of every citizen's social contract, this particular objection would fall.

depend is so dispersed and diluted that no one, whether student or vice-chancellor, can get his hands on it. . . . The central covenant on which universities stand is that it is the individual teacher and no one else who decides what he shall teach and in what direction he shall advance knowledge. Any vice-chancellor or dean or committee who issued directives on these matters would be breaking the covenant. To entrust these two categories of decision-making to committees, whether there were students on them or not, would not be a 'transfer of power', it would be imposing power where none has existed before. This freedom has been won after centuries of struggle, from Galileo to those who refused to teach Lysenko's genetics or Hitler's theories of race. . . . The other two basic categories of decision-making are who is to be taught and who is to teach: admissions and appointments. In neither of these matters is power concentrated.' (pp. 140–1).

All this explains very well how it happens that in a crisis—such as a student sit-in possibly leading to police intervention—the Vice-Chancellor or university President conceives himself to be defending the ark of the covenant, with desperately thin resources, while the student body perceives him as defending his colleagues' power base, with the entire capitalist system standing at his elbow. Mutual incomprehension could not be more complete. But there is a flaw in Sir Eric's argument. Power diffused is still power. Students, and the rest of us, may now have our lives profoundly affected by what is taught and by what knowledge is advanced in universities. If students, and beyond them the lay public, find that all the significant decisions are taken by one man or one committee, however benign or well-intentioned, that is transparently power. But if the decisions are shared by a hundred just men or a hundred just committees, power is still what those students are subject to, especially if the hundred are socially conditioned to decide most grave issues the same way, or to avoid discussion of them altogether. In the latter case, it is true, more can be achieved in the interstices of power—for example, by playing off one professor or department against another. But manoeuvres of this kind can never be more than marginal. In the United States, students—perhaps the whole society—became victims, not of an express centralised decision to de-humanise higher education, and to expand it by pursuing the Federal research dollar at whatever cost to individual or institutional self-respect, but of a conditioned response to economic opportunity, made by university faculty members whose culture had programmed them to react in that way and no other. Now that Pentagon research grants are being withdrawn as capriciously and illogically as they were originally made, the professors' condition may be pitiable. But while it all lasted, their collective power in relation to students was as unmistakable as the collective power of white suburbanites in relation to inner city Negroes. The point has been well put by Stanley

K. Sheinbaum, who coordinated the Vietnam Project at Michigan State University:

> 'On every campus from Harvard to Michigan State, the story is the same. The social science professor, trained (not educated) to avoid the bigger problems, is off campus expertising for his government or industry client whose assumptions he readily adopts. His students are mechanistically led through the same social science materials by a less competent instructor or graduate assistant, and they will be as little exposed to questions of judgment and the application of wisdom as was the professor in the first place.'[18]

It does not necessarily follow from the argument about the role of power within a university that the particular political model to be applied must be one man, one vote. Democracy comes in many disguises, even in a democratically governed society. But under modern conditions, with the university lying open to society and society lying open to the university, each feeding the other, it will be difficult for a university to adopt permanently a form of government radically different from the wider society's, and expect the difference to protect the institution from outside political influence. Only the lingering models of the monastery, the school, and the club have for so long permitted universities to get away with such superbly—and in their day, usefully—undemocratic forms of government. President Levi of the University of Chicago is perfectly correct to argue, as he does, that whate'er is least administered is best, that it is better not to know too much too accurately about one's colleagues and the costs of their activities in money, time, and space, and positively dangerous to expose the university to an attack of democracy, as though decision-making itself were the whole life of the institution. Almost any British Vice-Chancellor (though comparatively few American university presidents), would in private say the same.

However, universities ruled out that choice for themselves when they accepted large amounts of public money for research, and at the same time made themselves indispensable as public educators. In Chicago during World War II, President Hutchins knew less about the progress of the atomic pile on his own campus than some people in Washington did, and when Leo Szilard and his colleagues sent their now-famous letter to President Truman asking him not to use the atomic bomb on a Japanese city, there could be no way for the university itself to throw its weight behind the appeal, even if it had wanted to. That pattern, inevitable in war, remained in peace. There is a much more direct relation than is generally realised between the internal and external government of a university. Dr. Geiss in Hamburg describes it in this way: 'Political life in Germany is being normalised. In a democracy, if there are major forces

[18] *Ramparts*, April 1966. (Quoted in Peter Buckman, *The Limits of Protest* (London, 1970), pp. 42–3.

unrepresented in Parliament, it is normal for them to go on to the streets. Our turmoil here is thus a symptom of our normality. The new generation since the war has taken the democratic slogans for granted as measures of reality. Applied to the university, those slogans made the claims of German professors look totally ridiculous.'

The claims of professors—stripped of the pettiness and the pretensions— would be the same all over the world: claims that the full-time pursuit of excellence, whether in scholarship or tennis, requires a man to delegate his democratic rights in the institution to an oligarch whom he hopes he can trust. This is in effect what most democrats do most of the time, and would do, even in democratic universities. Many academics who sit on university committees are just as ignorant of the subjects discussed as students would be. But discussion of how democracy can be most efficiently worked has always been subsequent to the struggle—of workers, of women, of students—for the franchise. In all such struggles, the competence of the about-to-be-enfranchised to decide the questions that will be set before them is never really the issue. The issue is first, 'Can the upstarts be resisted?' and if they cannot, 'What adjustments must we make?' In other words, 'If they can vote us down, we must make sure that they know enough to vote as we would.' Paternalism so cynical would not be accepted by a reformist, let alone a revolutionary, today, but the point can be more neutrally made that power, in the medium-to-long run, creates the skill necessary to exercise it. Workers who get control do not long remain workers, students who appointed professors would no longer be students, as they are now understood.

In Britain, curiously, the force of this has lately been better realised in the relations between the Government or the Committee of Vice-Chancellors, on the one hand, and the National Union of Students on the other, than it has been in individual universities, some of which are still trapped in monasticism of a corrupt, Victorian-Gothic kind.[19] In the United States, the opposite has happened:

'Phase one of the student revolution transformed the legal relations which obtained on American campuses . . . Students participate in everything from the board of trustees at Princeton to key financial committees and alumni fund-raising groups on other campuses. Students also participate extensively in setting up degree requirements for graduate and undergraduate schools; they help design curriculum programmes, select faculty for promotion and tenure, and even serve on search committees for new university presidents and provosts.'[20]

[19] However, British students now sit on the academic Senate of fourteen of the forty-three universities, where in 1966 they sat on one only. This naturally falls far short of NUS demands for a form of *drittelparität*, but it is some indication that British dons, like the British aristocracy, know when to adjust to altered circumstances. (*The Guardian*, November 24, 1970).

[20] *New Society*, July 9, 1970.

The writer, Irving Louis Horowitz, is there guilty of extrapolating from the exceptional—and in America, there is always an exception to be found. However, he goes on to suggest that the next phase of student 'trade unionism' will be a demand to be paid for the administrative and academic chores which at present they are graciously permitted to perform gratis. Perhaps, but there will be difficulties, for the industrial power which students have acquired in some American universities and colleges is not matched at state or Federal level. Just as middle-aged, middle-class parents can no longer communicate with their student children, the parents' elected or appointed political representatives cannot communicate with student organisations. Since the typical American university is now a state university, this basic lack of franchise is bound to bring further trouble as the industrialisation of students proceeds. Practical wisdom demands an extension of the franchise, for if the Regents of the University of California operated under *drittelparität*, they could hardly have directed the policy of the institution more ineptly and expensively than they have done, faced with social forces for which they had neither sympathy nor understanding.

In the US, universities whose administrations and faculties are permitted to make political responses to political pressures will have a better-than-even chance of remaining islands of comparative sanity, and therefore places where good intellectual work can be done, in an increasingly paranoid environment. In Britain, paranoia exists, but chiefly as a localised academic vice; the societal vice is an excess of phlegm. From Japan and Italy—and even from France, until the intellectual coherence of M. Faure's law finds expression in the new institutions it is creating—Britain and America have nothing to learn about university government. In Germany, too, it will take a long time for the constitutional experiments of Bremen or Hamburg to reach, say, Wurzburg, and Anglo-Saxon academics are unlikely to borrow from the model until it has proved itself. But the model is latent within their own systems already, in the subtle pressure of central government no less than in the crude pressure of the student proletariat, and political pressure is most to be feared when it is deprived alike of recognition and an outlet.

CHAPTER SIX

What should students study?

1   LEARNING AS AN INTERNATIONAL CURRENCY

'Nowadays all the students must needs attend lectures on Virgil and Pliny and the rest of the new-fangled authors—what is more, they may listen to them for five years and yet get no degree: and so, when they return home, their parents ask them, saying, 'What art thou?' And they reply that they are naught, but that they have been reading Poetry. And then their parents are perplexed—but they see that their sons are not grammarians, and therefore they are disgruntled at the University, and begrudge sorely the money they have spent. . . . Let us pray, then, that all the Poets may perish, for "it is expedient that one man should die"—that is that the Poets, of whom there are but a handful in any one University, should perish, rather than so many Universities should come to naught.'

Epistolae Obscurorum Virorum (Germany, early sixteenth century),
edited by F. G. Stokes (London, 1911), pp. 484–6

'To the Higher Mathematics—and may it never be of any use to anyone.'

Oxford high table toast (traditional)

Every fresh outrage of action or repression in one of the world's universities—in London, New York, and California, arson of irreplaceable scholarly material; in Ohio and Mississippi, random shooting of students by the forces of order—recalls how far revolutionary movements in universities have come since the early days of the Berkeley Free Speech Movement and of the *Mouvement de 22 Mars* at Nanterre. Both these incorporated a severe but purposeful critique of the style and content of academic teaching in the universities concerned. It would now be a very naïve professor indeed who still believed that if he could just get the curriculum right, and discover enough competent and amiable people to teach it, peace would come dropping slow on the campuses, as on Yeats's isle of Innisfree. Students learn while they are still school-children that when the curriculum or the quality of teaching are under discussion, social and political pressures in the school or the community generally count just as much as commonsense or rationality. (A student at Harvard who talked to me at length about his Indianapolis high school said that his best teacher there—a teacher of American history

—had been fired, not for political reasons, but because parents complained that he was making their children read books outside the set text.) They learn that any attempt at reform, however strictly it seems to be confined to an educational context, sooner or later confronts an individual, or a system, which can only be worsted by direct or political action. Absurdly, students go on to suppose that because at every turn in the educational system there is an obstacle which cannot be removed by rational argument, there must be a conspiracy between the obstacles, that somewhere in a central computer there is an obstacular master plan, which must be searched out and destroyed before any local ground clearance can do any lasting good. In America especially, radicals whether of the Left or the Right are kept going by their conviction that there is a conspiracy against them (this is the real tragedy of any encounter between students and police in the United States) and the more distant the supposed source of the threat, the more potent it is. Thus, in Berkeley, Governor Reagan is a potent threat indeed, but he only became so after the balance of academic power within the university had shifted against undergraduates, who could then see only state-wide or global remedies for their diseases. In Berkeley it is, according to Professor Tussman, the faculty that is responsible for the 'joyless drift' of the undergraduate college, and is 'the vested interest most difficult to move. It acts out of conviction and habit, but what it has created and what it maintains is in educational, social, and human terms a disastrous failure.'[1] Similarly in England, as Eric Robinson has pointed out in an admirably tactless book, there has been much research on almost everything which students do or suffer outside their academic work, but of the impact of lectures, seminars, tutorials, reading: of the way in which they acquire new ideas and discard old ones; of how they learn to master procedures and pass examinations— of these things almost nothing is known, because the researcher could not find out without interrogating students on their teachers and teachers on their methods.[2] In the last three or four years, several British universities have jumped through this tact barrier, and Lancaster's Department of Higher Education, for example, reckons to investigate 'learning situations, the effectiveness of teaching, problems of assessment and examination, and the social, psychological and intellectual problems of students'. (Note 'students'—teachers are not supposed to have social or psychological problems.) But the lateness of the start only reinforces my point: that students the world over are not encouraged to pry into the faults and irrationalities of their own immediate learning environment, and are therefore the more prone to project their domestic discontents on to the wider society whose own faults and irrationalities are more glaringly

[1] Joseph Tussman, *Experiment at Berkeley* (London, Oxford, and New York, 1969), p. 67.
[2] Eric Robinson, *The New Polytechnics* (London, 1968), p. 106.

obvious to them. Even in Lancaster, the scholar hired to examine learning situations was soon given to understand that he would be wiser to conduct his researches in universities other than his own.

Architectural influences

All over the world, however, the organisation of learning at university level is now recognised as a problem. It does not follow from this that it is possible to hold a genuinely cross-cultural discussion about it. Even leaving aside linguistic difficulties, the area of potential misunderstanding is very large. Before embarking on just such a discussion, it may be worth noting what kind of things are held in common and what are not. Clearly, the physical environment and facilities are a common factor. A dreaming spire in Oxford, a hyperbolic paraboloid in Brasilia, or a tower block in Tokyo are interchangeable in function: they contain boxes, small or large, in which students may encounter a professor, each other, or a machine. Occasionally, but not often enough, routine university architecture is consciously used by someone as a device to express a significant academic or human idea. The driving spirits behind the University of Vincennes deliberately made their lecture rooms too small for more than thirty to forty people so that the traditional stance of the French lecturer—six feet above contradiction in an amphitheatre with seats for 500—could no longer be adopted. Saarinen's Law School at Chicago, as already noted, forces professors who want to collect their mail to cross the student lounge on the way. The new generation of British universities have been praised by one American university architect-planner for their 'continuous teaching environment, a physical form that preserves communication and contact between all parts of the institution while allowing external accretion and internal change.'[3] (He means that everything you need is in walking distance, and that the plan leaves room for new growth or second thoughts.) On the whole, this praise is deserved: the plateglass universities, planned all at once (by different people) with a great rush of creative blood to the head, express the best ideas of a whole architectural generation much more clearly than the bigger American campuses, whose one or two distinguished buildings are often surrounded by sprawling acres of reach-me-down mediocrity. Professor Perkin points out that the British innovation is also a revival of 'a very ancient and natural principle' which was first adopted by the medieval collegiate universities when it was still possible to interweave the activities of a university with the pedestrian patterns of a small town. 'It is only the coming of large-scale urban living, and above all of the motor vehicle and its dispersion of human activities as well as its danger to life and mental peace, which has disrupted the old, natural solution and made urgent a new, artificial one.'

[3] Richard P. Dober, *The New Campus in Britain: Ideas of Consequence for the United States* (New York, 1965), p. 9. Quoted in Perkin, op. cit., p. 90.

There is a touch of sentiment in this vision of mental peace in the medieval university, when one remembers all the brawling, not to mention the statute found necessary in fifteenth century Leipzig: 'A rule against throwing rubbish and pouring wine out of university buildings'.[4] However, the British belief that though twentieth century universities may as well be plumbed they ought not to be motorised has something to offer university planners elsewhere, who allow enrolments to top 100,000 and naturally begin to think of students as just another product on which economies of scale can be achieved.

Scholarship and nationhood

From the fact that university planners of whatever nationality can talk to each other, and from the generally depressing similarity of the shells which house constantly expanding numbers of researchers, teachers, students, laboratory operations, and books, it might be concluded that there is some similarity in the style and subject-matter of the inquiries conducted inside the shells. So there is, but there are qualifying factors. Scientific investigation, certainly, has a common pattern, a common language (mathematics), and common equipment, elementary or advanced. But even here, social or economic variations between countries find expression in outwardly similar laboratories. An English geologist in the United States remarked to me that the difficulty anyone has there in getting a car serviced or a television set mended is matched in laboratories by a shortage of technicians. Professors are expected to keep their own machines in working order, and because they are Americans, endowed with a mechanical aptitude and willingness that Europeans unwisely disdain, they generally do. Indeed, he said, it has often been possible in American laboratories to distinguish first-rate scientists from second-rate ones by the fact that the latter automatically believe the figures that they read off from their machines, whereas the former think it possible that the machine may be mistaken. Differences are of course even more apparent when it is a question of what to investigate, and how to use the results. 'I always think of Alvarez at Berkeley as the archetypical American physicist,' Professor Pietro Bassi at Bologna told me. 'He's a brilliant investigator and he's also prepared to use physics for projects like bombarding the Great Pyramid with particles to see if there's a burial chamber inside, or making a golf ball that emits signals when it's lost. Blackett wouldn't do that. Nor would I. Well, the Pyramid perhaps. But not the golf ball'.

In the humanities, the divergences in both style and subject matter are far greater than is generally realised. Indeed, there is a factor at work here which casts some light on the possibility or impossibility of a world

[4] For this and other first-hand descriptions of medieval student life, see R. F. Seybolt (translator), *The Manuale Scholarium* (Harvard, 1921).

culture. The life-cycle of academic man, the conventional progression from kindergarten to professorship, may be viewed in two ways. In one sense, it is a steady development from the local to the global. The mind, initially furnished only with the vocables and written signs of its native language, the civic problems raised by family and class-mates, and the natural history of local ponds, gradually acquires information and conceptual grasp and develops into the 'world authority' on a topic that may or may not bear any relation to the subject matter it studied at the age of five. In another sense, however, the line of development is not straight, but curved back on itself like the flight of a boomerang. It both begins and ends, or may do so, in achievements to which nationality and national cultures are almost irrelevant. Everyone has to learn how to compute, how to read, how to put his own national flesh on the bones of the 'generative grammar' that is posited by Chomskian linguistics. The most successful performer at these tasks—which must, incidentally, be the most difficult which any human mind ever undertakes—may then ultimately arrive at a comprehensive grasp of some fragment of human learning, a fragment so small that national differences are again hardly relevant to the scholars at work in that particular field. The subject may be literary, historical, economic, sociological, or anything the reader pleases. Once these broad fields are narrowed down to, say, 'Metrical problems in *The Rape of the Lock*', 'Hanseatic account-books', 'Achievement orientation in relation to family size in developing nations' or 'Social cost analysis in suburban transport'—I invent at random—Professor X from Boston can take tea with Professor Y of Osaka and akvavit with Professor Z of Uppsala without any of them feeling particularly embarrassed by their lack of a common general education. But between these terminal points of primal innocence and final specialisation it is possible to plot a curve of educational chauvinism whose high point falls at different ages in academic man's life, according to the way his own country organises its education, and the direction which his own academic interests take. Thus in Britain, where rigorous specialisation may begin at the age of fifteen or so, a classicist or historian may begin to deal in an international academic currency while a French or American boy of the same age and level of intelligence is still learning at an unsophisticated level about the glorious past of the USA or the cultural uniqueness of *la France*. On the other hand, a British graduate of the Cambridge English school or the Oxford Law faculty might travel round Europe for years without meeting an academic boon companion, while a French sociologist of religion would command a ready audience in London.

It would be absurd to interpret this general point as an argument for (or even against) specialisation at school level in any country. Most university graduates, after all, do not become professors and never attend an international conference. On the other hand, the direction of universities as such is determined by those that do. It is important that the drive behind their activities should be understood, and it is also important that when societies make choices about what shall be learnt by all their young people and what only by some, they should at least attempt to weigh up more distant international consequences than formerly needed to be taken into account. Otherwise, the phrase 'world culture' will remain limited in use to the generational and political self-expression of the international student movement.

All societies make choices, political and economic as well as cultural, in the matter of educating their young, and the nature of these choices is normally better concealed than any other kinds of choice that societies make. This is because the essential ideological damage, if there is damage, is done before the victim has the power to make an independent judgment upon it. At a later stage, a few individuals become capable of assessing in a balanced way what has been done to them and why, but even they can seldom quite shake off the influence, and over-reaction is commoner than detachment. A foreign observer is often the best guide, as the reader of de Tocqueville or Veblen on America, Flexner or Halévy on England, Matthew Arnold on France, Germany and Italy, or Ronald Dore on Japan, is well placed to realise. But here is an Englishman reflecting on the problem posed by his own country:

> 'We speak sometimes as if education were a fixed abstraction, a settled body of teaching and learning, and as if the only problem it presents to us is that of distribution: this amount, for this period of time, to this or that group. . . . Yet to conduct this business as if it were the distribution of a simple product is wholly misleading. It is not only that the way in which education is organised can be seen to express, consciously and unconsciously, the wider organization of a culture and a society, so that what has been thought of as simple distribution is in fact an active shaping to particular social ends. It is also that the content of education, which is subject to great historical variation, again expresses, again both consciously and unconsciously, certain basic elements in the culture, what is thought of as "an education" being in fact a particular selection, a particular set of emphases and omissions.'[5]

This theoretical statement introduces a close historical analysis of English *schools*, not universities. It is clear that the dimensions of the problem alter when universities are at issue, but not nearly as much as one is led to suppose by the antiquity of the university idea and the medieval flummery which academics like to gather around them. The case-studies in the preceding chapters should help to establish this. The continuity between school and university tends to be obscured in England, where the two grew up quite separately, and where elitist restraints on the

---

[5] Raymond Williams, *The Long Revolution* (London, 1961), p. 145 (Penguin edition).

distribution of university places combine to put universities in a class apart. But when Williams says, a page or two further into his analysis, that a child must be taught 'first, the accepted behaviour and values of his society; second, the general knowledge and attitudes appropriate to an educated man; and third, a particular skill by which he will earn his living and contribute to the welfare of his society', we are reminded not only of Governor Reagan before his election telling the Regents of the University of California that in future, members of the University faculty were going to be appointed on the basis of their willingness and ability to teach the morality of the surrounding community ('My God, are we going to teach anything at that low a level?') was Clark Kerr's comment afterwards); but also of the attempt by Anthony Crosland, as British Minister of Education in 1965, to make his new Polytechnics (State-controlled institutions which in most countries would be called universities) concentrate on 'vocational' education, while the universities themselves concentrated on 'academic' education. This last notion was rather quickly dropped, for it carried an unmistakable implication that academic education was for officers and vocational education was for men, but for my present purpose it illustrates rather well the thesis that as soon as higher education ceases to be the privilege of a numerically unimportant minority, and begins to draw in a proportion of the population similar to that which previously attended the upper forms of secondary schools, the values which the society has tolerated from the university begin to be phased out, and the values which it has thought appropriate for schools are phased in—whatever the students themselves or their professors want.[6] (Early in 1970 a British judge, sentencing some students from the University of Essex for attempted arson, wondered aloud, as judges will, what kind of instruction in civics these lads received at college. Oxford or Cambridge would have politely ignored the remark as a judicial *faux pas:* Essex, which has a public relations officer, issued an apologetic statement.) In this sense, the 'altruistic' demonstrations which the more privileged students of British universities have lately been staging in support of their less privileged counterparts in polytechnics, and their readiness to share recreational and social facilities across the demarcation lines which Government policy has drawn between the two types of institution, are based on a correct perception of political reality: 'If the bastards push *them* around now, they'll push *us* around soon.'

The great American private universities, it might be argued, have been protected from this kind of 'vocational' pressure for three reasons: first,

[6] The most striking example is the Japanese University Control Act, 1969. Long before the rise of fascism, schools in Japan were under close official control. Universities, on the other hand, enjoyed an extraordinary autonomy. After 1945, as the Japanese student population exploded, the Japanese Government made several attempts to obtain a controlling influence in university administration. In 1969, as a result of student outrages, it succeeded.

their professional schools at graduate level (Law, Business, Medicine, Divinity and so forth) already give a vocational edge to the university's entire concept of itself; second, there already exists in America the 'alternative philosophy' which Mr. Crosland was attempting to introduce into the English university system, for the state universities, though their contemporary attitudes and achievements are at their best hard to distinguish from those of Chicago or Columbia, originally grew from a highly vocational philosophy of education; third, the present reality of juvenile unemployment in the US and the future possibility of graduate unemployment in some categories, have begun to suggest to voters that 'unproductive' forms of higher education are a positive social good, for what does not produce must consume, and consumption is the twentieth century American's chief patriotic duty. In Japan, France, and Italy, by contrast, there is surprisingly little insistence that the universities should 'teach the morality of the surrounding community'. In Japan this tolerance of academic dissent represents a reaction, induced partly by consciousness of past mistakes and partly by the command of the American conquerors, against the former identification of the educational system with the Emperor and hence with the militarist regime which stood behind him. But in these countries there is widespread discontent with universities' failure to leave their multiplying graduates with skills that make an adequate contribution to the welfare of society. Perhaps the most striking symbol of this discontent, and of the community's insistence that when student numbers rise beyond a certain point, their civil privileges should be reduced rather than increased, is the alteration of laws or customs in order to allow police access to university campuses.

Nevertheless, whatever societies may say, universities themselves, above all in Britain, France, and America, are primarily concerned with the second aim of education that Williams lists: teaching 'the general knowledge and attitudes appropriate to an educated man'. It is this kind of teaching, intensified and particularised as it must be at university level, with which this chapter is concerned, though as Williams insists, this 'general' education cannot finally be separated from training in social values and the acquisition of a socially useful skill: 'If we believe in a particular social character, a particular set of attitudes and values, we naturally believe that the general education which follows from these is the best that can be offered to anyone: it does not feel like "indoctrination", or even "training"; it feels like offering to this man the best that can be given.'[7] So far, of course, the natural context for the discussion would be a liberal arts college, such as America possesses in profusion, ranging from the severe peaks of Reed, Swarthmore and the undergraduate colleges of Harvard and Chicago to some very lowly foothills; such as Oxford and Cambridge were until the reforms of the nineteenth

[7] Ibid., p. 147.

century began to bite and serious scientific research began; such as was, and remarkably still is, the 800-year-old Japanese Buddhist college at Koyasan, an intellectual and religious sanctuary high in the pinewoods above Osaka, which one much-travelled Japanese scholar slyly described to me as 'a Buddhist Cambridge'. (Its curriculum ranges from manuscript decipherment to flower arrangement.) These have all, in their way, been laboratories of general education, and for what they represent no replacement has yet been found, but they are all now suffering the *peine forte et dure*, and general or liberal education cannot any longer be discussed without allowing for the weights that prevent it from breathing easily: the research mentality by which academics are gripped and governments fascinated; the student movement's rejection of all educational paternalism, so that the everlasting argument about what to teach is entangled with a new version of the old one, 'by whom shall the style and content of teaching be monitored and controlled?'; and the popular belief, as yet insubstantial but bound to gather weight in due course, that the mass media and the revolution in educational technology have now superseded the nice little, tight little, college in a park.

'General education'

Before going further, I must try to clarify terms and procedures. The educational reformers' texts to which I shall refer are exclusively British or American. But I propose to avoid the word 'liberal', as in 'liberal education' or 'liberal arts', and to follow Williams in talking about 'general education'. This phrase, though less well defined in the thinking of Englishmen, is very familiar to Americans, as the titles of the 1945 Harvard Red Book *General Education in a Free Society* and Daniel Bell's challenge to Columbia, *The Reforming of General Education*, sufficiently indicate. What is meant is, I think, also something very close to the French *formation générale* and the German *Bildung*. In origin, the notion of the generally educated man owes a great deal to the Renaissance ideal of the *homo universale*: the man to whom nothing human or natural was alien, because 'the round world's imagin'd corners' had not yet been pushed out too far for any single human mind's comprehension of what lay between. The ideal is far from dead: indeed, the last decade or two's mounting concern about the crevasse between the 'two cultures', and the fretful search for workable forms of 'inter-disciplinarity' in higher education, represent a desire to construct an artificial alternative to the unattainable original. But there has been a significant redefinition, in terms of method rather than content, of the education that is implied by the ideal. This is of itself sufficient reason to abandon the phrase 'liberal education', which survives from a period before the Oxford-and-Harvard ideal of the well-groomed mind was modified by the narrower but stronger ideal of academic professionalism, imported from Germany in the middle of the nineteenth century. From that point on, the possessor of 'general education' was a man who had figuratively put his signature to what Northrop Frye calls 'the educational contract', meaning 'the process by which the arts and sciences, and their methods of logic, experiment, amassing of evidence, and imaginative presentation, actually operate as a source of authority in society'.[8] A much earlier, if not the earliest, English version of this idea is found in a sermon by the nineteenth century Oxford reformer Mark Pattison, who contended for the priority of research at the university while it was still primarily organised for the transmission of Renaissance culture. The university student, Pattison said, should be placed in a position where 'his intelligence is not only the passive recipient of forms from without, a mere mirror in which the increasing crowd of images confuse and threaten to obliterate each other; it becomes active and throws itself out upon phenomena with a native force, combining them or analysing them—anyhow altering them, imposing itself upon them . . .'[9]

It is only when general education is defined in this way that the sterility of the debate between 'liberal' and 'vocational' concepts of education can be clearly seen. In academic terms, the antithesis is as old as the medieval university itself, which as we have seen (Chapter Three) failed to apply its considerable reasoning power to problems whose surface difficulties were manual and practical. But socially, the force of the antithesis, in Britain at least, derives from Victorian assumptions that owners needed a store of information on which to base decisions, whereas workers only needed the 'three Rs', plus a single manual skill which would last them for the whole of their working lives. Eric Robinson, who correctly points out the baleful influence which these assumptions still exert in British higher education—with 'liberal' teachers boasting of their courses' uselessness and 'vocational' ones instilling techniques already half-way superseded— goes on to define a new enemy, 'academic' education, by which he means 'vocational education for those preparing for work in academic research'. The nub of his criticism is worth quoting, for it will find echoes far outside Britain:

'The implication of the very word "research" is of discovery rather than creation; this in practice imposes severe practical limitations on what is and is not academically acceptable as original work. The idea that original work consists in the discovery of what is there, rather than the creation of ideas to explain experience and of devices to improve it, goes far to explain, for example, the lack of attention and recognition which the academic world has given to writing (as distinct from criticism), to engineering design (as distinct from analysis), to the promotion of health (as distinct from the curing of disease), to

[8] Niblett, op. cit., p. 46.
[9] J. Sparrow, *Mark Pattison and the Idea of a University* (Oxford, 1965), p. 129.

legislation (as distinct from the interpretation of the law), to the visual arts and to music. . . . The complaint about the academically trained young man is not simply that he is slow to get the answers but that he asks the wrong questions and applies irrelevant criteria to his answers.'[10]

Academic man, in so far as he is how he is described in this passage, has never received—or has forgotten—general education in the Frye–Pattison sense of commitment to the 'process by which the arts and sciences . . . actually operate as a source of authority in society' and to the cultivation of an intelligence which 'throws itself out upon phenomena with a native force', combining, analysing, and altering. It is only when the Renaissance ideal is re-stated in this way that it becomes possible to see the skeleton of a general education that contains elements of 'vocationalism', 'liberalism', and 'academicism', all three, not as a compromise between the interests of different parties in the body politic of the university or the state, but as basic equipment for coping with the world. The same approach also suggests how the university, as an institution devoted to 'the higher learning', may compile an unabashed defence of its own controlling share in the general education of the minority (becoming a majority) of citizens who become or remain full time learners after the age of eighteen or so.

Education of this kind cannot be carried on in a school, or anything which constitutionally resembles a school (Polytechnics in Britain have not yet wholly broken free from this embrace) because in all societies schools do not contain within themselves the source of their own legitimacy. There are always phenomena upon which no schoolteacher dare 'throw himself with a native force', for the society which employs him will always prefer its molecular combinations to remain unchanged. The university, on the other hand, is in Northrop Frye's words 'the source of free authority in society, not as an institution, but as the place where the appeal to reason, experiment, evidence, and *imagination* is continuously going on'. (My italics). The hopeful but despairing Paris slogan of May 1968—*imagination au pouvoir*—suggests that this claim may as yet be slightly wishful, but 'a man's reach should exceed his grasp, or what's a heaven for?'

General education at university level is thus always, if it is genuine, remedial education. This is not to say that the appeal to reason, experiment, evidence, and imagination is omitted in British and American, French or Japanese, schools, though most British, American, French, or Japanese adult citizens would have at least one tale to tell to the contrary. But there is always a further, unstated appeal to social sanction, which at university is replaced, or ought to be, by an appeal to something which it is almost impossible to explain to a person who has not himself claimed it: the right to cause an intellectual disturbance. Historically, that appeal

[10] Op. cit., p. 103.

has been allowed by societies, first as a a freak exception to a general rule of social control, latterly as an acknowledgement of the fact that 'intellectual disturbances' in the physical and chemical world are capable of being turned to national advantage. (Even the Soviet Union has had to concede a degree of intellectual freedom to its scientists.) But only very recently has it become economically possible, and indeed necessary, for advanced countries to admit to this 'source of free authority' more young people than society itself is prepared to tolerate or able to control when they start to exercise their freedom.

Until 1968, this gathering crisis remained mostly hidden. Inevitably, once the political barriers came rattling down, the young felt the more betrayed by a society which only wanted to educate them as long as it could be sure that education would not make them too uppity. By the same criterion, much of the actual teaching they received in the university itself felt like a betrayal too—a constraint rather than a liberation. (Hence the rash of 'free universities'.) Of course, the acquisition of knowledge and reasoning power is always a constraint in one sense: it constrains from the uttering of nonsense. Radical students have sometimes found even this constraint insupportable. But their original perception—that many of their teachers had forgotten how to create an intellectual disturbance, or had no intention of transmitting that skill—was correct. It is a problem which cannot be solved, as political problems occasionally can be, on the streets. The question of what students should learn—as opposed to what employers expect them to have learnt—can only be solved within universities, and since student curricular experiments tend to be lively but short-lived, the spade-work is normally done by a few maverick professors or lecturers. In this section, I review three books about the 'general education' of students. I then briefly raise the delicate issue of who is to control the quality of university teaching, and how. Finally, I cite American interest in computerised instruction, British plans for the 'Open University', and a singular Harvard marriage between undergraduate teaching and publishable research, to demonstrate the infinitely various activities which, at a university, the word 'teaching' has to cover.

2 GENERAL EDUCATION: SUGGESTIONS FROM CHICAGO, BERKELEY, OXFORD

The books to which I refer are the following:

Joseph J. Schwab, *College Curriculum and Student Protest* (Chicago and London, 1969)

Joseph Tussman, *Experiment at Berkeley* (London, Oxford, and New York, 1969)

Michael Yudkin (ed.) *General Education: a symposium on the teaching of non-specialists* (London, 1969)

Other books could no doubt be found, but reportorial as well as critical considerations dictated the choice of these three. They all happen to have been published recently, out of university situations which are described elsewhere in this book (seven out of the ten contributors to the Yudkin book hold or have recently held teaching posts at Oxford.) Intellectually, the authors are 'mainstream' rather than 'counter-culture': the delirious deviations of 'free universities' are not for them, though Tussman acknowledges a debt to Alexander Meiklejohn's Experimental University at Wisconsin in the 1920s, and in general the European reader of the American books needs to be aware of a long and close association between college curricula and social utopianism in the US. (In England, educational utopians run schools, knowing that they would be run out of colleges. In America, they run colleges, knowing they would be run out of high schools. In this sense, A. S. Neill's Summerhill in England equals Black Mountain College—now defunct—in America.)

Institutionally, the authors of these books are not mainstream at all. Both Schwab and Tussman are profoundly and justifiably pessimistic about the ability or will of their own universities to reorganise their activities, and affront eminent faculty members, in order to revitalise undergraduate teaching. When in Chicago, I asked Schwab, who is a biologist, what proportion of his professional colleagues were interested in teaching as he understood it he replied 'perhaps thirty per cent'. Tussman, though a philosopher by trade, is not too nervous to use the word 'appalling' about 'the established teaching habits of the contemporary professoriate and the institutional structure [of Berkeley] which reflects and reinforces those habits'. An experimental college of students must anyway be marginal in a

237

university of 30,000. The English writers do not damn their colleagues' attitudes to teaching, and perhaps have less reason to, but their interest in interpreting their subjects to non-specialists necessarily isolates them somewhat in an educational system notorious for its encouragement of single track minds.

One of the most striking characteristics of the American books, though much less so of the English one, is the authoritative—even authoritarian—tone in which they are written. This may be partly a matter of age: both Schwab and Tussman have been university teachers for several decades, and are their own men. This gives them the power to organise courses and write books about them, not the power to organise other people's courses as well. But more important, they are educational reformers, and like their predecessors from Rousseau to Dewey, they cannot easily believe that their readers will disagree with them. Certainly they would be disinclined to lose the convictions and experience of an academic lifetime in a transitory fog of 'student participation', even though their convictions include the belief that students are in many ways sold a false prospectus of the education which modern universities actually offer.

Joseph Schwab, a faculty member of the University of Chicago, has managed to write a book on curriculum without, so far as I can discover, mentioning the name of Robert Hutchins, the president who made the university famous between the wars for a college curriculum which was designed to create (through a list of the world's 'Great Books' and other means) a common culture accessible to all students. Hutchin's curriculum was based on content.[11] Schwab's is based on method. It is, as undergraduate curricula must be, explicitly remedial. Schwab is unsurprised by students' vulnerability to their demagogues' deliberate or unconscious confusions of word, fact, and idea when he knows that even at the high intellectual level demanded of entrants to the University of Chicago, a student may not at school have been taught how to recognise a fact or look for it:

> 'His professor of chemistry, biology, even physics, has expounded inference, interpretation, and theory as if they were facts, and has exhibited facts, even laboratory facts, in such fashion that they appear to have presented themselves to the scientist wearing their meanings on their sleeves. His teacher of literature has imposed a critical doctrine and recited interpretations of literary works. Often he has not even revealed the existence of other doctrines, other interpretations . . . still

[11] 'The comic—or tragic—climax of this version of General Education has been reached in the *Syntopicon* published by the Encyclopaedia Britannica and the University of Chicago, in which one finds alphabetically arranged, the leading ideas of the Great Books, with citation of texts where each idea is treated.'—Reuben Brower, 'Reading in Slow Motion' (1959), revised and reprinted in Yudkin, op. cit., pp. 1–27.

less has he been concerned that students develop their own measure of the competences of interpretation and criticism . . .'[12]

The kind of introductory courses normally given by professional generalists to first year students do not, Schwab thinks, fill this gap in the average student's preparation, because they set out to survey wide fields of knowledge, give drill in supposedly fundamental facts, or instil the 'philosophical principles' of a subject without developing in the hearer the arts of recovery, enquiry, and criticism appropriate to the discipline under discussion. General education for non-specialists, or people who are only on their way to a specialism, should mean no 'truth' without the evidence and supporting arguments. 'It means—especially for history, philosophy, sociology, and psychology—no "truth" with its evidence and argument without some sampling of the alternative choices of principles, evidence, and interpretation which confer on these fields their characteristic pluralism: in psychology, for example, no B. F. Skinner without some Harlow; no Freud without a Harry Sullivan or equivalent *and* a stab at a "cognitive" theory of personality.'[13] Materials like this must however be properly representative of a discipline's problems and methods, or the course will, apart from anything else, be useless to a student who may need to discover a subject's particular 'feel' before settling on it as a specialism.

Schwab is distrustful of the student-run experimental colleges which attempt to re-draw the map of learning by arbitrary rearrangements of subjects which happen to look good together; and also of the contemporary academic world's permissiveness under pressure, with the dean of arts and letters permitting and encouraging students to 'do their own thing', or allowing their social class and ethnic origins to dictate their course assignments. But once a framework is set, there can and should be far more diversity in the system, and allowance for individual pushfulness, than is at present permitted. The scholastic aptitude tests used in America as a selective device by colleges are unduly verbal, and quite unfair to the possessors of special abilities or disabilities. The itch 'to make, to do, to shape, to alter' in art or craft is directly related to the similar itches to shape ideas in philosophy, mathematics or criticism; or to operate and modify institutions. (Note the parallel with Mark Pattison's formulation.) The university's business, unless its function is simply to keep bodies in custody till the labour market wants them, is to counteract the pressures of school and home which have in most students choked the child's instinctive feeling that both kinds of shaping belong together. Schwab also takes for granted that education in the humanities should concern itself with primary sources, 'novels, drama, music, and works of plastic art, treated in their particularity and not as instances of genera'.

[12] P. 20.
[13] P. 183.

Schwab's opinion about the class or group size which is ideal or even necessary for this kind of teaching is conventional: ten to thirty-five. Much less conventional, especially to an English ear, is his view of the examination and testing problem. British universities, as has already been observed, set enormous store by 'closed' examinations, externally set and marked. In Oxford, the 'myth of objective consciousness' which Theodore Roszak attacks so vigorously is embodied in the ritual demanded of the candidate who goes down to the Examination Schools for the academic Last Judgment: the symbolic lustration (white tie) and concluding bacchanal (champagne on the steps at the end). In Europe generally, only a few more or less experimental universities (Vincennes for example, and the British Open University) have adopted a version of the American credit system, by which a student accumulates the credits necessary for a degree by professorial consent at each stage of his academic career. In Italy, the form of examinations has hardly changed since the Middle Ages: the student defends his own knowledge verbally against the questioning of a panel of doctors, with his friends silently cheering him on from the public benches. In Japan, the university's own examinations count for rather less in the student's mind than the exams he has to pass on his way into the university, and the ones he has to pass to be admitted into the company of his choice after leaving university. Schwab knows that 'given the ugly start in schooling which most children suffer, it is not what a professor says which conveys what he expects of students, nor even what he himself is and does. It is what he asks for in examinations.' Therefore, the logic of his concern for method rather than content must be upheld at this point too: examinations 'must be tests of what a student can do, not merely of what he knows'—and will swiftly forget.

Schwab takes his sample procedure from the humanities, and assures us—as a scientist himself—that the sciences can be similarly treated. Two weeks before the end of the academic year, a work is set for examination. It is representative of the others whose meaning students have sought throughout the session, and it is accessible to the same disciplines, the same probing of its form and matter, structure and sense. It allows comparisons with other works used during the year. But it is fresh. The instructor has had nothing to say about it. Students may then choose their own ways of mastering the set work in advance of the formal examination, reading alone or in groups, consulting books or staff. For the examination proper, students need not be policed in the traditional, insulting fashion: they may bring their annotated copies of the set work, and exchange words with colleagues; it will not matter, if the examination and its marking are true tests of what has been assimilated rather than parroted. Schwab comments:

'This runs counter, of course, to the tradition of examinations. Students are collaborating; they are cheating, in fact; borrowing ideas from each other, criticisms, tips, and caveats. Which is exactly the point. They are doing on their own exactly what we have taught them to do. They are doing exactly what we do—unless we are poets or egomaniacs—when we undertake a similar work, for we, too, borrow ideas from colleagues and predecessors (and it matters very little whether we seek their help face to face or by way of their publications), and seek from colleagues charitable enough to give it, criticism of our thoughts and formulations. The examination, in short, is a continuation of the curriculum as well as a certifying device.'[14]

Berkeley: the Tussman College

Berkeley, where Joseph Tussman's Experimental College was founded in the fall of 1965, has taken its popular image as an *educational* institution from two prime sources: a book, *The Uses of the University* by its then-President, Clark Kerr, who half-described, half-satirised it as a 'multiversity', a 'City of Intellect', whose faculty entrepreneurs were 'held together by a common grievance over parking'; and from the Free Speech Movement of 1964, whose criticism of teaching at Berkeley was summed up at the time by two sympathetic faculty members:

'At Berkeley, the educational environment of the undergraduate is bleak. He is confronted throughout his entire first two years with indifferent advising, endless bureaucratic routines, gigantic lecture courses, and a deadening succession of textbook assignments and blue book examinations testing his grasp of bits and pieces of knowledge. All too often the difference between the last two years of a student's education and the first two is chronological rather than qualitative. It is possible to take a BA at Berkeley and never talk with a professor.'[15]

(Compare what Bolognese students say about their own education: 'Trying to talk with a professor is like seeking an audience with the President of the Republic', 'My work is not just intellectual but physical—to find a place in the lecture room', and—a rhetorical flight which deserves the original Italian—'*non parliamo degli appelli affollatissimi, dei bidelli tyranni, delle corse da un instituto all' altro per trovare un professore, delle altese snervanti, delle file in segretaria, delle firme di frequenza che sono un' inutile formalità*'.)[16]

Berkeley, then is constructed round scholars, with their departments, monographs, Ph.D. students, consultancies. Tussman's first argument is that students are not scholars, though some may become so. 'The American college student is simply a normal American who has behaved well in high school and who can afford to go to college. He is there because

[14] P. 218.

[15] Sheldon S. Wolin and John H. Schaar in *New York Review of Books*, March 11, 1965. Reprinted in Lipset and Wolin, op. cit., pp. 350–364.

[16] Giovanni Russo, *Università Anno Zero* (Rome, 1966), p. 26.

it is the natural place for him to be, not because the life of reason beckons
. . .' Tussman's reply to the uncoordinated riches of the courses offered
to all comers by the multiversity is a conservative one: a highly structured,
simple-seeming course of books drawn from three civilisations (Athenian,
seventeenth century English, and American), taught by six professors to
150 students, and centred on an abandoned fraternity house. To an English
reader it sounds like a reconstruction on a permanent basis of an old-
fashioned classical schoolmaster's sixth form reading party, and it is no
surprise to learn of the college's early internal strains, when students
unused to any form of externally-imposed academic discipline found
themselves committed to slow reading, in a fashion which Tussman
describes as 'sub-disciplinary' rather than inter-disciplinary, of Homer's
Iliad, Plato's *Republic* (in translation), Hobbes's *Leviathan*, Arnold's *Culture
and Anarchy* and other works: reading them, that is to say, 'because they
are better than anything that has been written about them', and because
they bypass the organising categories of the university—the administrative
departments which so easily come to be thought of as the watertight
compartments into which knowledge itself can be divided.

The curriculum is therefore inter-disciplinary for the professors, if
not for the students: they are required to teach subjects on which they
are not comfortably 'expert'. It makes no bow to the sciences, which
students in the Experimental College have to acquire elsewhere in the
University. Science students themselves, in Berkeley as elsewhere, are
mostly expected to spend their lower division years in technical preparation for their major subject. Their professors, Professor Tussman
writes, 'are sorry about it and wish someone would whip up a nice com-
pact liberal education which their students could swallow in their spare
time'. Teaching in the Tussman college is done by the usual techniques of
lecture and seminar, and by the less usual technique (in America) of the
tutorial, which with a staff student ratio of 1 : 30 is necessarily occasional
rather than regular. Tussman rigorously excludes the use of graduate
students as teaching assistants. There are few short cuts to good teaching,
he says, and this is not one of them. Graduate students should be immersed
in their fields as young technicians: it is fair neither to them nor their
pupils if they are asked to teach outside those fields. The college gives
no grades: a student passes or fails. It is too early to draw conclusions from
the subsequent performance of its students in higher divisions of the
university, and the college is at the time of writing a skeleton of its original
self. Berkeley in the last few years has not been an ideal place for conservative experiments.

All conservatism, in the appropriate context, becomes radicalism.
Professor Tussman writes: 'A sustained attempt to improve the quality
of education reveals, as perhaps nothing else does, how deeply we, as a
society, are imbued with the ideas and attitudes of competitive individualism. The university teacher receives the "already deeply disaffected and

disillusioned" sons and daughters of the American middle-class, whose "philosophy" and hence behaviour is a mirror-image of their parents':

' "Everyone should do what seems right to him." Apparently the ultimate moral principle, casually relegating law, politics, experience, authority, knowledge, humility, and all that, to the dustbin of history. . . . We do not see, apparently, that this is the classic characterisation of the state of war.'[17]

The college, in this situation, is a remedial educator in a rather different sense, charged with rebuilding from the ground upwards a theory of the state, so that students may at least know what they are dissenting from. It is at least evident that in Reagan's California, Hobbes's *Leviathan* is a fully contemporary text.

British generalists and specialists

The British book on general education which I discuss is more detailed and technical than either of the others, because its editor Michael Yudkin, a young biochemist, went about the job by asking several contributors to say how they would teach their own specialisms to strangers, and confined his own contribution to the teaching of science. However, Sir Isaiah Berlin and Mr. A. D. C. Peterson, in (respectively) foreword and conclusion, approach the subject with the broader brush of the historian of thought and the professional educationist. Mr. Peterson usefully quotes Aristotle:

'In modern times, people's views about education differ. There is no general agreement about what the young should learn either in relation to moral virtue or to success in life; nor is it clear whether education should be more concerned with training the intellect or the character. Contemporary events have made the problem more difficult and there is no certainty whether education should be primarily vocational, moral or cultural. People have recommended all three. Moreover there is no agreement as to what sort of education does promote moral virtue.'[18]

There is still no agreement, even when one remembers that the Greek word for virtue has a meaning which is as close to 'skill' or 'competence' as it is to 'piety' or 'good behaviour'. Peterson borrows from Aristotle and Bacon the concept—still dominant in the Western theory of schools and universities, if not in their practice—of a liberal or general education which enables a man to realise, in Matthew Arnold's phrase, 'his own best self'. But like Schwab, he too would define this education not in

[17] Pp. 103–4.
[18] *Politics*, VIII, 2.

terms of content, but in terms of the mind's power to operate in 'the four main modes of human experience': the analytical (as in mathematics and syntax), the empirical (as in the social and natural sciences), the moral, and the aesthetic, though these demarcations are apt to change with the changing conceptual frameworks of the experimental sciences. (As Mr. Peterson admits, the methods of the natural and the social sciences need to be differentiated much more sharply than he originally provided for.) This general education is in turn distinguished—though again, more sharply in theory than in practice—from 'polytechnical' education as developed by Marxist theorists, who see the fulfilment of the individual in the development of his capacity to serve the economic needs of society. Ironically, this Marxist formulation is precisely what European left-wing students object to in their own systems of higher education. In Britain, too, there is imminent danger of conceptual muddle, and the physical conflict that often follows from that, if the new, supposedly 'liberal' institutions called Polytechnics in the United Kingdom simply borrow the Marxist philosophy of polytechnical education and apply it to the economic needs of industrial capitalism. British educationists might be wise to find a different term either for the institutions or for the philosophy.

It is impossible to summarise here the arguments of Yudkin's contributors, except to say that most readers will find their own general education pleasantly stretched by one or more of the essays. But an idea of the approach may be gathered from the summarised principles of the general course in mathematics, by Alan Tayler, Alan Tammadge, and Philip Prescott:

'1. The content should be mathematics relevant to the present day, both intellectually and in its application. It should demonstrate its power and usefulness in applications that are likely to be relevant to most of the students. It should include the development of an abstract mathematical structure as an example of ordered mathematical thought and as an opportunity to gain some impression of the aesthetic appeal of mathematics.
'2. The method of teaching should be predominantly that of personal discovery by the student with some tutorial guidance.'[19]

Michael Yudkin's own essay on the teaching of experimental science criticises the common notion that because politicians and administrators may have to make decisions about space rockets or biological warfare they ought to learn electronics and biochemistry, rather than classics or English. The fallacy here is that scientific change is always at least twenty years further advanced than the full-time education of political leaders. Most of the ministers involved in decisions about nuclear tests today left university before the bombing of Hiroshima, and even Harold

[19] P. 111.

Wilson's Oxford economics, 1940s-vintage, was sometimes held to be of questionable use to a 1960s Prime Minister. The kind of 'scientific literacy' that matters is knowledge of when science is relevant, what kind of evidence should be sought, and how it should be weighed. Beyond this, if real understanding of the scientific world view is to be reached, a course must somehow convey the feel of doing science, which includes not merely the weighing of evidence but the outreach of the imagination. Most of the introductory or survey courses in science which Yudkin investigated in the United States simply impart information. Some teach a course in scientific method, but this account of the empirical steps taken in research is incomplete, for it glosses over 'the most ingenious step that a scientist takes—the creation of a fruitful hypothesis. Better is J. B. Conant's "case history" approach,[20] but although actual scientists' own accounts of their gropings towards new techniques, concepts, and solutions can teach undergraduates much, even these tend to ignore the false starts and inconclusive experiments.' Written with hindsight, they are logically rather than chronologically ordered.

> 'The conclusion seems inexorable. A true appreciation of experimental science can most easily be achieved by carrying out independent investigations. Through working in a laboratory, an undergraduate can come to see how intellectual and emotional elements are intertwined in science, and can gain his own understanding of those features which an external account cannot wholly describe.'[21]

Yudkin goes on to describe two problems, one physical and one biochemical, which can be investigated empirically in minimally equipped laboratories by non-scientific undergraduates, but which do not merely offer mechanical work leading to a rigged solution. Laboratory work of this kind is naturally not intended to replace altogether discussions and lectures on the more formal aspects of scientific inquiry, but it might well be used to supplement the courses of science specialists, who otherwise seldom see the wood of science for the trees of their own narrow subjects. It would be amusing if the effect of all this in Yudkin's Oxford were to return some scientific laboratory work from the specialist palaces in the Parks to the college cellars from which it sprang, so that Balliol classicists could learn to construct their own hypotheses for the mechanism by which the enzyme esterase catalyses the substrate ethyl acetate—to pick one of Yudkin's own examples. However, A. D. C. Peterson's melancholy account of the unsuccessful attempts that have in the past been made to get general education taken seriously in British sixth forms and at university entrance examinations holds out little promise of success this time. True, Britain is no longer quite bereft of inter-disciplinary or

[20] See *Harvard Case Histories in Experimental Science* (Harvard, 1957).
[21] Pp. 127–8.

general education at undergraduate level (the foundation year at Keele, the school of physics and philosophy at Oxford, and numerous 'broadening' experiments at the Plateglass universities come to mind.) Besides some honours courses are broader than others: a philosopher of science will range more widely than a physiologist. But as Peterson suggests, until every young person in Britain knows that he does not have to propel his mind very fast down a single track to obtain, first, a university place, and second, the best jobs the economy can offer, university-level general education will remain marginal as well as remedial. (However, see p. 39.)

Yudkin himself happily admits that his proposals will yield no dividend in scientific manpower, and though he might be proved wrong about that in the next generation, politicians take shorter views. Intellectually, though, the battle for general education to be communicated, if at all, through an introduction to the different ways of knowing—the empirical, the moral, the aesthetic, and so on—rather than through ingenious re-arrangements of subject matter, looks to be won.[22] The deciding factor, as often in protracted educational debates, was the impossibility of doing it any other way. Until very recently, intelligent people could still think it useful to impart or absorb an encyclopaedic smattering of the world's learning, and to keep up with the eighteenth century Enlightenment's idea of an Educated Man. A good many familiar features of our mass culture, from the BBC's Brain of Britain contest to the foot-in-the-door encyclopaedia salesman, rely on the afterglow of the same belief. Only in the past thirty years or so has it become totally absurd. It is not only that the world has exploded with the physicists and the astronomers, and imploded with the biologists and behavioral scientists. It is also that the world of learning is metamorphosed, and enlarged by geometric progression, when these and other disciplines are allowed to act upon each other, and to be acted upon by the contemporary world. With the rise of the Third World, for example, teachers of history are forced to face the question, 'if Caesar why not Akbar?', and many people who have just begun to consider themselves rather ignorant for knowing so little of the history of Western science are shortly going to be distressed by their ignorance of Chinese. In this light, survey courses which leave a student with one or two unsaleable textbooks and do not even teach him how to exploit the resources of a library seem a criminal waste of time, and the British alternative—the disease of premature and over-intense specialisation—seems a rather joyless denial of the human mind's pleasurably diverse capabilities.

The capabilities are of course not uniformly diverse in different people.

[22] I speak of Britain and America, but even in France there are straws in the wind. See John Ardagh's description in *The New France* (London, 1970), pp. 502–5, of Marcel Bonvalet's regime at the Nancy Institut des Sciences de l'Ingénieur. Bonvalet's inductive, participatory method of teaching is related, directly or indirectly, to the Vincennes programme and the Faure educational reforms, described in Chapter Four.

Liam Hudson explores in *Contrary Imaginations* the educational conclusions that might be drawn from the fact that you can ask a future Senior Wrangler with a 'convergent' mind how many uses he can think of for a brick and get a couple of conventional replies '(building things', 'throwing'), while if you put the same question to a 'divergent' arts boy you may get twenty times as many uses mentioned, from 'hotwater bottle' to 'nutcracker'. It seems likely that enthusiastic advocates of general education, if tested in this way, would show up as divergers. But Hudson, though he himself thinks that 'much of what passes for education in this country and the United States is a waste of everyone's time, pupils and teachers alike', points out the dangers of supposing that because conventional education is antipathetic to the divergent, possibly more creative mind, it must therefore stifle talent. Certain English and American schools (and universities?) may, he suggests, 'provide precisely the background of mild conformity and incompetence which reinforces the potentially original child's conviction of his own worth. They provide the ideal background against which to rebel.'[23]

[23] Liam Hudson, *Contrary Imaginations* (London, 1966), pp. 133–4 (Penguin edition).

Hudson's remark will serve to introduce two issues which in the last few years have floated to the surface of the debate in several countries about the quality of university teaching. These are, first, the issue of monitoring and control ('who is to judge whether teaching is being well done, and how is it to be rewarded?'); and second, the issue of excellence versus economy ('Can we afford to improve the staff student ratio in order to teach this subject better?'). The first is an issue for the most part domestic to universities, where it is fought out between professors and students, and between professors and administration. The second is an issue for administrators and for governments, which take understandable fright at the galloping expense of university teaching. (In Britain, for example, the only obvious way to reduce the cost of universities by a significant margin is to worsen the student: staff ratio, which now stands at 8 : 1. To present the sum very schematically: half a million students cost £500,000,000 p.a. exclusive of maintenance grant. At the existing ratio, they require 62,500 research and teaching staff, whose salaries, averaged for the sake of argument at £2,000 p.a. each, account for a quarter of the £500,000,000. A change in the ratio from 8 : 1 to 10 : 1 then begins to look like a very attractive economy.) But in one sense, the issue of control and the issue of economy are the same. No government or parent wants to pay money, and no student wants to pay time, for a style of teaching which can subsequently be shown to be ineffective, or which *is* ineffective, however hard it is to prove the charge. The trouble is that there exist no recognised standards, either of economy or of excellence, nor any theory by which standards might be set. Teaching is a little like the performance of a symphony: it is easy to count the players and record the metronome markings of the movements—but was it a good performance? Do you ask the orchestra, the audience, the conductor, or the critics? And if all four, how much weight do you give to the view of each?

I cannot hope here to do more than outline the problem, and then to present examples to show the astonishing diversity of the process which generically we call teaching. Most of the problems have been far more carefully investigated in the United States than anywhere else. I understood the reason at a graduate seminar in a big American state university, where a professor had just expounded a new technique for social measure-ment. A student put up his finger and said 'You lost me.' The phrase dis-closed a whole academic culture. A British student who had failed to understand part of a lecture would say—if he said anything at all—not 'You lost me', but 'I lost you.' (A French, an Italian, or a Japanese student would be lucky if he had the chance to speak.)

The course-assessment forms that litter American student union offices define the expectations—and disappointments—which the university teacher evokes. Here is one summing-up of an economics professor at a big Catholic university (Notre Dame, Indiana): 'This energetic prof. is a favourite among econ. as well as non. econ. majors. Both his Monetary Policy and his Macro. courses reflect his enthusiasm and deep grasp of this dynamic and constantly changing behavioural science ... Winterwise, he is a ski enthusiast and an excellent skier.' At Reed College in Port-land (Oregon), which is academically one of the top three or four liberal arts colleges in the US, students' ratings of their teachers are automatically sought by the faculty as part of the evidence on which professors are hired or fired. But even this was not enough for many Reed students, and in the summer of 1969 groups of them were demand-ing places on faculty appointment committees, and collecting from their friends subjective, open-ended assessments of the college's teaching. This was the kind of answer they got:

'This professor is very open and friendly, thoroughly academic, sometimes pedantic. He tends to make rather picayunish comments upon papers. He is very cheerful when drunk. I think he is very inter-ested in individual students' needs, and quite ready to respond to them helpfully. He is accessible, frequently using his home as an office.'

'B—— is boring, obnoxious, pseudo-hip. His reading list was bland and non-structured. He has no idea how to lead a class. He is also *the* politically naïve teacher in the college.'

'R—— very much wants to help his students. He tries to be responsive to students' interests and needs, but doesn't put much effort into study of formal returns from students. He digs being with us. His interest is a bit more selfish and aggressive than is ideal, but I think his presence is generally healthy here. He'll make it. He's very intelligent.'

This, perhaps, is at the far edge of academic permissiveness. For its opposite extreme there is no need to go further than the correspondences in serious British newspapers during December, 1968, after the Prices and Incomes Board (a Government review body) had suggested that students might possibly participate in the assessment of university teaching. The suggestion was described by Professor E. H. Gombrich, the art historian, as 'a blueprint for the destruction of civilisation', and it evoked from the Professor of Zoology at Southampton the judgment that 'to give merit awards on the strength of quality and quantity of one's teaching is as ludicrous as giving them on the basis of number of words published per annum'. The then Prime Minister, Harold Wilson, lost no time in dismissing the proposal out of hand—but then Mr. Wilson was himself once a university teacher.[24]

Of course, in many American universities and colleges, the evaluation of faculty by students became a narrowly political rather than a substantive intellectual issue. Even at Reed, one of those now-rare colleges where everyone seems to know everyone else, students' clumsily phrased attempts to protect the academic careers of teachers whom they liked and to edge out the others carried an undertone of bullying, which quickly drove the faculty behind its professional stockade. However, the seriousness with which Americans are prepared to discuss the problem is accounted for not just by political pressure from students, but by the scale of the academic industry, and by the tenure system. In a big state university, with up to 50,000 students, a single department may carry a staff that would have been large enough before 1939 to sustain an entire campus. It may have to select for employment or promotion a couple of hundred teachers a year. Seniors in such a department would be interested in any method that enabled them to judge the quality of men whose faces they may not recognise even after they have been working in the same building for years. The tenure system heightens the anxiety. American universities hire assistant professors in a comparatively carefree manner but the department's subsequent decision whether or not to give the man tenure as an associate professor is a very different affair. A mistake, as Stephen Orgel and Alex Zwerdling remark in a shrewd essay 'On judging faculty', institutionalises mediocrity. 'It means thirty years of cheated students and bad research; and when such men reach positions of power, their mediocrity is perpetuated through their own decisions.'[25]

But how is a student to know whether he is being cheated? The grosser forms of absenteeism ('Professor X is away in Washington today and his class will be taken by Mr. Y') sound easy to detect—but what if Professor X is so eminent in his field that a tenth of his time is worth half anyone else's? Nor can a student, except perhaps at graduate level, be expected to recognise the gaps in his teacher's knowledge of the subject matter. It is hardly easier for a department head. Even if he has the time, the inclination, and the effrontery to drop in on colleagues' classes, he cannot judge a man's success on more private occasions—for instance, at adapting his teaching style to the different needs of different students, of whom one may become an organisation man in an aircraft company, and another take up an academic career in the professor's own special

[24] However, see similar proposals seriously made by a Senate sub-committee on promotions in Bradford University. (*The Guardian*, October 17, 1970).

[25] In Robert S. Morison (ed.), *The Contemporary University; USA* (New York, 1967), p. 226.

subject. It is these difficulties, as well as the other pressures of the academic industry, which encourage university faculties to judge their members' performance solely or mainly on the quality or quantity of their published research. The presence of students on departmental committees is unlikely to reverse this tendency. But on the other hand, it will not necessarily destroy civilisation either.

4 NEW ROUTES TO LEARNING: THE COMPUTER AND THE OPEN UNIVERSITY

But what is teaching?
For example, this is teaching:

Since this is our first chat, I'll show you what I can do. When I just type a period at the left margin, it means I'm waiting for you to reply. Type your response on just one line, and always end it by pressing 'return' key. Got the idea?

.

No

Fine—you found the return key. Incidentally, if you make an error while typing, type a @, then press 'return', then you may type your response again. Try it.

.

Yes

Okay, let's move on. These topics are available.
SIGNAL (signals and waveforms)
WAVE (problem on waveforms)
COMPLEX (questions on complex numbers)
PHASOR (sequence on phasor representations)
RESISTANCE (problem on resistance of semi-conductor bar)
DIODE 1 (first instruction sequence on diodes)
DIODE 2 (second instruction sequence on diodes)
COMMENT (to record your comments)

.

COMPLEX

Let's try a few questions about complex numbers. I'll use 'J' to mean 'square root of minus one'. Now, consider the complex number 'Z = X plus JY' where X and Y are real numbers. What is the real part of Z?

.

X

Okay. What is the imaginary part of Z?

Y

That's correct, John. So the imaginary part of '1·5 — 'J7·2' is?

— 7·2

Right. When a complex number is written 'Z = X plus JY' it is said to be in the 'algebraic' or 'Cartesian' form. For what arithmetic operations is this form best?

Addi, subt.

Yes, for addition and subtraction. What is the sum of '1 plus J2' and '2 plus J3'?

3 plus J5

Correct, John. What is the result when you subtract '2 — J3' from '1 plus J2'?

1 — J2

Try that one again. Subtract real part from real part, and imaginary part from imaginary part.

2 plus J7

Wrong again. Try a slightly different one. What is (5 plus Jo)—(4 plus J1)?

6 plus J4

Apparently wrong answer. To stop now type 'stop'; to try next question type 'go'.

Go

The teacher in that example was a programme in a computer at Stanford University. The 'pupil' was a faculty member at Berkeley, fifty miles up the Californian coast. The time used was approximately fifteen minutes: readers in different countries may check that against their prevailing computer time-sharing prices, and see how much such teaching their education systems can afford. For full and expert discussions of both theoretical and practical possibilities in instruction-by-computer, the reader is referred to articles by Patrick Suppes, an enthusiast, and replies by critics.[26] A chillier estimate is made by Anthony Oettinger in *Run, Computer, Run*.[27]

Ultimately, I believe, the computer is bound to 'explode' the university in a new sense, by helping it to extend learning facilities into the student's home. Other, simpler modern technologies—for instance, cheap copying services, and the reprinting of rare books—are already having a similar effect. Oettinger's own conclusion, briefly, is that the computer does indeed have great potential usefulness in education, perhaps especially in elementary science courses at college level, but that the social disorganisation and poverty of the American school system will make it an uneconomic tool for children's use. For the present, Oettinger is more interested in the computer as an 'active participant' in the development of scientific theories, and he uses THE BRAIN (The Harvard Experimental Basic Reckoning And Instructional Network) to this end. 'A physical theory expressed in the static language of mathematics often becomes dynamic when it is rewritten as a computer program; one can explore its inner structure, confront it with experimental data and interpret its implications much more easily. . . . In disciplines where mathematics is not the prevailing mode of expression the language of computer programs serves increasingly as the language of science.' (p. 201)

And this too is teaching:

'*Exercise 2*
You have been engaged for several weeks researching among the private papers and possessions of a British politician named Jones (please note that Jones is a completely imaginary character, invented for the purpose of this exercise). You have discovered:

  1. A letter dated 9th December, 1909, from the then Prime Minister to Jones, referring to the recently passed Labour Exchanges Act, and saying: 'although the world has not yet had the chance to appreciate your invaluable labour, I shall always remember that you, my dear Jones, were the true progenitor of the Act.'

  2. Certain household accounts showing that over a fifteen year period Jones consumed ten bottles of brandy a week.

  3. Various newspaper cuttings and letters from party leaders dating from the 1906 election showing that Jones was definitely regarded then as a rising politician.

  4. Jones's marriage certificate dated 3rd May, 1903.

  5. A transcript of the court proceedings in which his wife successfully divorced him, March, 1911.

From standard parliamentary sources you know that Jones never achieved

[26] E.g. in *Harvard Education Review*, Fall 1968.
[27] Harvard, 1969.

office, and that in fact he faded out of politics during the first world war. From the parish register in his home village you find his date-of-birth as 20th August, 1873.

Communicate this information in the form of a brief piece of historical writing such as might appear in a secondary source.'

Arts Foundation Course Unit 7: Basic Problems of Writing History (Open University Press, 1971)

That was an extract from a correspondence package devised for the British Open University by the Professor of History, Arthur Marwick. This particular example, of course, leads on to Professor Marwick's discussion of sample answers: the real teaching lies there.

The Open University represents a new approach to the problem of quantity and quality in higher education. Like many British innovations, it has aroused rather more interest from experts and politicians abroad than at home. But it had 42,000 applications for its first places, and selected 25,000 (all adults, not 18-year-olds). The courses, transmitted by BBC radio and television, and backed up by correspondence packages and local tutoring, began in January 1971. The central academic staff is small—about four to each traditional 'discipline'—but can call upon outside help. Students will be able to call upon counselling services as well as local tutors, and may have access—when the technology matures and the expense comes down—to electronic video recordings and other equipment which the domestic, or 'exploded', university will need. The economic uniqueness of the institution, which has cost about three million pounds to found, consists in the fact that the costs of the university are only marginally proportionate to student numbers. It is as cheap to broadcast the weekly radio and television programmes to 25,000 as to one, and though this kind of economy cannot apply to the network of local tutors, the size of the guaranteed order has already enabled a specially designed and cheap microscope to be included in the £100 package of equipment which went out to the University's science students. However, the experiment's future, both political and academic, cannot yet be regarded as certain. The Conservative Party initially opposed the scheme (which was lovingly protected from economic crises by a Labour Minister, Miss Jennie Lee), and although the new Conservative Minister of Education seems sympathetic, the University's costs over the next quinquennium will be scrutinised in Whitehall with a very critical eye.

Probably the real importance of these last two examples—computerised instruction at Stanford and televised instruction in Britain—is not technical, nor even economic, but pedagogic. By its nature, the technique concentrates the mind of the men and women who design the courses, for by the time that the lesson reaches the student it is too late for amendment. Everything has to be foreseen, and after transmission evaluated.

Not surprisingly, the Open University staff, and their pilot courses, already exhibit a preoccupation with methodology; and television has a methodology of its own, expressed here perhaps in the 'case-study' approach to the teaching of the humanities. (For example, Mendelssohn's revival of the music of Bach will be treated, first as a problem in music and musicology, but also as a point of entry into questions about Romanticism, and standards of bourgeois taste.) Professor Marwick has been brash enough to make these considerations explicit nine months before transmission starts:

'All universities are concerned with teaching styles of thought and methods of criticism and study, not with purveying mere information. Conventionally it is accepted that these styles of thought and methods of criticism will rub off on the student as he works his way through his undergraduate career. Is this rubbing-off process really the best one? Might it not be possible to clarify and systematise just what these styles and methods are, then communicate them much more directly to the student? One of the most important disciplines imposed upon Open University teachers by the very nature of their teaching is that they must very clearly set out just what it is they expect their students to be able to do at the end of a course which they could not do at the beginning of it.'[28]

For universities everywhere, this process can only be sheer gain—and probably in the long run more effective than the student-teacher contestation method which I described in operation at Reed.

[28] The *Listener*, March 12, 1970.

There is one outstanding problem which these new techniques of instruction can never solve for modern universities. This is the relation between excellence in teaching and excellence in research. In this matter, emphases vary considerably from country to country. The North American university president who advised on the best way to make a young department grow—'Start with research and attract foundation grants; think about what you are going to teach after you've got going'— probably knew his way to the top of the graduate school charts. His undergraduates might be better off in Oxford, England, where a major obstacle to the introduction of any new subject is the difficulty of finding someone in each college to teach it. Yet in both universities, a substantial majority of staff would still hold to the academic shibboleth that if the functions of teaching and research are wholly separated into different communities, both suffer. That is difficult for an outsider to judge. What can be observed from outside is the tautening of the cable as the interests of teaching and research pull apart. At the Quail Roost symposium recorded in Professor Niblett's book,[29] one speaker remarked that subjects which cannot be researched into are today only with difficulty accommodated within a university curriculum. (That is one of the obstacles to general education: not many people want to be professors of general studies, and not many universities would employ them in that capacity.) A few moments earlier, another speaker had urged that our whole culture was in a major transitional stage from the 'golden age' of specialisation for largely material ends, to an age which used specialisms, but valued wholeness. Wholeness, unfortunately, is not researchable. An academic is hired to be a professor, not a guru.

Just occasionally—perhaps more often than anyone has a right to expect—the guru and the professor, the researcher and the teacher, are combined in the same person. I met Lawrence Wylie the way one meets people in America. I was visiting the Behavioural Sciences think-tank at Stanford, and Charles Tilly said 'If you're going to Harvard, you ought to see the man responsible for a book called *Chanzeaux*,[30] which

[29] Op. cit., pp. 208–9.
[30] Laurence Wylie (ed.), *Chanzeaux: a Village in Anjou* (Harvard, 1966).

is surely the best if not the only work of original research which a Harvard full professor has written with his undergraduate class.' So I went to Harvard, and met Professor Wylie, and read *Chanzeaux*, and wrote to his ex-pupils, and met one of them in France where she was doing postgraduate work, and but for a motor breakdown would have visited Chanzeaux itself, but that did not really matter since I knew it from the book.

Harvard, as most people will hardly need telling, is not as other universities are. Its difference from Berkeley was described to me one afternoon by one of the voluble 'Berkeley refugees', as the *New York Times* called them, who had recently found sanctuary in Harvard. 'Harvard,' he said, 'is old, smug, and sure. It pays more attention to students. Berkeley is upwardly mobile, on the make. There's less competitive backbiting here. They don't emphasise their Nobel prizes. You assume that your colleagues are good. At Berkeley, it's been said, anyone can be trumped and usually is. You have job tenure but not status tenure. If someone younger and hotter comes he gets a better lab. Harvard is relatively unbureaucratised. Each faculty has different appointment procedures and salaries. The University makes no attempt to arbitrate. According to Martin Meyerson, Harvard is like a bunch of small federalised grocery stores. Berkeley is like a supermarket chain.'

Harvard's contribution to the Chanzeaux book was twofold: money and tolerance. It has a lot of both. The book is dedicated to Clarence and Douglas Dillon, whose newly endowed Chair of the Civilisation of France was filled by Wylie in 1959, and who gave further support to students engaged on the project. The introduction salutes Harvard's 'chaotic, permissive nature which allowed Social Relations 108 to evolve from a traditional seminar into what students say is a state of mind'. How an undergraduate seminar on the sociology of a French village, attended by about a hundred students of successive generations over a period of eight years, became a book by eighteen authors would be, as Wylie says, an interesting study in itself. Alas, this is not that study. But the educational significance of the procedure adopted is too great to be left buried in the preface to a book which is of absorbing interest to lovers of France, villages, and social anthropology, but which only a rarely perceptive librarian would put on his education shelf.

Wylie's interest in western France dates back twenty years, to a study he made with his family of a village in the Vaucluse, Roussillon.[31] He was at the time a French teacher at Haverford, a small liberal arts college in Pennsylvania, and his sociological study was an occupation for a sabbatical leave. In 1957, on his next sabbatical, he wanted to study a similar community that was yet opposite in political and religious behaviour. That meant a community where most people attended Mass and voted to the right, but were not—like Bretons, Alsatians, and Basques—differentiated

[31] Laurence Wylie, *Village in the Vaucluse* (Harvard, 1957).

by language and culture from the rest of France. He talked to people in France who understood what he was about, and consulted the excellent maps which French sociologists of religion and political geographers have produced, showing the geographical variations in people's behaviour. He finally settled on *le pays des Mauges*, in the south-west quarter of the old province of Anjou. The great town of the district is Angers, on the Loire, whose Catholic university dates its existence from 1229, when Parisian masters displaced by the Carnival Riots (see p. 128) took refuge there. In the Mauges, Wylie's team write, 'some of the most interesting and maddening puzzles of French history are actually before the traveler's eyes, even though he may be unaware of what he sees. The very hedges surrounding the fields, for instance, have to do with that baffling question in European history of why, in some parts of Europe, farmers have traditionally lived on isolated farms while in others they have lived in villages. This distinction is a feature of two contrasting ways of life, manifested by the presence or absence of the hedges.[32] For whatever reason, this topographical feature, *le bocage*, coincides in the Mauges sociologically with conservatism and Catholicism, and historically with support for the Vendée rebellion in 1793 against the French Republican government. Wylie spent several weeks in the Mauges looking for a suitable village, talking with 'political and diocesan authorities, journalists and *notaires*, teachers and rental agents, priests and town secretaries'. His search ended in Chanzeaux, where he took a house, sent his two sons to school, and was with his family cordially accepted. They were probably the first Protestants who had ever lived there. In a year, he collected a great deal of information, but he then fell ill, and when he returned to Haverford, he had to put his notes away until he got better. Then he was appointed to the Harvard Chair. At Harvard, the Department of Social Relations asked him to give a course on French social structure. He had an undergraduate seminar with a dozen or so students, and he set them to work on the primary material he had collected on Chanzeaux.

As the year passed, and each course yielded a proportion of students who became passionately interested in this distant village that they had never seen, the instructional relationship between Wylie and his students became rather complicated. Students began making trips to Chanzeaux, on grants from parents, Douglas Dillon, the National Science Foundation, the Ford Foundation, or the Harvard Social Relations Laboratory. (In America, and especially in Harvard, you can usually raise money if you want something badly enough.) They brought back new information, and wanted to work on it. The seminars for new students continued year by year, but the Chanzeaux 'veterans', many of them now using their experience in their senior theses, wanted to continue their own discussion. In 1963 they began to meet Wylie informally for lunch every Saturday. Every year, a few of the keener 'neophytes' came too, in

[32] *Chanzeaux*, p. 3.

search of advice, and 'we had the best possible situation—students serving as teachers to other students'. It was not long before someone suggested that they had enough material for a book. They soon decided that individually written essays would not do: each of them knew too much about the subjects of other people's essays. The complexity of the task defies description. 'One student and I,' Wylie recalls, 'spent hours putting names on to cards and then another said, 'Why don't you computerise it all?' We ended up with forty-two variables on each of the 1,500 individuals living in Chanzeaux. We think we may have more information about this community than has ever before been had for any community, and there is probably not a page in the book which is only one person's work'. In spite of this, the book has not drowned in its own information, and the hundred or so participant observers of Chanzeaux have given the text a distinct, readable style. It was finished by the Harvard University's Press's deadline of July 1, 1965, after an all-night session in William James Hall, and published the following year, while Wylie was doing two years as Cultural Attaché at the American Embassy in Paris. A French edition, translated by Marc André Bera, was published by Gallimard in September 1970, and includes a chapter written by Chanzeans themselves in criticism of what *les Américains* said about them. (Wylie's team got the translation xeroxed and took the copies down to Chanzeaux in the spring of 1968.)

Wylie had four student co-editors, two boys and two girls. I asked him what had happened to them since.

'Of the boys, one is an associate professor of economics at Princeton and one is finishing his doctoral dissertation on the socio-economic implications of the cult of the Virgin in Spain. He has already published a book about a village on the island of St. Pierre. Of the girls, one has finished Harvard Medical School and will be a child psychiatrist. The other girl took her degree in Latin American studies and married an English professor at Stanford. Of the other students whose names appear on the title page, one subsequently did village work with the Peace Corps in Venezuela and is now doing "village work" with Puerto Ricans in New York City; another took off to advise the Tanzanian government about village development and has just written a book. Two are at Columbia: one is making a village study in Rumania as part of his doctoral work in anthropology; and the other, a doctoral student in sociology, is using his experience of the Chanzeaux project in support of his dissertation's thesis—that the educational system is an obstacle to students' self-education.'

I was curious to know what these sixteen students made of the Chanzeaux experience on looking back, so I sent them a short questionnaire and asked for comments. Eight replied, including three of the four co-editors. I was content with this response: if all had replied at similar length, the inquiry would have had to make a chapter on its own here.

All but one of the eight had parents who both went to college. All but one (a lawyer) are still in the academic world, as graduate or Ph.D. students, or teachers. The chief subjects they took at Harvard varied considerably: Government, Political Science, History of France, English, Mathematics, and other dabblings of the kind which American universities encourage. Four of them found other Harvard educational experiences worth mentioning: history tutorials with Tom Skidmore and Patrick Higgonnet; the 'T-group' course in undergraduate scoiology; David Riesman's freshman seminars in sociology—'usually great men who came and spoke to us about the relations between their lives and ideas'. (Great men never mind visiting Harvard.) Three of them are still in touch with people at Chanzeaux.

The other replies were more quotable than classifiable. The most fruitful questions I asked were the following:

(1) How far are your present occupation and pattern of relationships attributable to participation in the Chanzeaux project?
(2) Do you regard the work you were able to do with Professor Wylie as typical or atypical of opportunities for students at Harvard?
(3) Have you used similar methods in your own teaching (if any)?
(4) If you had been at Harvard during the 'revolution' of May 1969, where do you think your sympathies would have lain?

These are some of the replies:

To question (1)
'Totally . . . I am presently preparing a thesis on the 19th and early 20th century development of a suburb of Paris. Because of my participation in the Chanzeaux project, my approach to history is firmly colored by the belief that an understanding of continuity and change on the local level is imperative if one wants to study history generally. . . . The simple fact of having spent a summer working in the departmental archives of Maine-et-Loire, the municipal and parish archives of two towns, the diocesan archives of Angers, and some family archives was an extremely unusual opportunity for a college student, and helped me greatly in deciding that I wanted to go into local social history as a career.' (Ph.D. student)

'The Chanzeaux project was one of the most formative educational experiences of my life. What I learned from it, more than anything else, was co-operation and exchange. The lunches that we had in Quincy House and the meetings in the Wylies' apartment, discussing each other's papers, stand out very clearly. . . . Every episode I can think of has four or five people in it working together, re-writing each other's material, encouraging and pushing each other along. Our return to Chanzeaux in the spring of 1968 to record the reaction of the village to our book is a case in point. We all sat around in T-group-like sessions with the members of the Town Council while they talked about themselves and the difference between the way they saw themselves and the way we saw them.' (Professor of Economics)

'One effect of the Chanzeaux seminar was to interest me in Anthropology. So while everyone headed for a summer in Chanzeaux, I headed for an anthropology field station in southern Mexico, which then led to my going to graduate school in Latin American studies.' (Ph.D. student)

'Wylie has given me a standard to measure the mediocrity of most of the rest of academic social science and its essentially manipulative, bourgeois character.' (Graduate student in political science)

'Chanzeaux was the only *academic* thing in my entire 20½ years of school that I really *liked*. At least half of what goes on in universities should be like the Chanzeaux group, instead of all this nonsense about credit hours and final examinations. In addition to being a library (good) and an accrediting agency (bad), universities should involve some kind of communication between people. . . . When people will work together till dawn, with no sanction requiring them to do so, you know their work can't be *all* nonsense. . . . If I had not gone to Chanzeaux, gotten good references from Wylie and had my name on a *publication* (wow! an undergraduate!) I probably would not have been admitted to so supposedly high-grade a sociology department as Columbia's. . . . I'm doing my doctoral dissertation on how it came to be that education replaced property as the main obstacle to be overcome by the would-be upwardly mobile. . . . I doubt if I would have gone to graduate school if it were not for the draft.' (Graduate student in sociology)

To question (2)

'The opportunity to work with Mr. Wylie was an unusual stroke of luck for all of us. Student participation in substantial academic projects under a faculty member is fairly common at Harvard, but these projects rarely are as complex, prolonged, and involving as the Chanzeaux project.' (Partner in a law firm)

'The Chanzeaux project was atypical in its utter confidence in students, and in its entirely co-operative nature. Also it went way beyond the classroom in financial resources and facilities open to us.' (Ph.D. student)

To question (3)

'It is with some sadness that I admit that I haven't followed Larry's methodology as much as I would like to have in my own teaching. . . . I am myself very much caught up in the publish-or-perish pressure; and doing what Larry did is a total commitment. To some extent, also, I am young and still on the receiving end. For instance, I am involved now in the construction of an econometric model of the US financed by the Federal Reserve Board. This has been, at the graduate and post-graduate level, somewhat similar to the Chanzeaux project, the mentor being Franco Modigliani at MIT. The model has been built by Franco Modigliani and Albert Ando (professors), a team at the Federal Reserve Board in Washington, and half a dozen or so graduate students.' (Assistant professor)

'I am a course assistant this year, which means I do essentially nothing. The course is a required methods course. The professor is visiting this year from New York University, and he told me he often had his students do group work. "Why not try it here?" I said. So he did. The students were told to form groups with similar interests (4–6 students in one group) and come up with short-range projects in historical sociology. They did that fairly successfully, but the course was a disaster. There was bitterness about who might be doing more or less work than others. Groups split up and reformed. . . . The obvious flaw was that the class was convened as a group of people who needed to satisfy a requirement, not a group which was at least tentatively interested in doing research on a specific subject. More credit-hour nonsense.' (Graduate student)

'I have not yet taught, but when I do, I'll have students work as a group, without individual grades, on something that is a potential book, which takes fieldwork as its essential component.' (Ph.D. student)

'The Chanzeaux project was a forerunner for the kind of involved, loving, free exchange that is becoming more and more popular in undergraduate education in the US. Abandonment of authority by the professor, learning as a shared experience, and an emphatic humanism, are its hallmarks. . . . Similar courses, and "course-communities" are being formed with great frequency now, particularly in urban studies. It will always be a model for me in how to teach.' (Graduate student and writer)

To question (4)
'The day University Hall was seized I was in Widener Library. At about 5 o'clock that afternoon, Dean Ford ordered that the library be evacuated. It made a terrific impression on me that I had to stop doing my "studying thing" because the people who had occupied University Hall were doing their "revolution thing". . . . . If everybody could behave somewhat violently in the name of ends he felt were morally right, chaos would result . . . ' (Ph.D. student—left wing Democrat)

'My sympathies were with the strikers. Harvard is stuck up.' (Graduate student and writer.)

'There is no question here in my mind. I do, however, sometimes quarrel with the parochial politics of SDS, but I presume that at Harvard there are students—as at Stanford—who are generally more sophisticated and thoughtful, and ultimately more radical, with whom I would sympathise.'

'I was on the side of the insurgents. . . . But I don't think the administration was blindly serving the military industrial complex when they called the cops in. They were just scared. But they had no reason to be. Harvard is still enough of a community that it is not about to destroy itself (revolutionise itself yes, but not destroy). Columbia, on the other hand, is so fragmented and bitter that it just might burn down some day . . .'.

'Chanzeaux' represents one kind of teaching. It is for the reader to work out whether his country's economy could afford it, or its sociology permit it. (In France, for example, students are from their schooldays so tightly wrapped in cocoons of individualism that a comparably co-operative French investigation of, say, an English village would be almost inconceivable. In Japan hardly any teacher would sacrifice so much of his dignity to his seminar, nor would his students be easily persuaded that their own contributions to a book might be as valid as *sensei's*.)[33] Clearly, too, some subjects are more "human", or potentially human, than others. Even in the arts, a social inquiry involving fieldwork or participant observation is a very different proposition from a research project in English literature, requiring hours of solitary work in library or study. Nor will either publishers or readers be any happier with a flood of books indifferently composed by "course communities" than they are now with Ph.D. theses souped-up for hard covers by individual scholars. All the same, "Chanzeaux" deserves more imitators and adaptors than it has yet had. Almost every page of the book provides examples of the combination of objectivity, observation, and respect which Wylie drew from his pupils—by their own account, quite without over-direction and close supervision. But perhaps this anecdote gives some idea of all these things, and also a not unimportant sidelight on modern France:

'When one of us was invited to lunch with the Faligands and their cousins at the cousins' apartment in the suburbs of Paris, we saw enacted the 1965 version of the tale of the country mouse and the city mouse. Being from the country turned out to be no disadvantage. We were at table from one o'clock until well into the evening to celebrate Faligand's first trip to Paris—an unusual thing, for most Chanzeaux men have been to Paris, if only during their *service militaire*. In the presence of his two Parisian cousins, Faligand at first seemed somewhat subdued. The two young men had been born and raised in Cholet [a neighbouring town to Chanzeaux] but had come to Paris to work as soon as they finished school. One is a master tool-machine operator with his own

---

[33] I would like to cite here a comparably readable social-anthropological account (by an American) of a comparable Japanese village called Suye Mura: John F. Embree, *A Japanese Village* (London, 1946).

little shop. The other is a technician at IBM. Both of them are obviously intelligent, energetic, ambitious. Though they were kind to their cousin, whom they had not seen for several years, they seemed somewhat condescending toward him. The young men did most of the talking at first, but gradually Faligand began to take a more active part in the conversation. Little by little it became obvious that he was just as much a scientific technician as either of his cousins—perhaps more. He was skilled in auto mechanics, soil chemistry, botany, husbandry, accounting, marketing. He was also well informed on politics, problems of social security, questions of farm policy, and the Common Market. Besides, he was a member of Chanzeaux's town council and chairman of its finance committee. As all this became clear, the country-mouse city-mouse situation faded. These three men were much more on a level than they had thought.'[34]

Chanzeaux, in other words, is a useful example, not just of university teaching, but of something much rarer, university learning.

[34] Op. cit., pp. 341–2.

CHAPTER SEVEN

Aspects of inequality

1 SHARES IN SCARCITY

'On the one side, inequality harms by pampering; on the other, by vulgarising and depressing. A system founded on it is against nature, and in the long run, breaks down.'

Matthew Arnold, Lecture on 'Equality'

'College ought to be set aside for those of us who can really take advantage of it. The truly intelligent people are just having their talents wasted by having all these hacks around.'

Mario Savio, quoted in Robert S. Morison (ed.), *The Contemporary University, USA* (New York, 1967), p. 312.

Students talk about equality, demanding collective grades for themselves and free access to university for other people. Teachers are less free with the word. Outside courses in Political Philosophy, or Sociology of Education, the idea of equality is considered dangerous in most universities, especially the ones visited during the writing of this book. If there is one thing in common between Oxford, Berkeley, Tokyo, Hamburg, Chicago, Bologna, and Harvard, to name only seven, it is an aggressive inegalitarianism. They may not be the equals of each other, for the excellence of a university is in part a function of the Gross National Product which supports it, but they are not shy about claiming local superiority. They possess cultural goods which are desired by many, secured by few. The language which first-rate institutions keep for mediocre ones—'cow colleges' is the American expression—is as abrasive as the language in which individual scholars run each other down. There is excuse for this. It is often said in the educational world that if all schools/colleges/universities in the country under discussion were as good as the best, there would be no problem. It is less often admitted that if all were as bad as the worst everyone could go back to private tutoring. In the United States and in Japan the gap between the best and the worst is particularly wide, in spite of the accreditation system which Americans devised to protect the bad from contamination by the unspeakable. A scholar who once strolled into a gambling saloon in Las Vegas to while away time and lose a few dollars told me that he was cured of gambling for life by the notice on the wall which informed him that a proportion of his stake would go to maintain a student at the University of Nevada. But if American higher education had had to advance evenly—as school systems are expected to do in most countries, and university systems in some— it would never have advanced at all. The most common mistake which Europeans make in judging American college standards is to miss the fact that even if the bottom third of all graduates and all colleges is sub- tracted from the whole, the proportion of the age group with access at an enviably high level to the world of science and learning is still twice what it is in Europe. Yet in no country, however under-developed educationally, do people worry more than in the United States about the inadequacies and inequalities of the university system they have built. For comparatively few people, even university people, are able to travel abroad and see for themselves how fortunate, in any global perspective, they are. (Indeed, the trouble with the itinerant student agitators whom middle America so much fears is that they are not itinerant enough. A few million Federal dollars might well be better spent on buying fact- finding tours for campus radicals than on feeing FBI informers.)

Whether in a family, an office, a nation, or a world community, equality is a topic which is seldom debated coolly. One of the wisest men who ever addressed his mind to it—R. H. Tawney—did not attempt to subdue his passions while analysing the malign incompetence of the British school system. In the university world, the issue is still comparat- ively fresh. In Britain, until very recently, only a tiny proportion of the population reached a university. Whatever one's politics, one regarded this as an unalterable fact of life. The country, it was thought, had to be governed by an elite, and not everyone could be part of the elite. Animus was reserved for the rich rather than the lavishly educated. The numerical growth of students over the past decade may be the most obvious change in British universities and colleges, but the switch at all levels from defer- ence to egalitarianism is the more significant. In Japan, the concept of 'equality of esteem' among different universities was injected by the Americans after 1945, but has never properly taken. In France, the ideology of *egalité* is so firmly fixed in the constitution that few people bother to check up on its survival in practice, and the British representative at an OECD conference a few years ago had great difficulty, he told me, in convincing his French counterparts that the proportion of the British student body which came from the working class was more than twice the French.

Education differentiates, both intellectually and socially. It is not a coincidence that Britain, whose school system is notoriously unequal in structure, also makes children specialise earlier than any other country does. Most other people in most democracies judge the quality of a school by its success at diffusing knowledge and culture, by transmitting them from the few to the many. Britain transmits them under high pressure from the few to the few. However, inequality, intellectual and generational if not social, is built into the relationship between teacher and child, and admitted as a necessary evil, though some teachers are humble enough to say that they learn from their children as well as instructing them. At a university, social and generational inequality is supposed to diminish, but the intellectual difference is gloried in. University teachers, like their counterparts in school, are engaged in the transmission of knowledge and culture, but the tone of their institutions, and in many cases of their personal lives, is set by the ambition to be, if only for a week or an hour, the sole possessor and demonstrator of a piece of lore which is shared with no one else on earth. The researcher's cry of 'eureka!' is quite closely allied to the journalist's cry of 'scoop!' Both cries are followed by a powerful itch to communicate, and it is remarkable how easily this itch overcomes the absurd barriers which nations and universities erect against each other: Oxford may decline to recognise the Sorbonne's degrees, and the US may not be on speaking terms with the USSR, but sociologist talks to sociologist and physicist to physicist across both frontiers. Even so, the sequence of publication is itself interesting. The scholar who publishes to the public before publishing to his peers is held in deep suspicion throughout the academic guild. The conclusion to be drawn, unpalatable though it may be to a particular generation of young people, is that there can be no equality between ignorance and knowledge. This conclusion has been tacitly recognised in the counter, from the radical side, that 'their' knowledge, being metaphysical, embraces and therefore supersedes the verifiable knowledge which universities have dealt in since a different kind of metaphysics went out of fashion.

Huge pitfalls await the writer who attempts to discuss with an international frame of reference, the issue of equality in access to higher education. But like it or not, the issue *does* have an international frame of reference. OECD conferences address themselves to it; student leaders all over the world insist upon it; parents all over the world worry about the inequalities against them and rejoice at the inequalities in their favour. Most of the unconscious choices which societies make are expressed in whom they accept, and whom they reject, for higher education. The equality issue can be superimposed like a grid on different national situations, but most satisfactorily at the university stage, for two reasons: universities possess some international attributes denied to schools (for instance, limited interchangeability of staff and qualifications, and the *linguae francae* of scholarship); they are also at once critics and victims of all political and social development in their respective societies, and this gives the discussion of equality in tertiary education an edge that it cannot have at an earlier stage, however important that stage is to the individual's growth. At university level there are also peculiar difficulties, for there is one sense (discussed in the second section of this chapter) in which we have yet to conceive what equal opportunity in higher education might entail.

I had better first define terms. The sense in which most of us believe in equality for our own and other people's children is wishful but surely not unreasonable. We would like them to find in the educational system equal chances to develop their own inherently unequal powers to the limit of their ability, for a purpose of their own choosing and at a pace of their own choosing. In the West that statement now sounds like a truism, but it has taken several centuries to achieve that status, through the slow infiltration of Christian humanism and secular liberalism. Only thirty years ago, diametrically opposite philosophies of education officially governed the universities in three of the six countries reviewed in this book (though even in Germany and Japan fascist ideology found large pockets of resistance in the universities, and in Italian ones encountered widespread derision). Today, strangely enough, such cutting edge as the statement has is sharpest in the other three nations. In the United States, students of inherently equal ability (begging the question of racial gene pools recently raised afresh in the work of Professor Arthur Jensen) do not have equal chances if they happen to be black, and all students have experienced a mounting sense that they are being 'crowded' into courses and occupations which primarily suit the State's technocratic self-interest. In France, equality of opportunity between socio-economic groups is a long way off, and in Britain, though there is more equality of access, there are also no second chances: you study at the prescribed pace, or get out.

The wish, in other words, is nowhere matched by the reality. The millenium can never dawn, bearing in mind the divine discontent that is built into the process of learning, but it is still useful to distinguish different kinds of educational inequality, and to ask if they are all necessary. The first broad division is between the inequalities which arise from the manner in which education is distributed, and those which arise from the amount of education which is provided. The connections between the two are very complicated to trace. Sometimes *ad hoc* political decisions can produce real and sudden changes in the level of provision, as when Britain during the 1960s switched resources from 'imperial' defence to domestic education. It is arguable that this decision was provoked by a rising egalitarianism in the public demand for education, but it has not yet had more than a marginal effect on existing inequalities in distribution.

Provision

With the possible exception of the United States, the most important single source of inequality in education is the fact that there is not, and never has been, enough to go round. Edward Shils calls the ethos of student radicalism 'the ethos of a regime of plenitude', and universities 'selective institutions in a world of scarcity'. Dean Marc Zamansky of the Sorbonne defended examinations to his students in the words, 'Even a socialist society must be selective'—or as Hugh Gaitskell put it to the British, 'socialism is about priorities'. Shils goes on: 'Honours are scarce, first places are scarce, research grants and stipends are scarce, professorships are scarce, appointments in the higher civil service are scarce, so even are interesting appointments in the film industry, in television, and in market research.'[1] For that matter—not to make too much of the hopelessly contaminated activities just listed—really good sites for an anarchistic rural commune are also scarce, especially in crowded Britain and Japan. Moreover, the sheer scarcity of education is far worse than is generally realised. It is well said by Stuart Maclure in the same issue of *Encounter* that 'in most countries—and this certainly includes Britain—the only thing which prevents the educational system from going bankrupt is sheer inefficiency.' Ministers of Education must sometimes wake sweating in the night from a dream in which the whole army of intelligent but badly brought up or badly taught children, who now obligingly drop out of school half-way to intellectual fulfilment, suddenly present themselves for tertiary education. In a way, that is precisely what is beginning to happen, though professional posts and salary levels rather than intellectual fulfilment may be what most of the applicants have in mind. Only because it has so far happened, in Europe at least, on such a small scale is it possible for politicians and academics to talk as though nothing untoward were afoot, except that the universities are a little more crowded than usual, and manners are not what they used to be.

The most recent OECD analyses—working, as usual, with ridiculously out-of-date figures (for 1965/6)—conclude that as a proportion of the age group, the percentages of young people in higher education of some kind are: US 40·8; United Kingdom 11·9; France 16·7; West Germany 8·7; Italy 11·2; Japan 11·9. (OECD statisticians now consider the American and French figures calculated by this method to be misleadingly high, and the Japanese figure conceals the fact that most of the students are men: a Japanese boy is more likely than a British one to attend a university.) The correlation, once so bravely asserted by Harold Wilson and others in Britain, between the provision of education—especially higher education—and the achievement of economic growth remains unproven. The only certain fact is that if secondary education is extended in quantity and improved in quality, the children who benefit tend to stay on into the tertiary stage. But the discovery that if one gives Oliver Twist a larger first helping of porridge he will only ask for a larger second helping is not calculated to excite egalitarians or stir governments to fiscal generosity. In most advanced nations, the sixties and late fifties now look like a period of unprecedented affluence in higher education, which the middle classes were best poised to exploit, and which may have receded by the time other social groups are ready to claim their share. Probably only Japan, whose rapid economic growth gives her financial leeway,

[1] *Encounter*, May 1969, p. 48.

and whose universities are under-developed in relation to her schools, will be able or willing to do as much proportionately for higher education in the next decade as Britain and the US have done in the decade just past.

Scarcity, then, will remain, as will the miseries caused less by scarcity than by miscalculation: India has a glut of (mostly very ill-educated) graduates; the United States has at the time of writing a glut of Ph.D's, which is no more pleasant to the individuals concerned because it was correctly forecast several years ago. At the same time, it would be imprudent to be determinist about the level at which rich nations will in the future provide for their universities. There is still room for choice, especially in the wake of a rival's sudden and unpredicted success, like the launching of the first *sputnik*. In 1930, Flexner wrote: 'Nations have recently been led to borrow billions for war; no nation has ever borrowed largely for education.' Discussing England's ability to finance universities and research he pointed out that the British debt at the close of the Napoleonic Wars bore the same relation to the national wealth as it did in 1930, when Britain's obligations to creditors were frightening her politicians so badly. 'The previous debt was not extinguished, but it was virtually reduced to insignificance by the expansion of English industry by steam, coal, iron. Is it not conceivable that, if England similarly developed physics and chemistry, a comparable phenomenon would occur?'[2]

History has fulfilled Flexner's prescription, though in a rather odd way, for the willingness of both British and American governments to sink capital into education and research can in large part be traced to the physicists and chemists who between 1939 and 1945 succeeded so well, not in accumulating and generating wealth, but in spending and destroying it. Since then, it has become hard to distinguish as sharply as Flexner could between sums allocated to war and sums allocated to education. For Flexner, the discreditable underworld of the American university was vocational training, not military research. The institution was corrupted by the existence of courses, common even in famous universities between the wars, in non-subjects like 'book-reviewing' and 'principles of home laundering'. These still exist (one Middle Western state university got into trouble not long ago for running courses in tax avoidance) but for contemporary critics, universities are chiefly corrupted by excrescences like George Washington University's Human Resources Research Office (HumRRO) whose mission is 'to discover, develop, and apply human factors and social science principles and techniques to improve Army training and operational performance', and whose publications include a booklet called *Optimum Kill Power of Man*.[3] Both kinds of corruption stem from a conjunction of ideas that was in origin peculiarly American, but is not now confined to America: a community's belief

[2] Flexner, op. cit., p. 302.
[3] Ridgeway, op. cit., pp. 139–141.

that a university exists to deliver whatever intellectual goods are at the time in demand; and a university's belief that the problem of scarcity in education and research can only be solved by obedient submission to the chores which the community lays upon it. To this extent, the quick fading in Europe of the simplistic belief that universities, if they do as they are told, can be relied upon to produce economic growth for the people who pay their bills may be no bad thing. It returns us a little closer to the older assumption, made when nations were poorer, that learning and culture could only be had by people who were prepared to give up something else for them.

Distribution

However, the fiscal largesse of the past decade, whether or not it eventually succeeds in generating the technical and economic advance that all societies look for, has generated political pressures for equal distribution that cannot easily be resisted. One has already heard the suggestion that by 1990 the proportion of the European gross product devoted to education will reach twelve per cent (nearly twice Britain's current figure). Neither among nations nor among individuals is there any disposition to return to the principle of voluntarism in higher education, from which the Continental countries in particular are trying to shake themselves free.[4] Nations cannot, or think they cannot, afford to be left behind each other, any more than a European or American or Japanese family can afford to be left behind the Jones's or the Sato's down the street, whose boy is keeping ahead of theirs by attending, not just university, but graduate school as well. But if the resources available to universities have to be stretched thinner and thinner in relation to the demand made upon them, the issue of equality in distribution will become more acute. Arguments about distribution are always more painful in periods when the absolute level of provision is static or falling, for the simple human reason that a man may sometimes be persuaded, or fooled, into continuing to accept what he has while other people are being given more, but can hardly ever be persuaded to take less so that other people may be given some of his. Nor is it possible now, as it was when Tawney and Flexner were writing, to convince taxpayers that higher education is so rare a good that it would be spoilt if offered in too large doses, or to people for whom it has not normally been prescribed. In Europe the workers, and in America the Blacks, are becoming aware of what the educated have kept to themselves. They are not easy to convince that the delicate ecological balance of historic universities will be upset just by

[4] In Britain at the time of writing, a group of academics including Sir Sydney Caine (formerly Director of the London School of Economics) are trying to found a 'private' university by public subscription. The attitude of their colleagues to the project may be described as sympathetic but sceptical.

admitting them, and the middle classes who for the moment are still kings of the academic castle no longer have enough nerve to repel the assault parties. Only the character-type which was prepared to pay a high personal price for education was also prepared to insist that other aspirants too should show prior evidence of fitness for the cloister. This character-type is itself a product of the 'Protestant ethic' which has dominated the history of higher education in America, and deeply influenced it in Western Europe. That ethic has crumbled away from within during the twentieth century, as men and women whose savings had been wiped out in the German inflation after 1918 or the Crash of 1929 watched their grandchildren grow up to the assumption of unearned material prosperity.

It is the disappearance of this ethic, as well as the rise of what Professor Shils calls the 'ethos of the expansive ego', that accounts for the genuine, by no means wholly selfish, horror with which students now regard examinations. Examinations are useful, though inaccurate, mechanisms for regulating a regime of scarcity in a tolerable fashion. In the past, though most students prefer to forget this, they have been load-bearing buttresses of social justice in education, safeguarding the rights of the intelligent poor against the nepotic manoeuvrings of the rich and stupid. But their continued use as an administrative convenience is masking a fundamental change in our attitude to the test *qua* test. The Protestant ethic took much of its tone and mental sets from the struggles of seventeenth century Puritans to make themselves pleasing to God at the Last Day by thinking the right thoughts at the right time. This ideology was almost bound to devise, when it applied itself to education, an intricate elaboration and formalisation of the medieval examination system.[5] The device has worked pretty well for a century or two in the West. However, Professor Shils is able to tell us that it always causes trouble in India: 'The confrontation of a kinship-dominated culture of diffuse expectations, such as that of the student in his familial *foyer*, with the culture which demands specific performances as conditions for prospective rewards such as examination marks, appointments to particularly desirable positions, etc., creates much tension.'[6] Western students in their genera-

[5] Professor W. R. Niblett, of the University of London, has recently pointed out that the first university known to grade students was Louvain, where as early as 1441 masters were graduated in three classes, each with names published in order of merit: *rigorosi* (honours men), *transibiles* (pass men) and *gratiosi* (men passed as an act of charity). But far more common in the medieval period were the oral disputations which still survive as final examinations in Germany, France and Italy. Written honours examinations hardly penetrated Oxford and Cambridge until the nineteenth century, and then only for the despised minority who were studying seriously. 'The principle of proof of merit by examination result very much went with the stirrings against privilege of the growing middle class.' (*1969 World Year Book of Education*).

[6] Op. cit. The East, however, has its own terrors, exemplified in the Imperial Chinese examination system, abolished in 1905, which for formal futility has never been surpassed.

tional *foyer* are similarly alienated. They continue to write exams, even while exhorting each other not to, for the material career advantages of doing so are too obvious to be ignored. As a Harvard student put it in an essay on examinations which was much admired locally, 'the bureaucrat must be motivated primarily by his desire for a reward (money, status, prestige) which is external to the work process itself. . . . Students learn to sell their labor for money by selling their labor for grades'.[7] But once examinations are perceived in this way, rather than as competitive sports, the old zest goes out of them, alike in the setting, the writing, and the marking. Over the next few years, under pressure of numbers, more and more university teachers are going to wonder why they do it. In Britain, for instance, the weeks of valuable university term-time absorbed by examinations were not mentioned among the thirteen possible sources of economy, suggested in 1969 by the Ministry of Education to the universities—which rejected almost all of them. But if British taxpayers realised that they are paying handsomely for academics to scrutinise, not merely students' scripts, but each other's marking of the same scripts, and that this is done not out of sympathy for students but because dons in one institution cannot trust dons in another one to apply identical standards, they might well wonder if the scruple is worth the price.

Students now exhibit, or flaunt, their egalitarianism in many ways. It shows in the linked arms and co-ordinated charges of Japanese snake-dancers, the aggressively proletarian manners of Oxford middle-class radicals, the collective grades demanded by Italian *maoisti*, and the self-abasement of white American students before the Blacks (New York has even boasted a group which called itself the 'Committee of Concerned Honkies'). But students are seldom good guides to the structural inequalities with which their higher education systems are riddled. They lack information, and they are bound on the one hand to their own generation, and on the other to their own institution. There are certainly exceptions to this rule. British students were more clear-minded than many of their teachers in resisting a (Labour) government's attempt to perpetuate at tertiary level the kind of class divisions between institutions that have bedevilled British secondary education for generations. The Berkeley Free Speech Movement in 1964 was in part a continuation of the student-led civil rights campaigns in the American South. But it needs a cooler approach than most students can manage if the emotional egalitarianism of their generation is to be translated into more practicable measures relevant to the circumstances of individual countries.

Of course, there is a hard core of student egalitarians who want no improvement whatsoever in the circumstances of individual countries or universities, lest it postpone the day when the worm turns, the dead

---

[7] David I. Bruck in *Harvard Crimson*, April 28, 1969.

awaken, and the Revolution revolves. Discussion of this kind is designed to isolate rather than satisfy them, and it would be an insult to their intelligence to pretend otherwise. On the other hand, they insult their own intelligence if they pretend to themselves that equality is other than an elusive attribute of human societies, large or small, primitive or evolved. 'To find an absolutely homogeneous and egalitarian education,' said Durkheim, 'it would be necessary to go back to pre-historic societies in the structure of which there is no differentiation'. This is not to underrate Mao's or Castro's achievement in transforming the atmosphere, as well as the economics, of China and Cuba. But they did not begin with a bourgeois social democracy, whose semi-skilled workers know how much they would risk losing in a revolution that only substituted Djilas's 'New Class' of bureaucrats for the 'ruling class' as defined by classic Marxism. Revolutions only occur in advanced societies when they come by stealth, disguised as a technical innovation or a modest administrative reform, so that electorates can swallow them before they have time to take fright.

There are four types of avoidable inequality in educational achievement or opportunity which matter to modern societies: inequalities between classes (or races), between regions, between sexes, and between generations.[8] The most important, and the most neglected, is the inequality between generations, not least because it is the last inequality likely to be noticed by students, and for that matter by most people who immure themselves for life within the walls of a university. I deal with this separately, and here review the other three types.

University systems do not often present any of the three in pure form. But the clearest example of the university as an agent of division between classes is probably Germany. In 1965 only about six per cent of all German university students came from working class families, which account for half the country's population. Under four per cent came from farm families. Ordinarily, a German child destined for a university career has to have nine years preparation in a *Gymnasium*, finishing with the *abitur* exam at the age of twenty. Children not so destined attend other schools. This elitist structure, in which people knew their place and kept it, has been modified somewhat in recent years, and under the present plans of the Federal Government, the *Länder*, and the *Wissenschaftsrat* it would be modified much more drastically. At present, some young people reach university by transferring into *Gymnasia* from other schools, or by attending evening schools, and one of the new universities (Bochum, in the Ruhr) accepts industrial workers on short courses. In 1966, *Deutsches Studentenwerk* calculated that students needed about DM400 a month

[8] For this whole discussion in relation to the United States, see the rich and complex detail-with-commentary in Christopher Jencks and David Riesman, *The Academic Revolution* (New York, 1968), especially chapters 2, 3, and 4.

to meet expenses, excluding DM25 a month for university fees. But only 13·6 per cent were meeting eighty per cent or more of their expenses from public funds, though a quarter were being at least partly supported in this way. Traditionally, German students work their way through college: one out of every four earns money during the (seven-month) academic year as well as in vacations. The Federal Government has been considering legislation that would deny student stipends to those working against 'democratic order'.[9]

These arrangements are by no means the only barriers which German universities erect against social groups which have not in the past been considered worthy of an academic education. The inordinate length of courses (a minimum of five years from the *abitur* is normal) and the high risk of dropping out without a degree must make the loss of earnings hard for a working class family to accept, and students whose parents lack the traditional academic skills are encouraged to drop out by the absence, in most universities, of any effective guidance explaining the courses offered, and the careers to which they lead. Britain, by contrast, does its best at university stage to retrieve the waste and divisiveness of its secondary education: all students who need it have their fees and expenses paid by the State through local authorities, and suggestions that the grants be converted into loans have so far been bitterly resisted. Advisory services are poor at university entry, but professional at the career-choosing stage. Student drop-out rates are exceptionally low. The system is elitist in structure and in the assumptions which it breeds in the students who pass through it, but the reasons for this are historical and sociological rather than administrative.

The classical example of *regional* inequality in a single country's system of higher education is Italy (though Britain is not faultless: children from southern schools have a fifty per cent better chance of qualifying for university than northern children.) The bulk of Italian universities, including almost all the best ones, lie north of Naples. The whole country's university budget is approximately equal to that of the state of Michigan, so universities are almost entirely non-residential, grants are few, and although there are altogether over half a million students in Italy, who are free to attend any university they choose, 300,000 never attend classes, either because there is no room for them, or because they cannot afford to live anywhere other than at home. The concentration of the industrial working population in the cities which contain some of the best and most populous universities—Milan, Turin, Bologna—helps to keep the percentage of students of working class origin to a level (thirteen per cent) tolerable by international standards—if it is accurate. But the student whose parents are workers or agricultural small-holders in the Mezzo-giorno has a near-hopeless task. Even if he reaches a local university, he finds that its professors live in Rome. (Some of them, including one or

[9] Barbara B. Burn, op. cit., pp. 185-9.

two Cabinet Ministers, are content to draw the salary and send an assistant down to do the work.)

There is no classical example among the six countries of *sexual* inequality in higher education, for all are offenders, though naturally in
different degree. Among Western countries, Germany—especially the
Catholic, conservative south—is the most reluctant to educate its women,
but even Germans have not recently had, as part of their mental furniture,
documents like the old 'Code of Morals' for Japanese women which
insists that 'the minds of women generally are as dark as the night, and
are more stupid than men; they do not notice what is before them, and
they slander innocent persons; they envy the happiness of others, and pet
their children, all to the discredit of their husbands. Women are stupid,
therefore they must be humble and obedient to their husbands'.[10] Even
so, the Japanese stress on literacy in an otherwise undeveloped society
extended in the Code also to women, for girls were 'to study the foregoing
lessons from their infancy by reading and writing, so that they don't
forget them'. The Americans, in reforming Japanese higher education
after 1945, tried to moderate the deep bias in Japan against giving equal
status and opportunity to women, and the few girls who arrive (by
competitive examination) at the University of Tokyo get the same
education. But at Waseda, one of the leading private universities in
Japan, the figures tell their own tale: only a tenth of the undergraduates
enrolled are women, with the vast majority placed in the Schools of
Literature and Education; and in the graduate division the proportion
sinks to a fifteenth, almost all in Literature. (A Japanese woman is always
more likely than a Japanese man to understand English.)

The Government has probably made the situation worse rather than
better by establishing two national women's universities, and most women
go to colleges that are little better than finishing schools for brides. Even
the best women graduates of the best universities find competition for
jobs in society heavily rigged against them. There is no natural place
for women on the career ladder which Japanese call the 'escalator'—
even the profession of social work, badly though it is needed, is only
embryonic—and altogether, the girls whom Tokyo department stores
station at the foot of their escalators, to do nothing whatsoever but bow
to each customer on his way to a higher floor, stand pretty well for the
place of women in the Japanese educational system. Only in the student
movement itself is it easy to discern a grass root emancipation. One
particularly articulate girl, chairman of her dormitory at Nara Women's
University, told me that the boys at Kyodai nearby were frightened of
the girls' intellectual seriousness. She was herself harshly realistic about the
prevailing attitude to women in the society against which she and her
companions demonstrated: 'Japan today is prosperous and it is going

[10] Code reprinted in Isabella Bird, *Unbeaten tracks in Japan* (London, 1880), vol. 1,
pp. 323–6.

back towards keeping women in their own homes. In pop songs the girls say they want to be exactly the sort of women their lovers expect, and in the marriage ceremonies the tradition of over-affectionate women is reviving: good wives and snug homes.' For young women like her in modern Japan, there is an explicit choice to be made between Leftist politics ('Marx-shugi') and domesticity ('My-home-shugi').

Three countries: three examples of different inequalities. But of course, most countries have all three types mixed to varying degrees. There are some surprises. Consider this league table:[11]

Percentage of female enrolments in university-type higher education

	1955/6	1960/1	1965/6
France	33·2	37·2	40·5
USA	34·6	37·0	39·2
Italy	26·7	26·6	33·4
Britain	24·2	24·3	25·3
W. Germany	17·3	20·3	20·6
Japan	12·4	13·7	16·4

These figures show that sexual inequality in higher education, unlike class and regional inequalities, tends to diminish with expansion of numbers and the arrival of national affluence. (As always with comparative educational statistics, other differences between countries and systems affect the interpretation of the figures. France comes above the US in this table mainly because her higher technical education is concentrated outside the university sector. In no country is a woman engineer a common phenomenon.)

There is one very familiar, and most intractable, example of 'mixed factor' inequality in access to higher education: the position of Black students or would-be students in the United States. The example is of general interest, not merely because it is racial, but because with the possible exception of social inequality in France, where the Communist Party has campaigned under the slogan of '*l'Université aux fils des travailleurs*', this is the only example of an inequality which universities have been expected, both by the victims and by the public, to ameliorate by their own action. In Britain, in Italy, in Japan, and even in Germany, student political pressure on their university authorities to correct social inequalities by their admissions policy or other means has been astonishingly rare. Most students prefer generalities to particulars, and miss the targets which universities present because they are too busy taking aim at 'the System'. However, as Nathan Glazer describes it:

'. . . the demands of the black students have been concrete, and have gone directly to curriculum and university organization. They want

[11] Source: OECD.

specific courses on American Negro history and culture, and African history and culture. They want programs to recruit more black students, tutor them, and support them. They want more Negro faculty. Whereas the impact of the white radicals has been met by administrators as that of an external invading army, which they have tried to appease with educational changes which scarcely interested them, the attack of black students has been directly on educational issues, and can be met to some extent by changes in curriculum, and by student and faculty recruitment.'[12]

The separatism implicit in these demands surprised even liberal Americans who by 1968/9 were rapidly losing their capacity to be astonished. One famous liberal arts college, Antioch, gave its black students the separate courses and dormitories they demanded, only to be ordered by Washington to desegregate or face the loss of Federal funds. The rational objections that could be, and were, raised against the rush for *négritude* were overruled, even in Yale and Harvard. It was far from clear, for example, that the cause of Negro higher education would best be served by rich white universities which raided poor black colleges in the South for professors to teach their own newly-acquired and—by comparison with the black bourgeois students in a college like Morehouse—much less teachable students, drawn from the ghettoes of New York, Chicago, or San Francisco. No one doubted that many intelligent young blacks who felt lost and alienated in big white universities would feel happier studying the origins of slavery than parroting the grammar of Beowulf, though some might have found Beowulf easier than the academic jargon which, as Black Studies prospectuses showed, knows no barriers of colour, creed, or class. (One 'Malcolm X Liberation University' proposed 'discussion of the semantics and dynamics of prejudice and racism, cultural and political paranoia, psychology of paternalism and tokenism, and the effects of racism on motivational and perceptual variables'.) On the other hand, no one disbelieved the tactless woman who wrote to the *Washington Post* arguing that 'if the study of Swahili were made compulsory in our high schools and ten prizes a year were offered to the top ten scholars, all ten would go to Woodrow Wilson School, two to Chinese students and eight to whites, six of those Jewish'. But all these objections were in the end irrelevant. One of the angriest apostles of Black Studies, Nathan Hare of San Francisco State College, used the same image which the Japanese use to express the kind of socio-economic advancement he was looking for, 'The goal is the *elevation* of a people by means of one important escalator—education.' Neither private nor state universities in the US could easily resist a demand thus phrased. In the American university, 'the service of the community'—with whatever reservations and sophistications that phrase is loaded—comes before

[12] *The Public Interest* (No. 13, Fall 1968), p. 18.

institutional self-preservation. It is true that on many campuses, faculty and administration were terrified that the Blacks would burn the books if their demands were not granted. But anyway, once the Blacks—or any other group in American society—had focussed its anxieties and deprivations on the university, and had articulated them well enough for at least some white professors to concede that an intellectually respectable case had been made, satisfaction could not be denied. The more famous the university, the quicker it moved to make the best of the situation. It was expedient to set up a Department of Afro-American Studies, complete with four-year degree course and the hope of graduate work, before any other university could move to the draw. When Berkeley published its proposed Black Studies Curriculum[13] in the spring of 1969, it stated that the programme would require 'six outstanding Black scholars with doctorates'—doubling the number of black faces on Berkeley's Senate—and would also need to tap 'the rich reservoir of Black intellectuals who do not bear advanced academic credentials'—a very diplomatic definition.

The American academic scene is so *mouvementé* that it is impossible to predict how such departments will look five years hence, what coherence the subject matter will have, and what respect future employers will accord to a BA (Afro) of Berkeley or Harvard as opposed to a more conventional qualification from a lesser university. (Besides, other parallel changes have been simultaneously taking place: at Berkeley, for instance, the foreign language requirement and its associated departments are virtually extinct, and a man who so chooses may major in nothing-at-all, by picking credits at random from the entire course menu.) Professor Shils does not expect American universities to manage the 'service function' of mitigating the effects of society's racial biases any more happily than it has managed other service functions in the past, and suggests that Black Studies faculties teaching black perspectives 'in some ill-guided American universities and colleges' will have 'the same academic qualities and standards as departments of home economics, physical

---

[13] Subjects, listed under fourteen disciplinary heads, were as follows: African anthropology, Afro-American anthropology, comparative Black anthropology; survey of African art, introduction to Afro-American art, contemporary Afro-American art; Afro-Americans and the Theater; social control and the Black community; economics of racism, current economic problems of Afro-Americans; survey of Afro-American literature, the Black writer in America; US history from a Black perspective, African contributions to Western society; language of the ghetto, Black speech styles, Black non-verbal communication; music and the Black man, contemporary Afro-American music, history of African influences on Western music; Black thought in the twentieth century; political problems of Black Americans, the American Government in Black perspective, racism, colonialism and apartheid; psychology of racism, Black economic and social psychology; social welfare legislation and policy from the Black perspective; sociology of the Black family, Black social movements, Black social institutions, urbanisation of Black people. (See *Washington Post*, March 16, 1969).

education, hotel administration, or chiropody'. Maybe so. But the difference is that an American whose university refuses to offer a course in hotel administration will pick the subject up somewhere, while black Americans, who have learnt that a famous university confers prestige on every subject it touches and earning power on every student it admits, have no other place to take either themselves or their culture for the seal of approval. The implied compliment to the university is real, if unwelcome, and a marginal, short-term devaluation of academic standards in one sector of an already heterogeneous system could be cheerfully accepted if it held out some hope of fuller Black participation in the intellectual life of society a generation hence.

Black American students' attempt to make universities do for them what they cannot collectively do themselves have no exact counterpart elsewhere. But both the pressure and the comparatively ready academic response deserve a few imitators. It would be pleasant to see Japanese students demonstrating for more female companionship (and perhaps for the Chair of Amoristics which Sir Thomas Beecham once said he would like to see in every British university), British admissions tutors under pressure to discriminate in favour of applicants living north of the Trent, and German or Italian universities forced by a strike of maintenance staffs to curtail and demystify the process of acquiring academic qualifications. Utopia, it has been remarked, can only be realised by trench warfare.

2 AGE—THE GREAT DIVIDER

'It is time that we had uncommon schools, that we did not leave off our education when we begin to be men and women. It is time that villages were universities, and their elder inhabitants the fellows of universities with leisure—if they are indeed so well off—to pursue liberal studies the rest of their lives.'

Henry David Thoreau, *Walden*

The last inequality which I propose to discuss is of a different order of magnitude from the others. Indeed, it is so striking, widespread, and—it is thought—ineradicable that hardly anyone attends to it. This is the generational inequality between the man of twenty-five who has had access to a university and the man of forty-five, equally able and educable, who has not. People can talk for hours about the generation gap without mentioning this readily measurable aspect of it. The measurements vary from country to country, but here is Adam Walinsky, who was one of Robert Kennedy's speech-writers, sketching the American situation in an interview with a Middle Western Catholic university's student magazine:

'If a guy is 28 years old, when he got out of high school the proportion of high school graduates going on to college was less than half what it is now. . . . That is the great divider in our country right now, the people who have college education and the people who don't. This is the single greatest status divider, running through all ethnic groups, all places, all parts of the country. And no one's figured out how you give a guy something like that if he missed it coming out of high school, then got married, and now has kids and a mortgage. It's hard to pay off.'[14]

In Sweden, another country with a rapid higher educational growth rate, today's forty to forty-five year-olds belong to a generation in which one person in twenty qualified for university entrance. One in five of today's twenty year-olds possess the same qualification. By 1975 the proportion will be one in two.

Adult education, as traditionally understood, cannot cope with a

[14] Notre Dame *Scholastic*, February 28, 1969.

282

problem this size, though in America it at least tries. There, nearly half the adult population is touched by some form of continuing education, whether it is a housewives' painting class or a professional refresher course at a famous university law school. More and more of this education is conducted on campus by accredited university teachers. It is easy—for anyone who can spare the time and the money—to drop in on and out of a university. In Britain a quarter of the adult population is touched by further education in some form, but the walls of the universities themselves are far harder to leap. The full-time residential mature student in a British university is such a rare personage that half the staff can point him out in the quad. He is the one with six children, a grey beard, or some other sign of advanced years. Most people who discover too late that they want a degree register for an external degree with London University. There are 33,149 of them—a body equal in size to three Oxfords. Many local authorities refuse to pay anything towards their expenses, which are less than a tenth of the cost of a young undergraduate-in-residence. Some of these 33,000 oppressed students probably overlap with the 40,000 who applied to take degrees through the television, radio, and correspondence courses of the Open University, which opened at the beginning of 1971.

Neither Germany, France, Italy, nor Japan have travelled even as far as this. In Japan, for example, the first adult education courses run by the Ministry of Education were not instituted until 1923, and even then only as part of an official propaganda drive against democracy and individualism. The drive was not short of good technical advice—as early as 1911, a committee on 'Correspondence Education' recommended the use of films and slides—but the will to extend the outreach of the university and its associated ideas has never been conspicuous. In the 1964 Ministry of Education budget, adult education received ¥2,000,000,000 (£2,315,000) while school education received ¥430,608,000,000 (£498,200,000). Yet most teaching even of the traditional Japanese culture—music, cooking, flower arrangement, and other arts—has to be done in the adult sector, for the schools concentrate on teaching subjects considered useful for the modernisation of Japan. One Japanese educator puts the blame on the academic tradition which modern Japan originally selected for itself: 'Since 1868 universities were established according to the German system, and Germany happened to be a country in which the university was not closely connected with adult education. At present, though many university teachers are interested in adult education, their contribution has to be made not through the university, but in books and through the mass media.'[15]

However, it is not just abstract social justice, but the practical consequences of the social role in which the university is now cast, that force

[15] Kanji Hatano in Brian Groombridge (ed.), *Adult Education and Television* (London, 1966 and Unesco), p. 87.

the issue of generational inequality on our attention. This role is summarised by the sociologist Daniel Bell:

'In a post-industrial society the University, because it is the place where theoretical knowledge is codified and tested, increasingly becomes a primary, if not the central, institution of the society. To this extent, the University becomes burdened with tasks greater than it has ever had to carry in its long history. It has to maintain a disinterested role as regards knowledge, yet become the principal service agency of the society not just in training people but as the source of policy advisers. At the same time "human capital", rather than money capital, becomes the scarce resources of the society. The identification of talent, the motivation and training of persons, becomes a self-conscious task for the entire educational system.'[16]

Effective discharge of these functions entails a constantly heightening tension between the university as innovator, and the university as conservator. It is necessarily the first institution to sense in its own structure the approach to a biological threshold, as described by Donald Schon, President of the US Organisation for Social and Technical Innovation, and the BBC's Reith Lecturer for 1970:

'We've reached the point where adaptation is no longer possible on generational grounds. That is to say, we cannot any longer adapt to change on the basis of one generation dying out and another coming into being. . . . That's no longer possible, because periods of fifteen years require such major change that the concept of one's professional identity may need to be altered in order to meet it during that period.'[17]

It seems a bad time for the University, of all institutions, to plunge deeper and deeper into the war between the generations; and a good time to relieve the burden of the new tasks by questioning a few of the old ones. Here then are three world-wide assumptions about universities which a visitor from another planet might think remarkable:

1. Full-time education, whether residential or not, in a university is designed to receive the survivors of the school system. It is an able adolescent's *rite de passage*, which ends three to five years after it began, unless he is clever or determined enough to proceed to graduate work at his own, his wife's, or the State's expense. The longer he spends in higher education while he is young, the greater his ultimate reward in money or esteem.

2. A university degree is, like Holy Orders, indelible. The recipient, whatever he has actually learnt and whether or not it is still worth remembering, is certified as an educated man for the term of his natural life. If he becomes a university teacher, he is granted absolute security

[16] *Encounter*, June 1970.
[17] *The Listener*, July 2, 1970.

of tenure at the age when most of his ex-pupils begin to feel most in need of re-education.

3. *Extra universitatem, nulla salus.* Outside the University, there may be mental good works, but no academic salvation, no alternative source of legitimacy. There is therefore no danger in multiplying very quickly the number of people with a vested interest in preserving the educational system substantially as it is, and in making more and more certain that the most intelligent of our children do not escape its embrace until they are old men of twenty-five or so.

Parallel with these assumptions about higher education is another more general assumption that we make about society itself, and the role which knowledge plays in it. We assume, that is, that the future will be like the past, only more so. An alternative version of this assumption is that the future in Europe and Japan will be very like the present in North America. Either way, we conclude that more and more people will be educated for longer and longer before they are released to earn a living, and that this huge investment in money and time has to be justified, not by the pleasure it gives, but by the discoveries and theories it yields, which makes life more agreeable and less comprehensible for everyone else.

I do not imply that all these assumptions are wholly wrong. Even if they were, universities would survive. But their culture would be so painfully different to those who know them best that the assumptions will continue until it can be shown that there are alternatives. What follows is a tentative attempt to suggest a few.

'Higher education is the stage that intervenes between school and life.' Behind this assumption there is an invisible tug-of-war, fought between the historical development of education and the development of the educated man, as our civilization understands him. The educational system has grown by accumulation, like a coral reef. The process can be most easily traced in Britain, where a thread of scholastic continuity in the organization of both schools and universities runs back to the Middle Ages. Formal learning could once be confined to children, young people, and a few adult professional scholars. Only simple skills of reading, writing, and reckoning were needed to distinguish the elite from the mass, and very few people lived long enough to require re-education for a new age. They were too busy living—though not too busy to argue furiously, during the seventeenth century, about what an educated man should know, and about how technology could be introduced into the university curriculum. At every stage when an advance was made in the number of people reached by the educational system, or the number of years which the most promising pupils were expected to spend in the system, it was easier to extend the buildings, train more teachers, budget more money, and put a fresh load on to the curriculum than it would have been to make a radically fresh start. Nor was there any pressure upon teachers from society to make them act differently. The system despatched, from board school as from Balliol, men who performed as they were expected to perform, because the system itself had dictated the expectations which people had of it. No one thought of asking or testing how men and women in adult life had been helped or hindered by the education they received in childhood or adolescence, and as a proportion of total educational research, inquiries of this kind are still scarce to the point of invisibility today.[18]

The arrival, first of 'secondary education for all' and now—over the horizon—'higher education for all' made no difference to the basic structure of the system in any of the countries here reviewed. In Britain, for example, the Robbins Report (1963) is the ultimate source of most current projections of places needed in higher education, though its figures have been revised upwards several times in the past five years. Robbins did not propose any relaxation of the competitiveness needed to obtain a place in a British university. On its own estimates, over a million adults in Britain had over the previous three decades qualified for university entry but had not sought it, or had not been granted it. Criteria of ability and need rather than qualification would multiply that million many times. As one critic of Robbins has recently remarked:

'Have these people now to spend the remaining thirty, forty, or fifty years of their lives without that education? Robbins makes no provision for those who haven't made it up to now, nor for those who won't have made it in the next decades. . . . The provision of higher education for all who want it also implies *at any point in their lives*. At the moment there is a critical path to higher education, and if you don't get it by the age of twenty-three or so, you might as well give up.[19]

Knowing all this, any self-respecting and self-interested young person in Britain naturally seeks to enter higher education when he leaves school, and to stay there as long as he can, whether or not he is ready to make the most of it. British higher education, at the age of entry, offers for the student's choice a variety of camp-sites on the new map of learning that was undreamt of in the comparatively narrow academic climate of fifteen years ago, before the new universities were launched and before the

[18] In one of the exceptions—a survey recently conducted for the Carnegie Commission by the National Opinion Research Center—four out of five 1961 college graduates thought that their colleges ought to have helped them to 'formulate the values and goals' of their lives, but only one in five considered that his college had succeeded in giving this help.

[19] David Page, 'Against higher education for some', in David Rubinstein and Colin Stoneman (eds.), *Education for Democracy* (London, 1970), pp. 213–4. Mr. Page, a painter, and an Oxford graduate, has taught in a German university, a British College of Art and a British secondary school.

Government began to invest heavily in higher technological education, with associated liberal arts courses. If British working class families suddenly woke up to what is offered, the arithmetic of university places would have to be done all over again, for there is now a clear official commitment to find places for at least the great majority of those qualified. But once installed in their Architectural Award study bedrooms, British university students may be forgiven for feeling secretly or openly resentful of the paternalist prescription made for their lives. It is not that they are denied the chance, at least at school, to choose what they will learn: they swing from science to arts, and Government reports and statistics follow panting behind. But whichever they choose, they are almost always stuck with their choice. If they decide ten years later that their choice was mistaken, their chance of return is small. (See pp. 318–23.) Why, they would be asked, should they be given two bites at the academic cherry, when there are another few million people in the country who were once themselves potential students, but who missed their chance of the first bite?

All British post-school education is heavily subsidised by the fate of the generation immediately before. To an extent, the same is true of education during the school years: contemporary British primary schools are able to achieve excellence because it has been politically possible to forget the educational fate of the men and women prepared for life in the 1970s by the slum schools of the 1930s. But only at the later stage does the disparity between generations reach grotesque proportions. If parents hitherto content for their children to have all the chances made a determined bid for redress (or, of course, if Britain had proportionately as many students as California) the fiscal impossibility of providing all students with full tuition and maintenance grants at a real cost to the State of about £1,500 a year each would be obvious even to the National Union of Students. Perhaps the bid for redress should be made before Britain gets well started on the graduate grind and Ph.D. paperchase which America may be able to afford—fiscally if not psychologically— but which other countries cannot and should not.

Unfortunately, it cannot be taken for granted that the mature student— the person who comes back to full-time advanced learning over the age of thirty or so—is man for man or woman for woman as good an investment of public funds and university teachers' time as someone straight from school. Common sense, and various pieces of research in different contexts, would suggest that the stronger motivation of returners must outweigh the superior quickness of younger students, whose attention must first be distracted from their identity crises. Many university teachers would agree. Others will tell you that a good student in his twenties often possesses an 'edge' of originality and disrespect which is far more stimulating to teach than the soberer intelligences of early middle age. Clearly, the indications for policy must be quite different in the sciences from what they are in the arts, both because the difficulty in catching up on developments in a rapidly changing field is formidable, and because most scientists do their best work before they are forty. (Against this must be set the advantage, for the community at large and especially for schools, of having in their midst people whose science is alive rather than twenty years dead.) Otherwise, no one really knows very much about the process of learning in people who return to full-time education from other occupations in which they may or may not be using their minds. No systematic study, for instance, appears to have been carried out in Britain during the period when two years' National Service was still required of young men, and the pros and cons of doing it before or after (or in the middle of) a university career were much debated by dons.

The advantages for the university and its governance of diluting the institution's predominantly adolescent culture are too obvious to need stressing. It is not that mature students can be relied upon to keep the peace and take what they are given meekly. Some of them would probably arrive already trained in a tough school of Leftist trade-unionism. (This has already happened at the University of Lancaster, at Bochum in Germany, at Vincennes in France, and at many urban colleges in the US.) University administrators would then find themselves under more serious—because more rational—pressures than they were before, when the attackers were only the 'kids', as American professors revealingly tend to describe their undergraduate students. But the pressure would be of a kind more appropriate to the old ideal of a 'community of scholars' than the pressures now raised by generational revolt in institutions that are gradually losing all sense of scholastic community.

Politicians and civil servants would be unlikely to undertake the radical reforms which justice to the generations would require, simply to buy themselves peace in the universities. (In country after country, they have shown themselves comparatively uninterested in what happens to the universities, as long as there is peace on the streets.) But it would be easy for a single nation or two to try on a small scale a system of 'post-school credits' for higher education. The credibility of such a system would depend on the record of that country's political leaders. If—as in Britain with the tax rebates promised after 1945 as 'post-war credits'—they had previously welshed on obligations to pay deferred benefits in full and on the nail, the scheme might fail however much educationists wanted it to work.

The potential level of demand for 'mid-career' higher education, from wholly or partly qualified people who had not taken it at the first opportunity, is impossible to estimate accurately. Even the application figures for Britain's 'Open University' do not help much, for they arise from a population which has always been encouraged to associate full-time education with childhood. Different expectations would yield different results. Very much would also depend on the exact nature of the financial assistance offered. But Joseph Trenaman, who in the 1950s estimated the proportion of British adults who had ever taken any further education courses of any kind at twenty-six per cent, went on to suggest that nearly forty-five per cent of the adult population were resistant to new ideas and cultural values; but that the other half were potentially 'pro-educational'. They were likely to be susceptible to an educational approach at some level, though in only ten per cent of them was there a sustained interest in education. He concluded that the whole provision of education for adults, both formal and informal, was a reinforcing rather than a remedial·process. It depended on 'degrees of latency'. Demand for active organised participation only surfaced under certain conditions, and until the conditions were known, it could not easily be predicted from the statistics for current behaviour.[20] However, current behaviour in the US certainly supports Trenaman's theory that adult education is reinforcing rather than remedial. The people who want it most are the people who in absolute terms least need it—the ones who have already had seventeen years in school and college. The people who most need it—the Black poor—cannot use it. It follows (and for Britain and the US, which constantly try to economise on schoolteaching, it is important to make this clear) that no scheme for 'second chance' higher education can be a substitute for a school career which leaves a child with a good set of formal intellectual skills and a desire to learn more of something, no matter what. That is what the theologians would call a 'necessary but not sufficient' condition of susceptibility to more education later in life. It was the argument of chapter six that 'general education', to be worth the name, must impart those skills and that desire. Teachers have always known this; industrialists have only lately begun to appreciate the point which is made, for instance, by Professor Torsten Husén of Sweden in a paper on 'recurrent education', prepared for OECD's Centre for Educational Research and Innovation:

> 'The person who speaks and writes his native tongue and one or more foreign languages fluently, who commands the fundamentals of mathematics, who has learned how to learn and is able to continue studying on his own . . . that person will possess extremely useful tools which will enable him to cope with changing conditions and requirements. We know that the greatest difficulties of retraining for new and more highly-skilled occupations are encountered by those with the poorest formal education.'[21]

Professor Husén assumes, as anyone must who observes the evolution of higher education systems, that 'an ever-increasing number of those at the top of the qualifications hierarchy will have pursued their formal

---

[20] See the discussion in J. F. C. Harrison, *Learning and Living, 1790–1960* (London' 1961), pp. 354–358.
[21] OECD ref. no. CERI/EG/SG/69.03.

education until they are at least twenty-five'. He calculates that a person whose work depends primarily on technical know-how will in future, given the rate of scientific and technological advance in most fields, be obliged to renew his own personal fund of knowledge at the rate of five per cent a year. This will compel the individual to submit himself for systematic further education at regular intervals. If there has been a revolution in his speciality, he may even have to be retrained completely, from the point in his own education where specialisation began.

Conventionally, a 'knowledge worker' who envisaged this happening to him would regard it as a personal disaster. But is it? And is it in fact essential that all potential university students—people who are destined by ability and inclination to perform intellectually-demanding jobs during their lifetimes—should take on board all their ballast of formal education before they are twenty-five? Peter F. Drucker, for one, thinks not, and he is one of the very few writers to have drawn a constructive conclusion from the observable fact that a knowledge worker in mid-career tends to become devastatingly bored:

> 'In business and in government, in the armed services, and in the university there is a lot of talk about "retreads", about "recharging a man's batteries", about the need for "sabbaticals" and for "going back to school". But it needs to be recognized that this is not a problem of the individual, but a generic problem grounded in the ambivalence of the knowledge worker's status. It is a result—probably an inevitable one—of the hidden conflict between the knowledge worker's view of himself as a "professional" and the fact that he is within an organization, and a successor to yesterday's craftsman rather than to yesterday's "professional".
>
> 'Yet we cannot expect to shorten the working-life span of the knowledge worker through extending his years of schooling even further. Indeed we should go the other way and shorten the years the young man spends at school and university before he starts in knowledge work. The problem cannot be made to go away. But it can—and must —be converted into an opportunity. We must make it possible for the middle-aged knowledge worker to start a second knowledge career.'[22]

The Director of the OECD Centre for Educational Research, Mr. J. R. Gass, is another who has reached a similar conclusion. The 'education society', he writes, is in an inescapable dilemma; it is compelled towards more and more education, but it now shrinks from the political and sociological implications of putting an increasingly large percentage of young adults in institutions of higher education:

> 'The basic flaw lies not in expanding facilities for higher education but in *compelling* young adults to enter higher education when their

[22] *The Age of Discontinuity* (London, 1969), p. 273.

motivations would in all likelihood lead them to more active social roles. In most OECD countries today the young adult who fails to enter higher education *immediately* on leaving secondary school embarks on a path of personal development which *excludes* the highest social, professional, and economic opportunities. Few people return to higher education after they have tested themselves in society, to the extent that they are aware of their own abilities and have a personal view of how they wish to change or to fit into society. . . .

'This . . . is a plea for a "second option" in higher education through the occupational system, in which those wishing to pursue their studies would have no greater or lesser opportunities than those doing so immediately after school. It was done after the 1939–45 War—why not now? . . .

'The real terrain of argument is the socio-economic feasibility of such a radical departure in educational structure. Is there not an unresolvable conflict between the income needs of the adult with family responsibilities, and the possibilities of financing such a reform? Could career patterns be adjusted in such a way that a more flexible relationship between occupational experience and the educational system would be viable for the individual and society? What would be the effect on the labour market of school-leaving at, say, 16–18, followed by access to higher education between the ages of 22–30 and even later?'[23]

Questions of this kind, hardly asked a year or two ago, are now belatedly beginning to be explored officially within the circle of OECD countries. This is not a book of solutions to problems which are strictly insoluble by single individuals. Nevertheless, the following unofficial sketch of a 'post-school credit' scheme may not be wholly out of place. . . .

'Post-school credits'

Every young person who leaves school does so with a certain number of 'college credits' in his book. The *bachelier*, the *abiturient*, the high school graduate, the holder of two 'A level' passes (which are the equivalent terms for France, Germany, the US, and Britain) is granted, say thirty, credits. Whether he acquires these by examination, as in Europe at present, or by continuous assessment, or by a mixture of means, does not affect the scheme, and can be decided independently by different countries. His thirty credits entitle him to three, four, or five years higher education at a university of his choice, or at a time of his choice. (In practice he might well obtain both the desired college and the desired year, but legal entitlement would have to be more cautiously drawn.)

The time at which he chooses to take up his entitlement will depend on many factors; personal, academic, and national. The bachelor physicist

[23] J. R. Gass in the *OECD Observer*, No. 40 (June 1969).

who will never win his Nobel Prize if he does not make it by the age of thirty-five will use all his credits immediately and obtain more, on the strength of his undergraduate work, to last him through graduate school and Ph.D. The intending social scientist who wants to work abroad for a few years before graduating and embarking on a professional career will be able to do so. The couple whose chief desire is to marry early and raise a family may decide to return to college together when they are thirty-five or so and send their children to the university school. All of them will take advice about the likely state of the university market in the relevant years before making their decisions.

The boy or girl who was unsuccessful at school, or who left too early, to possess the full thirty credits will nevertheless not have left empty-handed. No one, even if he has never passed an exam in his school career, will have nothing in the 'bank'. But a child who chooses to enter the labour market with only the basic number of credits will have to earn the others later on if he wants higher education. He will attend evening classes, take short courses in community colleges, or submit independent work to an Admissions Board, in order to exercise his statutory right to attend college.

Financially, it is clearly impossible to make prescriptions that could have any national, let alone international, validity. Even within the boundaries of a single nation, such a thoroughgoing reconstruction of the system would have near or distant effects on individuals and on the economy which could not be assessed in advance without resources open only to governments. But certain principles may be suggested.

For the scheme to work at all, the individual must have confidence that if he postpones his university career in whole or in part, he will not be penalised financially, either during his whole working lifetime, or during his three or four years' absence from the labour market. 'Penalisation' is of course a matter of degree. No businessman earning an executive's salary could seriously expect the State to sustain his own and his family's standard of living at the same rate while he took his educational sabbatical. On the other hand, a manual worker could reasonably expect that his family would not be made to suffer for his education, even if a degree subsequently increased his earning power. The manual worker might have better opportunities to earn money casually at a time of his own choosing, but the businessman could more easily exploit the private insurance market to provide against a planned return to university ten or twenty years distant. The State ought to be able to keep the cost to itself of each individual mature student close to present levels, when all the economic pluses and minuses had been calculated, especially since there would in most cases be no need for residential accommodation to be provided for students separately from their own family units,[24] which

---

[24] In Britain at the time of writing, the student accommodation problem is regarded as one of the most formidable obstacles to the expansion of higher education.

would be commercially or municipally housed in the ordinary way. Within limits which would have to be determined by statute, the State could even use the level of individual grants as a way of adjusting the demand for university places in a given year or quinquennium.

Obviously, the unique British system whereby an aided student (the vast majority) receives the entire cost of his university education, less maintenance in vacations, would have to be abolished. As a device for extending the working class share in higher education, and assisting the birth of a British meritocracy, this system has been invaluable, though it is far clearer today than it was twenty years ago that its usefulness is severely limited by the prior handicaps which innately gifted working class children tend to suffer in bookless, unstimulating homes and—too often, even in 1970—in bookless, unstimulating schools. The British university grant and residence system has primarily been used by the children of the intelligentsia and the bourgeoisie to consolidate their own position in society. Raising the school-leaving age, opening up the institutional dead-ends in which British secondary and further education is so rich, and abolishing the guillotines which at successive examination stages cut children off from higher education for the rest of their lives, would in absolute and possibly also in proportionate terms bring many more working class children into higher education than a level of student assistance which the Exchequer, already faced with a serious backlog of public investment in health, education, and welfare, cannot afford if student numbers are to grow as fast as parents will want them to. (The sums are comparatively simple. If projections continue to be revised upwards as fast as they have been since the Robbins Report was published, there will be close on a million students in all types of higher education by 1980, at a true cost, including tuition as well as residence and maintenance, of almost fifteen hundred pounds p.a. a place.)

Students in Britain are now, in the sight of the law, just as adult at the age of eighteen as they will be at the age of thirty-five. They are just poorer. Poorer, that is, considered as isolated individuals. In fact, of course, the thirty-five-year-old has obligations, while the eighteen-year-old is likely to have patrons (sometimes called parents). Under a post-school credit scheme, the State is bound to treat both men alike according to their tax-assessed resources and obligations, and bound to allow a normal combination of cost-benefit and political criteria to determine the proportion of all students' university expenses which are met out of public funds. (For example, the level of public support is clearly pitched too low if an intelligent man is compelled to spend six years obtaining a qualification which he could have obtained in three, but for the need to spend university vacations earning money in dead-end jobs.) Under this system, parents will naturally cease to support their children in full through college, though if the Government expects a young single student to earn, say, a quarter of his expenses, it is unlikely to object if he is able to shift that part of the burden to his friends or relations. Parents, on the other hand, may well be needing the money themselves to spend on their own mid-career education. They could also be encouraged, as they are in America, to make tax-deductible gifts to the institutions which they or their children attend, to minimise for universities what will during the coming decade, in all the countries I am discussing, become a dangerous degree of dependence on central or local government funds.

It is idle to suppose that a measure of this kind can be introduced into any country's system of education without penetrating straight to the roots of it, withering some plants and making others flourish exceedingly. Almost any feature of the system that comes to mind, and a good many features of the surrounding society, will be profoundly affected. For example: the existence of selective secondary schools, assessing pupils by different standards; the governance and life-style of universities, especially residential ones; the content and method of university teaching; employers' reliance on the education system as a grading mechanism; job mobility and pension rights; the age of maximum salary and responsibility in businesses; public attitudes to the role of trained intelligence in human affairs—all these and many others would be modified. However, some features of the existing system that one might wish to change would not necessarily be affected. For instance, the single most powerful influence on the steep rise in graduate school enrolments in the US is reluctance to leave school, caused by the alternative prospect of being drafted to help fight a hated war. A scheme to spread formal education across a larger span of life might leave this trend unaffected, for no one will postpone education if he thinks that postponement might lose him his life, health, or self-respect.

On the other hand, it is also idle to suppose that profound changes in the organisation and administration of tertiary education can long be avoided. The change suggested, for example, is less drastic politically than the introduction of *numerus clausus* into the university systems of France, Germany, and Italy, which would exclude from higher education many people who could otherwise have expected at least a taste of it. The changes—structural, sociological, and political—that are liable to follow an uncontrolled student population explosion are already familiar. These will continue, even if at a slower pace than in the past decade. More insidious is the creeping inflation in the length of full-time education: a trend which runs directly counter both to the rhythm of intellectual renewal and innovation, and to the powerful biological and psychological drive towards early maturity.

To reiterate both points: most vocational training—and that includes the training of doctors and lawyers—has a half-life of not more than ten years. But as Bentley Glass of the State University of New York pointed out to the Commission on the Year 2000, this is also true of much that we call not vocational training, but fundamental education. Darwin or Mendel could have mastered the biology of the 1930s, with a short refresher course. But the man who acquired his biology qualification in the 1940s, and has taught the subject to children ever since, may need more than a short refresher course to master the biology of Watson and Crick. Again, student revolts have come and gone for well over a century, but never before have so many people's physical, intellectual, and emotional readiness for family formation and full economic responsibility preceded by a decade or so their chance of achieving these natural human desires. There is an inescapable limit to the demands which education-before-life can be allowed to make on life itself, even on the life of would-be professional scholars. As this limit is approached, one would expect a vague malaise, if nothing stronger, to show itself in academic communities—a discontent, not just with the immediate environment, but with everything that formal education has historically been about. That is precisely what has been happening on American campuses during the past few years, and this disenchantment with intellectuality needs to be distinguished very carefully from the anti-intellectualism of the Right—a much more familiar phenomenon in the US—which most lately surfaced to applaud the shooting of innocent students at Kent, Ohio.

None of the suggestions on the foregoing pages will be quickly or easily adopted. They are put up to be criticised, not swallowed. But it is time to dispel the notion that the twentieth century can change everything in its intellectual universe except its educational system and *curriculum vitae*. Culturally, that is on a par with the economic doctrine—fervently believed within living memory—that slumps are inescapable, unemployment culpable, and the levying of income tax a sin.

CHAPTER EIGHT

Four voices from the crowd

'Parents had no Manner of Authority over their Children, nor Children any Obedience or Submission to their Parents; but everyone did that which was good in his own Eyes. This unnatural Antipathy had its first rise from the beginning of the Rebellion . . . '

The Continuation of the Life of Edward, Earl of Clarendon

Not long ago an English writer, Tony Parker, persuaded the Home Office to let him live in a British prison for several months, talk to the inmates, and publish some of the conversations. The book, when it appeared, was widely hailed as a masterpiece. Mr. Parker, I am pretty sure, is too modest a reporter to care very much for that hyperbole: all he had done was to challenge the British official assumption that convicted criminals were people that one only talked *about*, not *to*.

The severest critic of modern universities would hardly compare them with prisons. Even in these cost-effective days, perhaps their most powerful allure, for both students and staff, is their character as places—almost the last places, in the developed countries of the world—where a man is at least temporarily free to choose most of his own times and seasons for attendance or absence, work or idleness. But before the end of a book which, like so many of its kind in the last few years, talks at some length *about* universities and their inhabitants, I wish to allow a few students to illuminate the subject-matter in their own way. I sought these people out, on both sides of the Atlantic, for their expressiveness and individuality rather than for their radicalism, though like many of their fellows in 1968/9 they sympathised with the activists even if they did not actually fight with them, and their conversation naturally betrays some of the preoccupations of their time and place. I have, except in one case, changed their names. The real people would, I am sure, stand by what I recorded on tape, and John Birtwhistle has thought too carefully about what he says to wish to hide behind an alias. But universities would be poorer places than they are if students risked everything they said being taken down in evidence against them. Apart from anything else, it makes it so difficult for them to change their minds later.

The plurality of America is expressed more vividly in its system of higher education than almost anywhere else. Beside the great universities which aim to teach all qualified comers and research in most known disciplines, there are colleges and universities with more limited aims and constituencies: colleges for Catholics and Baptists, Jews and Negroes, progressive intellectuals and reactionary halfwits. The restriction is *de facto* rather than *de jure* and is now seldom absolute, at least in the better institutions of each genre. A Jew sits on the governing body of the Catholic University of Notre Dame, and a few whites can usually be seen defying convention or their families on the campuses of Howard or Tuskegee. Morehouse College in Atlanta, which educated Martin Luther King, is of all the Black schools the strongest on esprit de corps and the proudest of its intellectual achievement in the face of fearful financial odds. An English observer, taking in its middle-aged, hard-used buildings, enthusiastic choir, tree-fringed lawn, cheerfully cynical students, compulsory chapel and paternally disciplinarian faculty, was forcibly reminded of a sound public school back home. This atmosphere needs to be borne in mind during the following interview. Ellis Murray, a slightly-built, springy history student, active in college journalism and politics but by local standards a moderate reformist, was as shrewd about the other schools as about his own. He explained Harvard's liberal policy over the admission of Blacks and the provision of a Black Studies programme by saying: 'Harvard has a lust to be first—and to be first you've got to tolerate.'

ELLIS

C. D. How has the reality of Morehouse matched up with your expectations?

E. M.   I visited the place before coming. You have five or six institutions in the Atlanta University Center, filled with black minds, so, I thought, undoubtedly you have to have some of the brightest black minds, some of the most politically and racially aware black minds in the nation. I found that to be untrue. I found that here you have some of the most complacent, lethargical, apathetic, indifferent people on this earth. And why? Because these are people who have always looked at white society with this admiration, love, lust, and they are unwilling to give that up, or to look at reality, because it scares them. It's not beautiful. We Americans, we're a sensual people, we like to look at something and say 'It's beautiful', and there's the same attitude here. There are individuals, yes, but not in such a degree that I had expected. It has something to do with the fact that they are second and third generation students in their families. The average parental income here is six or seven thousand dollars. They're people who for practical purposes believe they've made it in the world, when for all practical purposes they have not. A Ph.D. once challenged Malcolm X's philosophy and Malcolm looked into the audience and said 'Do you know what they call a Ph.D. whose skin is black?' The man said 'What?' 'A nigger'. This is true. If you have a Ph.D., or if you're James Brown with your money, or Sammy Davis Junr. with your talent, or if you're Edward Brooke with your power, you're still a nigger. Martin Luther King wrote of the world where your first name is nigger and your last name is boy, where your wife is never given the courtesy of being addressed as Mrs., where your grandmother is called by her first name by a seven or eight year-old child that she has to call Mister or Master.

C. D. Is it possible to criticise Martin Luther King here?

E. M. Oh, yes, he is indeed criticised here. And he deserves criticism, because he's a human being. This is one thing I'd like to stress. Black people have been looked upon as superhuman beings for a long time. They have been expected to endure more and they have endured more. But for some strange reason they're still expected to endure more. Too many of them expect themselves to endure more than a human being. For example James Earl Ray, who was recently sentenced to ninety-nine years gaol for murdering Martin Luther King: when I walked into my classroom and informed my teacher that as far as I was concerned he should not have been electrocuted, he should have been castrated and then burned, she fell back in horror. But why? This is a human emotion and I am a human being. I reserve the right to have the emotions of a human being, and when someone that a human being loves is killed, that human being has no choice but to feel sad and angry. I reserve the right to release that anger and have it known, whereas someone like Abernathy says, 'Well, I believe that we should love James Earl Ray, I don't think he should be punished.' I look on that as the statement of an idealistic idiot. To look upon James Earl Ray only as a victim of American society is foolish. You can refuse to accept racism: it is a hard long process, but it is possible. Look at the black people who have; look at the few white people who have.

You've been in North Carolina. The poor white trash there: everyone likes to feel superior to somebody and they can feel superior to black people because of what the society's taught them, even though they are the last rack of the ladder. One of the reasons why there is a black bourg-eoisie—and I mean that mentally rather than economically—is that people like to feel superior to something. Once X has his Ph.D. and looks back and realises that Y doesn't—or that Y didn't go to college at all—then he knows he's superior. He may not go around saying he's superior. Indeed he may go around saying that all men are created equal. But philosophically and scientifically that statement can be torn apart. For idealistic purposes that statement's fine, 'all men are equal, all men are brothers'. But in America people have been so idealistic that they've closed their minds to the reality and that's why there's so much hell going on in the society.

I shall always strive to continue my education. When I came to More-house, I had this idea that I wanted to obtain a Master's and a Ph.D., and then I ran into a couple of people with their Master's and their Ph.D.s whom I found totally ignorant. And I wondered, is it worth it? Is there a better education? And I found I learned more in many bull sessions than in many lectures. I used to travel round the country exploring and we had many bull sessions on those trips. In fact it was an experience I had on one of them that made me somewhat anti-liberal. We were going to Jekyll Island, Georgia, from Greensboro, North Carolina. I was the only black person in the car—there were seven of us. Everybody seemed very friendly, very liberal. They did not condemn Martin Luther King, they did not condemn civil rights. They agreed with it, moderately maybe, but they agreed that even black people should have civil rights. On the way back we stopped at this barbecue pit, and the waitress came out and she looked at me and said 'I'm sorry but we don't serve coloureds.' She suggested that I get out and take a walk while she served the white boys. Of course, everybody was hungry. And I refused. First of all, it would be foolish of me to get out of the car in Spartanburg, South Carolina, and take a walk. I don't know Spartanburg, South Carolina. What I know of it told me not to get out and take a walk. I would have expected those fellows to have felt the pain that I felt, even in a moderate degree, and to have refused to have eaten there; to have said, Well, 'let's go on somewhere else, where all of us can be served, because if she says she don't want to serve you, what she's really saying is she doesn't want to serve anybody.'

But that's not what happened. These very liberal people decided they were hungry, and their hunger superseded the inhumanity, the degrada-tion, that I had received. So they ate, and they told me they would take me somewhere to eat. So I told them, 'Don't bother, take me back home.'

Another example: I've been in several speech contests, and one of them was the 'World Peace through world law' contest. I remember travelling to New York City with a group of people who were supposedly very liberal. Again I was the only black student. One fellow was a minister. There were three students assigned to each room. The fellows thought that I was out of the room (actually I was in the bathroom) and I heard this discussion as to who was going to sleep with the nigger tonight. These people are liberals.

A third example. This was with a Jewish student, who was a very nice guy. He invited me to dinner. When I went to his home I found out that I was the first black person ever to come to dinner—you know, hurrah hurrah, I'm supposed to give 'em a Dewey button. I also found out that the fellow's father owned a store. In the store he employed six black people, one of whom had been working for him for thirteen years. Now why hadn't he ever invited this fellow—the first employee he's ever had— to dinner? All during the dinner they talked about civil rights. We went into the library and we talked about civil rights. I told them I was highly insulted because there we were in the library with beautiful books many of which I had read, and they felt that the only thing I could adequately articulate was something about civil rights. It showed me that liberals are caught up in their own bag, their own little world. It's the same world that Kipling described, you know, the white man's burden. As far as I'm concerned the white man's burden is the white man, and if he carries that burden he'll do very well.

I had the offer of a place to do journalism at Wisconsin. Well I didn't want to do journalism at Wisconsin, but I also held ambivalent attitudes to going to a white college. This is a time in American history when black nationalism is coming to the forefront, when people of black skin realise that they are a nation within a nation, that they have a *pathos* and that they should explore that *pathos* (I guess that's the right word.) This is one reason why I came to Morehouse College.

C. D. Which way will Morehouse jump? There's a drain of black intelligence —students and professors—to northern white universities which want to get in on the Black Studies act. Unless their place is taken by northern black revolutionaries who want the benefits of pure black education, there's little apparent future for this college.

G. M. That's partly why I don't know if I shall return to Morehouse next fall. The reason I have these reservations is that education in Morehouse College is a static thing: it's not active at all. I believe that a student should be involved in all educational processes. One of the experiences at Wesleyan is sending students all over the country—I was interviewed by two last week—to interview radicals on campus, and they're going to come back and teach teachers in what I term 'the student experience'. Originally they were just going to put it in a book but I suggested they hold a class when they got back and they called their instructor and he said 'Right, that's great.' That's the sort of thing that should happen here. I don't want to go. I like to run toward challenges not away from them. But I'm a freshman, and I don't want to end up four years from now saying, 'The most foolish thing I ever did was to stay here.' Morehouse College sometimes goes around calling itself 'the Harvard of the South', and sometimes they laughingly call Harvard 'the Morehouse of the North', but one of the questions a revolutionary student here would ask is 'Is it worth being the Harvard of the South? Do we want to imitate Harvard?' And they would answer, 'No, we don't have to imitate anybody.' There are a lot of students here who could have been and were accepted by other institutions. And the reason they came here was that here is a place that is not chained to government—it's not like Harvard, that receives ninety per cent of its funds from the government; we're not chained to the state; we're not chained to the Church (although we're supposed to be supported by the Baptists we receive less than one-tenth of one per cent from the Baptist Church); so you have what you can consider an independent institution, that can make the radical changes that a lot of other places cannot. However, the administration doesn't look at it this way. It says, 'From where do we get our money? From liberal whites, from business, from philanthropic societies, more and more from the government. So we've got to look good.' I can't accept this. I don't see why we have to look good. Does a Yale student have to look good? When I was at Yale, I was walking round with a shirt and tie on. A lady walked up to me and said 'You must be a freshman.' I said 'Why do you say that?' 'Well when freshmen first get here they walk around with shirt and tie on but then they learn.' You're not there to look good. You're there to *be* good and to learn, really learn. I have a friend, I call him Dad. We constantly have debates about society. He thinks it's beneficial to look good, because it's politic. I say it's not beneficial to look good because it's hypocritical. This college cares how you look. The college cares how you talk. The college cares how you eat, what are the rules of the cafeteria—you can't go into the cafeteria with your shirt pulled out. Yale has a beautiful dining hall, several dining halls, with food greatly superior to the slop we get here, but they don't give a damn how you look when you go in there, because you go there to eat. I don't give a damn how you look because you come here to get an education.

I'm not one of those that think education will be the saviour of society—which is another mistake many people on this campus make. First of all it was money: black people had to get some money. Until they found out there was a ceiling on how much money black people could get and then it was education. That's what Booker T. Washington was talking about. Of course he wanted a different kind of education; he wanted you to be trained. Whereas Du Bois wanted something to stimulate the mind. Morehouse College is known for producing professional Negroes. Yet Morehouse, without realising it, refuses to stimulate or create one black mind. I have run into several people here that I would go so far as to say actually were geniuses. They are being depressed: that bright flame which glowed in their mind when they got here is now going out, because they are being conditioned not to be men, they are being conditioned to be professional Negroes. You want to be with black people, yes. But unfortunately, to really understand black people, it looks like you're going to have to go to a white institute that *has* black instructors teaching black courses. In six weeks, Harvard set up a Ph.D. programme in Black Studies. In two years, Morehouse College hasn't even got a really good minor in the subject.

How has the college opened itself up to the community? Every now and then they'll say to interested students, 'Go out and tutor'. But this is only a give, and there has to be give and take: you see, that community has a lot to teach the college, as well as the college having a lot to instruct the community with. There are several projects that the students are designing. Whether or not the administration will accept them is another thing. Money is a factor I agree: the college has a hard time getting money, they have to just about beg when they get it. This is one of the reasons why you begin to hate money. Money's such a hang-up. It's like a chain around your neck.

The twentieth century black student has a problem. I guess he looks upon life the same way Dickens describes it in the *Tale of Two Cities*—'the worst of things and the best of things'. This is the way we have to look at it. In conversation, this is how people put it to me: 'Yes, it is the best of things, but it's also the worst. It would be good if we could just pick the best and leave the worst, but we can't. You can't just close your eyes to the evil in the society and become a bourgeois middle-class negro, and say, "Well, I've made it, and everyone else can't because that's life."' This is why I'm beginning to dislike what the Nixon administration is doing—or maybe it's American society that's doing—to individuals like James Brown. 'There's a black man who used to be a shoe-shine boy and now he has made it.' That's right but that's an individual. Now look at that individual and compare him to the masses. One, he's an entertainer. Now everybody's not an entertainer. Or take President Nixon's presentation of himself to the Republican convention: 'I am the personification of the American dream, I'm a poor boy who made it.' But he's got to admit that he's a white boy who made it. I think that poor fellow's sole desire was to become President of the United States, and now that he's President it's like a child who always wanted a swing and now that he's gotten a swing he's just sitting there swinging.

I contend that there's no black American. There are only black men in America. The only American is the white American, because the American is the person who has partaken of the American experience. It goes back to what Malcolm said about being a diner. He said, 'If you sit me at the table while you're eating and refuse to give me food you can't call me a diner. I'm just there.' That's the way black people feel in America: we're just here. One day we'll cross what the old spirituals call the river

Jordan, but actually I'm not interested in what's on the other side of that river. I'm interested in what's here. I realise that I'm just here and I don't want to be just here.

C. D. And you don't want to emigrate?

E. M. No. I don't want to emigrate. But, if the worst comes to the worst' I'll go to Africa if I think that over there I can find what I want. If over there I can find not only peace of mind but that degree of prosperity that is a driving factor in everyone. If I can go there and find what Malcolm X found in his tour, and if I can give something there, not just find something, yes I'll go. A man without a country is a very lonely man.

CAROL

Carol Johnson is taking anthropology at Berkeley. We sat talking in the sun in the open-air canteen at the edge of Sproul Plaza after listening to Mark Schorer lecture on Conrad's *Heart of Darkness*. But that was not the first occasion I met her. She had agreed to lead a 'Pursuit of Happiness' class, arranged by the student-run free university ('Center for Participative Education') which is in but not precisely of the Berkeley campus. A few people turned up at her apartment for the class, clearly lacking any notion of what happiness was or where to look for it. Carol, large-boned and auburn-haired, sat calmly in her chair, talking now and then about her astrology teacher, and sewing one of those bedspread-like costumes to which the Berkeley climate is so kind. Eventually she suggested a picnic up-coast at the weekend. I do not know whether or not it ever took place. But I do remember a casual remark of hers that made me feel more English and more old than anything else I heard in the United States. We were talking about travelling, and I said that for me, the most enjoyable journeys were train ones. 'I have never been in a train,' she said.

C. J. I was born in La Jolla (pronounced 'Lahoya'), right near San Diego. Cal's got a new campus there now. My father majored here at Berkeley—a double major in physics and electronics. That was one of the reasons I came here.

C. D. Not to do anything like that?

C. J. No. He thought maybe but I knew not. I knew by the time I was in tenth grade, two years before college. Physics here has some women in it and most are at the top of the department. The women who go into the sciences either have to be very good or they don't stay in. It's not my bag anyway. I'm majoring in anthropology. I came in languages, but I switched to anthropology because you can study languages anyway. In fact now I believe I can study anthropology anyway because I learnt more when I was studying at the project on my own than I did from teaching. It's a good department. I've heard it's the best in the US.

C. D. What influenced you in choosing what to do?

C. J. I never had any anthropology till I came here. I first went into it because I was interested in sociology, and I became disgusted with sociology because it is so, like, statistically oriented. You sit in a chair and you deal with statistics and with people that you aren't involved with personally. That's no way. Besides anthropology is much more human, and it deals with what for me are more religious kind of things, with a human being as an animal and how he fits into the ecology of the world, how he used to fit in and how that's changing, the huge distances of time and space that have happened.

C. D. When I asked you if you did astrology courses to understand the world, you said 'no but perhaps to keep it sacred'. When did you come to feel this way?

C. J. Perhaps I shouldn't say this but I think it was because of drugs. I think for me it was almost directly that. I wasn't brought up in any religion. The first time I started going to church was the Unitarian Universalist church. But that was still socially oriented: it was trying to deal with social problems and human problems but I wasn't really religious. Now I can pray in my own way. But I don't think I could ever pray in a church. I wasn't brought up that way.

I started taking drugs about two years ago, when I was sixteen. Actually I started smoking marijuana when I was fifteen. After that it was something different because I smoked only with a fixed family that I knew. It was a family ritual: I didn't smoke outside that group. They were young, not very rich, and lived in the country. I don't think everybody should take drugs. I think some people are very sensitive and aware to things without them, and when they do take drugs they disorient themselves. I had a lot of troubles doing anything and I was frustrated as well.

Since then I've taken LSD and I've taken mescalin. I've eaten peyote. I've only eaten peyote twice and I've taken mescalin two or three times. I don't really want to take more at this time. You can't get pure acid and you get things that are sold as 'speed' which are against what you can learn from that. Speed turns into an ego, like, 'there you are, there's your golden ego, you can do anything', whereas acid can often be breaking down your ego.

I get drugs from friends. One time I bought from someone I later found out was involved in an underworld thing, but I don't like that sort of thing at all. The Mafia and a couple of other groups like them are too capitalistically oriented for me. I think the ideal thing would be if there were enough of it so it could be free, and there wouldn't be pressure on the people who don't want it. It happens now. Like, in high school it used to be that you'd save up and go out and buy candy and boys would buy cigarettes and I guess some guys dirty books: well now it's the same thing with drugs. I think you have to have a level-headed approach to it. I've usually smoked at home instead of out at parties or dances. I have occasionally smoked at my mother's home and I'm thinking of taking some marijuana down next time for her to try maybe. We've talked about it before when I told her I was turning on. She's very open-minded about things except that she's not eager to change but she accepts things very readily and she's willing to draw parallels. She said, 'Well it sounds like a religious experience or like taking a walk on a beautiful day.' She's really great.

My mother and father have been divorced since I was about three. My father hasn't had a very happy life. He's been married three times since then. He travels a lot. He says he's happy though. He comes up to visit and I go down to visit. He does business round the country and he'll fly into SFO or Oakland on the way home. Also he's recently taken up flying small planes—the business executive thing. He lives in San Diego, like my mother. He pays some money to keep me going here. That's part of the legal support money but we've been having some trouble lately because I felt he was trying to control me through the money so now he's only giving me half of what I had before and at the end of this quarter he's going to cut it off. That's good because he's got my brother who's getting ready to go to graduate school and he needs money and my little sister, my half sister, will be going to college soon and she'll need money. He has pretty expensive tastes and I don't want him to go bankrupt because of me. If I really want to go to school I can do it, get a scholarship and so on. I have a scholarship right now because I had honours at entrance here and I have a 3·7 average right now which is an A minus and in my major I've got a 4·0 average but I've only taken five or six classes in that. For me in school the problem is not the grades but the feeling I have that I must learn *everything*. It's hard for me to accept that I can't do that. I drive myself very hard and then I have two weeks between courses to recover—catch cold or bronchitis or something and lay in bed—but I'm kinda tired of it. Typical frustrated intellectual hippy!

My high school didn't have that much to offer me but there were a lot of books my mother and brother had that I wanted to get into. When I was ten I saw a Japanese version of *The Idiot*, an underground movie made in Kyoto about thirty years ago, and when I went home I borrowed the book from my brother. It took me about three months to read it but I got through it and I read it again. (And Thoreau the same way though he wasn't so hard to understand at all because his philosophy is easier.) That film—it was kind of odd, Japanese people depicting Russian people being watched by American people, but it came through and later I could identify that film with the book.

My brother's a philosophy major here and he wants to go to Divinity School, either at Harvard or a place in New York or there are a couple of others somewhere else. He said to me about two years ago, 'I used to think I wanted to be a monk and live in seclusion but I'm not that kind of person and other times I think I want to be a super-intellectual and pull everything apart but I'm not that kind of person either.' He's looking for something half-way between.

C. D. Is there any tradition of this in your family?

C. J. No. My mother I guess is a middle class drop-out like a lot of other people. She dropped out, I mean, from participation in politics and so on. She's gotten back into that now though. When I went to junior high school I used to badger her about not voting and now I realise what her position was which was that it wasn't going to do any good anyway. She was before her time. She and my father were both very heavily influenced during the McCarthy era. They were just getting out of college at that time and he was here, Berkeley, which was the centre of what they call communism.

C. D. If you drop out yourself now—leave school and go and live up coast, as you were suggesting—will you come back?

C. J. I don't know. Everyone's trying to talk me out of it because I'm doing very well in school but school isn't helping me deal with the problems I'm really worried about. No, they're not really describable. But school is something separate from real life and it demands most of your time. Also it's an object-oriented sort of thing. You're working for something and the satisfaction is sort of doled out to you in small portions. I think that learning, intellectual pursuit, has to be self-driven. I don't think it's much good when it's just rambling around in a lot of things and putting out a lot of money, $125 a quarter or for the people that come from out of state $500 a quarter. I don't think it's worth it for me right now. I want to start realising life again for a while. I might come back though.

C. D. Did you give up living in the dormitory because it stopped you doing things you wanted to do, or for what reason?

C. J. The dormitory was just absurd. It's hard to explain this—I tried to explain to my father—but I think it's a very unhealthy atmosphere. It's like a mental hospital. Most mental hospitals that I've ever seen or read about don't really help people to get over their paranoia but make them even more unable to deal with life. The dormitory is made out of metal and plastic. I took acid in the dormitory once and I didn't feel comfortable at all because—the ecology was so unecological! It was like being in a cage. It's not just things like not being able to have a man in there if you want to—any place you're at you can wheel around things like that though I don't like to, I like to be honest with whoever I'm at—it's the fact that it's an institution, governed by housemother, which wouldn't be so bad if there were the feeling of a mother, a mature central figure, but I don't feel she's especially mature at all, and I don't think that most places of this kind really have someone the people can look to, someone for the girls to identify with. She was a very nice woman, but she was separate from us, and we weren't even an 'us', we were just stumbling around in the hall and bumping into each other. I'm really affected by my environment and I tend to read things into it. I'd feel more comfortable in a wood house. I don't like television, and houses made out of stucco with built-in appliances, what Ray Bradbury I think calls push-button living. That's part of anthropology too because one of the main differences between human beings and other animals is that we use things to cut us off from our environment and from other animals. I guess that's what science fiction writers have been occupied with a lot: the star child, and being encased in plastic while you travel around the city, and the cities on the moon with a big plastic dome over them. I think it's really a shame. I think we should get back to where we came from. I think our bodies are biologically more adapted to three million years ago. We live a life with anxieties and no fulfilment.

In anthropology too we studied personal space. The professor was talking about how in South America people would sit right up close to him when he was talking and there was very close personal contact, whereas here you can be walking down the street of one of our big cities and you consciously avoid brushing against people. It's almost a paranoia.

C. D. Do you live close to anybody in particular?

C. J. I'm pretty close to my room-mate, I think. I lived with a guy last summer but that didn't work out at all. You need independence a whole lot, at least I do, the right to decide for yourself what you're going to do at a particular time, to decide for yourself what you're going to think. The social pressures are pretty heavy. If you're very steadily involved with one person you want to please them, you want them to be happy with you. I think I did let that affect me, but also when you have two people and you want to do something you have to compromise usually unless you are both thinking of the same thing. I realise life demands compromise but at the same time you have to know what you really want before you can ever compromise and I didn't at the time. One of the things he said to me when we first got together was, 'you seem really happy and I want to be happy'. Well I don't like having people depending on me. I fall through, like, I come on like I'm really strong and know what I'm doing and I don't like to have someone looking up to me every minute and saying 'what do we do now?' It works the other way too. Some people demand that you do that to them, some very dominant men, they seem to want you to ask permission—and I don't ask permission! I was going out with a guy last year and I decided I wanted to go to a concert of some kind and I arranged it without him because I was the only person that wanted to see it and I was sure he wouldn't have wanted to go. So I told him one night when he called me up to ask what we were going to do and I said well I'm going to go this place and he was angry at me for about two weeks because of that. I guess what I'm looking for if I'm looking for anything is someone who's got more things to be interested in than being in love. There's so many different things that people are capable of as individuals that they can share with each other because of that. If you become dependent on just the relationship and forget about all the other things that are going on in your lives the relationship just becomes boring.

I want to have children and a strong home life and things like that. I used to have this careerist thing—I wanted to be a doctor, I wanted to be a lawyer. I don't have anything against that, in fact that's what I really want, but I don't want to settle down with anybody until I've found somebody that I'm sure loves themselves and is capable of loving other people besides me: you know, friends, and lovers may be, or children.

I'm Aquarius. For women Aquarius supposedly is generally an unhappy love life and dissatisfaction that way. It's easy for me to be dissatisfied because I'm really a serious person, and a lot of times the courtship kind of relationships are so superficial that they don't add much to your life, except maybe dinner once in a while when you can't afford it, and that isn't worth it. The only time I can say that I really really found love was a time when it wasn't even like falling in love with anyone else and it was one of the few people in the world that I could say, 'you decide anything in the world and I'll trust you, like, we could be standing on a cliff and you say jump over and I'll jump'. And it wasn't built on courtship or dating but on real friendship. Not sexual. I think he kissed me once and put his arm round me and pulled my pigtails but there was a, I guess, platonic bond that for me means a lot more. It's so hard to explain . . . for me it's more important, for a lot of people it's not.

C. D. You said your astrologer makes mistakes . . .

C. J. Yes. My astrologer gets flustered when he's not prepared. He was trying to cast charts without doing them beforehand and he got very hung up about the fact that he was doing it before two or three hundred people, and he wanted to come on well, so . . . I don't take his courses for credit. I decided as soon as I started that I wasn't going to take his classes for credit because if I did I'd feel directed, and also because credit is such a material thing, it's like getting a pat on the back for having done something to somebody's approval and here is something that you want to do solely for yourself. I think just about all the people taking the class are serious about it because the astrology class itself is intended for people who already know a little. Like, he's not giving you a general thing of what astrology is but he's telling you how to cast natal charts, how to interpret what they mean. I've been interested in astrology about a year. I think it does affect what I do. Up till about a month ago, I just realised last night, I was using it to understand myself and to justify faults in myself, but I don't think that's a good way to use astrology. It's rather a way to tie everything together in a big bundle. I feel extra-sensory vibrations are present in a 'cosmic consciousness' sense, universal life vibrations throughout the whole universe. They've been getting more and more scientific proof that various things on earth are affected by things that happen way out far distant, like menstruation and the moon, or the tides and the moon. The main thing that I'm trying to get at in astrology is a sense of connecting things together, people together, the universe together; not really understanding it, but accepting it. Astronomy does this for me too: the distance, and realising that those clouds are not even clouds, they're not like a ball of cotton at all. But we're not even here really; we're ninety per cent nothing. That's my attitude to science now, a kind of wondering attitude. Astronomy started from astrology, didn't it, and they're still very closely connected. The class are going to go down to an observatory down south somewhere. They have a programme on astrology which they say they've had on their files for a long time without anyone wanting to see it.

C. D. What other courses are you taking?

C. J. Russian language, Etymology of Chinese characters (comparing modern and ancient forms and trying to figure out where they came from and what they mean), Astrology and the Pursuit of Happiness, Dostoievsky, and French Phonetics (that's required for the French major here and if I get it I'll probably try for a double major in French and Anthropology). Last quarter I was taking a course in Primates (that's, you know, bones—physical anthropology) and I was also taking a course in folk lore and a Philosophy course. I'm a sophomore now—thirty-nine units I had since last quarter. But I feel as though I've aged about ten years since I came here. I was really eager to come. I was thinking first of going to Reed[1] but I didn't know too much about it or have too much faith in it and I thought if it was too strong there wouldn't be any place in it for me.

  We're the best educated generation there's ever been in America and we're the ones who've been taught more about American ideals than

[1] Reed College, Portland, Oregon. See pp. 249–50.

anyone except maybe the people who created them. I think that's the reason why a lot of people are refusing to take anything less. They learn to expect freedom, to expect that the Constitution will be true. My mother wasn't taught to expect it: she was taught that it was something people wanted but couldn't necessarily have. We are. I think it's good. We're also taught that everyone has the right to life, liberty and the pursuit of happiness, which isn't true at all as you have to bind yourself to someone who'll give you money so you can eat, and a woman especially has to bind herself. You aren't free to pursue happiness. Women don't get such good jobs. My mother has been a secretary most of her life and has had to work for people intellectually inferior to her, who treated her like dust. Even when she was working for the university and had to correct all these professors' papers and letters and things. She was part of the machine. She was there to be given orders and make up for discrepancies without saying anything about it. My mother used to lose pay when she had to take care of me and my brother when we were ill. That seemed strange. I know it's the way it happens and I guess basically I'm a socialist but I don't think political things change it. You have to work from the bottom up instead of from the top down and so that starts with yourself. That's my main beef about the people who are protesting here: they protest, but they are still totally within the tradition of the university and of this kind of life. They're still operating on the assumption that if you talk about something you'll solve it. If you think something is right you should do it, and by your doing it other people will be affected, and see how it's done.

In each of the countries I visited while engaged on this book, competition for access to higher education is naked and unsparing, whether it is to get into the right university (as in Japan and to a lesser extent in the United States), or into any university (as in Britain), or into one of the *grandes écoles* that are considered better than a university (as in France). Competition at this intensity claims victims in many ways. Not all young people get to university who should; not all who do get there find what they wanted or expected. I am presenting here two witnesses in support of the previous chapter's thesis: that some of the misery caused by the global guillotine at eighteen-plus might be alleviated by a more flexible attitude to the 'learning periods' in a person's lifetime; and that students who drop out of university, or who enter it late and out of step as 'mature students', are not (as academics often suppose) marginal to the whole enterprise, but rather a key to its fundamental reform. Even statistically, drop-outs are far from marginal in those countries (such as France or Italy) where in some universities and some fields of study up to half the students who register do not complete their course. But these are countries whose universities are open to all qualifiers, and their student drop-out rate is therefore to be regarded as a substitute for a selection process rather than as a fault in the institution itself (though of course, it may be that too).

In Britain, statistically, the student drop-out rate is comparatively low (about 10 per cent, rising to 25 per cent or so in certain technological institutions that have only recently been granted university status). Mature students, defined as persons over the age of 30 who are attending universities full-time as undergraduates, represent only 3·5 per cent of the British student body, and if the most hospitable university—that of London—were left out of account the percentage would be considerably smaller. But because of these low numbers, and because the British academic scene is still on a small enough scale for the teachers of such men to know them personally, the two people whose experiences I record in the following pages jumped out at me from the surrounding landscape in the universities to which they belong (or belonged).

They are perhaps even less representative of their contemporaries than the two Americans. John is unusual among drop-outs in that he clearly possesses a better critical mind than most students who remain in the system. Joe is gaining nothing economically by breaking off his career to attend university, whereas most British mature students are seeking to improve not merely their education but their qualifications (and hence earning power.) Both men are pretty far to the Left, which is no more a general truth about drop-outs and drop-ins than it is about orthodox students. But they have in common a useful worm's eye view of that outwardly highly civilised institution, the British university. How did they arrive there, and what did they find?

JOHN

John Birtwhistle is twenty-two. He lives in a London flat surrounded by books, records and the other essentials of middle-class professional life. He is a parson's son, and is more conscious than most in his generation of the living threads that bind the activity which he thinks proper for him to the activity which his parents thought proper for them. Except perhaps in its eighteenth century doldrums, Oxford has always at once stimulated and sheltered such men, and they have usually repaid the debt with almost excessive affection. Nevertheless, John left Oxford ot his own free will. This is why.

J. B. When I think about what I learnt at school, I find I have kept a ragbag of odds and ends. Take a particular subject, history, where there are some things we all know in common—1066, Bad King John, Round-heads and Cavaliers, Enclosure of the Common Land, and so on. These are some of the high points of English people's awareness of their history. They can, of course, be shown to represent some of the major forms of society which have ruled that people, and the transitions between those forms. But in school they are seen as isolated events, from which one gets very static ideas such as that Britain 'is' a monarchy. The meaning of the process of industrialisation, for example, is made elusive. School doesn't give us any way of understanding industrial exploitation, the accumulation of capital, the rise of the bourgeoisie and of the working class. School just gives us events, not processes, and encourages us to take up attitudes towards them which have nothing to do with history. For example, kids take sides between Roundheads and Cavaliers. Most of them prefer the hippies to the skinheads, although the Roundheads were the more historically progressive: the point is that they are encouraged to take sides on grounds of style, not history.

Nor is it just that historical events are drained of their true meaning: the school fills them up again with a false meaning which supports the ruling British myths and institutions. Take the way in which the force of Christianity is mystified. I can remember stories about missionaries which portrayed some of the motives of these men, but not their actual effects. They were seen as spreading the gospel, or tracing some river, and it escaped notice that they were acquiring land, spearheading the White Man's invasion and afterwards instructing the natives to obey the new regime. A narrower, but striking example: I remember at school drawing cross-sections of the Davy safety lamp. We were told Davy was a very good man who wouldn't take any profits from his invention: it was given to mankind for safety in the mines. Well, I since read that as soon as the Davy lamp came in, accidents in mines actually increased, because the device was an excuse for the bosses to push men down into the more dangerous parts of the mine.

Lastly, the ragbag of events is not linked up with the present industrial, racial and national struggles. So the present order of society, and the rule of industrial bosses, is not seen as temporary, like the others. Schools have a subject called History on their timetables, but they don't teach anybody to think historically.

Here is one of the roots of student rebellion. What activated discontent with our teaching was a series of events which exposed the foundations of our society as very flimsy. We were in sixth-forms in the early sixties. Suez had shown the uneasy status of Britain's ruling class, and affected the whole culture. The atom bomb terror, dramatised by the Cuba crisis in 1962, showed that the State was against the People. Millions were spent on weapons, while the Freedom From Hunger Campaign was pointing out that the world was hungry. I had joined CND before Cuba, and thinking about pacifism was a way of criticising the church for its hypocrisy on social questions. Religion was finally killed by *Honest to God*, which said the external forms didn't matter. Political rulers at that time were represented by the complacent Macmillan, and by the Profumo scandal. Naturally, we turned against teachings that pretended all was well, that didn't begin to explain what was wrong or how it could be changed.

At first, the world became hostile and incomprehensible. I was interested in Existentialism and adopted a sort of stoic humanist pessimism: 'To know is to suffer' . . . A man, like Pascal's 'thinking reed', is at least *aware* of what happens to him. It was CND, and some revolutionary books I read by accident, that converted this mood into an active search for understanding about how to change society. The great virtue of CND was that a myriad philosophical and political ideas rattled around in it. I picked up an outline theory of the State, on broadly Anarchist lines, from the people who talked about direct resistance against a civil power that was preparing to destroy us all and yet itself survive in its own deep bunker. A lasting effect of mass movements lies in the future action of people for whom they provide decisive political education. There's a parallel between CND and the Algerian struggle in France, and Civil Rights in America, which were tributary to the present student movement; and the student movement itself is all the time helping to form the members of future political groupings.

So politics made me feel my education had not supplied any tools for understanding the world. On the other hand, I did nose out a few books which, while academic rather than revolutionary, did seem to raise the interesting questions. These writings helped determine my expectations of university, by conveying a particular idea of what disciplines like Economics and Philosophy could be about. For instance, Bertrand Russell writes about how philosophy is *both* a technical subject, and yet can inform a way of life. Galbraith's *The Affluent Society* quotes Marshall on the title page: 'The economist, like everyone else, must concern himself with the ultimate aims of man.' Of course, when I got to Oxford I found that Russell's work had been not so much refuted as pushed aside by 'linguistic' philosophy. From Keynes, let alone Marshall, politics had been eliminated.

However, universities are quite ready to take in people of my state of mind—even though they know that the syllabus does not answer to it. They spot people who do not yet think like them, but who seem the 'right kind of chap' to be licked into shape. You must leave politics aside and grind your nose on their idea of professional rigour. At worst, you become part of their tradition of amiable eccentricity.

For example, when Balliol gave me a scholarship, it was on the basis of essays answering their questions about aesthetics, existentialism, Marxism, and goodness knows what, done for a paper titled Philosophy. That is, at the point of entering university, I was rewarded for practising philosophy according to my own conception of the discipline. But these problems then never appeared in the course, and people were actually prevented from studying them. It's like a misleading trade description. I'm just trying to express the sense of frustration and indignation people feel when they are told that philosophy is about calculating abstract sequences in formal logic.

Perhaps it seems a bit strong to say students are actually prevented from learning what interests them? The myth of the tutorial system is that it favours individual development. But in fact, everyone may have separate tutorials but everyone does the same topic in the same week: it's easier for the tutor. And if you are going to get anything out of spending time with the man, you have to establish a common language with him. In practice, this can only be *his* language, the language of the exams it all leads to. For example, a tutor pretended not to know what I meant by the term 'contradiction', used in a Marxist sense. (That is, there can be contradictions in the real world, whereas formal logic thinks they hold only between propositions.) Now this tutor was also an examiner, and if I'd used the term 'contradiction' like that in an exam, he would have marked me down—yet it is a perfectly rigorous philosophical usage.

It seemed to me that this kind of systematic narrowing and distortion of students' minds was particularly out of place in the course I was reading. First, the speed of change in its subject-matter, society, means that the student is as likely as the teacher to have truths to contribute. Then, 'Philosophy, Politics, and Economics' was originally conceived as a study of modern society as a whole, just as 'Greats' enquired into *ancient* culture. You'd think the three component disciplines could link up with each other, with Philosophy criticising the rest. In the early days, men like G. D. H. Cole did teach all three. Of course, they say there are technical reasons why that's no longer possible, arising from the development of the disciplines. But this is not a datum: a discipline develops along particular lines at least as much through the sociology of professionals and their pretensions to 'science' as it does through its inherent qualities. And one might say that if Economics, for example, 'develops' so that it doesn't refer to Politics, then it has ceased to enquire into real phenomena, which don't divide into academic compartments. At the very least, the teachers could be allowed to specialise themselves up into the air, while allowing student more freedom to make their own syntheses.

As it is, the chronic fragmentation of learning supports the political status quo. For example, if Economics and Philosophy are taught in separate water-tight compartments, economists can get away without challenge to their philosophical claims, of which the most important is that their 'science' is 'positive', unbiased. And disciplines like Marxism, which are both scientific and *synthetic*, are dismissed by Oxford as foreign unreadable woolliness. There is a prevailing intellectual arrogance, splendidly illustrated by the closing sentences of Warnock's *English Philosophy Since 1900*, by which they protect their professional interests by calling soft-headed anyone who thinks beyond the confines they have clamped on the disciplines. It has a lot to do with English intellectuals never having had to argue with a powerful Marxist movement, so that even bourgeois philosophies like Existentialism have not been constructed here, and can't be studied here because they raise the spectre of Marxism.

For a while, I responded by taking my interests away from the syllabus and into the peripheral Oxford institutions, the student societies. Student sub-cultures have always acted as a longstop, so that those who are turned off the course are still not lost to the ruling class: for example, student drama supplies personnel to the BBC. But tactless interference by the university in these sub-cultures can sometimes upset this clever safety device. I was in continual trouble over societies. They would haul me up on such ludicrous charges as distributing literature without their permission.

Well finally, for not filling in some petty registration forms, they fined me and forbade me to be an officer of *any* university society again, ever. As far as the student movement in general is concerned, it is a mass of authoritarianism like this which built up a stock of bitterness. More than a hundred people at a philosophical meeting voted in protest at their action, but it was not reversed. A year or so later, we had progressed to direct action: officers of six societies refused to register, there was a big crowd outside the Clarendon building, and the Proctors had to claim that registration had always been voluntary anyway. But as far as I personally was concerned, they had already severed my last bond with Oxford.

I know what my mistake had been all along. My college was renowned for the MPs, civil servants, etcetera that it produced, and my very naïve mistake was to think it could be induced to make a revolutionary for a change. That is, I thought that if one knew what they knew, one could use it for a different end—but no.

C. D. I suppose this is true only in the Burgess-Maclean-Philby sense, that if you go through this cursus honorum you may end up in a position where you can do a vast amount of damage.

J. B. Yes. My mistake was backed by a long tradition of 'permeation' in the Fabian sense, of working your way up until you can drop the correct word in the PM's ear. (This fallacy was shown up by the Labour Government's recruitment of intellectuals in '64, and their subsequent disillusion.) The great con at Oxford is the idea that first you must become proficient in 'their' subject, and only then can you criticise anything. But their discipline is a complicated mistake from the start. The social sciences as a whole express the mentality of the ruling class and its servant elites. If 'I' succeed in such a system, in fact the system has succeeded *over* me. I would have been socialised into all the detailed ways of thought of the rulers. So more and more of us are throwing over the Fabian tradition, which seeks only to *reform* the system.

To have a revolutionary theory, which helps *overthrow* the system, you must be thinking about revolutionary practice in which you yourself are engaged; and there's no magic whereby a person whose whole experience is within privileged and bureaucratic organisations can solve the problems of the great mass of the people.

This is important for the student movement, because one of the excuses some leftist people have for ensconcing themselves in universities is that they think they are producing 'counter-culture'. This excuse neglects the fact that the social forms of counter-culture cannot be symmetrical with the forms of the prevailing culture. The culture which really counters the authority and property relations of prevailing society must be formed by the class that counters the ruling class. It is to be developed with the working class, at the point of their antagonism with authority and property.

It took two years at Oxford for this to dawn on me. The intellectual work demanded of me, and that which interested me, diverged more and more: at the same time, I felt the artificiality of living entirely among intellectuals, almost all of the same age group and sex. As Hazlitt put it, better able neither to read nor write than able to do nothing else. A year after passing Prelims., I asked to leave Oxford on personal grounds, intending to come back in a year. I went to live at the World's End, Fulham, where I got clear about two matters in particular.

First, our society is divided on class lines. This seems elementary, but I had known it only in theory. My prep school, for instance, was in a large country house: the local youth were thought to be very savage and both masters and boys called them VPs, or 'village perds'—irrevocably 'lost', damned souls. One was taught to think oneself better than most of the human race. I now lived in what was called a 'play street', but which was full of oil and glass and abandoned cars; while down the King's Road the richer residents had keys to let their own children into grassy squares. In the mornings I worked in the basement of a hotel, otherwise reading and writing, or just observing London. Very roughly, how you think is a product of the sort of practical problems that you face from day to day. You develop a different view of society when you reject the elite role for which the university processes you. I never went back to university. While I was in London, the May Events happened in France —showing that even advanced industrial societies are open to revolution from within. On another front, the people are showing heroic resistance to American might in Vietnam. These two struggles convinced me that to spend time on 'Politics, Philosophy and Economics' is not to be a person of the present age.

The second thing I confirmed in London was the possibility of doing intellectual work independently of institutions. For if you reject universities, there remain the real inquiries of politics, philosophy, and economics of which the academic course is a distortion. I returned to Oxford city, editing a magazine for the student movement, using public libraries, surviving without full-time work. One of the bits of rhetoric used against the student movement is that Karl Marx read books in the British Museum Library, rather than blow it up. But that gives the game away, because *anybody*, whether they've got qualifications or not, can work in a public library. Way back in 1840, Carlyle wrote that universities are obsolete as soon as you print books. Just look at the lecturers, reading from a manuscript which they keep artificially in that form, year after year, not publishing it as a book because then the medieval rationale of lectures would collapse.[2] It really seems very natural not to be a member of the university.

I was, however, still not at all satisfied with my way of life. So far, I had merely joined the end of a long line of destitute, free-floating Grub Street intellectuals, and this is a long way from working politically with the proletariat. One has to find the material for intellectual work in the fabric of social life itself, and put any mental skills one has at the service of people who are working to change society. So I came back to London and got involved in community politics with council tenants, Social Security claimants, and young people.

[2] See p. 106 for the medieval attitude to lecture-publication.

It seems that there is now emerging a whole social group who are roughly in my position. After all, when a university throws out a student or young lecturer, or if he takes himself off, he does not disappear into the blue: he becomes an implacable life enemy of the system. People are now getting together in all our big towns and setting up the infrastructure, such as community newspapers, for a radical intelligentsia. That is, if one sees that the universities educate intellectuals to serve the ruling class, we are educating ourselves to serve the people.

The project of being a revolutionary means different things at different points in history. A defining factor at the moment is that there is no revolutionary political party in England which is both theoretically 'correct' and also has a mass base. At the same time, the old problem remains for the intellectual to overcome his social division from the masses. An intellectual has to find means of translating ideas into action, and of apprehending the interests of a class other than that into which he has been educated. In the absence of the Party, these functions are starting to be carried out through community politics, and the theoretical self-criticism of the action groups involved. People take up jobs in the community, so as to have a natural role in its politics and also some understanding of the community's dynamics. They then try and help make explicit the revolutionary meaning of that politics. This is very different from the kind of 'community action' which is merely charitable or reformist. Tenants' struggles and the like are about people taking their own affairs into their own hands, and that is a revolutionary principle.

The Left is now asking itself whether the Anarchists were not right about the libertarian, populist, decentralised form of revolutionary organisation. The student movement is important here in that it follows some of the principles of proletarian democracy—sovereign general assemblies, changing and recallable officers, and so on. And it is, of course, free from the old Communist Parties. On the other hand, the movement does not always understand the related principle that to be on the side of the people you have to be working with them. What really oppresses students is not *within* the university: it is the boundary of the university itself, which cages them inside theory and prevents practical unity with the forces that are changing society.

JOE

Joe, with his flat vowels, black horn-rims and leather jacket, looks as completely at home in the soulless corridors of the University of Manchester Arts Faculty as John must have done on the steps of the Clarendon Building in Oxford. He is a slightly alarming person for an ill-prepared lecturer to find in a student seminar, for he is apt, with transparent seriousness and innocence, to drop into the conversation remarks like 'The third time I read *La Nausée* . . . ', and even if he does not pronounce the title as a Frenchman would, most lecturers in English Literature are happy if they have read the book once. Joe's account of his long struggle for admission to the University of Manchester (no other university would do, for he has a house and family in the city) must speak for itself. Other 'drop-ins' in less overcrowded subjects than English might be luckier (though there are only thirty-seven other such students in the whole of the University of Manchester.) The University of London, compelled towards catholicity by the foreigner at its gates and by the diverse interests of London's citizens is much more receptive. Oxford too. There is a retired American sugar manufacturer at Balliol, studying the Book of Common Prayer, and not long ago, a stockbroker in the prime of his life came up to read Comparative Religion under a most distinguished professor. (Whether or not the stockbroker got religion, the professor got distinctly rich.) But however that may be, this is how one great British university looked to a man who came to it late enough to know that it is with universities as with life: if you want anything badly, you must be prepared to fight for it.

Joe. I was born in 1939. I went to primary school, got my eleven plus, and went to Stockport Grammar School a year early, while I was still ten. The system was very bad academically. We were rushed through O levels—I took five at the age of fourteen—just to get the minimum requirements for university entrance. I went into the Sixth and took A levels at sixteen. You were then regarded as university potential, but it didn't work with me. I failed my A levels, and for various reasons I left school and got myself apprenticed at Renolds Chain. On day-release from them I went to technical college at Stockport and took my Ordinary and Higher National Certificates. I was by then twenty-one, qualified as a design draughtsman in general engineering.

When I was about twenty-three, I made tentative enquiries about mature entrance to university. Because of the way things were set up here in Manchester, I would have had to use my technical qualifications and come to the university to study engineering. I did not want to do that. What with this, and the financial problem, and general lack of information, I was put off, and I did not reconsider the idea for a long time. Meanwhile I went to WEA classes, including one from the Professor of Comparative Literary Studies here. He asked me if I would like to come to university, because I showed interest in writing. I explained that I didn't feel I could at that moment, and he said, 'Get in touch when you want to.'

After this there was another gap, until I was twenty-nine. By then I was a freelance engineer in the petroleum industry. There was a colossal boom in the industry at the time, and my wife too was at work. I could save. I decided that I would try again as a mature student. My wife worked for a lecturer in psychology here. I asked him how to set about trying, and he suggested a few individuals to see, but his knowledge was only vague (he's now out of academic life, running his own market research company.)

In June 1968 I wrote to the University asking for information. The Joint Matriculation Board, whose offices are here, sent me a standard application form. I had to list my academic history. The first surprising thing to me was that my technical qualifications were sufficient for entrance, being rated as A levels. I sent the form back filled in and said that I really wanted the form for mature entrance. Whom should I go to? 'We don't deal with it,' they said. 'See the University.'

I did not know who would be the best person. Even at the Extramural Department, nobody knew what the requirements for mature students were. They agreed that there *was* a system, and suggested that Mr. So-and-so might know about it. But he didn't. By this time I had picked up a bit so I went to the Registrar's department. 'Yes, there is provision,' they said, 'but we don't know where.' This was not just one of the secretaries, but a person in authority.

By this time I realised that I was getting nowhere, so I got a copy of the University prospectus, which had a list of lecturers. I picked out of the English Department list the nearest to my home, and went to see him. I told him my problem. He agreed it was best to approach an individual department, and he had a word with Professor T. I came and saw T, bringing him my academic record and some of the writing I had done, and told him what I wanted to do. He had to ask his secretary what the procedure was. This was in September 1968.

I had decided from the prospectus that I wanted to do a joint degree in English and philosophy. (English by itself here is weighted down with medieval studies.) Professor T said I had left it too late for that year. I said I wanted to come straight away, and couldn't I be squeezed in as a mature student? He gave way a bit. By this time I was on the UCCA[3] last-minute entrance list. It seemed as if I had made it. After two interviews with T I put everything down on the form and left it at that. The next thing I knew was a rejection slip in the post after a few days. I telephoned T, who said it wasn't the English Department that had rejected me but Philosophy, because they were doing the vetting. I telephoned the man responsible at his home, and he said, yes your application came to us, but you have no A levels, and neither the recommendation from T nor the mature student details were on the form. Try again next year. I said ok.

People in the University would not say how I should set about getting in. It was up to me to convince them. I was later told that there are two schools of thought on this: one is to make mature entrance easy, the other to make it difficult, as an exercise in overcoming obstacles.

By this time it was late September 1968. I had to accept that I would have to wait a year. So I applied again through UCCA channels, for the

[3] Universities Central Council for Admissions—a clearing-house system for student applications to different universities.

same course (just English and Philosophy). Replies came back at the turn of the year. I was surprised when the first thing I got back from UCCA was another rejection. I got in touch with T again, and asked the reason. 'There's a tremendous demand for places,' he said, 'and no room for mature students. Besides, it's a difficult course.' I did not know how I could convince him, though he had verbal evidence that I had covered a lot of the reading. By this time I was blazing. I realised that if you were not extremely persistent you had no chance of getting in. I had gone through every channel, and I had had to find them out myself.

So at this point I wrote to the Professor of Comparative Literary Studies, who all those years ago had suggested I approach him. By this time he was teaching in the University of Wales. I had not written to him before because I had not thought it necessary. I couldn't understand why the system was beating me. I wanted to get into the University of Manchester—it had to be Manchester, because my home and family were here—in an orthodox manner, not through personal preference. An ordinary lad of twenty-three could not have appealed to anyone. Of course by the end I would have lied or connived at anything to get in because it was such a corrupt system.

I did not think the professor would remember his conversation with me, but he did, and replied saying that he had written to the person who dealt with entrance to the General BA course in the Arts faculty. I got to see him, and he was interested in the range of things I had covered beside my academic studies. I was granted entry to the General BA, which is lower than the Honours course I had asked for. After that I followed the normal procedure. On the day you enrol you are herded into a lecture hall of the Arts faculty and register. This decides what subjects you study. Most of the kids are completely bewildered by having to decide in about three minutes what they are going to study for three years. No prospectus came in advance through the post and it would only be words anyway.

You have to do four subjects and it's just 'What do you want to do? Do the lectures clash? Are the subjects compatible? Do they think you are suitable?' I tried to intimate the Joint Honours course I really wanted and chose English Literature, American Literature, Philosophy, and Logic. They refused this. I had to replace Logic with Greek Civilisation. I know one or two kids who had to choose subjects in which they were not the least bit interested. The whole registration business goes on for days and the system's like Kafka. You queue in line and if you're at the front of the queue when the doors close at the end of one day it's no guarantee that you're still at the front next morning. To one group of people they issued tickets saying they were next in line, then herded all the people without tickets into another room without telling them what for. I realised myself that they were being kept waiting for the ones with tickets, but all those poor sods thought they were going to be interviewed.

Repeatedly the English department prides itself on the number of mature students it has got. There are a few mature women, but all of them have got in with A levels through normal academic channels. I don't know anyone who has got in through the theoretical channels: 'qualifications not directly concerned' or 'presenting himself for interview and writing an essay'. English has always been my interest since grammar school. The philosophy is backing up my interest in the working of society in general. Politically, I'm an active member of the Communist Party, but that's not the reason for the trouble I had. A young Tory from Wilmslow[4] would have had the same difficulty. It was just gross inefficiency.

Financially, I could only come to university because for the previous five years my average earnings as a freelance engineer had been about two thousand pounds. The year I entered it was nearly four thousand pounds but that was exceptional. I got a maximum grant for myself and my children and a twenty-five pound increment for each year I had spent in industry over the age of twenty-five, which made another one hundred and twenty-five pounds a year. So I get about six hundred pounds a year at the moment. In my last year of work I reduced my standard of living as far as I could tolerate so that the shock wasn't so great, and I saved. That would be my advice to anyone contemplating a similar step. My wife works full time as a secretary, on twelve pounds a week. We have children of ten and eight, and a mortgage on a house in Heaton Moor.

My father came from the lower end of the working class. He was a young boy in Salford during the Depression. He educated himself through night school after coming out of the Navy in 1945. He's now a professional electrical engineer for a hospital management board. At the age of fifty-six he's just enrolled in the Open University.

I regarded this time as a three-year break from my job, to enlarge my interest in literature and general studies. My wife didn't mind—she could see I was unhappy as I was. I'm not sure whether or not I shall go back to what I was doing. I wanted to get myself into an existential situation where I could face myself with other opportunities even though I might choose my original career. I suppose I do hope that someone somewhere will want the range of experience and education I shall have had—in commerce and engineering, in literature, writing, and contemporary ideas. But the more I see of the University the less I think it's even remotely practical, except as a machine for giving people degrees to get jobs with. I can't imagine anything more sterile than working permanently in this place. With the libraries and things that there are here, if anybody had the sort of interests that I have, the University could be the creative bomb that it's supposed to be. I have three or four articles I would like to write on literary critical theory, but there's no outlet except for essays on aspects of Wordsworth or Tennyson. Philosophically, I'm grateful to

[4] A prosperous suburb of Manchester.

have been exposed to the English materialist philosophers—Berkeley, Hume and so on—because they have deepened my understanding of Marxism, but when I told a philosophy tutor here that I wanted to do some political philosophy in order to 'get to grips with Hegel', he replied: 'No one in this University understands Hegel.'

In the preceding pages, I transcribed in their own words the university experiences and *weltanschauung* of four students in two countries. The device is more likely than any words of mine to succeed in making the nature of the contemporary student experience 'transparent'. However, the scope of this book is not limited to Britain and the United States. Is it possible to discuss the culture of universities, and of the people in them, as though it were something international in reference and scope? The difficulties are great. English ears, at least, will have picked up important cultural differences between the last two speakers: the first unmistakably the mental stuff from which the self-questioning Puritan Revolution, and the curricular counter-culture of the Protestant Dissenting Academies, were forged in other centuries;[5] the second an amalgam of tough continental reasoning styles with the British working class's disposition to take what comes and see it through. A much more serious difficulty than such internal differences is that slippery word 'culture' itself, which means somewhat the same thing anywhere between London and San Francisco, but changes its meaning between London and Paris. Bernard Gensane of the University of Vincennes makes the point neatly:

> 'In England "culture" can mean simply a way of life. In France it is a vaguer notion, close to the German concept of *Kultur*, or as Edouard Herriot put it, "*Ce qui reste quand on a tout oublié*". To simplify greatly: to create a counter-culture in England is to put forward a new way of life. But in a Cartesian society, one has to offer a whole new way of thinking . . . '.[6]

John Birtwhistle's criticism of his contemporaries who want their counter-culture on the cheap suggests that he is leaning towards the French usage. However, this national difference is partly why French intellectuals find English ones trivial (when I asked Hélène Cixous which British academics if any she could visualise as contributors to *Poétique*, the new literary-theoretical magazine she was about to launch, she replied

[5] See my discussion of Puritanism in *A Future for the Free Churches?* (London, 1962), Ch. 2; and Irene Parker, *Dissenting Academies* (Cambridge, 1914).

[6] *New Society*, June 25, 1970.

that there were none); and why English intellectuals often find French ones unintelligible even when the language itself presents no barrier and when—as in the case of Structuralism—the latent ideas sound interesting. The French are trying to change their system of ideas: the English are merely trying to cure diseases of their national life-style, such as the 'boiled cabbage cut in sections' to which Eliot referred in a famous passage. I use the word 'culture' here in the Anglo-American sense: the culture of universities is analogous to Lewis Mumford's 'culture of cities.'

Enough has already been said in this book to indicate the limitations of internationalism as an attribute of university *structures*. Instead, there are certain available models for a university, which different countries (or, as in the dis-United States, different cultures within a single country) have at various points in time adopted and modified to their own social and political climate. On the other hand, the structures are sufficiently similar for individuals to have similar problems within them, to react to global events in the same way, and to travel freely between one institution and another, in spite of a quaint official reluctance to recognise each other's academic passports on arrival. There is also something close to an international market in student political ideas. A crude mental brotherhood exists between Maoists in Italy, say, and Maoists in Japan—though their strict adherence to the formula also suggests that the doctrine has not been interiorised and subjected to the modifications which would be necessary to give it a cutting edge in the individual's own culture (If Mao's followers were, like Mao himself, poets they would appreciate this more easily.)

The level of sophistication at which Marxist ideas, whether orthodox Communist, Maoist, Anarchist, or whatever, have been developed and applied varies considerably. If there were an international student army in the sense that some would have us believe, it would possess—in the unlikely event of its reaching agreement on so vital a distribution of power—a German strategist, an American tactician, a Japanese drill-sergeant, Italian apologists, and French street-fighters. (The British, I suppose, would drive the ambulances, for in Britain, according to M. Gensane, protest 'out-manoeuvres the system; it goes under or beside; and it lives, by and large, in a peaceful coexistence with the system. . . . In France, protest goes against the system'.) Variations of this kind are dependent, not only on differences between young people from different political societies, but on the age-groups into which students fall. German students are older and, if not wiser, cannier than others; British students, who do no national service and as yet include comparatively few graduate students, are hardly out of their teens; American students have had their adolescence and university careers artificially prolonged to the age of thirty by the Vietnam War and draft avoidance. Indeed, were it not for the collective infantilism to which the American university culture itself condemns them, and for the labour market's unreadiness to receive them, no one would regard American students as young people at all. Nicholas von Hoffman, in a book on the hippies, brings this out:

> 'Our working definition of youth now includes superlatively well-educated people who have all the skills needed to build or destroy on an impressive scale. People were shocked at the students' ability to out-think and outmanoeuvre the university's officials at Berkeley in 1964–65 . . . and penetrate the Pentagon itself in the face of 5,000 soldiers. They shouldn't be. A 24- or 25-year-old "youth" with several years' political experience in mass movements, who may also be a candidate for a doctor's degree in chemistry or history, can be a skilful and resourceful opponent.'[7]

London School of Economics administrators, looking back over a decade of American-style agitation from Ralph Schoenman[8] to Paul Hoch,[9] would endorse that judgment with a heavy sigh, wondering only why so superlative an education should produce so much trouble for educators.

Within each nation, collective (as opposed to individual) variations between this university's students and that one's are seldom very great, at least among the elite institutions which draw students from all over the country. More remarkable, perhaps, in the global village where communication is supposed to be instantaneous, is the rather slow, fan-wise movement of revolts and other fashions from metropolitan universities to up-country ones. What Tokyo does today, Kyushu does tomorrow; what Berlin does today, Wurzburg does tomorrow; what Chicago or Berkeley do today, Kent State or Kansas do tomorrow, whether it is sitting in the dean's office or adopting the midi-skirt. The influence of mass media can easily be overrated, especially by the mass media themselves.

Still, the particular variations between institutions have been stressed in this book. Academics insisting that their problems are unintelligible to an outsider sound pedantic and absurd when the listener knows that ten or a thousand miles away a similar set of students is staging a carbon-copy sit-in along a carbon-copy corridor. But if they did not believe in their institution's uniqueness, they would despair of being educators, and because they believe it, they make it come true. Students, who disbelieve it, despair of being students for the very same reason. They have been encouraged to think that there is a global plot against them, to whose success local action, though worth undertaking for its own sake as a tournament and a discharger of tension, can make but little difference.

---

[7] *We are the people our parents warned us against* (New York, 1967), p. 49 (Fawcett Crest edition).

[8] See my *The Disarmers: a Study in Protest* (London, 1964), Ch. V.

[9] Cf. Paul Hoch, *Academic Freedom in Action* (London, 1970); and *LSE: The Natives are restless* (London, 1969).

This is seen most clearly in Japan, where the submersion of the individual in the snake-dancing mass of multi-coloured plastic helmets, and the preoccupation with symbolic, sacrificial action, allow fantasies of imminent global victory to erase all concern with particular, proximate institutions. Even at the level of political systems, students' assumption that the oppressor is monolithically uniform and coherently malign is mistaken. As Alasdair MacIntyre puts it in his critique of Marcuse: 'The feeling of impotence that many have is not misplaced. They are impotent. But they are not impotent because they are dominated by a well organized system of social control. It is lack of control which is at the heart of the social order. . . . The most impressive fact of our time is the accidental character of most of the policies which government is forced to embrace.'[10]

But if students are blinded by romantic globalism to the rich particularities which surround them, their own spectacularly corporate behaviour in crisis or ecstasy blinds many adults to the dominant feature of contemporary youth culture, which remains its preoccupation with the human self, its 'egopetalism'. By egopetalism—'seeking the ego'—I mean something different from the more stable adult vices of egotism and egocentricity. The egopetal personality or culture is more restless. It cultivates its garden but cannot wait for the flowers to open, it tries to 'blow its mind' as a boy blows a bird's egg. It seeks, inevitably, a personalised education, and reacts to the more stereotyped product it is offered as does any consumer in a supermarket—by pressing demands for individualisation which could be easily met by the old corner grocer's shop, but which primitive post-industrial technology has not yet learnt to satisfy. Like most significant changes in human sensibility, egopetalism represents part-action, part-reaction; part outreach for a future that has not yet become feasible, part detestation of past social controls which seem the more horrifying because they have not been personally experienced. The Berkeley professor who blamed the student revolt on 'the fall-out from Dr. Spock' got it only half-right. The students of the 1960s in Britain and America were not the first generation to enjoy the relaxation of sexual and other controls, for many of them were the children of revolutionaries. ('Dad, we're not interested in the *history* of radicalism,' one of them remarked when his father began to tell him about the struggle of progressives for the ear of California during the 1930s.) The novelty of the sixties' generation was that they were the first birth-right permissives, able not merely to act liberated, but to give every appearance of enjoying it. To the unliberated, the enjoyment is far worse than the act, and the young paid for their pleasure with broken heads and smarting eyes. They were butchered, so to speak, to make a policeman's psychotherapy.

Egopetalism is also the necessary link between those puzzlingly differ-

---

[10] *Marcuse* (London, 1970), p. 71.

ent generations—different in all the countries covered by this book with the partial exception of Japan, whose militant student movement started much earlier—of the silent, apathetic fifties and the licentious, activist sixties. Differences of this kind are never total, and the unusually exhausting political style of contemporary activists is already beginning to return the less dedicated to the torpor from which they so suddenly emerged. In Germany, as Günter Grass has pointed out, students who bother to vote in their own elections are once more a minority.[11] By 1970 in Berkeley, demonstrations involved more schoolchildren than students (interestingly enough, the decline of the Campaign for Nuclear Disarmament in Britain could be measured from the point where its marches became children's outings) and student vigilantes were patrolling the campus to warn the unwary against taking notice of notoriously unstable demagogues. Similar trends could be observed in France, Germany, and Britain. Lewis Feuer tries to explain the phenomenon:

'Sociological generations have their own law of time. . . . A generation is a group which in adolescent years is shaped by a critical historical experience; a generation defines its character by its response to that critical situation. And if the critical situations alter drastically within a few years, persons who biologically are only a few years apart may yet be sharply differentiated as "generations".'[12]

There is clearly much in this. History does often conveniently provide watershed events to separate those who were adolescent before them from those who were adolescent during or after them: Suez for the British, Vietnam for the Americans, Algeria for Europeans, the 1960 renewal of the Japan–America Security Treaty for the Japanese. Events like these also precipitate what Professor Feuer sees as the main general cause of student movements in the numerous countries he surveys: the 'de-authoritisation' of the elders implicated in these events. Child psychologists might surely suggest that we might attempt here to make correlations with the 'critical historical experiences' of the elders themselves. If it makes a difference to be at university before or after Suez or Vietnam, it may also make a difference whether your parents compiled their image of the world before or after the Depression.

However, underneath this speeded-up flux of generations, whether the flux is attributed primarily to political or to technological causes, a certain groundswell, less subject to sudden reverses, ought to be discernible. Egopetalism seems to me to be one of the possible ties that bind the contracted personalities of the fifties, with their zeal for familial reconstruction and private professional advancement, to the expanded personalities of the sixties, with their zeal for peer-group harmonies and private

[11] *Encounter*, September 1970, p. 27.
[12] *The Conflict of Generations* (New York and London, 1969), p. 373.

emotional advancement. The necessary connections have been most acutely made by the British sociologist Donald MacRae:

'When there is no certain, continuing human future, then politics are inevitably devalued, and at once more permissive, wide-ranging, and radical, but also less serious, though potentially more desperate. Even the human person, once the arena of learning, will, and sustained choice, has come to seem less coherent, more arbitrary, impermanent, and thin. The external and internal world of the young is a contingent one. . . . All this must be seen in the political context of the Left since the death of Stalin. . . . Without the polarization round the cadres of bolshevik orthodoxy, with their ethic of being "a good student", of asceticism in politics, denial of choice in public affairs, servile obedience, and readiness to be manipulated for a determinate future by the masters of Soviet policy, the student Left has swung—and will swing—widely. The gain is, of course, enormous. . . . But the perplexities about student behaviour, about the new generational subculture, are in part a consequence of this transformation.'[13]

'Everyone,' said Lord Clarendon the seventeenth-century historian, looking back over the destruction which to his way of thinking the Puritan Revolution had brought—'everyone did that which was good in his own eyes'.[14] In a period of rapid change, de-authoritised elders, and a glut of advice expertly communicated, there really seems little else to do. The culture of contemporary students the world over is still, however, shot through with the ultimate questions about life to which Professor MacRae calls attention: the question 'why anything should exist rather than nothing'. The question worried Carol at Berkeley, who took astrology because it seemed to tie the loose ends of the world into one big bundle; it had worried John Birtwhistle at Oxford, when he adopted the 'stoic, humanist pessimism' of Pascal's 'thinking reed': 'to know is to suffer'. It is echoed from the other side of the globe by Hiroaki Yamazaki, a Literature student at Kyoto University who was killed during the students' battle to prevent the Japanese Prime Minister from leaving Haneda Airport for a visit to Vietnam in October 1967. After his death there was found among his possessions, along with Marx's *Philosophical and Economic Manuscripts*, J. N. Shklar's *After Utopia: the decline of political faith*, and Kierkegaard's *Diary of a Seducer*, Yamazaki's own microscopically-written diary:

'I know very well that I have little courage. I am essentially an opportunist. Even my courageous support of one side remains sus-

---

[13] *Journal of Contemporary History*, Vol. 2, No. 3 (July 1967).
[14] Christopher Hill, *Puritanism and Revolution* (London, 1958), essay on 'Lord Clarendon and the Puritan Revolution'.

ceptible to attack from the other. In short, I am not qualified to live. I am a weak human.

'I came into existence eighteen years and ten months ago. What have I done to live during this period? I can feel no sense of responsibility, either for the present or for the future. I constantly find myself doubtful if not indifferent, and I borrow others' words to defend myself. What on earth am I?'[15]

[15] Quoted by Junro Fukashiro (education correspondent of *Ashai Shimbun*) in *Japan Quarterly*, Vol. 16, No. 2 (April–June 1970), p. 152.

CHAPTER NINE

Malaise des clercs ?

1 THE FUTURE OF SCHOLARS

'A scholar's wisdom comes of ample leisure; if a man is to be wise he must be relieved of other tasks.'

Ecclesiasticus 38, 24

'The vast holidays, the majestical temper induced by the work, the fact that no effort is needed to keep the place or attract the students, the petty cliques which form among the professors, the induced sense of superiority to ordinary industrious beings, gradually corrupt the noblest and finest natures, and I have never known a man made a professor without becoming more or less deteriorated.'

William Robertson Nicoll, in a letter (1905)

Scholars were students once, as matrons were once nurses and generals (occasionally) privates. The gradual shift from the latter state to the former can be represented as a process of elimination, or as a process of socialisation. The unfit are discarded, or the worthy taught the values of the guild. The military and medical analogies are not quite fair, for by their own unremitting insistence scholars are students still. A matron is seldom seen to pick up a bed-pan or a general a rifle, but the scholar, though he may consider it bad form to attend a colleague's lecture, does read and annotate books. In America there is a new breed, *Scholasticus tactilis* or *mcluhanensis*, which considers even this unnecessary; and everywhere it is fashionable, and possibly even true, to claim that reading is an activity for which time is occasionally found after the sit-in has been busted, the revised statutes passed, and Miss X's love-life listened to yet again. Writing, however, continues. Somehow, and especially in America, the three or four published articles a year which are expected of the normally ambitious continue to appear, and scientific journals continue to grow exponentially.

About scholars as people, there are few international generalisations that can usefully be made. At twenty, generational identity can sometimes override national and cultural difference, and in a cosmopolitan coach-load of students, Art from Kansas and Miguel from Spain and Michio from Japan will quickly find something to say to each other about the world, sex, or the University. At fifty, the scholar has thrown a port-like crust of personal and national identity. He talks easily to strangers of any nationality if they are in the same subject, the more narrowly defined the better, but for other conversation he is dependent on friends and acquaintances who share the same, highly-localised source of gossip. You may talk to him about Visigothic vowel shifts or the structure of long polymers, or alternatively about who has got tenure, a salary rise, or a new building for his department; but in between there is a gap in sensibility: he may or may not know anything of the world, or of university institutions other than his own, and his private life will usually be a somewhat liberalised version of the style prevailing among people of the same background and income group in his own country. It is always something of a shock when these privacies are allowed to show through—as in the footnote which a British social historian, aggrieved at criticisms of university teachers, appended to a recent book: he had only taken ten days' holiday with his family the previous year, he said, and he had during the fortnight read five reports in preparation for an international conference.

Yet scholars, no less than other men, become more intelligible when their home life can be set against their professional work and public attitudes. Opportunities of this kind have been one of my chief pleasures in working on this book. The young Japanese literary scholar who held that the present generation of Japanese students was the worst the country had ever had, because they were so undisciplined, would have sounded unsympathetic on a public platform, and might have had a hard time during one of the compulsory self-criticism sessions which Japanese revolutionary students impose upon their professors. But as an admirer of British domestic life, he asked me to his home, a tiny, two-up, two-down house on the outskirts of Kyoto, where he lived with his wife, two shy children, and as many books as could be fitted in, including no fewer than sixty assorted dictionaries and concordances, from the £90 Oxford New English Dictionary downwards. The dictionaries alone must have cost the price of a car, and it was easy to see that the discipline he expected of students was no less than the discipline he demanded of himself and his household.

National and personal differences of this kind naturally emerge most clearly when the scholar migrates from one culture to another. David Riesman tells of a Japanese professor, truer to his national type, who let his house for a year to a visiting American academic, and later suffered the exquisite humiliation of being approached by colleagues who said: 'While you were away, Professor Z and his wife asked us round to dinner. It was most interesting: we had never been to your home before.' Jacques Barzun, discussing the perils of offering permanent or visiting professorships in American universities to men from Leyden or Paris or Oxford, recalls a scholar reared and trained in Germany who was found after a few semesters to have ingeniously excluded women from all his classes. Nor would American students take very kindly to the professor at the

Sorbonne to whom a French student acquaintance of mine sent a belated essay with a covering note of apology. She had done so, she told me, partly in the hope of securing some small human contact in the Sorbonne's desert of impersonality, but she received back from the professor not merely her essay but also her own letter, duly corrected for French style and expression, with no further comment.

Professors differ widely from country to country in their attitudes to sponsorship of research and frequency of publication, their accessibility to students, their concepts of academic independence, whether curricular or extra-curricular, and above all in the conditions of work they enjoy. A Japanese professor without an alternative source of income, whose professorial salary locates him firmly in his country's lower middle classes, is impressed by the five thousand pounds a year British economist with his Government consultancies and foreign holidays, or by the Parisian lawyer making fifty thousand francs a year out of selling *polycopiés* of his courses to students; but all stand astonished together at the offers made by top American universities to men whom they really want. Jacques Barzun cites an actual proposition made to a man who was already receiving twenty thousand dollars or so a year: 'We will pay you ten thousand dollars more than your present salary. You need not teach. You will have twelve thousand dollars for research assistants and books. You may be away from the campus every third term. If you do want to teach, you will receive additional compensation at the rate of one thousand dollars for each semester course.'[1] 'To keep these figures in some kind of proportion, it is necessary to take account of high expenses and taxation, a vast differential between the best and the worst paid at the richest and the poorest universities, and more recently, a severe money shortage which has put several famous campuses into deficit and may signal a few years' pause in the rate of American academic growth. (However, as Riesman and Jencks point out, 'People have been predicting financial crises in higher education since the late 1940s, and thus far none has materialised.'[2] The obstacle to the United States' spending three or four per cent of the gross national product, instead of the present two per cent, on higher education by 1985 is political rather than economic: the voters, especially in volatile states like California, learnt to hate the University.)

All the same, there *is* a crisis of the professoriate which is internationally shared, even if it is not expressed as dramatically as in Hiroaki Yamazaki's posthumously-discovered diary, or in the Sorbonne wall-posters of '*une jeunesse qui l'avenir inquiète trop souvent*'. For 'scholars were students once'. They cannot precisely share their juniors' generational solidarities, urgent need of a mate, and apprehensions about the imminent parachute drop into the job market jungle. But there is also a *malaise des clercs* which is common to both constituencies. Both are related to 'critical

[1] *The American University* (op. cit.), p. 39.
[2] Op. cit., p. 540.

333

historical experiences' which have begun to fade. Both suffer from the consequences of the numbers explosion in their ranks. Both, more philosophically, are affected by the ways in which knowledge is organised and expanded. I take these three points in order.

(1) For the contemporary academic profession, considered as a profession rather than as an aggregate of individuals with highly trained intelligences, the critical historical experience in all the countries visited is not Vietnam or Suez or the Korean War, nor even, except in the most obvious personal ways, the period of global conflict between 1941 and 1945, but the decade 1930–40. This was the decade which made political allegiances existential, and which also decided, probably for the rest of the century, where the world's intellectual centre of gravity would lie. The intellectual migration from Europe to America in this decade, and the experiences of the individuals concerned, have been explored in two recent books, Laura Fermi's *Illustrious Immigrants* and Fleming and Bailyn's *The Intellectual Migration (Europe and America, 1930–1960)*,[3] which contains the personal reminiscences of such men as Leo Szilard, Paul Lazarsfeld, and T. W. Adorno. According to Mrs. Fermi's file, out of perhaps twenty thousand professional people of all kinds who came to the United States during this period at least two thousand were scholars of greater or lesser eminence. It has already been pointed out that by then, America had already surpassed Europe in scientific achievement, and that even without the rise of Nazism, the superior organisation of the American scientific community, and the more welcoming climate in which scientists worked, would have anyway created the conditions for a brain drain.[4] However, scientific skill is an international commodity. Nothing short of cultural despair and personal danger could have propelled so many artists, art historians, literary critics and psychoanalysts on the same journey, to put down fresh roots in a culture which many of them secretly or openly despised. (Adorno himself eventually returned to Europe, and Mrs. Fermi recalls one German woman psychoanalyst who declined to come at all on the grounds that she would not be able to get her laundry done properly in Topeka.)

The Manhattan Project is the monument to the excellence of the immigrant physicists, but the total effect of the whole invasion upon American academic life was also proportionate to its size. A hundred or two names would have been lost among a thousand campuses, but two thousand concentrated for the most part in the institutions best able to use and appreciate their talents, reacted upon each other as well as upon their hosts. On the soil of Europe, Pole might ignore Hungarian and German Jew insult Czech Jew, but in Columbia, Berkeley or Chicago they found it easier to make new connections, human and intellectual,

---

[3] See bibliography, p. 355.
[4] James A. Wilson, 'The Emigration of British Scientists' in *Minerva*, Autumn 1966.

simply as exiled Europeans. Paul Lazarsfeld suggests that major academic innovations can often be traced to people who belong to two worlds, but who are not safe in either of them. 'The best historical examples are Wilhelm von Humboldt who, as a hanger-on at Weimar, belonged to the lower Prussian aristocracy and created the University of Berlin in 1807. Another is Guillaume Budé, who was a hanger-on among the French humanists but who had access to the Court of François I and spent his life developing the Collège de France in opposition to the anti-human-istic Sorbonne.'[5] An outstanding twentieth century illustration of this thesis, though his innovations belonged to the relations between science and government rather than to academic life itself, is the late Lord Cherwell (Professor F. A. Lindemann), whose sense of discomfort in pre-1939 Oxford probably pushed him closer to that other congenital misfit, Winston Churchill.

Many of the migrant scholars paused in England on the way; some stayed, and in the smaller British academic world their influence was disproportionate to their numbers. In Britain, as in America, it is easy to detect the passionate feelings which migrant European academics of this generation still have for the country which found them a home, especially if they are obliged to listen while radical students sneer at 'democratic tolerance'. But Britain's inability to absorb more than a hundred or two scholars into her small, under-financed, and inflexibly structured universities was almost as tragic a loss to British science and learning as the migration itself was to the countries from which they came. Many of the refugees would have preferred to stay but, as Charles Weiner says, 'There was just not enough room or money or will. The Depression was taking its toll, and the universities had not yet experienced large increases in enrolment.'[6]

It is hard to express what a university and its surrounding culture gains from a transfusion of this kind. As a boy, hitch-hiking round Italy between school and Oxford, I was once given a lift by the late Sir Francis Simon the physicist and his wife, on the hot dusty side-road to San Gimignano. They asked me to their north-Oxford home in my first term. To the product of a strict English classical education, the culture shock was wholly salutary. Here, for instance, was a scholar who, because he was a scientist and also because he was a European, not only found English domestic heating ludicrous but knew exactly how it should be improved. I afterwards realised that thermal efficiency and heat loss were an obsession of Francis Simon's which made his friends smile, but that did not erase the impression. No English scientist, even though similarly met and equally kind, could have meant quite the same, for there is a spark which is struck from a slight heightening of the cultural tension as one national cast of mind encounters an opposite one at a different stage

[5] Fleming and Bailyn, op. cit., p. 302.
[6] Ibid., p. 219.

of development. It is part of the point which I am trying to make that the occasion of the encounter was trivial and non-academic. I could not have understood a word of Professor Simon's classes, nor did he, to the best of my recollection, understand Greek. He simply stood for the richness and strangeness which I had been led to expect of a university but which, I now realise, belong only to very few universities, at particular historical moments.

For clearly, intellectual migrations on a 1930–40 scale do not easily occur, even with a Hitler to provoke them; and even if they did occur, other conditions would have to be met for their impact to be comparable. No body of Japanese scholars migrating to Europe or the US could have the effect of those Europeans between the wars, who knew so quickly what they liked or disliked in their adopted countries and why, and who were close enough to the younger culture, emotionally and linguistically, to invigorate and be invigorated without a lengthy acclimatisation process. Nor could strangers, even if counted in thousands, today pierce the plumped-out cushion of the American academic world as easily, or in as many different places, as the innovators of 1930–40.

(2) This brings me to the second *malaise des clercs*. For when a higher education system undergoes massification or very rapid growth, and no longer draws for staff exclusively or primarily on people whose own families and teachers have been bred up to the idea of a university, it tends to become more rather than less parochial. However many pints of intellectual new blood are transfused into its veins, the body remains comatose. Anyway, it is a question where to find suitable donors. In a mass system, they can only come from abroad, or from a social group which possesses the necessary talents but has previously been unfairly debarred from access to higher education. In America, the Blacks are at present the obvious candidates for this role, now that the European brain drain of the last forty years has slowed down. But Black scholars, themselves for the most part educated as children at a dismally low level of the same system which trained the whites, cannot be expected to secure changes in American universities comparable with those that were initiated in the previous generation by foreigners, whose cultures had fostered their abilities carefully and denied them only the chance to spread wings and fly where they would. Changes initiated by Black students and scholars will be political rather than intellectual. Changes in thought will follow changes in structure—if, that is, either change occurs. For a mass system can only change radically when a substantial minority of people within it want change, and even then success is not guaranteed. (Radical change is not to be confused with ad hoc responses to pressure, followed after a decent interval by the mixture as before.)

In Britain now, there may well be more people of transatlantic origin working in universities, especially in the politics and social science fields, than there were European refugees in British scientific laboratories before 1939. In Canada American university teachers are so common that xenophobic resistance has been building up. But apart from leading an occasional demonstration and intensifying the general pressure for advanced degrees and more elaborate certification, their cultural influence has in Britain been less than the domestic demographic changes which have been taking place. In 1964/5 the British Association of University Teachers found that twenty-five per cent of lecturers and senior lecturers were under the age of thirty-one and seventy-one per cent under the age of forty-one. As novelists like Kingsley Amis (*Lucky Jim*) and Malcolm Bradbury (*Eating People is Wrong*) discovered early on, the first-generation university teacher in Britain was a symbol of social unease at a time when most people in universities and outside were still worrying about the problems of first-generation university students. There was something essentially ridiculous about a man whose human reactions, sexual problems, and cultural disorientation marked him down as a somewhat overgrown student, but whose professional milieu and hopes of preferment demanded the rapid or pretended assumption of asceticism, utter reliability, and the whole *apparatus criticus* of the Academy.

Nor did the intimate scale of the old British academic system offer professors and appointment committees any techniques for deciding which out of half a dozen unknown young men with the same formal qualifications was the most suitable for incorporation into the academic guild. The problem in Britain and Germany is not yet as acute as Professor Oscar Handlin makes it sound in the US, where with fifteen thousand members of the American Historical Association and similar numbers in other such bodies, the system of informal recommendation by intermediaries has broken down; and where the carefully-undefined duties of a university teacher, and general anxiety to avoid trouble with the militant American Association of University Professors, explain 'the tolerance of plagiarists, loafers, incompetents, drug-takers, lunatics (mild) and promiscuous sexual prowlers.' But the new atmosphere is certainly not one in which skill at teaching is likely to count for very much in the making of appointments, unless students can find 'political' ways to make it count, and—much more difficult—intellectually satisfactory ways to make it count in favour of the right people. For when every second letter of recommendation asserts that the subject is an 'excellent teacher', and when none of the parties in the case have ever been forced to think what good university-teaching might be, a published article is the only solid rock on which an appointment can be made and subsequently defended. (It may even be the best available criterion, but no one knows.) It is curious that Sir Sydney Caine, Director of the London School of Economics, 1957–67, can admit this fact of academic life freely with one breath and with another revert to the more typical British stance that 'in the essential academic business of a university all that is desirable is that those responsible for taking decisions should be fully aware of any relevant student points of view.'[7]

Fog patches of this kind suggest that there is after all something to be said for the traditional German view that only original work should count towards appointment at a university, since at least students then know where they are: they pick up crumbs from the great man's table, or remain unfed. However, under modern conditions that view has become a form of romanticism. In part, this is because in a mass system of higher education, many or most students are not strongly motivated to pick up crumbs, unless they are absolutely necessary for the process of qualification, and expect or need their teachers to pick up a spoon and feed them.

(3) But in part, the source of the trouble lies much deeper, in the method by which the university organises and expands knowledge. Here, too, lies the most intractable symptom of the *malaise des clercs*. A modern university, that is, keeps a table laden with dishes rich and various beyond the means of a Medici prince or a Chinese emperor, while around it sit no great trenchermen, but only nibbling courtiers, victims of what Professor Handlin calls 'morcellisation'. From that style of eating, there fall fewer crumbs. Professor Handlin continues:

> 'The university which sought a historian or a historian of the United States confronted dozens of potential candidates. But once it focussed on "an expert in Reconstruction (1865–1876)" the choice narrowed down nicely, sometimes to a uniquely qualified individual who was therefore worth every penny paid. . . . The disadvantage, not so evident at first, grew out of the neglect to inquire whether the man who knew all about Cassius County in the election of 1872, or about fish eyes, or about metal stress, knew anything else.'[8]

No reader should suppose that this is a sudden development, or one that lay unnoticed until the student revolutionaries of the 1960s forced it upon our attention. Two 'great men' of the inter-war generation saw no less clearly what was happening, and deserve at this distance in time to be quoted at some length:

> '. . . the modern professionalism in knowledge works in the opposite direction so far as the intellectual sphere is concerned. The modern chemist is likely to be weak in zoology, weaker still in his general knowledge of the Elizabethan drama, and completely ignorant of the principles of rhythm in English versification. It is probably safe to ignore his knowledge of ancient history. . . . Effective knowledge is professionalised knowledge, supported by a restricted acquaintance with useful subjects subservient to it. . . . Each profession makes pro-

[7] *British Universities* (London, 1969), pp. 91, 149.
[8] *Encounter*, July 1970, p. 25.

gress, but it is progress in its own groove. Now to be mentally in a groove is to live in contemplating a given set of abstractions. The groove prevents straying across country, and the abstraction abstracts from something to which no further attention is paid. But there is no groove of abstraction which is adequate for the comprehension of human life. Thus in the modern world, the celibacy of the medieval learned class has been replaced by a celibacy of the intellect which is divorced from the concrete contemplation of the complete facts. . . . The leading intellectuals lack balance. They see this set of circumstances, or that set; but not both together. The task of co-ordination is left to those who lack either the force or the character to succeed in some definite career.'

A. N. Whitehead, *Science and the Modern World* (Cambridge, 1926), pp. 244–5

'. . . even the accomplished intellectual is a far from satisfactory person. His involvement with the world is only cognitive, not affective or conative. Moreover, the framework into which he fits his experience is the framework of the natural sciences and of history treated as though it too were one of the natural sciences. He is concerned mainly with the material universe and with humanity as a part of the material universe. He is not concerned with humanity as human, as potentially more than human. One of the results of this preoccupation with the material universe is that, on the rare occasions when the intellectual does become affectively and conatively involved with the world of human reality, he tends to exhibit a curious impatience which easily degenerates into ruthlessness.'

Aldous Huxley, *Ends and Means* (London, 1937), p. 198

Theodore Roszak has collected, by casual excerption from academic journals, some chilling examples of the ruthlessness which stems from a dissociation of intellect and sensibility—examples none the less chilling because they could each separately be defended as contributions to the ultimate welfare of mankind.[9] Some such dissociation is common to all trades and professions—it is certainly a basic tool of investigatory journalism—but it is especially dangerous in academic life because in our would-be scientific world culture the 'results' of 'research' are almost universally accepted as in some larger sense 'true'. In the last ten years, even quite unsophisticated people have come to realise that newspapers and television may print or screen hastily-gathered half-truths, for want of time or in hope of gain. But academics, though notoriously as prejudiced as, say, British judges in their private or political utterances, are generally believed to be disinterested in relation to their professional specialty. The more rapid the fission of subject specialisms, the harder it becomes to

[9] See *The Making of a Counter Culture* (op. cit.), pp. 269–289.

nail this misapprehension, for it is in the connections we make between different ideas and events that our personal prejudices or inadequacies shrug off their 'academic' disguise and bare themselves for public inspection. An expert on Cassius County in the election of 1872 might even hope to escape without revealing at any point how he himself might have voted in that election, or how he might have responded to the result. A man attempting to make sense of a larger fragment of Black and White relations in the United States could only withdraw from the subject emotionally at the price of writing a pointless book.

True, as the academic community enlarges and the pace of innovation accelerates, dissenting murmurs are being heard. Roszak's books are one example. The American Dr. James Shapiro's recent abandonment of research, after the group which he led had by isolating a single gene brought genetic engineering a stride nearer, alarmed the scientific world. A young British Ph.D. student in experimental psychology, working on the transfer of memory from one animal to another by transplant of brain extract, publicised a similar decision at about the same time. Commenting on both events, a London newspaper's science correspondent said: 'Such defections are viewed within the scientific community as damaging and pointless. . . . Many believe the fear of new knowledge, or its rejection, can lead only to stagnation and eventually to the decay of the human spirit. This argument, however, does not fully meet the situation. Things are moving too fast in some branches of science for their implications to be comfortably absorbed by society.'[10]

That last sentence has of course been true ever since the invention of the steam engine, if not the wheel. '*Acceleration d'histoire? C'est tarte à la crème*' (custard pie) I once heard a French professor snap at a pupil who had had the temerity to mention the idea. But there are analogies between the knowledge explosion and the population explosion. Both have been with us for some time but have only recently begun to matter acutely; both arise from strong instinctual drives which it is hard to control or take pleasure in controlling. So far no human society has formulated any device for steering its own intellectual drives, apart from the totalitarian method of thought-control and proscribed publication (exemplified in the careers of Lysenko on the one hand and Teilhard de Chardin on the other), and the democratic-individualist method of 'if you don't like the research project drop out and join a commune'. Still less can control of any kind be contemplated in the international sphere, where nations are still squabbling over the outfall of the day before yesterday's technology, such as the standardisation of colour-coding for electric cables, or the desire of the world's younger fishing fleets to take their rightful share in exterminating the blue whale.

Man has taken the last eight hundred years or so to evolve fully from *homo sapiens* to *homo scholasticus*. On the way, he had to fight bitterly,

[10] Anthony Tucker in *The Guardian*, July 21, 1970.

and sometimes pay with his life, for the principle that everything which can be known should be known, wherever the knowledge may lead; and for the principle that because the truth about the universe is too large and uncertain to be contained within any intellectual system which can be invented, tolerance of apparently dangerous new ideas is a precondition of progress, and in some circumstances of survival. Herbert Marcuse achieved fame of a sort by questioning the value of the second principle, and asserting that 'the emergence of a free and sovereign majority' will depend on the sustained efforts of militantly intolerant minorities. His critic Alasdair MacIntyre calls this the most dangerous of all Marcuse's doctrines, because the purpose of tolerance is not, as Marcuse thinks, the protection of truth, but the protection of rationality. MacIntyre goes on:

'The institutionalisation of rationality was one of the great achievements of bourgeois society. Of course the very fact of institutionalisation can be used to try to isolate the practice of rational criticism and so prevent it being exercised upon the social order, and there is a continuous pressure upon universities and other institutions to make the practice of rational enquiry merely instrumental to the purposes of government. These assaults upon rational enquiry in the interests of the established social order have to be resisted. . . . But the defence of the authority of the university to teach and to research as it will is in more danger immediately from Marcuse's student allies than from any other quarter.'[11]

That is not true in the University of California, where Marcuse works, and as we saw in Chapter Three, the 'institutionalization of rationality' in universities was originally a work of feudal rather than of bourgeois society, but let this pass. Within his own terms, MacIntyre's critique is unassailable. Its weakness—which does not save Marcuse, but is relevant to the present discussion—is that it treats the modern university as though it were nothing more complex in its organisation and perilous in its power than the members of the Aristotelian Society in public session, rationally criticising the social order and the official philosophy. If this were all that the university is, no one but a gross totalitarian would object to this defence of it. But MacIntyre is incorrect to say, or imply, that institutionalisation of rational enquiry leaves us with no problem except to preserve its autonomy, and to keep governmental contaminants out of the universities. For the university of itself persistently applies its skills of teaching and research to projects which are rational only in the sense that they assume that two plus two do make four, and that a sentence with a subject and an object also needs a verb. Of course, decadent academic professionalism is nothing new in universities, nor in intellectual life as a whole. But as Whitehead pointed out, 'In the past, professionals have formed unprogressive castes. The point is that professionalism has

[11] Op. cit., p. 91.

now been mated with progress. The world is now faced with a self-evolving system, which it cannot stop.'

To talk in terms of 'stopping it', or of 'control' is to raise spectres which no twentieth century man, least of all a liberal academic, can bring himself to contemplate. But it would be just as irrational not to recognise that the mighty engine of academic professionalism, with its drive to *know* come what may, is a machine with a built-in bias that is independent of political systems, however they are constructed, and of the social will, however it is ascertained. The machine may or may not succumb to crude pressures: it may or may not prefer a lavishly-financed Defence Department research commission of modest intellectual appeal to a somewhat more absorbing inquiry for which funds have to be begged here and there. But it can always be relied upon, outside all magnetic fields of this kind, and wherever it has complete freedom, to investigate first the topic which advances the interests or engages the sympathies of *homo scholasticus*. This may sound obvious, but it is not yet obvious to many that no university will ever voluntarily devote to integration or assimilation of what it knows a quarter of the energies it spends in exploring what it does not yet know. No inter-disciplinary devices however subtle (and most of them in most universities are somewhat primitive) can ever quite catch up with the academic mind's instinctive tendency towards ramification. The intellectual world works rather on the principle of Pandora's box: every demon that escapes needs at least two more to catch it. The principle can be seen in action in any university department. A Professor of Sociology, say, is appointed. A methodological dispute ensues, and is settled by the appointment of professors to represent mathematical sociology and participant sociology. Debates about content and demarcation are followed by the creation of posts in inter-disciplinary fields like the sociology of religion, the sociology of education, the sociology—to borrow from Heinrich Böll's Schmeck—of the mackintosh. The implicit hope is that the counter-tugs of each will prevent the department as a whole from slicing its drive, and that a stream of published articles will travel straight down the academic fairway.

As long as the university remained a specialised institution, of which nothing else was expected but the diffusion and advancement of learning, society had little reason to interfere with its choices, except to limit their expense or muffle their subversive effect. However, in any advanced nation the university is not now a specialised institution, but a fourth or fifth estate of the realm. Early industrial culture had most of its tributary sources outside the university. The transforming technologies of print, power, and transport owed little or nothing to the institutions described in this book. The sceptical distance maintained between the iron-master and the professor meant that the mistakes and brutalities of the first industrial revolution came under a retrospective critique which could not alter what had happened, but which at least had power to secure amendments and avert repetitions. The millowners and the railway contractors could not be taught imagination, not even by a William Morris or a Matthew Arnold, but they eventually had to bow before the evidence, just as the most virulent and mythopoeic forms of racialism in the end have to bow before the sociologists and the anthropologists, when they can get a hearing.

Post-industrial culture, on the other hand, is being defined by the universities themselves. They select its controllers and invent its technologies. A retrospective external critique will not be possible, partly because there is no external stance available to the critic *except* an instinctual, non-rational one, partly because the speed of the developments does not allow time for the critique to be mounted before the next irreversible change is upon us. The professor who claimed that history had always been accelerating only had to listen to his own Concorde to be reminded that all acceleration eventually encounters a boom. True, modern civilisation has also devised the cybernetic principle—the self-steering mechanism which the first industrial revolution lacked, so that all its effects were inordinate, like the bills which an imperfectly cybernetic computer cannot stop sending you. But at present, it seems wistful to hope that this principle will be at hand to throw the switches when the codified and tested theoretical knowledge issued by the university turns out to have set the world on some as yet unforeseen collision course. Can the university seriously be expected to become its own physician, as well as its brother's keeper?

Homo scholasticus is already unhappy with some of these roles. Similarly, no doubt, there were ascetic medieval monks who were sorry when the monastic system became full-blown and all-embracing, in the manner described by Dom David Knowles:

'During the eleventh and the greater part of the twelfth centuries monasticism reached its peak of influence. . . . The material result of this was seen in the numberless religious foundations, in the vast and ever-increasing army of monks and *conversi*, in the great buildings that began to dominate the landscape and the rich estates controlled by the monks. From being in the early eleventh century primarily a religious and an educational force, they became towards its end, both by force of numbers, by virtue of their appeal to all classes, and by sheer economic weight as landlords, an immense social power.'[12]

For the monasteries, this development led ultimately to dissolution. In the 1960s, the academic orders have had a warning that if they stand pat on their rationality as the monastic orders stood pat on their piety, even a dissolution of the universities cannot in the long run be ruled out. It is largely an accident of timing that the warning was couched in Marxist

[12] *The Religious Orders in England* (Cambridge, 1948–59), vol. iii, p. 457.

phraseology—the phraseology of a political system which is itself dying. The fault here was society's, for creating an intellectual proletariat of unemployed juveniles, whose condition the phraseology fitted, just as the nineteenth century industrial proletariat had begun to disappear.

However, the post-industrial state has in sight no alternative to the university as codifier, tester, regulator, and civiliser. It is well that universities and educational systems should be made as efficient as they can be, and as just as possible to all regions, classes, sexes, and ages in their distribution of their cultural and (indirectly) economic goods. The inclusiveness, the open-plan living, which this implies for academic man in his institutions is one of the safe predictions that can be made for the future. Inclusiveness need not entail the acceptance of Ph.D. programmes in any subject, however humdrum, that can plausibly be dressed up in academic robes. Nor need it prevent positive discriminations being made between people who actually want what a university can provide, and people who really want something quite different. But it does entail the honouring of intellectual integration alongside intellectual fission, even if this means that Nobel Prize winners no longer come first in the academic pecking order. It almost certainly entails the presence in strength on the campus of the non-rational or the supra-rational, expressed in religion formal and ecstatic and the creative arts formal and ecstatic, not just as a subject to be analysed but as a sacrament to be celebrated, and as a Distant Early Warning System to be monitored.

There is still one thing needful. Granted even the perfect university in the perfect society, a prudent citizenry will nevertheless allot funds and pay a control group handsome salaries to live as they choose and learn as they choose, on condition that they attend no school, apply to no university, and drink sherry with no professors. For how terrible, how very terrible, it would be if somewhere in the recesses of the human mind there *were* an alternative to the university as mirror to the knowable world, and there were no private, altogether extramural person left with the eyes to see and the voice to tell.

Appendix A

Members of the University of California Board of Regents (1970) and samples of their incoming mail

The Honorable Ronald Reagan, Governor of California.

Congressman Ed Reinecke, Lieutenant Governor.

Robert T. Monagan, Speaker of the Assembly.

Max Rafferty, Superintendent of Public Instruction.

Allan Grant, President of the California State Board of Agriculture.

Joseph A. Moore, Jr., President of the Mechanic's Institute.

Wendell W. Witter, investment banker. Alumni representative.

Charles J. Hitch, President of the University of California, formerly Assistant Secretary of Defense in the Kennedy Administration.

Philip L. Boyd, banker and rancher.

W. Glenn Campbell, Director of the Hoover Institution on War, Revolution, and Peace.

John E. Canaday, public relations counsel to Lockheed Aircraft Corporation.

Edward W. Carter, President of Broadway-Hale Stores, Inc.

William K. Coblentz, lawyer.

Frederick G. Dutton, lawyer. Formerly Secretary of the Cabinet in the Kennedy Administration.

William E. Forbes, President of the Southern California Music Company.

(Mrs.) Catherine C. Hearst, wife of the President of the Hearst Publishing Company, whose grandmother, Phoebe Hearst, was the University's first woman Regent.

(Mrs.) Elinor Raas Heller, formerly Democratic National Committeewoman.

DeWitt A. Higgs, aeronautical lawyer.

Edwin W. Pauley, founder and chairman of Pauley Petroleum, Inc.

Robert O. Reynolds, Director of Air West Inc., and President of the California Angels baseball team.

William M. Roth, financial executive, formerly a US representative in the 'Kennedy Round' negotiations.

Norton Simon, Director of Norton Simon, Inc. and a member of the Carnegie Commission on the Future of Higher Education.

William French Smith, lawyer. Led Reagan's delegation to the Republican Convention at Miami, 1968.

Dean A. Watkins, co-founder and Chairman of Watkins-Johnson Co., and a trustee of Stanford University.

The month's communications, laid before the Regents at their meeting in April, 1969

Resolutions adopted by the Kiwanis Clubs of Palo Alto, East Bakersfield, and Hacienda Heights, respectively, deploring violence in educational

institutions at all levels, and giving their support to those segments of
the State, local communities, educational institutions, and citizenry
who are striving to maintain order and solve the problems which
exist in the schools and colleges; and urging greater communication
as a means of working out these problems in an orderly fashion.

Two letters from citizens, deploring campus violence and suggesting
measures to bring disruption to a halt, such as: a one-year moratorium
on campus disturbances, in return for which the administration will
have an in-depth study of the educational system conducted; issuance
of student identification cards and revocable licenses to permit campus
entry; and increased penalties for disruptive students.

Letter from a Santa Barbara resident, referring to reports that a class on
the tactics and practice of guerrilla warfare will be held on the Santa
Barbara campus, and demanding an explanation of why such a class
is permitted in a University building.

Letter from a Los Angeles resident protesting that persons holding positions
of prestige on the public payroll, such as University faculty members,
be permitted to align themselves with subversive activities.

Letter to Chancellor Heyns and The Regents, signed by fifty-one faculty
members, graduate students and employees of the Department of
Bacteriology and Immunology, Berkeley campus, dated February 21,
and transmitted through the President, expressing concern over the
declaration of the state of extreme emergency on that campus, and
urging that this declaration be rescinded.

Copy of a letter to the Governor's education adviser from a San Francisco
attorney, alluding to, and critical of, actions and statements made by
the Governor pertaining to the University; expressing the view that
elected officials should accept responsibility for action on the political
and sociological conditions that have created campus problems and
face up to the necessity for taking action to correct the abuses and that
they should stand firm against violence; and demanding that the area
south of the Berkeley campus be cleaned up.

Resolution signed by thirty-nine students at Berkeley, expressing support
of, and confidence in, Chancellor Heyns and his conduct during the
period of the recent strike.

Communication from a history instructor, Canada College, urging that
American society devise constructive programs to ensure equality for
all Americans, black and white, in order to broaden the base of American democracy.

Resolution adopted by the Oakland Republican Assembly, noting that
a German National student militant has applied to the Department of
State for a visa for entry into the United States, for the declared purpose
of speaking at the University of California and other American universities; and recommending to the Department of State that his application
be summarily denied.

Letter from a San Diego resident, expressing the view that, because of the size of the University, it is impossible for The Regents to exercise close review and control over such matters as tenure, over-age appointments, student publications, and student fund administration; suggesting that, rather than delegating authority in these matters to the administration, The Regents should look more to the taxpayers; and proposing that a Board of Vice-Regents be established for each campus composed of qualified citizens in the local community, this Board to be delegated the responsibility for matters such as those listed above.

Communication from a UCLA Professor, transmitted through the President, urging that the proposed Standing Order amendment under which the Board would reassume direct charge of the appointment of all tenure faculty be rejected for several reasons, among them: that adoption of the proposal would be fatal to decentralisation, which he considers has been successful; and that reassumption of responsibility for faculty appointments would imply Regental expertise in an area where such expertise cannot and should not be expected to abound.

Two communications urging that power to hire faculty be returned to the Board of Regents.

Letter from a citizen in San Diego, objecting to Speaker Monagan's proposal for graduated fee increases, on the grounds that it is distasteful and objectionable to low income as well as high income families, and expressing the view that the most democratic approach is equal treatment of all students.

Letter from a Davis student, telling of his concern over misappropriation of student funds by student governments, and expressing his thankfulness that The Regents ultimately control use of such funds.

Copy of a letter to President Hitch from Lieutenant General Stanley R. Larsen, expressing concern over the possibility of changes in the ROTC program on University campuses which may be detrimental to the continued viability of the program; noting that Secretary of Defense Laird has urged universities to delay any change in the status of ROTC pending a thorough review of possible problem areas by the Army, Navy and Air Force; and requesting deferral of any adverse action pertaining to the ROTC program in the meantime.

Resolution adopted by the Executive Board of the Santa Cruz County Democratic Club, urging that returning Vietnam veterans be given first priority in enrollment at the University and State Colleges and that entrance requirements for them be no higher than for other potential students.

Communication from a Davis student, transmitted through the President, stating the need to expand the gym facilities on the Davis campus.

Memorandum from an Oakland resident, requesting that a course on 'Geometrical Optics' be removed from the Physics Department and be considered as part of the curriculum of the School of Optometry.

Copy of a statement adopted by 440 delegates at the 1967 State convention of California Congress of Parents and Teachers, in support of strong family life education in California's public schools.

Letter from a former non-academic employee, requesting intervention by The Regents in his formal grievance regarding termination of his University employment for reasons he considers unjustified.

Appendix B

Preamble (*titre premier*) to the *Loi d'Orientation de l'Enseignement Supérieur*
(Paris, November 12, 1968)

THE AIMS OF HIGHER EDUCATION

Article 1

The Universities and other institutions to which the provisions of the present law apply have as their mission the advancement and communication of knowledge, the development of research, and the training of the minds of men.

The Universities must strive to develop advanced learning and discovery to the highest level and at the most appropriate pace, and to make them accessible to everyone who has the necessary will and aptitude.

They must meet the needs of the nation by providing it with leaders in all fields and by taking part in the social and economic development of every region. In performing this task, they must adapt themselves to the evolving democracy which the industrial and technological revolution demands.

Teachers and researchers must be assured of the means whereby they may carry on their activities in the atmosphere of independence and calm which is indispensable for reflection and intellectual creativity.

Students must be assured of proper means for resolving upon a field of study and for making the best choice of the career to which they will devote themselves; and to this end, the Universities must impart to them not only the necessary knowledge but also the essentials of intellectual development.

The Universities make room for the cultural, sporting, and social activities of students: this is essential for a balanced and complete education.

They shape the leaders of the country's educational system and—without prejudice to the adaptation of different categories of teacher to different special tasks—protect the overall unity of education. They enable teaching methods and bodies of knowledge to be continually improved and brought up to date.

Higher education must be open to former students and to people who have not been able to continue their studies, so that they may, according to their abilities, better their chances of promotion or branch off towards another profession.

The Universities must contribute, especially by taking advantage of the new means by which knowledge is diffused, to the provision of continuing education for every section of the population, and for all useful purposes.

Generally speaking, higher education—which includes all education after the secondary stage—contributes to the cultural advancement of society, and through this, to an enhancement of every man's responsibility in the determination of his destiny.

(translated by Mary Stiff and Christopher Driver)

Appendix C: The New

Provisions of the *Loi d'Orientation,*

Composition and constitution

Representatives elected by council members of the universities and other related but independent establishments, with a third of the seats reserved for *les grands intérêts nationaux*. The Minister of Education presides.

NATIONAL COUNCIL FOR HIGHER EDUCATION AND RESEARCH

AND

Representatives elected by council members of the universities and other establishments, voting in separate electoral colleges for teachers and students. Half the teachers elected must hold the rank of professor or *maître de conférence*.

REGIONAL COUNCILS FOR HIGHER EDUCATION AND RESEARCH

▲

A university is a group of education and research units, in a combination approved by the Minister. It may or may not correspond to a region: that is, in a given region there may be several universities.

Each university council is composed of faculty, researchers, students, and non-teaching personnel, elected by their respective electoral colleges. Lay people, chosen with regard to their activity in the region, must comprise between a sixth and a third of the council's membership. The maximum total membership of the university council is eighty.

The university has financial autonomy. It is directed by a president, who must be a professor, elected for a minimum of two years and a maximum of four. He may be re-elected once.

UNIVERSITIES

▲

These are the component parts into which the old Faculties were broken down under the Act. They may be former Faculties or sections of Faculties, or new institutions. They have varying statuses: some are 'public establishments of a scientific and cultural nature'; others have the attributes of a university department. Regardless of their status, they will have legal and financial autonomy. Each unit is administered by an elected board composed of teachers, researchers, students, and non-teaching personnel, selected in separate assemblies by universal and secret ballot. Teachers must constitute at least half the board, and only students who have completed a year of university study and qualified to continue may vote.

The boards are headed by an elected director, and may not have more than forty members. Special science boards, composed only of faculty, researchers, and scientifically competent people, determine research curricula and the distribution of funds.

EDUCATION AND RESEARCH UNITS

French University

1968, diagrammatically presented

To do long-term planning of higher education and research, in relation to other national plans.
To be consulted about the distribution of Exchequer funds among the different universities and other establishments.
To harmonise university statutes and advise on the conditions for obtaining national degrees.
To advise the Minister of Education in cases of dispute between a Rector (responsible for co-ordinating all branches of education within his *académie*) and a university or regional council.

To contribute in their district to the planning, coordination, and programming of higher education and research.
To maintain links with the bodies responsible for regional development.
To advise on the categories of laymen to be appointed to serve on university councils.

To be inter-disciplinary. Universities must 'associate arts and letters with sciences and technical studies as much as possible. They can, however, have a dominant field of specialisation.'
To determine their educational activities, research programmes, pedagogical methods, and methods for testing students' knowledge and aptitudes, within the limits laid down by the Act, decrees, and regulations.
To arrange, together with other interested organisations, for the units of education and research to provide continuing education.

To determine their own status, internal structures, and links with other university units. They are also responsible for their own educational activity, research programmes, pedagogical methods, and procedures for testing aptitude and verifying knowledge. (The elected boards state the conditions under which examinations shall be sat, but the designation of boards of examiners, the award of degrees, and the selection and placement of teachers are the exclusive prerogative of teachers who hold professorial rank.)

Notes:
Académie denotes an educational district: each one is headed by a Rector, representing the Minister of Education, and includes at least one university.
Maître de conférence is a person who holds the *doctorat d'Etat* and is waiting for a professorial Chair to be vacated.

Appendix D

Guide to the universities of Paris

Paris I. Mainly in the place du Panthéon. Does law, history, economics, politics, geography, archeology, art history. The ministry's favourite, with a leading Byzantine historian as the presiding genius.

Paris II. Also mainly in the place du Panthéon. Law and economics. Described in a student brochure as the reactionary part of the law faculty. At the inaugural meeting for freshmen a student asked if Professor Maurice Duverger was there. Quarrels a lot with Paris I about rooms and lecture theatres.

Paris III. Rue de la Sorbonne. Censier, Institute of Anglo-American studies. Modern languages and communications. Traditional approach, and accused of Anglo-Saxon influences.

Paris IV. Mainly in the Sorbonne and the Grand Palais. Classics, history, philosophy, geography, modern languages, and so on. Mostly what remains of the Sorbonne. Scholarly, with many new ideas.

Paris V. Mainly in the rue de l'Ecole de Medecine and in various hospitals. Medicine, pharmacy, technology, psychology, sociology. Described as having a 'vocation de masse.'

Paris VI. Quai Bernard, Halle aux vins and in various hospitals. Medicine and science. The doctors feel ill at ease because outnumbered by the scientists. Described by some students as 'the rut', by others as 'la continuité'.

Paris VII. Halle aux vins, Censier, Charles V and other places. Natural science, biological sciences, languages, history. The with-it university, described by some students as 'l'aventure.' Influence of Professor Culioli, and of Edgar Faure's chief adviser. Methodological research.

Paris VIII. Vincennes. Experimental university open till 10 pm. Accepts unqualified students. Quarrel because the crèche has not been re-opened this year. Said to have difficulty in existing as a university. Left-wing, filled with ideas, energy and enthusiasm.

Paris IX. Dauphine. Experimental university. Economic sciences and languages. Contains the centre for urban studies which is restive.

Paris X. Nanterre. Arts, law, economics, social studies. Now traditionally the most restive university. Many hard-working people determined 'to save Nanterre.'

Paris XI. Sceaux, Orsay, Montrouge. Law, medicine, science. Institute of nuclear sciences. Technology. Presided over by close collaborator of M. le Ministre.

Paris XII. Créteil, Saint-Maur. Under construction. Now has about 1,000 students in various arts subjects. Next year due to receive 5,000 in medical, para-medical and environmental studies.

Paris XIII. Saint-Denis, Villetaneuse. Under construction as an example of multi-disciplinary studies. Isolated but the architects are enjoying themselves. Will have literary, legal and computer studies.

Source: Douglas Johnson in *New Society*, December 10, 1970

Critical bibliography

A list of books possibly relevant to the study of universities on an international scale would be almost as daunting as the British Museum catalogue. Nor would there be much point in listing here the unsystematic
collection of books which I have read or referred to in the course of
writing. (The pleasingly unsystematic shelves of the London Library
encourage this method.) However, curiosity about the university
institutions and higher education systems of other countries is bound to
grow, and where useful material in a tolerably accessible form exists, it
would be churlish not to mention it. Serious scholars will be aware of the
gaps, and look elsewhere.

INTERNATIONAL COMPARISONS

Classics:

Hastings Rashdall, *The Universities of Europe in the Middle Ages*, revised
   edition by A. B. Emden and F. M. Powicke, 3 vols., Oxford, 1936.
Matthew Arnold, *Schools and Universities on the Continent* (1868), edited
   by R. H. Super, Ann Arbor, 1964.
Abraham Flexner, *Universities: American, English, German*. New York,
   1930. Reprinted by Oxford University Press, 1968, with a critical
   introduction by Clark Kerr.

Contemporary:

Barbara B. Burn, *Higher Education in Nine Countries*, with chapters by
   Philip G. Altbach, Clark Kerr, and James A. Perkins. New York, 1971.
   (This book is referred to in the Introduction.)
Anthony Kerr, *Universities of Europe*. London, 1962. Short factual surveys,
   now necessarily dated.
Joseph Ben-David, *Fundamental research and the universities*. OECD, 1967.
   A short but provocative study of the relation between academic
   organisation and the pace of scientific discovery in developed countries.
Eric Ashby, *Universities: British, Indian, African*. Harvard and London,
   1966. Flexner's heir, in experience and grasp, though not in savagery.
Eric Ashby, *Community of Universities*. Cambridge, 1963.

Donald Fleming and Bernard Bailyn (eds.), *The Intellectual Migration (Europe and America, 1930–1960)*. Harvard, 1969.

Laura Fermi, *Illustrious Immigrants*. Chicago and London, 1968. Both these books paint a vivid picture, the first in scholars' own words, the second through personal acquaintance and subsequent research, of academic cross-fertilisation under pressure of events.

(Bibliography)

Richard Schwarz (ed.), *Universitat und Moderne Welt: ein internationales Symposion*. Berlin, 1962. Contains a bibliography of 'scholarly literature on problems of higher education' which lists publications (of uneven merit) from several different countries, including most of those covered in this book.

(Reports)

Reviews and comparisons of national policies for education and science are conducted by international bodies such as Unesco and OECD. See their catalogues.

(Periodicals)

Comparative articles, or explanations of national situations to an international scholarly audience, are often to be found in *Minerva, Daedalus* (the Journal of the American Academy of Arts and Sciences), *Archives Européennes de Sociologie*, etc., and sometimes in national journals devoted to higher education problems, such as the *Universities Quarterly* in Britain. *Encounter* is another useful source. Most of the countries reviewed here have national or private institutes for research in higher education, which publish bulletins.

Students:

S. M. Lipset (ed.), *Student Politics*. New York, 1967. Encyclopaedic treatment by a formidable but not too pontifical American social scientist and his contributors.

Julian Nagel (ed.), *Student Power*. London, 1969. Essays, predominantly by Left-inclined sociologists, about the student movement and its causes in Britain, the United States, Western Germany, France, and Italy. With an attempted international chronology of student unrest 1964–68.

Lewis S. Feuer, *The Conflict of Generations*. New York and London, 1969. Surveys a century and a half of student revolt in several countries, and recalls personal experience and acquaintance in Tokyo, Moscow and Berkeley, where the writer was Professor of Philosophy during the Troubles.

Stephen Spender, *The Year of the Young Rebels*. London, 1969. Personal account of a world tour of the universities chiefly affected by the 1968 student uprisings.

Barbara and John Ehrenreich, *Long March, Short Spring*. New York, 1969.

Two footloose American graduate students describe what European students were thinking and feeling in 1968.

Anthony Sampson, *New Europeans*. London, 1968. (pp. 397 ff.) Footloose British journalist does the same.

Daedalus (Winter, 1968), issue on 'Students and Politics'. (American Academy of Arts and Sciences, 280 Newton Street, Brookline Street, Boston, Mass. 02146.)

INDIVIDUAL COUNTRIES AND INSTITUTIONS

(1) *United States:*

Americans, so much more self-conscious about the educational process than any other nation, have described and criticised their universities to each other tirelessly. The foreigner's problem is to select, which is most easily if lazily done by choosing an internationally familiar name—a Richard Hofstadter or a David Riesman—and following it through the catalogues, picking up from the actual books the references which sound promising. The encyclopaedic scope and depth of American scholarship at its best can thus be made to work for weaker spirits. The underlying historical and sociological trends of American higher education need to be grasped in this way before the season's paperbacks, and the rapid shifts of fashion in protest and analysis, can be 'placed' by an observer from a different culture. The following are a few key works in different genres.

Richard Hofstadter and Wilson Smith, *American Higher Education, a documentary history*. Chicago, 1961 (two vols.). Contains adroitly-selected fundamental texts, from John Harvard's time onwards.

Laurence R. Veysey, *The Emergence of the American University*. Chicago, 1965. An historical explanation of what makes American universities different from, and more various than, any other.

Richard Hofstadter, *Anti-intellectualism in American Life*. New York, 1963. An astringent and erudite commentary on a strand of American behaviour which has deeply influenced the way scholars and students in the United States see themselves.

Christopher Jencks and David Riesman, *The Academic Revolution*. New York, 1968. (Paperback with a new foreword, 1969.) Much the most complete, well-written, and up-to-date sociological description of American higher education as a whole. It has been criticised in detail (see especially the defensive reaction of the Negro colleges to early drafts, *Harvard Educational Review*, Vol. 37 No. 3, summer 1967). But it will not be soon superseded.

Clark Kerr, *The Uses of the University*. Harvard 1964
and
Jacques Barzun, *The American University*. New York, 1969. The former President of the University of California and the former Dean of Faculties and Provost at Columbia University describe the inner

reality of the system, created in the past twenty-five years, which one of them has called 'the Federal Grant University'. Both books are highly readable, not to say malicious.

Andrew Greeley, *The Changing Catholic College*. Chicago, 1967. A Catholic sociologist's objective and irreverent description of one type of 'minority group' higher education in the US.

W. R. Niblett (ed.), *Higher Education, demand and response*. London, 1969. See the essay on 'Elite and popular functions in American higher education' by Martin Trow, a Berkeley sociologist of academic life on both sides of the Atlantic.

James Ridgeway, *The Closed Corporation*. New York, 1968. A *New Republic* journalist's well-muckraked account of universities as businesses, and of who pays whom for what kind of research on famous and not-so-famous campuses. It is fallible in detail, has no solutions to propose, and the tone of feigned astonishment becomes wearying—but it was a badly-needed book.

Jerome Skolnick and others, *The Politics of Protest*. New York, 1969. A report, prepared for the National Commission on the Causes and Prevention of Violence by a team based upon the Berkeley Center for the Study of Law and Society, exploring the motives and behaviour of black militants, student rioters, and anti-war demonstrators.

Kenneth Keniston, *Young Radicals*. New York, 1968. The Yale psychologist's attempt at a typology, based upon sympathetic personal interviews. The hopeful conclusion stands up less well to recent developments than the finding by Erich Fromm and Michael Maccoby that radical students are more 'life-loving' than either conservative students or the general population, but that the radicals themselves include a 'necrophilic' segment who 'use the ideology of revolution to rationalise their inner deadness and their impulse to destroy rather than create.'

Alvin C. Eurich (ed.), *Campus 1980*. New York, 1968. A useful anthology of essays, with a preface by Arnold Toynbee, on where American higher education, at its many different levels, expects to be by the end of the decade. The exercise can be recommended to other countries.

Daedalus (Winter, 1970). Issue on the governance of universities.

(*Individual institutions*)

COLUMBIA: Jerry L. Avorn, Robert Friedman, and others, *Up Against the Ivy Wall*, New York, 1968, and London (under the emasculated title *University in Revolt*), 1969.

The Cox Commission, *Crisis at Columbia* (Report of the Fact-Finding Commission appointed to investigate the disturbances at Columbia University in April and May, 1968). New York, 1968.

BERKELEY: S. M. Lipset and Sheldon S. Wolin (eds.), *The Berkeley*

Student Revolt, facts and interpretations. New York, 1965.

CHICAGO: William Braden, *The Age of Aquarius: Technology and the Cultural Revolution.* Chicago, 1970.

Many of the interviews in this book were conducted with participants in the 1969 sit-in at the University of Chicago. Unfortunately, it came to my attention too late for discussion in the text.

HARVARD: Richard Zorza, *The Right to Say 'We'.* New York and London, 1970.

These microcosmic accounts of student uprisings do much to convey the tone of the institutions affected, even when allowance is made for the partisanship. For Berkeley, the following official or semi-official reports may also be consulted:

The Byrne Report (on politics and government in the University of California). Regents of the University and *Los Angeles Times,* May, 1965. Not published in book format.

The Muscatine Report (*Education at Berkeley*). University of California (Berkeley and Los Angeles), 1966.

The Foote Report (*The Culture of the University: governance and education.*) *Daily Californian,* January 15, 1968, with minority dissent, April 4, 1968; published by Jossey-Bass (San Francisco), 1968.

(2) Japan:

Robert King Hall, *Education for a new Japan.* New Haven and London, 1949.

Rationale of the reforms imposed upon Japanese education by the American occupying forces' education experts after 1945.

Japan Ministry of Education, *Higher Education in Post-War Japan.* Edited and translated by John E. Blewett, S. J., Sophia University, Tokyo, 1965.

A Jesuit scholar at Japan's leading Catholic University interprets what the Japanese were trying to do with their higher education in the fifties and sixties.

Michio Nagai, *Nihon no Daigaku.* Chuo Koron Sha, Tokyo, 1965. American edition (*Higher Education in Japan*) forthcoming.

A critique of the contemporary Japanese university by an historically and internationally minded sociologist.

The same writer's *Daigaku no Kanosei* (Chuo Koron Sha, Tokyo, 1969) is a proposal for an 'experimental university commune' in Japan.

Ronald Dore, *Education in Tokugawa Japan.* London, 1965. Describes the historical background to mass education in Japan.

Herbert Passin, chapter on Japan in James S. Coleman (ed.), *Education and Political Development.* Princeton, 1965. (pp. 272–312).

David and Evelyn Riesman, *Conversations in Japan*. New York and London, 1967. Diaries of a two-month visit in 1961, and confusingly organised. But the writers' extraordinary breadth of academic and cultural contacts make this book an excellent introduction to the 'feel' of Japanese intellectual life.

Robert Jay Lifton, 'Youth and History: *Individual Change in Post-War Japan*', in Erik Erikson (ed.), *Youth: Change and Challenge*. New York, 1963.
The writer, a friend of the Riesmans', has studied in Japan the impact of historical change on individual psychology, especially in the young. His views should be compared with:

Kazuko Tsurumi, *Social Change and the Individual*. Princeton, 1970. An authoritative, highly particularised book on Japanese ideology and personality before and after the 1939–45 War. Part III analyses the attitudes of members of the Japanese student movement at the period of which the Riesmans write.

Bernard Béraud, *La Gauche Revolutionnaire au Japan*. Editions du Seuil, Paris, 1970. The writer, a contributor to *Combat* and other French journals, speaks Japanese, resides in Tokyo, and has a wide acquaintance among Japanese student leaders.

Stuart Dowsey (ed.), *Zengakuren: Japan's revolutionary students*. Ishi Press (Box 1021, Berkeley 1, California), 1970. Six well-informed Japanese students from Waseda, edited by a sympathetic American, describe the background both to the student struggles of 1947–70, and to the University Control Act of 1969.

Stefano Bellieni, *Zengakuren Zenkyoto: rapporto su una generazione in rivolta*. Feltrinelli, Milan, 1969. Official replies from the various sects of the Japanese student movement to questions about their theory, strategy, and tactics, with an historical introduction (to the end of 1969).

OECD, *Reviews of National Science Policy: Japan*. OECD, 1967.

Fukuji Taguchi, 'Japan in transition', in Bernard Crick and William Robson (eds.), *Protest and Discontent*. London, 1970. Analysis of the contemporary Japanese political situation by a professor of politics at Meiji University, Tokyo.

(*Reports*)

Japan Ministry of Education, Report on measures to meet problems facing university education in Japan, by the Central Council for Education, April 30, 1969.

Japan Ministry of Education, Draft outline of the Preliminary Report on the Basic Design of the Reform of Higher Education in Japan, by the Planning and Research Department, December 23, 1969.
These reports, both couched in rather vague Japanese English, are reprinted in *Minerva*, the first in VIII, 1. (January 1970); the second in

VIII, 4 (October 1970). The substance of the text of the University Control Act 1969 is translated in Dowsey, op. cit., pp. 176–178.

(Periodicals)

Japan Quarterly. Asahi Shimbun Company, Tokyo. Relevant articles on university subjects appear frequently: for example, vol. XVI No. 2, Junro Fukashiro on 'Student Thought and Feeling', and the results of the Asahi Shimbun public opinion surveys on the issue of university strife (divided between surveys of the general public and surveys of professors and students).

Waseda Guardian. Room 1, Student Union, Waseda University, Shinjuku-ku, Tokyo. An enterprising, irregularly published sheet edited with very modest resources by students of English, for international consumption. Usually moderate in tone.

Jerry Dusenbury, 'Japan and the Foreign Student', in *Student World*, Vol. LX No. 2, second quarter, 1967 (issue on 'the internationalisation of the University.' World Student Christian Federation, 13 rue Calvin, Geneva.

The writer, an American, describes the fundamental hostility of the Japanese to foreign students and professors in their universities.

Joseph Roggendorf, 'The Japanese Student Movement as seen from Europe', in *Sophia*, vol. XVIII, No. 4 (1969). A German Jesuit compares the situation in Japan with what he saw on re-visiting West Germany in the summer of 1969. His sympathy with radical students is human, not political.

(3) Britain:

Here too, though to a lesser extent than in the United States, the problem for the student of higher education is knowing where to start his reading. Most of the general books about British universities have been written not by outside observers, nor even by full-time scholars, but by successful scholar-administrators. They are strong on policy, weak on flavour. The following are exceptions, one or two for each of the main branches into which the British university 'system' is divided:

Jasper Rose and John Ziman, *Camford Observed*. London, 1964. Two young scholars' ironic but serious examination of Oxford and Cambridge as centres of teaching, research, and civilisation—just before these institutions succumbed to an epidemic of reforming zeal comparable with the nineteenth century Royal Commissions.

W. H. G. Armytage, *Civic Universities*. London, 1955. Wide-ranging and historical, full of felicitous quotation.

'Bruce Truscot' (E. Allison Peers), *Redbrick University*. London, 1943. Though now something of a period document, this book taught a whole generation to think critically about institutions previously taken more or less for granted.

Michael Beloff, *The Plateglass Universities*. London, 1968. A much slighter book by a young Oxford political scientist, which nevertheless captures the mood of the new British universities in the first flush of youth. It should be read with, e.g.:

Asa Briggs, 'Development in Higher Education in the United Kingdom: nineteenth and twentieth centuries', in Niblett, op. cit., pp. 95–121, and with a comprehensive factual description for an international audience:

Harold Perkin, *New Universities in the United Kingdom*. OECD, 1969.

On particular subjects, relevant to all British universities, books consulted should include the following:

Peter Marris, *The Experience of Higher Education*. London, 1964. An early (for Britain) sociological attempt to discover what students made of the education thought good for them by their teachers.

A. H. Halsey and Martin Trow, *The British Academics*. Faber, 1971.

Richard Hoggart, 'Higher Education and Personal Life' in Niblett, op. cit. The most sensitive analyst of British popular culture, now at UNESCO, describes what the recent changes in the relationship of universities to society have been doing to actual people. See also the *Listener* (April 9, 1970).

Raymond Williams, *The Long Revolution*. London, 1961. Contains a characteristically careful, if sometimes opaque, analysis of the unconscious *intention* behind the shape of education in England.

Alexander Cockburn and Robin Blackburn (eds.), *Student Power*. London, 1969. British student radicals reflect on their gains.

David Martin (ed.), *Anarchy and Culture*, The Problem of the Contemporary University. London, 1969. British academics reflect on their losses.

Eric Ashby and Mary Anderson, *The Rise of the Student Estate in Britain*. London, 1970. An eirenic historical account, fully alive to the contemporary questions about university governance.

(Reports)

Committee on Higher Education, Higher Education. Cmnd. 2154, London, 1963. (The Robbins Report) HMSO.

Department of Education and Science, A Plan for Polytechnics and Other Colleges. Cmnd. 3006, London 1966. HMSO.

Committee of Vice-Chancellors and Principals, The Quinquennium 1962–67. London, 1968.

University Grants Committee, University Development. Quinquennial reports, 1935–69. London, HMSO.

(Individual institutions)

For books about universities in Britain, both general and particular, see the interesting critical bibliography in V. H. H. Green, *The Universities* (Pelican 'British Institutions' series, London, 1969) whose text itself, however, is over-weighted towards Oxford and Cambridge.

For the fullest critical and statistical anatomy of an (admittedly untypical) British university, see the *Franks Report on Oxford University*, 2 vols., Oxford, 1966.

For an anatomy of radical students, see Tessa Blackstone, Kathleen Gales, Roger Hadley, and Wyn Lewis, *Students in Conflict: LSE in 1967* (London, 1970), in which a London School of Economics research team applies the School's long tradition of serious social investigation to domestic uproar.

(4) *France:*

The French university structure has been broken up and re-formed too radically for existing accounts to be reliable. (The *Institutions Universitaires* volume in the admirable 'Que-Sais-je?' paperback series is under revision.) However, for the background to the events of May, 1968 at Nanterre and the Sorbonne see, for example:

Raymond Poignant, *L'Enseignement dans les pays du Marché Commun.* Institut Pédagogique National, Paris, 1965.

Report of the Robbins Committee (already cited), appendix V (on French higher education).

Theodore Zeldin, 'Higher Education in France, 1848–1940', in *Journal of Contemporary History*, vol. 2, No. 3, 1967, pp. 53–80.

Raymond Aron, 'Quelques problèmes des universités françaises' in *Archives Européenes de Sociologie*, vol. III, No. 1, 1962, pp. 102–122; and numerous articles in *Encounter* (see indexes) by the same author.

Literature on the May events is already vast, but see for instance:

Edgar Morin, *La Brèche*. Fayard, Paris, 1968. A wide-ranging, topically-minded sociologist's analysis.

Patrick Seale and Maureen McConville, *French Revolution 1968*. London, 1968. Two journalists of the London *Observer* record what happened in the mind and on the streets.

J. Sauvageot, A. Geismar, D. Cohn-Bendit, and J-P Duteuil, *The Student Revolt: the activists speak*. London, 1968. (Editions Seuil, Paris: *La Révolte Etudiante*.)

For the ongoing situation, see:

John Ardagh, *The New France*. London, 1970. (Originally published as *The New French Revolution*, London, 1968, but since revised.) A bilingual British journalist's description of contemporary French life. See chapter 10 (in the revised edition) for education before and after the Faure reforms; and chapter 11 for an account of French intellectuals.

Catherine Valabrègue, *La Condition Etudiante*. Petite Bibliothèque Payot, Paris, 1970. An alert mother's account of everyday conditions in French universities, through student eyes. A short paperback in easy French.

For official figures and statements of intent, see:

Ministre d'Education Nationale, Statistiques des enseignements: tableaux et informations. Annual.

Ministre d'Education Nationale, Declaration de M. Edgar Faure devant l'Assemblée Nationale, le 8 Octobre 1968.

Loi d'orientation de l'enseignement superieur. Paris, 1968. (Librairies Imprimeries Réunies, 7 R. St Benoit, Paris VIe.) Badly translated in *Education in France*, No. 38, January 1969 (French Embassy: FACSEA, 972 Fifth Avenue, New York 21, NY).

Edgar Faure, *L'Education Nationale et la participation*. Plon, Paris, 1968.

Edgar Faure, *Philosophie d'une réforme*. Plon, Paris, 1969.

Edgar Faure, *L'âme du combat*. Fayard, Paris, 1970.

(5) *West Germany:*

Serious scholars are supposed to be able to read German. There is therefore much less up to date literature on German universities accessible in English than might be supposed. For the traditional system, see:

Friedrich Paulsen, *The German Universities and University Study*, translated by F. Thill, London, 1906. (*Die deutschen Universitäten und das Universitätsstudium*, Berlin, 1902). Also Abraham Flexner (op. cit.).

For what happened next, see:

Edward Y. Hartshorne, *The German Universities and National Socialism*. London, 1937.

Frederick Lilge, *The Abuse of Learning: the Failure of the German University*. New York, 1948.

For the period including the post-war years, see:

Dietrich Goldschmidt, 'Teachers in Institutions of Higher Learning in Germany', in A. H. Halsey, Jean Floud, and C. Arnold Anderson (eds.), *Education, Economy, and Society*. Glencoe, 1961, pp. 577 ff. (Translated from H. Plessner (ed.), *Untersuchungen zur Lage der Deutschen Hochschullehrer* (Gottingen, 1956), vol. I.)

Juergen Fischer, 'The Universities and the Reform of Higher Education in the Federal Republic' in Walter Stahl (ed.) *Education for Democracy in West Germany*. New York, 1961. This describes the proposals tabled by the *Wissenschaftsrat* in 1960.

R. H. Samuel and R. Hinton Thomas, *Education and Society in modern Germany*. London, 1949.

Secratariats of the Standing Conference of Ministers of Education (KMK) and of the West German Rectors' Conference (WRK), *Higher*

Education in the Federal Republic of Germany: Problems and Trends.
German Academic Exchange Service (DAAD), Bonn, 1966. This is an
explanatory pamphlet for foreign consumption, with tables, useful
addresses, and a bibliography of German sources.

Edward Shils (transl.), Report of the *Wissenschaftsrat* on university reform
(1966) in *Minerva*, April 1970, pp. 250–267. The previous eight pages
contain the same writer's translation of Wilhelm von Humboldt's
original memorandum (1809–10) on the foundation of the seminal
University of Berlin.

Wissenschaftsrat, *Empfehlungen zur Struktur und zum Ausbau des Bildung-
swesens im Hochschulbereich nach 1970*. This immensely long report (a
forty-page 'summary' was issued to the press in June 1970) awaits
translation.

OECD Reviews of National Science Policy: United Kingdom and
Germany. OECD, 1967.

Council of Europe, *Reform and expansion of higher education in Europe
1962–67*. Strasbourg, 1967.

Ralf Dahrendorf, 'Starre und Offenheit der deutschen Universität: die
Chancen der Reform', in *Archives Européennes de Sociologie* vol. III,
No. 2, 1962, pp. 263–293. Dahrendorf, an internationally minded
sociologist with a strong political bent, is probably the best authority
on German higher education related to German society. His talk, 'The
Crisis in German Education' at the Institute of Contemporary History
in April, 1967, is summarised in the *Journal of Contemporary History*,
vol. 2, No. 3, 1967. See also his *Society and Democracy in Germany*
(London, 1968), especially chs. 5, 10, 20.

Eva Weller and Wilfried van der Will, 'Protest in Western Germany',
in Nagel (ed.) *Student Power* (op. cit.) pp. 45–59. See also running reports
on the German student situation in *Encounter*, by Melvin J. Lasky,
John Mander, and others.

Detlev Albers, Gert Hinnerk Behlmer and Werner Loewe, 'Bremen
zwischen Technokratie und Demokratisierung', in *Studentische Politik*,
2—1970. Forschungsinstitut der Friedrich-Ebrt-Stiftung, 53 Bonn Bad
Godesberg, Kolner Str. 149.

Hans Peter Ipsen and Eberhard Grabitz (eds.), *Das Hamburger Universitätsgesetz: Seminarreferate und Diskussionen; Gesetzestext.* Appel,
Hamburg, 1970.

(6) *Italy:*

OECD Reviews of national policies for education: Italy. OECD, 1969.
Libro bianco sull' Università. Edizioni Abete, Rome, 1968.
Adriano Buzzati-Traverso, *Un fossile denutrito: l'università italiana.*
Mondadori, Milan, 1969. (o.p.)

Giovanni Russo, *Università Anno Zero*. Armando Armando, Rome, 1966.
These last two titles are referred to in the text. Many other similar titles—*Si puo salvare l'Università italiana?*, *Problemi e prospettive urgenti dell' Università*—indicate the appetite of the Italian public to read about the problems they cannot solve.

Federico Mancini, 'A Letter from Italy' in *Dissent XVI* (Sept.–Oct. 1969) p. 413ff.

Luigi Barzini, *The Italians*. London, 1964.

Giovanni Bertin and others, *Scuola e società in Italia*. Laterza, Bari, 1964, (pp. 181ff. for social survey of University of Bologna graduates.)

Edith E. Coulson James, *Bologna, its history, antiquities and art*, London, 1909.

Università di Bologna, *Annuario 1965–66*.

THEMES

The literature on access to higher education, on what universities should teach, how they should be governed and related to society, and what their ultimate purposes might be, is naturally enormous, and I have only skimmed the surface of it. Besides, it is more readily accessible, on the educational shelves of libraries, than accounts of recent events in other countries' institutions. This section therefore merely lists a few books, some already mentioned in the text or in other sections of this bibliography, which the writer found enlightening as a way into the subject.

What should students learn?

Daniel Bell, *The Reforming of General Education*. Columbia, New York; and London, 1966.

Paul Goodman, *Compulsory Mis-education* and *The Community of Scholars*. New York, 1964.

Michael Yudkin (ed.), *General Education: a symposium on the teaching of non-specialists*. London, 1969.

Marjorie Reeves, 'The European University from Mediaeval Times', in Niblett, op. cit., pp. 61–93.

University governance

Clark Kerr, *The Uses of the University* and
Jacques Barzun, *The American University*
have already been cited.

Sir Sydney Caine, *British Universities: purpose and prospects*. London, 1969.

E. P. Thompson (ed.), *Warwick University Ltd*. London, 1970.

Together, these books show how the wheels go round in British universities, and dramatise the distance between the conservative official academic mind, and its left-wing critics.

Proceedings of the Overview Committee on Governance of Universities (April 5–6, 1968) and of the Conference on Governance of Universities (November 14–16, 1968). House of the Academy, Boston, Massachusetts, 1969. (Inquiries to the Managing Editor of *Daedalus*—q.v.)

Proceedings of the international conference of university administrators in Bellagio, Italy, 1969. (Forthcoming).

Aspects of equality

R. H. Tawney, *Equality*. London, 1931.

Emile Durkheim, *Education and Society* (translated by S. D. Fox). Glencoe, 1956.

Michael Young, *The Rise of the Meritocracy*. London, 1958. (It is interesting to note that this short and classic satire has only just been translated into French.)

Ralf Dahrendorf, *Democracy in West Germany*. (Already cited.)

A. H. Halsey, Jean Floud, and C. Arnold Anderson (eds.), *Education, Economy, and Society*. A first-rate reader in the subjects which the title links.

John Vaizey, *Education in the modern world*. London, 1967.

J. W. B. Douglas, J. M. Ross, H. R. Simpson, *All our future: a longitudinal study of secondary education*. London, 1968.

Peter F. Drucker, *The Age of Discontinuity*. London, 1969. A long-sighted philosopher of business discusses (especially in Chs. 12–17) the social implications of the 'knowledge society's rate of growth and change.

Daniel Jenkins, *Equality and Excellence*. London, 1961.

Daniel Jenkins, *The Educated Society*. London, 1966.

A Protestant theologian and social critic raises, from a background of discussions with the *Frontier* circle of British Christian intellectuals, issues that were later and more noisily raised by radical students.

Malaise des clercs?

A. N. Whitehead, *Science and the Modern World*. Cambridge, 1926.

Aldous Huxley, *Ends and Means*. London, 1937.

Arnold Nash, *The University and the Modern World*. London, 1943.

Sir Walter Moberly, *The Crisis in the University*. London, 1949.

A philosopher and mathematician, a novelist and philosopher, a scientifically-trained theologian, and a theologically-minded university administrator, exercise their minds on the twentieth century crisis, and the issues of intellectual integration. Stylistically, the first two books wear better than the second two, but all contain ideas worth reviving.

Herbert Marcuse, *One Dimensional Man*. London, 1964.

Raymond Williams, *Culture and Society*. London, Source books for left-wing critics of modern society.

Plenary Sessions of the Commission on the Year 2000: the future of intellectual institutions (November 1–2, 1968). House of the Academy, Boston, Mass. (Proceedings duplicated by *Daedalus*).

Index

For convenience in use, the index of this book has been divided. An index of personal names appears first. The reader wishing to pursue individual institutions, general themes, or academic disciplines through the text should turn to the second index. Neither index covers the appendices and bibliography.

Index of names

Professional education, 130–31, 143, 232
Property Owners Association (Chicago), 51
Protestant Dissenting Academies, 324
Psychoanalysis, 161, 334
Psychology, 162, 166, 239, 247, 340
Public Accounts Committee (Britain), 201

Recurrent education, 220, 284–95
Reed College, 232, 249–51, 256, 309
Regents of the University of California, 88–94
Religion and religious institutions, 13–14, 46–7, 55, 59, 62–3, 68, 113, 126–32, 156, 181, 190, 193–4, 196, 258–9, 273, 329, 344
Religious studies, 181–2
Robbins Report, 42, 151–2, 175–6, 189, 199, 286, 293
Royal Manchester College of Music, 29
Russian, 309

Salaries, professorial, 49, 55–6, 72–3, 89, 104, 106, 137, 204, 333
San Francisco State College, 86, 279
Santa Cruz (University of California), 132
Scandinavian universities, 196, 282, 289
Schools and school systems, 36, 72–5, 116, 152, 189–90, 196, 225, 230, 235, 247, 254, 275, 279, 287, 289, 293, 312, 328
Sciences Politiques, Ecole de ('Sciences Po'), 164–5, 169
Scientific and technological research, 36–8, 71, 87, 95, 117, 130–31, 136, 138, 156, 197, 201–2, 208–9, 228, 244–5, 254, 288, 334–7, 339–40
Selection for university places, 151–2, 153, 157
Sexuality, enjoyment or exploitation of, 82–4, 142, 147, 197, 327
Size of universities, 58, 76, 79, 159, 167, 334–5
Social Service Administration, 47
Sociology, 30, 39, 88, 137, 162, 166, 168, 209, 222, 239, 258–65, 304, 342–3
Sociology of religion, 229, 259, 342
Sorbonne (*see also* Paris, University of), 61, 132, 160, 268–9, 333
Spanish College (Bologna), 193, 196–7
Staff, University, conditions and attitudes, 36 (Manchester); 49–50, 58 (Chicago); 71, 94–5 (Berkeley); 114–17 (Bologna); 136–7, 148–9 (Balliol); 160–5 (Vincennes); 183–4 (Lancaster); 209–15

(Germany). General refs.: 204, 228–9, 236, 249–51, 280, 284–5, 331–44
Stanford University, 51, 86, 253, 255, 257 (Behavioural Sciences Institute)
Statistics (as a subject), 39, 208
Strasbourg, University of, 168
Student numbers, growth of, 121–2, 150, 157, 159–60, 169, 175–6, 189, 228, 248, 270, 287, 294, 335
Students (moods, conditions, demonstrations)
  Manchester: 31–2, 33, 35–6, 318–23
  Chicago: 47–8, 59
  Japan: 67–8, 71–3, 76–7
  Berkeley: 83–4, 97–9, 303–10
  Italy: 114–21
  Medieval Paris and Oxford: 126–30
  Balliol and contemporary Oxford: 143–147, 312–18
  Vincennes: 162–4
  Lancaster: 182–7
  Germany: 209–15
  Other refs.: 220–4, 236, 238–43, 249–51 (Reed), 257–65 (Harvard 'Chanzeans') 267, 274–80, 283, 296, 297–303 (Morehouse), 325, 344
Students, sociology of, 140–4, 151–3 (Balliol), 182 (Lancaster), 261, 264, 270, 275 (Germany), 276 (Italy), 277 (Japan), 282–3, 287, 291, 294, 311–12, 325
Summerhill School, 237
Sussex, University of, 30, 149n, 176, 177
Systems engineering, 180

Teaching, economics of, 248, 253–5, 258–9
Teaching (undergraduate), 48, 59, 70–71, 78–9, 127–9, 136–7, 139–40, 149, 161–2, 164–5, 225–65, 287, 296–323
Teaching methods, 161–2, 164–5, 168, 250, 252–6, 257–65
Teaching, *see also* Curriculum
Tertiary education, *see* Higher education
Textile technology, 36
Theology, *see also* Religion and Religious studies, 47, 126–9, 181, 213, 306, 319
Tokyo, University of ('Todai'), 61, 68, 70, 72, 73, 74, 266, 277
Tsukuba (Japanese academic city), 79
Turin Technological University, 217
Tuskegee Institute, 297
TWO (The Woodlawn Organisation, Chicago), 52–4
Tyzack Report, 199–200